TOWARD AN UNDE
OF THE MOTHER OF OUR LORD

Mary for Evangelicals

TIM PERRY

FOREWORD BY WILLIAM J. ABRAHAM

IVP Academic
An imprint of InterVarsity Press
Downers Grove, Illinois

For Rachel

"Many women have done excellently,

but you surpass them all."

Proverbs 31:29 NRSV

InterVarsity Press
P.O. Box 1400, Downers Grove, IL 60515-1426
World Wide Web: www.ivpress.com
E-mail: mail@ivpress.com

InterVarsity Press® is the book-publishing division of InterVarsity Christian Fellowship/USA®, a student movement active on campus at hundreds of universities, colleges and schools of nursing in the United States of America, and a member movement of the International Fellowship of Evangelical Students. For information about local and regional activities, write Public Relations Dept., InterVarsity Christian Fellowship/USA, 6400 Schroeder Rd., P.O. Box 7895, Madison, WI 53707-7895, or visit the IVCF website at <*www.intervarsity.org*>.

Design: Cindy Kiple

Images: Scala/Art Resource, NY

ISBN-10: 0-8308-2569-X
ISBN-13: 978-0-8308-2569-1

Printed in the United States of America ∞

Library of Congress Cataloging-in-Publication Data

Perry, Tim S., 1969-
Mary for evangelicals: toward an understanding of the mother of our Lord / Tim Perry.
p. cm.
Includes bibliographical references and index.
ISBN-13: 978-0-8308-2569-1 (pbk.: alk. paper)
ISBN-10: 0-8308-2569-X (pbk.: alk. paper)
1. Mary, Blessed Virgin, Saint. I. Title.
BT603.P47 2006
232.91—dc22

2006020879

P 18 17 16 15 14 13 12 11 10 9 8 7 6 5 4 3 2
Y 20 19 18 17 16 15 14 13 12 11 10 09 08 07

Contents

Abbreviations 7

Foreword by William J. Abraham 9

Introduction: *"So How's Mary Today?"*. 13

PART 1: MARY IN HOLY SCRIPTURE

1 Anonymous Mother of the Heavenly Man:
Mary in the Letters of Paul 21

2 Ambiguous Protector of the Family: *Mary in the Gospel of Mark* 32

3 Scandalous Mother of the Messiah: *Mary in the Gospel of Matthew* . . . 41

4 Poor Prophet, Pondering Mother, Persistent Disciple:
Mary in Luke/Acts 63

5 Woman of the Hour: *Mary in the Johannine Literature* 97

PART 2: MARY IN THE HISTORY OF CHRISTIAN THOUGHT

6 New Eve: *Patristic Roots of Mariology* 119

7 Mother of God: *Formalizing the Patristic Heritage*. 148

8 Queen Mother: *Mary and the Medieval Imagination*. 177

9 Decline and Exaltation:
Mary from the Reformation to the Nineteenth Century 209

10 Queen of Heaven, Mother of the Church, Sister in the Struggle:
Mary Through the Twentieth Century to Today. 239

PART 3: TOWARD AN EVANGELICAL MARIOLOGY

11 Virgin Mother: *Mary in the Mystery of the Incarnation*. 267

12 Chosen One: *Toward a Doctrine of Mary's Person* 285

13 Advocate: *Toward a Doctrine of Mary's Work* 296

Acknowledgments. 309

Name Index 311

Subject Index 313

Scripture Index 317

Abbreviations

ANF	*Ante-Nicene Fathers*
CD	Karl Barth, *Church Dogmatics,* trans. and ed. Geoffrey W. Bromiley and Thomas F. Torrance (Edinburgh: T & T Clark, 1936-1977)
CWE	*Collected Works of Erasmus* (Toronto: University of Toronto Press, 1974-)
FC	Fathers of the Church (Washington: Catholic University of America Press, 1947-)
FCMC	Fathers of the Church: Medieval Continuation (Washington: Catholic University of America Press, 1989-)
HG	Bede, *Homilies on the Gospels,* trans. Lawrence T. Martin and David Hurst, 2 vols. (Kalamazoo: Cistercian, 1991)
KJV	King James Version
LW	*Luther's Works,* American edition (St. Louis: Concordia, 1955-1986)
NAB	New American Bible
NIV	New International Version
NJB	New Jerusalem Bible
NKJV	New King James Version
$NPNF^1$	*Nicene and Post-Nicene Fathers,* Series 1
$NPNF^2$	*Nicene and Post-Nicene Fathers,* Series 2
NRSV	New Revised Standard Version
PJ	*Protevangelium of James*

Foreword

Over twenty years ago I was honored to preach at the St. Patrick's Day celebration in the Roman Catholic Cathedral in Seattle. When I went home later in the year to Ireland, my mother asked me what I had been doing lately and I told her about the service. She looked at me in pain and said plaintively, "Billy, you didn't really do that now, did you?" At that moment, I knew I had crossed a line that thousands of evangelicals have crossed in the last generation. We had simply ceased to see Roman Catholicism as the theological enemy; we had entered into a whole new relationship in which neither side could ever be the same again.

We do not yet know the full story behind this extraordinary development. Of course, we can chart crucial causal factors that deserve mention. The collapse of Christianity in the West, the impact of the Ecumenical Movement, the consequences of Vatican II, the brilliance of Pope John Paul II, the cross-fertilization of scholarly collaboration, the quiet influence of personal friendships—these have systematically changed the landscape in which we now operate. Yet they are not the whole story, either humanly or spiritually speaking. It will take decades to unravel the work of the Holy Spirit in breaking down barriers and opening up new vistas in the Western church as a whole. Moreover, we know it will take decades to come to terms with the theological issues that will need to be revisited and reconceptualized on the other side of this informal ecumenical revolution.

In the work that has opened up before us, reflection on Mary is obviously a critical topic. Evangelicals are nervous about Mary; the old stereotype of Roman Catholics worshiping Mary is extremely difficult to dislodge from the imagination. Yet even before they get to the more substantial theological issues related to Mary, evangelicals recognize immediately that she is a pivotal agent in the Gospel narratives who cannot be ignored. This was recently brought home to me dramatically when one of my students noted how odd it was to preach about all the other leading figures in the Gospel materials (John the Baptist, the disciples, the rich young ruler, Herod and the like) and ignore Mary. Once this hit home, he began not only to preach about Mary but also to think seriously about the place of Mary in the Christian faith. He is now embarked on a study of the significance of Mary for Christian discipleship.

We might also rename the interest identified here as the significance of Mary for Christian piety. This is a natural place for evangelicals to begin; they will find it relatively easy to explore how the life of Mary speaks to their ongoing participation in salvation. They will naturally pursue this interest in terms of the texts that speak of Mary; so their first move will be to explore the full range of biblical texts. However, it is obvious that the theological work cannot stop there. On the one hand, there is a rich tradition of interpretation of the relevant texts that become pertinent if the full meaning of the text is to be mined. In the last generation, evangelicals have rightly turned to the whole history of exegesis as a source of insight. Thomas Oden's work on the exegesis and commentaries of the church fathers has proved to be especially important in this regard. Thus, the study of Mary in Scripture cannot in the end be confined to Scripture.

On the other hand, once the tradition of commentary is engaged, a whole network of theological issues quickly becomes visible. At one level, what is at issue is the place of the saints in the life of faith. Clearly Mary stands secure in any list of saints, so she opens a door that cannot be closed. How should we think of the saints? Should we be content with a minimalist vision that sees every believer as a saint? What do we do with those who exhibit conspicuous sanctity and thus become a unique source of inspiration? What is involved in the canonization of saints in Eastern Orthodoxy and in Roman Catholicism? How do we respond to claims about the intercession of the saints? What are the metaphysical and ontological assumptions at stake in the invocation of the saints? How are these assumptions to be articulated and defended? What vision of salvation undergirds the place of saints in faith and piety? What is the epistemological significance of the impact of saints (both negatively and positively)?

At another level, Mary becomes intrinsically important. When they think of the incarnation, many students initially think of Mary as a kind of vessel for the life of the Son. They reduce the issue to that of a "rent-a-womb" lease. However, this quickly dissolves once they begin to come to terms with a real incarnation in which the eternal Son of God assumes real human nature in the womb of Mary. At that point, the debate about Mary as *Theotokos* catches fire and the race is on to come to terms with the early christological debates. Questions about Mary quickly multiply thereafter. What light does she throw upon the nature of sin? What is the significance of her positive response to God in sorting through the tangled debate about grace and freedom? What is the import of Mary for such topics as sexual ethics, the gender of the ordained, the character of feminism and the nature of the church?

Tim Perry's contribution to the discussion about Mary is a great place for evangelicals to start in their exploration of Mary. His writing style is absolutely splendid. There is a wonderful economy and clarity of expression that is sustained from beginning to end. The whole flow of the narrative is very pleasing; and the transitions between units of thought and chapters work very well. I found myself both ready to move on and keen to see what was up ahead. The last section provides a very useful conceptual grid for thinking through the fundamental issues that need to be engaged in a theology of Mary.

Taken in the round, this is an outstanding piece of work. It sets out to provide an evangelical theology of Mary and succeeds admirably in this respect. I would expect this volume to become a landmark study of Mary from within the evangelical tradition. It should become the point of departure for future work on Mary within evangelicalism. Clearly such a text is badly needed, given the interest in Mary that has suddenly sprouted in the last fifty years. I can also see folk building on this work, say, on the significance of Mary for evangelism or spirituality.

This book will certainly be provocative to evangelicals; however, it is provocative in the right sort of way. It brings out how intimately Mary is tied to issues of Christology, and evangelicals are clearly on the side of orthodoxy here. It also implicitly sends the message that the debate has really taken off in the last generation and evangelicals can no longer stand on the sidelines. The book clearly sends a challenge to the Reformed version of evangelicalism in that it integrates the positive Marian commitments so well with that tradition, say, on predestination. The more telling provocation will be to those who have a leaner version of *sola scriptura,* and who thus are more ready to set Scripture against tradition rather than rely on tradition to interpret Scripture. In addition, I especially commend the way in which the argument draws on elements of the evangelical tradition, for instance, on the nature of intercession and on the place of the gifted intercessor. It will be very interesting to see how Anglican evangelicals in England will handle the book as a whole. I predict a certain reticence given the tensions with the Anglo-Catholics. However, this part of the work may open up further channels of conversation in Britain. Moving further afield, the book as a whole is certainly a model of what evangelical-Roman Catholic dialogue can be at its very best. Its primary contribution will lie in helping evangelicals get a grip on the relevant history and on the theological issues at stake. I will be very surprised if Roman Catholics do not welcome it for both its tone and content.

The big unanswered question here is what vision of the epistemology of theology is in play. In more conventional terms: is there any deep difference in the end between a Protestant and Roman Catholic position on Scripture? In this volume, both appear to involve an appeal to Scripture as primary and tradition as a secondary hermeneutical warrant; but they diverge on how the tradition is going to be identified. Another way to get at this is to note that many have charted a connection between Marian doctrine and the adoption of papal infallibility. It will be interesting to see whether or not Perry can avoid the move to adopt some vision of papal infallibility, once he fully internalizes the robust vision of Mary adopted here. It would, of course, have been a distraction for this question to be taken up and resolved in this volume. However, it is lurking below the surface, and it will need to become central in the future discussion that this book will rightly evoke.

William J. Abraham

Introduction

"So How's Mary Today?"

I hope readers do not blanch at the somewhat irreverent title. It summarizes nicely the project to follow, the wider cultural context of its publication and my own personal journey over the last four years. I consider these here in reverse order.

My Journey with Mary

In 2001 I published a column about Jesus' sex in *Faith Today,* which reflected on Mary in God's plan.[1] I contended that evangelical Protestant silence failed to reckon seriously with the biblical material. The first two chapters of Luke's Gospel present her as powerful, fully in control of herself, her body and her sexuality. In her humble, yet confident, assent to God's will, she conceived a child without a husband. Her response to Gabriel is the epitome of secure obedience, a goal toward which every believer ought to aspire. I concluded that evangelical Christians should say of Mary: "Blessed are you among women, and blessed is the fruit of your womb" (Lk 1:42).

Since the column's publication, my preoccupation with Mary has grown. Two key events stick out. First, during a casual conversation a senior colleague confidently asserted that had he been at the Council of Ephesus (431), he would have supported the Nestorian party's insistence on the Marian title "Christotokos."[2] That a theologian trained at the evangelical movement's best theological schools would expose his ignorance of the theological issue at stake, namely, the unity of Jesus' person, suggested to me that the lack of Marian reflection in

---

[1]Tim Perry, "Ask a Theologian," *Faith Today,* November/December 2001, p. 46.

[2]For a full account of the Nestorian controversy and the Council of Ephesus, see Justo L. González, *A History of Christian Thought,* rev. ed. (Nashville: Abingdon, 1987), 1:353-67.

modern evangelical theology was more than imagined. In this instance it appeared to have led to an impoverished and possibly unorthodox Christology. Second, the Center for Catholic and Evangelical Theology's annual conference in June 2002 invited speakers from across the theological spectrum to write on the theme "Mary: The Mother of God." Timothy George's "The Blessed Virgin Mary in Evangelical Perspective" and Jaroslav Pelikan's "Most Generations Shall Call Me Blessed" underscored the relative silence of Protestant theology generally and evangelical theology particularly.[3] I concluded that the perceived gap was real and needed to be filled.

Armed more with passion than knowledge, I pursued this elusive woman, hoping to introduce her to an audience unfamiliar with and suspicious of her apart from Advent and Christmas. My search led, eventually, to Saint Paul University in Ottawa, Ontario, where I enjoyed the institution's hospitality as a sabbatical scholar for the 2004-2005 school year. In my opinion, no library in Canada could have served me better. Closeted in my studio, I read familiar biblical passages far more closely than ever before, followed by a reading of the fathers and the theologians of the Western tradition from the medieval era to the present. As I did, a humorous image captivated me. While we theologians debated perpetual virginity, immaculate conception, bodily assumption and other such matters, Mary sat above us, smiling and saying nothing, undisturbed and utterly mysterious.

A colleague at Saint Paul's would often ask me, "So how's Mary today?" At the start of my sabbatical, I would detail where my research had taken me since our last conversation, and this in turn would lead to substantive bibliographic discussions and theological debate that have made this book far better than it would otherwise have been. Toward the end of my sabbatical, however, when the question was asked, all I could answer was, "She's fine. I'm not so sure about me." I was exhausted.

However tiring, my journey has been fascinating, even entrancing at points. I have discovered much about Marian doctrine and devotion that I did not know before, grasped more deeply those aspects that I did know, and come to appreciate and understand—though not to embrace—a piety that for some Christians deepens devotion to Jesus. In a peculiarly Protestant way, I have come to share the attraction that Mary has continued to exert across numerous divides created by religion, confession, gender, culture, geography and history. But do I know

[3]Both essays were presented at the 2002 annual meeting of the Center for Catholic and Evangelical Theology held at St. Olaf College in Northfield, Minn., and published in *Mary: Mother of God*, ed. Carl E. Braaten and Robert W. Jenson (Grand Rapids: Eerdmans, 2004), pp. 100-122, 1-35.

Mary? Hardly. There is one more book on the market—my own—and she's even more mysterious to me now than before.

I have come to learn, gladly, that this is the point. Christians East and West, Roman Catholic and Protestant, are fascinated with Mary because we are fascinated with Jesus. She directs the faithful away from herself, always to her Son. This has proven to be the most profound (and intensely personal) discovery made throughout this project; I trust it is also one for readers who complete this book. At its intellectual and devotional best, thought and practice about Mary is not really about her. It is about Jesus. It is about understanding more deeply the mysterious reality that is the assumption of human nature by God the Son. It is about seeing—rather than merely conceptualizing—the gospel that he brought, a gospel in which God freely elects and humans freely receive. It is about emulating the life of a disciple wholly devoted to his service, even when the requirements and implications of such service are unknown or unclear.

Mary and North American Evangelical Protestantism

Another happy discovery made along the way was that my own interest in Mary was coming to be shared by North American Protestant theologians. Over the ten years or so, a trickle of Marian interest has steadily turned into a stream and shows signs of continued increase for some time. Over the last two years, this fascination has generated cover stories in *Christianity Today, Christian Century,* and even *Time.*[4] I leave it to the sociologists of religion to seek out and explain the causes of this growth. I wish to highlight one: what Timothy George calls an "ecumenism of the trenches."

Against an increasingly hostile, intolerant and powerful secularism, Roman Catholics and evangelical Protestants in North America have found themselves thrown together, allies in the fight for the lives of those whom the culture regards as disposable. In front of abortion clinics, courthouses, legislative assemblies, and even in jail cells and at adoption centers and hospices, many of us made a radical discovery: we are one in Christ. Our unity is a gift of God already given; our disunity reflects the all-too-human ability to abuse, ignore and deny that which God has already done. In this case, the Father has elected one people, saved them through the work of one Lord and united them by one Holy Spirit. Ecumenism is not about negotiating a series of treaties among divided

---

[4]Timothy George, "The Blessed Evangelical Mary," *Christianity Today,* December 2003, online at <http://www.christiantiytoday.com/ct/2003/012/1.34.html> (accessed April 20, 2005); Jason Byassee, "What About Mary?" *Christian Century,* December 14, 2004, pp. 28-33; and David Van Biema, "Hail, Mary," *Time,* March 21, 2005, pp. 48-55.

churches, but about those churches learning to accept what God has accomplished and discerning together what unity-in-the-truth means and implies.

Unity-in-the-truth in the light of our disunity means that serious disagreements persist over just what is the truth, and as a result visible unity is at present and for the foreseeable future impossible. Two decades of increased cooperation on issues of social justice can neither undo nor should they gloss over the Protestant Reformation. Mutual suspicion and recrimination may be subsiding, but doctrinal differences—serious, church-dividing ones—remain, especially for those of us who are convinced that truth is unity's basis and goal. Mary has from the Reformation's second generation been a lightning rod for debating the nature of salvation, hermeneutics and the mediation of grace from God to God's people, to name but three of the more serious issues.

But unity-in-the-truth as a gift of God already accomplished in the cross and resurrection and poured out in our hearts by the Holy Spirit also means that what unites—namely, the triune God—is infinitely greater than what divides. Taking this to heart, growing numbers of traditionally minded Roman Catholic and Protestant theologians in North America have set about to articulate as clearly and as charitably as possible where we can agree and where we cannot. This has led to many fruitful semiformal and informal conversations that in turn have led not only to greater mutual understanding and appreciation, but also to a deeper perception of just how intractable some of these difficulties, humanly speaking, are. Still, conversations are ongoing, and God has been known to work miracles. I hope that this book helps to contribute to these conversations and at least does not provide the Holy Spirit with another human impediment to be removed if the visible unity for which our Lord prayed is to become a reality.

Having said all that, I recognize that what I have written will not resonate with many in the global evangelical Christian family. My perception of the way things actually are arises from and is directed to my North American context. I recognize that brothers and sisters in contexts where Catholics and Protestants are rivals will perceive matters differently. To be blunt: in North America, Mary is not nearly as controversial, polemical and even intimidating as she is in, say, Northern Ireland, Latin America and some parts of Asia. I hope that, had I written from one of those situations, I would have written substantially the same book; I recognize, however, that I would have said some things (very) differently.

I also acknowledge that I run the risk of being accused of being out of touch with the concerns of evangelical Christians in those kinds of situations. Granting that in at least some cases these accusations will be legitimate, I invite these as yet unknown critics to read, to reflect and to consider whether there is anything applicable in what follows before they dismiss it entirely.

Outline of Study

This brings us, finally, to a summary of what is to come. I have followed a simple method rooted in my own theological and ecclesial convictions: Scripture, tradition and reason. Following the Protestant Reformers, I take as axiomatic that Holy Scripture is divinely inspired and is therefore the necessary, sufficient, clear and authoritative guide for theological construction.[5]

I therefore begin with the Mary in the New Testament. Paul presents Jesus' mother as an anonymous guarantor of his Jewish humanity (chap. 1). Mark names Mary but is ambiguous about her character; she may well be one of Jesus' opponents (chap. 2). On the surface Matthew's Mary is not so much a character as a device to display Joseph's virtue; nevertheless his treatment of Mary's scandalous pregnancy moves her out from the shadows of anonymity (chap. 3). Mary is three dimensional only in Luke, where she is a prophet, mother and disciple (chap. 4). In this threefold portrayal, I discern a move toward a symbolic representation of the corporate faithful that comes to the fore in the Johannine literature (chap. 5). Whether at the wedding banquet or the cross, Mary symbolizes the corporate faithful's response to Jesus; in its canonical context Revelation provides the most symbolically charged portrayal of Mary: Heavenly Queen.

Of course, the Reformation's call to *sola scriptura* neither means nor implies that Scripture may be interpreted rightly by anyone, being guided solely by reason and/or the Holy Spirit. Rather, contemporary interpretation of Scripture must be tested against two secondary sources, the first being tradition.[6] Scripture is not to be interpreted randomly or arbitrarily, but within the context of the historical continuity of the Christian church—what C. S. Lewis calls "mere Christianity."

When it comes to Mary, unfortunately, the label *tradition* casts a wide net, for no woman has been the subject of more (and more sustained) thought over the last millennium and a half. I have found it necessary, therefore, to truncate my discussion more than I would have liked. A survey of depictions of Mary in early Christian art has been bypassed entirely, and Marian piety is mentioned only when and where it was a stimulus to doctrinal development. My focus is

---

[5]On this point I wholly agree with the definition of inspiration offered by the *Catechism of the Catholic Church* (Ottawa: Canadian Conference of Catholic Bishops, 1994), 3.2.106: "To compose the sacred books, God chose certain men who, all the while he employed them in this task, made full use of their own faculties and powers so that, though he acted in them and by them, it was as true authors that they consigned to writing whatever he wanted written and no more."

[6]For a recent articulation of the relationship between Scripture and tradition by evangelical and Roman Catholic theologians that clearly delineates points of agreement and disagreement, see Evangelicals and Catholics Together, "Your Word Is Truth," *First Things,* August/September 2002, pp. 38-43.

doctrinal. Even this account, however, is far from exhaustive. Eastern theologians after John of Damascus are not mentioned at all, and I have hit upon only the most significant Western ones. I have been forced by the limitations of space, time and personal competence to paint with a broad brush. Nevertheless, I hope that the portrait of development presented in part two is fundamentally sound.

Chapters six and seven exposit the church fathers. As the heritage of the undivided church and a point of contact that unites diverse members of the Christian family, the fathers provide a real, secondary guide and authority. I hope to show in these two chapters that Mariology was largely in place by the end of the patristic era. The developments of the medieval era (chap. 8) merely clarify, expand and intensify the doctrine that is already present. The Reformation and its aftermath drive chapter nine. From the sixteenth through the nineteenth centuries, similar concerns led to diametrically opposed strategies: silence and exaltation. Chapter ten concludes part two by bringing twentieth-century documents into consideration. I argue that a confluence of factors has brought Mary to the forefront of ecumenical (and especially Catholic-evangelical) dialogue.

Finally a persuasive interpretation of the data must be offered. This is the task undertaken in part three. In chapter eleven, I examine the possibility, ground and starting point of a Mariology that grants pride of place to Scripture and legitimate, but less significant, weight to tradition, concluding that a christologically grounded Mariology that begins with Mary's motherhood is not only possible but also a necessary dogmatic enterprise. Chapter twelve then offers a prequel of sorts, discussing Mary's place vis-à-vis the doctrine of election, while chapter thirteen builds on chapter twelve, discussing Mary's relationship to the church. In each chapter, traditional Protestant objections will be squarely faced. Thus, chapter eleven deals with Mary's perpetual virginity while chapter twelve addresses immaculate conception, mediation and coredemption, and chapter thirteen takes up her bodily assumption, heavenly reign and intercession.

PART ONE

Mary in Holy Scripture

1

Anonymous Mother of the Heavenly Man

Mary in the Letters of Paul

Because I have adopted a chronological approach, the investigation of the New Testament data concerning Jesus' mother begins with Paul's letters to Philippi, Rome and Galatia. Their authorship is not seriously disputed, and the range of dates offered for the composition of each is relatively narrow. Certainly all three had been written by A.D. 60 and therefore quite likely predate the earliest canonical Gospel, Mark. Although none mention Mary directly, five passages in these letters invite reflection on Jesus' birth. Any mariological study, therefore, ought to consider what light they cast on the later Matthean and Lukan accounts of Jesus' nativity.

The second section explores the most relevant passages: Galatians 1:19, Galatians 4:4 and Galatians 4:28-29. The first two refer respectively to "James the Lord's brother" and to Jesus as "born of a woman" and "born under the law." Their relevance is clear. The third, a reference to Isaac being "born according to the Spirit," will be examined because it is understood by some to indicate Paul's familiarity with the virginal conception.

The first section, however, turns to two liturgical formulations found in Philippians and Romans that actually predate Paul.[1] They provide a window

---

[1]For a balanced statement of the arguments for and against Pauline composition of Phil 2:5-11, see Ralph P. Martin, *A Hymn of Christ: Philippians 2:5-11 in Recent Interpretation and in the Setting of Early Christian Worship* (Downers Grove, Ill.: InterVarsity Press, 1997), pp. 42-62, 315-19. For Rom 1:3-4, compare V. S. Poythress, "Is Romans 1:3-4 a Pauline Confession?" *Expository Times* 87 (1975-1976): 180-83, which argues that Paul uses pre-Pauline phrases to construct his own hymn, with James D. G. Dunn, *Romans 1-8,* Word Biblical Commentary 38A (Dallas: Word, 1988), p. 5, which contends that the hymn is wholly pre-Pauline.

into the Christ-centered belief and worship of the first disciples.

Pre-Pauline Witnesses

Philippians 2:5-11 and Romans 1:3-4 are intriguing.[2] While neither mentions Mary directly, both suggest that a notion of preincarnate existence was familiar in the worship of the earliest followers of Jesus and at the same time stress his complete humanity.

Philippians 2:5-11. The history of interpretation of Philippians 2:5-11 fascinates even casual biblical interpreters.[3] Decades-old debates continue even as standard or classic proposals are commonly recognized. Commentators continue to disagree over the meaning of the passage's unique vocabulary, its poetic structure and liturgical setting in Pauline and pre-Pauline Christian worship, the pastoral purpose to which Paul puts it and its christological content. It poses challenges unique in New Testament studies, not to mention theology, and theologians venturing into this territory must tread cautiously. The passage reads as follows:

> Let the same mind be in you that was in Christ Jesus,
> who, though he was in the form of God,
> did not regard equality with God
> as something to be exploited,
> but emptied himself,
> taking the form of a slave,
> being born in human likeness.
> And being found in human form,
> he humbled himself
> and became obedient to the point of death—
> even death on a cross.
> Therefore God also highly exalted him
> and gave him the name
> that is above every name,
> so that at the name of Jesus
> every knee should bend,
> in heaven and on earth and under the earth,
> and every tongue should confess

---

[2]The importance of Phil 2:5-11 and Rom 1:3-4 for Christology is aptly summarized in the title of a collection of essays on the Philippians text. See Ralph P. Martin and Brian J. Dodd, eds., *Where Christology Began: Essays on Philippians 2* (Louisville: Westminster John Knox, 1998).

[3]The standard guide remains Martin's *Hymn of Christ*, the updated version of his classic study *Carmen Christi: Philippians ii.5-11 in Recent Interpretation and in the Setting of Early Christian Worship* (Cambridge: Cambridge University Press, 1967).

that Jesus Christ is Lord,
to the glory of God the Father. (Phil 2:5-11)

The first stanza's description of the movement of Christ—from being in the form of God through emptying himself to being found in human form and subject to a human death—appears to acknowledge a preincarnate form of existence. If so, then this constitutes New Testament evidence for an understanding of the incarnation that, if not yet philosophically or theologically precise, nevertheless animated early Christian liturgies. Does such a view lie in the text? Or is it seen only in the light of centuries of reinterpretation after the Council of Nicea in 325, which dogmatically defined Christ's preincarnate existence? Does Philippians 2:6-7 admit the preincarnate existence of Christ?

The denial that it does takes two forms. First, some precritical commentators suggest that the passage refers to the divine Christ after his incarnation. John Calvin insists that the act of self-emptying (Phil 2:7) is a moral one. Incarnate as a human being, the divine Christ refuses the divine attributes rightfully his, thereby offering an example of humble service par excellence for the Philippian church.[4] While Calvin rightly considers the hymn's pastoral context, he ignores the more immediate hymnic context in which Christ's self-emptying takes place. The first stanza clearly encapsulates the downward movement from being in the form of God to becoming human. It seems to refer to incarnation.

More recently, some have argued against incarnation for reasons opposite to Calvin's. The verses describe the human Jesus; enfleshment of a divine person is not present. James Dunn insists that the hymn contrasts the human Adam with the human Jesus (cf. 1 Cor 15:21-58).[5] For Dunn, "the form of God" in which Christ is found (Phil 2:6) is none other than "the image of God" in which Adam was created (Gen 1:26-27). Yet where Adam tried to "snatch at" or "rob" (translated "exploited" above) equality with God, Jesus did not, embracing instead the path of radical obedience.[6]

Dunn's argument is open to two criticisms.[7] First, any reference to Adam may only be inferred, and its basis, Dunn's equation of "the form of God" with "the

---

[4]John Calvin, *Commentary on the Epistle to the Philippians,* trans. John Pringle (Grand Rapids: Baker, 1979), p. 57.

[5]James D. G. Dunn, *Christology in the Making: An Inquiry into the Origins of the Doctrine of the Incarnation* (London: SCM Press, 1980), p. 114.

[6]Ibid., p. 117.

[7]The criticisms are set out in L. D. Hurst, "Re-enter the Preexistent Christ in Philippians 2:5-11?" *New Testament Studies* 32 (1986): 448-57; and idem, "Christ, Adam, and Preexistence Revisited," in *Where Christology Began: Essays on Philippians 2,* ed. Ralph P. Martin and Brian J. Dodd (Louisville: Westminster John Knox, 1998), pp. 84-95.

image of God," is tenuous. However evocative the Adam/Christ contrast may be, it is not explicit. Second, granting the contrast does not demand rejection of preincarnate existence; it may strengthen it. L. D. Hurst writes that

> if the point of the passage is to present an ethical example of humility rather than to teach soteriology, the implied contrast could . . . be between the heavenly Christ who, being in divine form, did not consider an equality that he possessed something to retain, but willingly assumed humankind's predestined (Ps 8:5) state as "a little lower than God"; Adam, on the other hand, aspired to an equality . . . to which he had no right, and unwittingly was made lower . . . than his previous state.[8]

While it is possible to see in Philippians 2:6-7 both an Adam/Christ contrast and an emergent understanding of incarnation, I continue to see early moves toward a doctrine of incarnation. Paul contrasts two ways of thinking—one selfish, the other selfless—by reminding the Philippian Christians of Christ's example as summarized in a familiar hymn. The one who was in the form of God, that is, the one whose nature was that of God, did not consider his equality with God as something to be held on to, but emptied himself of his rights and privileges precisely by assuming the form of a slave, by being made in the likeness of human beings. The form of God/form of a slave parallelism is best preserved when it is understood to refer to incarnation.[9]

If this exegesis is correct, the (undeveloped) idea of Christ's preincarnate existence known to the early church could be expressed without reference to a virginal conception. Might this silence imply that the earliest Christians therefore were ignorant of it? Is it a later invention drawn on by Matthew and Luke? This silence should not be dismissed too quickly. We shall return to it again.

Romans 1:3-4. The creedal statement in Romans 1:3-4 is just as fascinating as the previous passage and should be considered in the context of Paul's greeting to the church in Rome:

> Paul, a servant of Jesus Christ, called to be a apostle, set apart for the gospel of God, which he promised beforehand through his prophets in the holy scriptures, the gospel concerning his Son, who was descended from David according to the flesh and was declared to be Son of God with power according to the spirit of holiness by resurrection of the dead, Jesus Christ our Lord, through whom we have received grace and apostleship to bring about the obedience of faith among all the Gentiles for the sake of his name, including yourselves who are called to belong to Jesus Christ,

---

[8]Hurst, "Christ, Adam, and Preexistence Revisited," p. 88.

[9]Gordon Fee, *Paul's Letter to the Philippians,* New International Commentary on the New Testament (Grand Rapids: Eerdmans, 1995), pp. 202-20, esp. p. 203 n. 41.

> To all God's beloved in Rome, who are called to be saints:
> Grace to you and peace from God our Father and the Lord Jesus Christ.
> (Rom 1:1-7)

Most modern scholars follow Rudolf Bultmann's argument that Romans 1:3-4 is a Pauline incorporation of an early Christian creedal confession.[10] Joseph Fitzmyer presents the evidence evenhandedly, beginning with vocabulary: (1) the fragment contains the only reference in Paul's uncontested writings to Jesus as son of David (cf. 2 Tim 2:8); (2) it contains Paul's only use of the verb *horizō* (literally, "limit, determine, define"; translated "declared" above); and (3) Paul's use of the Semitic phrase "spirit of holiness" is similarly unique. Fitzmyer adds two interpretive points: (a) the contrast of "flesh" and "spirit" does not carry Paul's usual moral tone; and (b) the association of sonship with resurrection is part of the earliest apostolic preaching (cf. Acts 13:33). Fitzmyer also observes that the lack of reference to Christ's death or crucifixion "is surprising if Paul were freely composing these verses (compare 1 Cor 2:2)."[11] Alone, this final piece of evidence is weak, but it does support the pre-Pauline hypothesis.[12]

Romans 1:3 presents Jesus as *descended* from David's seed. Although the Greek verb can mean "to be born," it more often denotes "to come into being," a minor grammatical point with significant theological implications. If the former reading is correct, the verse simply describes Jesus' human descent; if the latter reading is followed, it alludes to the preexistence of the divine Son.[13] John McHugh agrees and adds that Paul thus acknowledges the virginal conception![14] While the verb cannot bear the theological weight that McHugh intends, the debate over preexistence is harder to adjudicate. Whether a human birth or an incarnation is meant, the context stresses Jesus' humanity. Hence, "according to the flesh" (Rom 1:3) does not carry the moral tone that Paul often employs (e.g., Rom 8:4-9; Gal 3:2-3; 5:16-19).[15]

Standing parallel with "descended" is "declared" (Rom 1:4). "Appointed" probably better captures the notion that it is *God* who appoints Jesus as his

---

[10]Rudolf Bultmann, *Theology of the New Testament,* trans. Kendrick Grobel (London: SCM Press, 1965), 1:49.

[11]Joseph A. Fitzmyer, *Romans: A New Translation with Introduction and Commentary,* Anchor Bible 33 (New York: Doubleday, 1993), p. 230.

[12]I assume with Douglas Moo that "it is necessary at least to maintain that whatever Paul quotes, he himself affirms"; see *The Epistle to the Romans,* New International Commentary on the New Testament (Grand Rapids: Eerdmans, 1996), p. 46 n. 31.

[13]Dunn, *Romans,* p. 12.

[14]John McHugh, *The Mother of Jesus in the New Testament* (Garden City, N.Y.: Doubleday, 1975), pp. 273-77.

[15]Fitzmyer, *Romans,* p. 234.

Son through his resurrection.[16] Appointed, however, does not mean adopted. Jesus' divine sonship is assumed throughout (cf. Rom 1:2). Jesus' appointment as God's Son was a public disclosure of what had been true all along. God's Son was revealed as God's Son in his resurrection. This further suggests that "with power" (Rom 1:4) properly modifies "appointed" rather than "Son of God." If "appointed to be the Son of God with power" is preferred, then the text portrays Jesus as a source of power or as enthroned with heavenly power,[17] sharply contrasting Jesus' preresurrection state as David's descendent with his postresurrection state as God's Son. On the other hand, if "appointed with power to be the Son of God" is preferred, then it describes the resurrection as the mighty act of God the Father to vindicate his Son publicly. If "appointed" underscores the dramatic and public nature of Jesus' revelation as Son, then the second reading of "with power" better highlights the extraordinary nature of Jesus' resurrection.

The last parallel statement, "according to the spirit of holiness" (Rom 1:4), stands over against "according to the flesh" (Rom 1:3). The phrase, unique in Paul, is a wooden rendering of ***ruakh qodesh*** (e.g., Ps 51:11 [MT 13]; Is 63:10-11).[18] Context helps to focus its range of meaning. First, it cannot be a reference to *the* Holy Spirit, at least as he is understood in full-blown trinitarian doctrine. Neither, as was argued above, should it be read in terms of the moral flesh/spirit dualism found elsewhere in Paul. Third, a material/immaterial reading would overemphasize the contrast.[19] The contrast between Romans 1:3 and Romans 1:4 stresses the vindication of Jesus as Son of God, not a change in essence or status. Thus it does not mean a move away from the material world of flesh to the immaterial world of the spirit. It is best read as saying that the creative power of God (cf. Gen 1:2) is now active in Christ as the forerunner of the general resurrection.

The universal nature of the resurrection is underscored in the Greek phrase translated "by resurrection from the dead" (Rom 1:4). The early church understood Jesus' resurrection not as a singular occurrence, but as the beginning of the general resurrection that itself signaled the day of the Lord.[20] Thus Peter and John proclaimed that in Jesus is the resurrection of the dead (Acts 4:2), and Paul declared the risen Lord to be the beginning of the harvest of those who had died

---

[16]Dunn, *Romans,* pp. 13-14; and Moo, *Romans,* pp. 48-49.

[17]On these two portrayals, see Fitzmyer, *Romans,* p. 235; and Ernst Käsemann, *Commentary on Romans,* trans. Geoffrey W. Bromiley (Grand Rapids: Eerdmans, 1980), p. 12.

[18]Dunn, *Romans,* p. 15.

[19]Ibid.

[20]N. T. Wright, *The Resurrection of the Son of God* (Minneapolis: Fortress, 2003), esp. pp. 242-45.

(1 Cor 15:20). This creedal formula affirms that by raising Jesus from the dead God publicly vindicated him, showing him to be his Son.

Paul sums up when he resumes his own writing at the conclusion of Romans 1:4. By being raised, Jesus Christ is shown to be the Son of God. Through him all who believe share in this resurrection life and are thereby united with him. As has been made obvious by God's mighty act of resurrection, it is appropriate to speak of his Son as "Jesus Christ, our Lord" (Rom 1:4 NRSV, NIV; Rom 1:3 KJV). Paul uses this confession to summarize and to introduce the gospel of God, which is the gospel he has been commissioned to take to the Gentiles. Through it he affirms that this gospel is from first to last the gospel of God's Son.

Mary in Galatians

Galatians 1:19. We move now from wholly pre-Pauline material to three passages in Galatians. The first is part of a larger defense of Paul's apostleship (Gal 1:11-24). Upon returning from Arabia (Gal 1:13-17) to Jerusalem to visit Peter (Gal 1:18), Paul "did not see any other apostle except James the Lord's brother" (Gal 1:19). Who is James? What is his relationship to Jesus?

The first question is straightforward. James is neither the son of Zebedee nor the son of Alphaeus (cf. Mk 3:17-18; Acts 1:13). He is most likely mentioned in Mark 6:3 as one of Jesus' brothers. He was prominent in the Jerusalem church (cf. Acts 15:13; 21:18-19), and Paul includes James with Peter and John as one of its "pillars" (Gal 2:9). Indeed, after Peter left Jerusalem (Acts 12:17), James became leader of the Jerusalem church. He was known for his devotion and asceticism, and he died as a martyr in 62.[21]

The second question is more complicated. The obvious significance of *adelphos* is "uterine brother." As such, it is defended by Richard Longenecker and assumed by James Dunn.[22] But is it possible that this conclusion is premature? It is, after all, widely agreed that the semantic range of *adelphos* encompasses meanings ranging from common ideological and religious adherences to various family relations. While Paul is not using "brother" to refer to James and Jesus' common religion, it is not clear that he means uterine brother; legitimate alternatives are "cousin" or "stepbrother."[23] Context (Gal 1:11-24) does not permit a final determination. That James and Jesus are from the same family is indubita-

[21]Richard N. Longenecker, *Galatians,* Word Biblical Commentary 41 (Waco, Tex.: Word, 1990), p. 39. See also Josephus *Antiquities* 20.200.

[22]Longenecker, *Galatians,* p. 39; and James D. G. Dunn, *The Theology of Paul the Apostle* (Grand Rapids: Eerdmans, 1998), p. 183.

[23]See "ἀδελφός," in James H. Moulton and George Milligan, *The Vocabulary of the Greek New Testament* (London: Hodder & Stoughton, 1930), pp. 8-9.

ble; that they are both children of Mary is possible but not established. Thus this verse alone does not refute ancient beliefs regarding Mary's perpetual virginity. On the other hand it underscores Paul's assumption that the Savior is, in fact, a human being.

Galatians 4:4. After defending his apostleship and rehearsing his history with other apostles, Paul outlines his gospel: both Jews and Gentiles are saved by faith apart from the law (Gal 2:15—4:7). He concludes with a piece of ancient Christian liturgy (Gal 4:4-6) that may be reconstructed with Paul's expansions in square brackets:

> [But when the fullness of time had come,]
> God sent forth his Son,
> born of a woman,
> [born under the law, in order to redeem those who were under the law,]
> in order that we might receive adoption as children.
> And because you are children,
> God has sent the Spirit
> [of his Son into our hearts,]
> crying, "Abba! Father!"[24]

Absent the Pauline elements we have a simple six-line declaration concerning God's sending of the Son and the Spirit. The sending language is used in the Bible with respect to divinely appointed messengers, whether heavenly (cf. Gen 24:40; Zech 7:12) or human (cf. Judg 6:8; Jer 7:25).[25] When Spirit and Son are set side by side as above, the case for the Son's preincarnate existence is clarified: if "the Spirit was the Spirit before God sent him, the Son was presumably the Son before God sent *him*" to be born of a woman.[26] We have here still another step on the way to a fully developed doctrine of the incarnation.

To find in the phrase "born of a woman" support for the doctrines of the incarnation and even the virginal conception is pious—but bad—eisegesis. On the contrary, the phrase is a Hebraism synonymous with "human being."[27] This safeguards against overinterpreting the allusion to preincarnate existence. As an identification of humanity, "born of a woman" does not describe the manner by which the Son of God became a human being. The phrase's omission of a father is not Paul's subtle endorsement of a virginal conception or birth. Rather, the

[24]F. F. Bruce, *Commentary on Galatians,* New International Greek Testament Commentary (Grand Rapids: Eerdmans, 1982), p. 195.

[25]James D. G. Dunn, *The Epistle to the Galatians* (Peabody, Mass.: Hendrickson, 1993), p. 215.

[26]Bruce, *Galatians,* p. 195.

[27]Raymond Brown et al., *Mary in the New Testament: A Collaborative Assessment by Protestant and Roman Catholic Scholars* (Philadelphia: Fortress, 1978), p. 43.

expression emphasizes the full humanity of the Son of God in order to set it over against the adoption that believers have received as a result.[28]

The phrase "born under the law" is Paul's way to move from Jesus' humanity to his Jewishness. Not merely the son of a woman, he was also a son of the law. Paul thus anchors Jesus in specifically Jewish history, thereby highlighting that in Jesus the representative role played corporately by Israel has been taken up by one man. Born of a woman and born under the law, he represented both Gentile and Jew, thereby reconciling both to God (Gal 4:5).

Galatians 4:28-29. The final fragment comes from Paul's allegorizing of the story of Abraham and Hagar (cf. Gen 16:15; 21:1-14). His opponents in Galatia are Ishmael, the child of the slave and "born according to the flesh." His converts are Isaac, the child of the free woman and born according to God's promise. But Paul introduces a notion foreign to the Genesis account: that Isaac was born "according to the Spirit": "Now you, my friends, are children of the promise, like Isaac. But just as at that time the child who was born according to the flesh persecuted the child who was born according to the Spirit, so it is now also" (Gal 4:28-29).

Martin Dibelius argues that this designation drew upon a Hellenistic-Jewish reading of the story that, having been heavily influenced by Greek mythology's semidivine heroes, had come to understand Sarah to have been miraculously impregnated by the divine, without any contribution of Abraham.[29] If so, this is a textual precursor to the virginal conception of Jesus and an indication of Paul's awareness of this miracle. It is, however, highly unlikely. Not only does it rest on questionable interpretations of texts in both Paul and Philo, it seems to run afoul of Paul's understanding of the roles of both parents in the conception of Isaac as found in Romans 4:19. Dibelius's reading does not stand; and washed away with it is any evidence of Paul's awareness of the Lord's virginal conception.

Conclusion

Having completed a close reading of texts in Paul, we are left with very little direct information about Mary. She is the anonymous mother of the heavenly man. Still, four conclusions will guide the remainder of the exegetical work in part one.

---

[28]Dunn, *Galatians,* p. 215.

[29]Martin Dibelius, "Jungsfrauensohn und Krippenkind: Untersuchungen zur Geburtsgeschichte Jesu im Lukas-Evangelium," in *Botschaft und Geschichte: Gesammelte Aufsätze von Martin Dibelius* (Tübingen: Mohr, 1953), pp. 1-78.

Preincarnate existence of Christ. It is highly probable that the earliest followers of Jesus believed in Christ's preincarnate existence. When they worshiped, they understood Jesus as having entered the realm of human existence from another kind of existence. He was Son before he was born. The notion that preincarnate existence is the invention of later Gentile Christians departing from Jewish-Christian faith and practice is wrong. Rather, preexistence emerged through the community's worship of the risen Lord inside of three decades of the events themselves, within the lifetimes of at least some of the first disciples, and in a way that did not threaten its commitment to monotheism.[30]

The early church believed that a preincarnate Christ became a human being, and it devoted itself to him in worship and adoration. It thereby sowed the seeds for what would become—through three centuries of further worship, reflection, debate and controversy—the doctrine of the incarnation of God the Son.

Humanity of Christ. The same passages that indicate belief in preincarnate existence also unreservedly affirm Christ's humanity. He was "born of a woman, born under the law," and his "brother" was James. In the mind of the early church, the preexistent Christ was also a human male who entered the world in the most natural way—birth. Therefore, just as we ought not to read the conclusions of Nicea into the affirmations of preincarnate existence, so also we must not overinterpret those asserting Christ's humanity. The preexistent Christ became a human male. The texts do not say how. Paul indirectly mentions Mary only with respect to her role as Christ's mother. He says nothing regarding Christ's miraculous conception.

Awareness of Mary and the virginal conception. It is odd that a series of texts acknowledging both the preincarnate existence of Christ and his complete humanity would say absolutely nothing about his virginal conception. And yet this is what we have. Must we therefore conclude that the Christians who composed these hymns and creedal formulas, not to mention Saint Paul, did not know of the virginal conception? The two earliest strata of evidence do not indicate knowledge of Christ's miraculous conception, Mary's virginity or even her name. While this cannot prove a lack of knowledge—absence of evidence is not, after all, evidence of absence—it does force the careful reader to ask "why not?" It is likely that Paul and the communities whom he quotes were unaware of the virginal conception and Mary's identity.

It does not follow, however, that the Matthean and Lukan accounts of Jesus'

---

[30]Larry Hurtado, *One God, One Lord: Early Christian Devotion and Ancient Jewish Monotheism* (Philadelphia: Fortress, 1988), and idem., *Lord Jesus Christ: Devotion to Jesus in Earliest Christianity* (Grand Rapids: Eerdmans, 2003).

conception and birth are later Greek mythological additions to a purer, more Jewish, original Gospel. It remains conceivable that Matthew and Luke drew on Christian traditions of which Paul was unaware, but which were rooted in other apostolic witnesses (cf. Lk 1:2). Certainly, the themes contained in these passages harmonize well with Matthew's and Luke's nativities.[31]

Subordinate place of Mariology. Mary is anonymous. There is evidence of devotion to Jesus, to be sure. In the only indirect reference to Mary, "born of a woman" highlights the humanity of her Son. She clarifies beliefs about Jesus. This anonymity provides a theological axiom crucial to the remainder of the study: Mary is to be studied, doctrines about her developed and debated, and she is worthy of devotion only insofar as these deepen our understanding of the person and work of her Son, her Savior and ours. Mariology is always subordinate to Christology. Thus, while as a cradle Protestant I would not have chosen his words, I affirm his intention when Pope John XXIII wrote that "the Madonna is not pleased when she is put above her Son."[32]

---

[31]Brown et al., *Mary in the New Testament,* pp. 43-44.

[32]Quoted in Hilda Graef, *Mary: A History of Doctrine and Devotion,* vol. 1: *From the Beginnings to the Eve of the Reformation* (London: Sheed & Ward, 1963), p. v.

2

Ambiguous Protector of the Family

MARY IN THE GOSPEL OF MARK

Mark's treatment of Mary offers no account of the miraculous conception, nothing concerning Jesus' birth and almost no development of her character. She appears once (Mk 3:31) and is mentioned once more by name (Mk 6:3). Nevertheless, these significant appearances address one of Mark's central themes: natural, good institutions (i.e., religion, family and community) can hinder discipleship. After examining these accounts in detail, we will assess whether their references to Jesus' brothers are more evidence against Mary's perpetual virginity.

At the climax of the Gospel, a woman named Mary appears at the cross (Mk 15:40), at the tomb (Mk 15:47) and is a witness to the resurrection (Mk 16:1). While the Mary in each instance is the same person, whether she is the mother of Jesus is unclear, reinforcing Mark's ambiguous portrait.

True Family of Jesus

Context: The source of Jesus' power (Mark 3:19-30). Mark introduces Jesus' mother in a moment of narrative tension. Jesus has been teaching, healing and appointing disciples around the region of Galilee (Mk 3:7-19). Demonic powers know and proclaim Jesus' identity but are warned by Jesus to be silent. Jesus charges the Twelve not only to teach but also to expel demons. Mark's Jesus is a secretive teacher and wonderworker who awes crowds and authorizes others to act similarly. But whence does his power come? By what authority does he expel demons and commission disciples? These questions drive the narrative, beginning in Mark 3:19.

Jesus has returned to Simon and Andrew's home (cf. Mk 1:29-30; 2:1). The crowds have followed, pressing in such that he and his disciples cannot eat. The scene then switches to a group of antagonists: literally "those from him" (Mk 3:21). Although some understand this phrase to refer to the crowds or the disciples, most agree that it denotes Jesus' mother and brothers (Mk 3:31).[1] They are coming from Nazareth to Capernaum "to restrain him" (Mk 3:21). The verb is more violent than the NRSV's translation suggests. Mark uses it to describe the arrest of John the Baptist by Herod (Mk 6:17) and the hostile desires of the chief priests, scribes and elders toward Jesus (Mk 12:12; 14:1). The notion is one of forcibly taking control of a person. Their motive is clear: "People were saying, 'He has gone out of his mind'" (Mk 3:21). What people? Not the crowds; they are amazed at Jesus' teaching, surrounding him in hopes of healing. Not the scribes; they have their own accusation to make. Those concerned for Jesus' sanity were the relatives.

Leaving Jesus' family on the road from Nazareth to Capernaum, Mark now introduces the reader to a second group of opponents. Scribes have already made the trip from Jerusalem. These are not the local (and relatively minor) opponents whom Jesus has previously encountered (Mk 2:6, 16), but a delegation from the capital.[2] Their charge is grave: Jesus is an emissary of Satan. While this seems to be much more serious than the charge of insanity, the difference is not one of kind, but degree. Given the close association between mental illness and demonic influence in first-century Palestine, Jesus' family likely thought a demon controlled him (hence the need for forcible restraint).[3] The scribes' accusation reverses and intensifies this indictment: Jesus controls a demon, indeed Beelzebul, the ruler of demons (Mk 3:22).[4] The most powerful social institutions of Jesus' day, family and religion, question his authority. Jesus must answer.

Demonstrating his authority even over his opponents,[5] Jesus "called" the scribes (Mk 3:23; cf. Mk 3:13-15) to listen first to a political parable. It is absurd to think that Jesus drives out Satan by the power of Satan. Just as a kingdom riven by civil war is easily conquered and just as a royal family (i.e., "house"; Mk 3:25) internally divided is effortlessly supplanted, so if Satan "has risen up

---

[1]For crowds, see Henry Wansbrough, "Mark iii.21—Was Jesus out of His Mind?" *New Testament Studies* (1972): 233-35. For disciples, see R. T. France, *The Gospel of Mark: A Commentary on the Greek Text,* New International Greek Testament Commentary (Grand Rapids: Eerdmans, 2002), p. 166. For crowds, see John R. Donahue and Daniel J. Harrington, *The Gospel of Mark,* Sacra Pagina 2 (Collegeville, Minn.: Liturgical Press, 2002), p. 129; Robert H. Gundry, *Mark: A Commentary on His Apology for the Cross* (Grand Rapids: Eerdmans, 1993), p. 171; and Morna Hooker, *The Gospel According to Saint Mark* (Peabody, Mass.: Hendrickson, 1991), p. 115.

[2]France, *Mark,* p. 168.

[3]Hooker, *Mark,* p. 115.

[4]Gundry, *Mark,* p. 172.

[5]Ibid.

against himself and is divided, he cannot stand, but his end has come" (Mk 3:26).[6] Jesus then shifts the image from internal division to external attack. The "strong man" (Mk 3:27) must be tied up before a burglar can plunder his property. The strong man is Satan, the burglar is Jesus. The house—retaining the political imagery from the previous verses—refers not to the body of a demoniac (cf. Mt 12:43-45) but to Satan's household or kingdom. At the outset of the Gospel, John the Baptist foretold the coming of "the one who is more powerful" (Greek *ischyroteros*; Mk 1:7). He is now here. Jesus' exorcisms bind the strong man. By exorcising demons, he plunders the strong man's goods. The picture is now one of conflict between rival kingdoms—a point that Matthew's version of the story makes especially clear (cf. Mt 12:28). Accordingly Jesus' judgment on the scribes is harsh: to speak as they have is to identify the work of the Holy Spirit with the work of Satan. This is an eternal sin (Mk 3:28-30).

Jesus' mother and brothers (Mark 3:31-35). Mark now draws us outside. Jesus' family has arrived from Nazareth:

> Then his mother and his brothers came; and standing outside, they sent to him and called him. A crowd was sitting around him; and they said to him, "Your mother and your brothers and sisters are outside, asking for you." And he replied, "Who are my mother and my brothers?" And looking at those who sat around him, he said, "Here are my mother and my brothers! Whoever does the will of God is my brother and sister and mother." (Mk 3:31-35)

Mark's deliberate arrangement of the scenes shows that we are dealing not with two overlapping stories, but one:[7]

a Jesus' family seeks to restrain him (Mk 3:20-21).
b The scribes question Jesus' authority (Mk 3:22).
b' Jesus responds to the scribes (Mk 3:23-30).
a' Jesus responds to his family's demands (Mk 3:31-35).

This close linkage requires that Mark 3:31-35 be read not as Jesus' rejection of his family but rather in a manner similar to that of his response to the scribes, that is, as his response to his family's rejection of him.

As this second movement opens, Jesus and his disciples remain inside, trapped by the surrounding throng. Outside is Jesus' family. The irony is rich. Jesus, having just demonstrated his authority over the religious leaders, is now

---

[6]For an account of the real-world political strife on which Jesus may have drawn for this parable, see Donahue and Harrington, *Mark,* pp. 130-31.

[7]Amunay Yoonprayong, "Jesus and His Mother According to Mk 3.20.21, 31.35," *Marianum* 57 (1995): 513-643.

called to give an account by another potentially hostile power—his family. But their authoritative claim on Jesus is being made from the outside. They are separated from Jesus' disciples. Mark's physical setting mirrors a deeper spiritual reality that is about to be made evident.

Jesus' mother and his brothers sent word and called to him (Mk 3:31). With no account of the virginal conception and miraculous birth of Jesus, it is only natural that Jesus would have had brothers and sisters. While grammatically possible to argue that *adelphoi* means "cousins," the linkage with "mother" without clarification supports a simpler reading: "siblings."[8] Based on Mark's descriptions of the relationships between half brothers (Philip and Herod Antipas in Mk 6:17) and full brothers (James and John in Mk 1:19), the semantic range here encompasses only full and half siblings, that is, people with at least one parent in common.[9] To translate *adelphoi* as anything other than "brothers" here fails to take the text seriously.[10] At most, "brothers" leaves open the possibility that they are Joseph's sons but not Mary's.

Mark declares that despite their blood ties, Jesus' family is distant from him both physically and spiritually.[11] They must send word and call to Jesus. The NRSV implies that the crowd passes the message to Jesus. Robert Gundry, however, contends that "since Jesus has been addressing the scribes . . . and since he will speak to them *about* the crowd (vv 33-35), it looks as though 'they' and 'them' [through whom the message is passed] are the scribes."[12] This reading is preferred because Mark's sandwich technique indicates that Jesus' family and the scribes are acting in concert to challenge his authority.

Jesus' reply is therefore best understood as being directed to the scribes. It begins, like the last one, with a question: "Who are my mother and my brothers?" And, looking at the crowd encircling him, Jesus identifies only those who do God's will as his true family. What God's will is, however, is unclear. The

[8]Jesus' punch line (Mk 3:35) makes sense if the brothers, sisters and mother all have a close blood relationship to Jesus. When examining the Matthean parallel (Mt 12:50), Catholic theologian John P. Meier makes an observation equally applicable to Mk 3:35: "The whole thrust of the metaphor is weakened if we must interpret the natural point of comparison to mean: 'Whoever does the will of my Father in heaven is my male cousin, my female cousin, and my mother.' The full force of the aphorism is retained only if the natural relationships mentioned are all equally close and blood-related, at least in the eyes of the redactors of the Gospels"; "The Brothers and Sisters of Jesus in Ecumenical Perspective," *Catholic Biblical Quarterly* 54 (1992): 13-14.

[9]Ibid., pp. 19-20.

[10]France, *Mark,* p. 179.

[11]Stephen P. Ahearne-Kroll, "'Who Are My Mother and My Brothers?' Family Relations and Family Language in the Gospel of Mark," *Journal of Religion* 81 (2001): 14.

[12]Gundry, *Mark,* p. 178 (emphasis original).

thrust of the encounter suggests that it involves recognizing Jesus' authority, following him, listening to him and cooperating with him. Jesus establishes the spiritual boundary between those "inside" and those "outside" at which Mark's physical setting has hinted. No social connection guarantees Jesus' acceptance. His own family is outside, opposing Jesus and his message.[13]

Rejection of Jesus in Nazareth

Following Jesus' redefinition of his family to embrace those who do God's will, Mark presents four parables in quick succession, each disclosing the nature of God's kingdom: the sower (Mk 4:1-9), the lamp (Mk 4:21-25), the growing seed (Mk 4:26-29) and the mustard seed (Mk 4:30-32). Accompanying these stories are two short explanations of Jesus' pedagogical purpose (Mk 4:10-20, 33-34). Immediately thereafter follow three accounts of Jesus' deeds that authorize and exemplify the previous words: he stills a storm, demonstrating his authority over creation and chaos (Mk 4:35-41; cf. Gen 1:2); he exorcizes the Gerasene demoniac, showing again that God's kingdom has invaded Satan's (Mk 5:1-20; cf. Mk 3:23-30); and he restores a dead girl and hemorrhaging woman, proving that the salvation he brings restores life[14] even at the cost of transgressing purity laws (Mk 5:21-43; cf. Lev 15:19-33).[15]

Mark now temporarily dams his cascade of events; it is time for readers to make a decision about Jesus. Through the narrative that follows, he asks: Having heard his words and seen his deeds, will you now accept Jesus' call to discipleship and enter the kingdom of God? Again, Jesus' mother and family are deeply embedded in the context of unbelief through which Mark makes his invitation:

> He left that place and came to his hometown, and his disciples followed him. On the sabbath he began to teach in the synagogue, and many who heard him were astounded. They said, "Where did this man get all this? What is this wisdom that has been given to him? What deeds of power are being done by his hands! Is not this the carpenter, the son of Mary and the brother of James and Joses and Judas and Simon, and are not his sisters here with us?" And they took offense at him. Then Jesus said to them, "Prophets are not without honor, except in their home-

---

[13]On the social role of the kinship unit, see Joanna Dewey, "The Gospel of Mark," in *Searching the Scriptures: A Feminist Commentary,* ed. Elisabeth Schüssler Fiorenza (New York: Crossroad, 1994), p. 478.

[14]Wendy Cotter, "Mark's Hero of the Twelfth Year Miracles: The Healing of the Woman with the Hemorrhage and the Raising of Jairus's Daughter (Mark 5.21-43)," in *A Feminist Companion to Mark,* ed. Amy-Jill Levine (Sheffield, U.K.: Sheffield Academic Press, 2001), pp. 54-78.

[15]Marla J. Selvidge, "Mark 5:25-34 and Leviticus 15:19-20: A Reaction to Restrictive Purity Regulations," *Journal of Biblical Literature* 103 (1984): 619-23.

> town, and among their own kin, and in their own house." And he could do no deed of power there, except that he laid his hands on a few sick people and cured them. And he was amazed at their unbelief. (Mk 6:1-6)

Jesus has returned to Nazareth to teach in the synagogue. His hearers are amazed, their reaction reminding readers of the preceding parables and miracles.[16] But their astonishment quickly turns to rejection; Jesus' hometown has joined the opposition with the religious leaders and Jesus' family. Mark slowly alienates Jesus from all social groups—religion, kin and now neighbors—moving steadily toward a climax in which Jesus will be rejected by his nation and God's kingdom will be given to outsiders.[17]

The carpenter, the son of Mary. Mark 6:3 has bearing on our study of Mary and Jesus' siblings. The Synoptic parallel accounts, along with John's similar declaration in a different setting, mention Joseph either indirectly (Mt 13:55) or by name (Lk 4:22; Jn 6:42). Only Mark names Jesus as the carpenter. Both facts are germane. While a minority of Markan manuscripts describe Jesus as the "son of the carpenter," most scholars accept "the carpenter" as the authentic rendering.[18] Mark's use of the definite article indicates that Jesus is well known to the townspeople in this role. Indeed, their unbelief suggests that they cannot conceive of him as acting outside of it. R. T. France phrases it aptly: "To the people of Nazareth, Jesus is the local boy, and they know of no reason why he should have turned out to be any different from the rest of his family."[19] Joseph's absence both here and in Mark 3:31-35 is easily explained. Far from being a subtle acknowledgement of Jesus' virginal conception, Joseph's absence suggests that he had died and did not figure in his son's adult life.[20]

The phrase "the son of Mary" may be more controversial. Ethelbert Stauffer argues that it insultingly insinuates illegitimacy.[21] The townspeople were offended because they thought he was a bastard. This interpretation, however, has not carried the day. Compelling counterevidence shows no ulterior intentions.

---

[16]That the references to "wisdom" and "deeds of power" in Mk 6:2 are clearly intended to evoke memories of the parables (Mk 4:1-34) and the miracles (Mk 4:35—5:43) is made clear by the reference that Jesus "could do no deed of power" in Nazareth because of the people's unbelief (Mk 6:5).

[17]Hooker, *Mark*, p. 152.

[18]Ibid.

[19]France, *Mark*, p. 242.

[20]Ibid.

[21]Ethelbert Stauffer, "Jeschu ben Mirjam: Kontroversgeschichtliche Anmerkungen zu Mk. 6:3," in *Neotestamentica et Semitica: Studies in Honour of Matthew Black*, ed. E. Earle Ellis and Max Wilcox (Edinburgh: T & T Clark, 1969), pp. 119-28.

Standing in parallel with "the carpenter," the phrase indicates familiarity.[22] More recently, Tal Ilan has provided extrabiblical examples in which men are identified by their mothers, but without any aspersions.[23] The simplest understanding is best. Jesus is "the carpenter, the son of Mary," a local manual laborer whose father had died some years back. We may paraphrase their exclamation to reflect its small-town gossipy nature: "Who is this guy? Is he not the carpenter? You know, Mary's boy?" The description says little about Mary. At most, Mark has reinforced the depiction of Mary as an opponent.

James and Joses and Judas and Simon and . . . his sisters. Jesus has four brothers whose patriarchal names (Jacob, Joseph, Judah and Simeon) suggest that Mary was raising a pious Jewish family.[24] At least one of these, James, became a follower of Jesus and a leader in the early church (Gal 1:19). Some identify Jude with the writer of the New Testament book of the same name because its author claims to be James's brother (Jude 1). Allusions to the Lord's brothers in Acts 1:14 and 1 Corinthians 9:5 suggest that some and quite possibly all of these eventually joined the church. The sisters of Jesus are never identified.

End and Beginning of Jesus

Our final stop in Mark is the cross and tomb. The male disciples have fled (Mk 14:50); only female disciples bear witness to Jesus' final hours. Three are named because of their status as witnesses to Jesus' resurrection: Mary Magdalene, Mary the mother of James and Joses, and Salome (Mk 15:40). After Jesus' death, the two Marys remain with Joseph of Arimathea to inter the body (Mk 15:43, 47). Finally, on Easter morning all three return to the tomb to embalm the body (Mk 16:1).

It is tempting to identify the second Mary with Jesus' mother. Not only would it harmonize Mark's account with John's (Jn 19:25-27), an appeal can be made on the basis of their sons' common names (cf. Mk 6:3). This reading, however, is unlikely. First, had Mark wanted readers to know that Jesus' mother was at the cross and the tomb, he would have said so. Why say "Mary the mother of James the younger and of Joses" when "Jesus' mother" would do (cf. Mk 3:31; 6:3)? Second, the names Jacob and Joseph were too popular in first-century Palestine to assume that they refer to the same persons. Further, if it is Jesus' mother, then she reconciled with Jesus before his death. This would further har-

[22]Harvey K. McArthur, "Son of Mary," *Novum Testamentum* 15 (1973): 38-58.

[23]Tal Ilan, "'Man Born of Woman . . .' (Job 14:1): The Phenomenon of Men Bearing Metronymes at the Time of Jesus," *Novum Testamentum* 34 (1992): 23-45.

[24]Gundry, *Mark,* p. 296.

monize Mark and John (cf. Jn 19:25) and is historically possible, but it undermines Mark's theme of alienation as a consequence of discipleship (cf. Mk 3:31-35). Finally, the description of James as "the younger" or "the less" seems to distinguish him from James the son of Zebedee among the Twelve. If so, then this Mary is the wife of Alphaeus (cf. Mk 3:18). These texts do not challenge the reading of Mary as opponent.

Conclusion

Three conclusions drawn in chapter one are reaffirmed by the exegesis now completed. First, Jesus is a human being. He lived in the webs of family, religious and social obligations common to first-century Palestine. Although he redefined them, ignored them and transgressed them for the sake of the gospel, at no point is he aloof. The second conclusion is related: like Paul, Mark demonstrates no awareness of the virginal conception of the Lord. The best explanation for the absence of Joseph is his death; to argue otherwise is baseless. Although this does not prove Mark's ignorance of the miracle, it does suggest it. Third, Mark, like Paul, does not write a Mariology, nor is he concerned to give attention to mariological themes. He proclaims "the good news of Jesus Christ, the Son of God" (Mk 1:1). Characters, including Mary, further that aim. This introduces the first of Mark's unique contributions.

Ambiguity of Mary's pre-Easter place. Mark has used Mary to develop a constant theme: discipleship to Jesus is costly, straining and severing intimate ties. Mark has replaced Paul's anonymity with ambiguity. Mark numbers Mary among Jesus' opponents; she believes that he is insane, she wants to restrain him, she is not present at his death. She is "a foil for authentic discipleship."[25]

Is Mark's Mary an active enemy of Jesus and his mission? This conclusion moves just beyond what a close reading allows. Jesus' active opponents in Mark 3:20-35 are the scribes, not his mother and brothers. Being the guardians of God's revelation, they most of all should have recognized Jesus' identity and the source of his power. They alone attributed to Jesus an alliance with Beelzebul; they alone blasphemed the Holy Spirit. Jesus' redefinition of family, on the other hand, is a response to misunderstanding. The family's opposition is a misguided attempt to act for Jesus' (and its own) well-being. Mary may well be acting in this scene with the best of intentions toward both her firstborn and her other (step)children.[26]

---

[25]Elizabeth A. Johnson, *Truly Our Sister: Mary in the Community of Saints* (New York: Continuum, 2004), p. 218.

[26]Ibid., p. 220.

Jesus had exposed himself and his family to great danger. Mary organized the family at Nazareth to bring him home. These are not the actions of an enemy. These are the actions of a strong and loving mother who is concerned with preserving the lives of her children: "In this light, a feminist perspective espies the exercise of female power in the action of Miriam of Nazareth, who, no stranger to Roman violence and the havoc it could wreak on human lives, goes to persuade her child out of the line of fire."[27] Far from undermining Mark's theme of costly discipleship, this underscores how easily the gospel's call is missed and how, even when intentions are noble, Jesus' way can sunder deep bonds. When we read Mary's actions as caring and her intentions as good, we glimpse how expensive the cost of discipleship is. Mary is an opponent of Jesus for the best of reasons—to protect those she loves (including Jesus) from harm.

Mary's other children. As we have now seen, Paul (Gal 1:19; 1 Cor 9:5) and Mark (Mk 3:20-21; 6:3; cf. Mt 12:46; 13:55-56; Lk 8:19-20) refer independently to Jesus' brothers. This is true also of Luke (Acts 1:14) and John (Jn 2:12; 7:1-10). The most natural conclusion is that after Jesus' birth Mary and Joseph had a normal sexual relationship that resulted in the conception and birth of at least six more children (cf. Mk 6:3). The continued virginity of Mary is not a concern of the New Testament authors. Had the question not arisen as a result of later theological debates, it would not arise here. But it did arise later and has caused exegetes to try to determine just what the relationship was between Jesus and his siblings. We can conclude that the actual grammar of the texts leaves room for debate. Grammatically, Jesus' "brothers and sisters" may or may not have been other children of Mary. For Roman Catholic and Orthodox Christians the matter is largely settled: Mary is ever-virgin (Greek *aeiparthenos*; Latin *semper virgo*). For many Protestants this is also where the debate ends: the Bible strongly insinuates that Mary had a family of her own after the birth of Jesus.

Are we at an impasse? Not necessarily. Protestants must also ask after the Reformers and the Protestant confessions. We must also be willing to see whether the doctrine logically required by others is clearly taught in Holy Scripture and whether it clarifies or grounds doctrines that traditional Protestants believe to be true. These questions will be taken up in parts two and three.

---

[27]Ibid., pp. 220-21.

3

Scandalous Mother of the Messiah

Mary in the Gospel of Matthew

With his elaborate story of Jesus' origins, one expects Matthew to say more about Mary than either Mark or Paul. Mary does not, however, figure prominently in Matthew. Although she is mentioned in the genealogy (Mt 1:16), with the miraculous nature of her pregnancy described (Mt 1:18-23) and the birth of Jesus narrated (Mt 1:25), Matthew focuses on Joseph, "a righteous man" (Mt 1:19). Thus, the genealogy is *his*—Joseph, David's heir. Mary's conception is announced in *his* vision. God must persuade *Joseph* to marry Mary. In the birth account, Matthew downplays Mary's pain and joy and stresses that *Joseph* had not had sex with her. Matthew's central theological point is that Jesus is not Joseph's son, but the Son of God; he is still Joseph's and therefore David's heir.

Matthew's perspective is androcentric.[1] In a story of sexual scandal, atypical pregnancy and birth, Mary's presence only exposes Joseph's nobility. As a result, it is difficult to scan Matthew's opening chapters without a sense of irony. And yet closer inspection may well undermine readers' irony. While

[1]An androcentric perspective is an authorial perspective that takes exclusively or predominantly male points of view with respect to the events it narrates. See Elizabeth Schüssler Fiorenza, "Breaking the Silence—Becoming Visible," *Concilium* 182 (1985): 4; Richard Bauckham, *Gospel Women: Studies of the Named Women in the Gospels* (Grand Rapids: Eerdmans, 2002), esp. pp. 1-17; Janice Capel Anderson, "Matthew: Gender and Reading," in *A Feminist Companion to Matthew,* ed. Amy-Jill Levine (Sheffield, U.K.: Sheffield Academic Press, 2001), p. 28; and Elaine Mary Wainwright, *Towards a Feminist Critical Reading of the Gospel According to Matthew,* Beihefte zur Zeitschrift für die neutestamentliche Wissenschaft 60 (Berlin: de Gruyter, 1991), pp. 27-28, 55-58.

Matthew does not say much about Mary in his opening chapters, what he says is significant.

Warren Carter argues that Matthew's Gospel is a "counternarrative" or "a work of resistance."[2] Addressed to disciples after the destruction of the temple in A.D. 70, it constructs an alternative worldview and community to those provided by Roman power and the synagogue-centered and text-centered Judaism of the day.[3] True Jewish identity, it claims, is found among the people claiming Jesus as the Davidic Messiah.

If Carter is correct about the centrality of the church/synagogue dispute,[4] then Matthew's Gospel is designed to bolster a minority view still within Judaism and to call into question the views of the others.[5] As such, it "affirms a way of life marginal to the dominant structures. It challenges its audience to live this resistant way of life faithfully in its present circumstances" because Jesus the true king had come and would come again.[6] Reading the birth narrative (and two other Marian passages) in the light of Carter's proposal shows that an apologetic motif runs parallel to Matthew's christological concerns. This subtheme adds insight and complexity to an understanding of Mary that has, until now, remained seriously underdeveloped.

Historical Value of the Birth Narratives

Paul, Mark and the Christian communities in which they operated demonstrate no awareness of the circumstances of the Lord's birth. Just what is revealed when the light of their silence shines on Matthew's and Luke's opening chapters? Are they history or fiction? The birth narratives do not present history, at least not in the popular sense of the word. Rather, both narratives reflect early Christian understandings of Jesus' origins, and both have been theologically

---

[2]Warren Carter, *Matthew and the Margins: A Socio-Political and Religious Reading,* Journal for the Study of the New Testament Supplement 204 (Sheffield, U.K.: Sheffield Academic Press, 2000), pp. 1-2. Most scholars date the writing of the Gospel somewhere between 75 and 85. See Raymond Brown, *The Birth of the Messiah: A Commentary on the Infancy Narratives in the Gospels of Matthew and Luke,* 2nd ed. (New York: Doubleday, 1993), pp. 45-48.

[3]When discussing Jewish faith before the A.D. 70 disaster, one can easily speak of "Judaisms." Conflicting emphases on the temple, Bible, land and synagogue were all viable. After 70, claims to temple and land were silenced, leaving the early rabbis and Jesus' followers. See Daniel J. Harrington, *The Gospel of Matthew,* Sacra Pagina 1 (Collegeville, Minn.: Liturgical Press, 1991), pp. 10-16.

[4]This handy abbreviation is, of course, anachronistic; Matthew's community still attended synagogue. See Robert Gundry, *Matthew: A Commentary on His Handbook for a Mixed Church under Persecution,* 2nd ed. (Grand Rapids: Eerdmans, 1994), pp. 190-203.

[5]Rabbinic teachers are still (grudgingly) granted some authority in Mt 23:3.

[6]Carter, *Matthew and the Margins,* p. 1.

tailored to suit Matthew's and Luke's own objectives.[7]

In *The Birth of the Messiah* Raymond Brown presents two arguments against reading the infancy narratives in Matthew and Luke as simple history. The first is what he calls "the problem of corroborating witnesses."[8] The likelihood that the Evangelists, Jesus' boyhood neighbors and members of his family were witnesses of Jesus' birth is remote. We exclude the Evangelists because, while the Gospels and Acts can claim to be rooted in apostolic memory, the first to proclaim the gospel were absent from Jesus' birth. The Nazareth townsfolk are rejected because they knew Jesus best of all, yet seemed to know nothing of the miracle (Mk 6:1-6; cf. Mt 13:53-58; Lk 4:31-32). Even Jesus' family is ruled out. If Mark 6:3 indicates that Joseph died before Jesus' ministry began, there is no way that Joseph recounted the events to the disciples. Mary is a better candidate, for we know that she joined the postresurrection community (Acts 1:14). But if it is plausible to posit her as a source for Luke (see chap. 4), discrepancies between the stories exclude her as Matthew's source. Finally, in the second century James was considered to be a possible—albeit secondhand—witness. But the fanciful, legendary nature of the *Protevangelium of James* makes this doubtful (see chap. 6). Brown concludes that "we have no real knowledge that any or all of the infancy material came from a tradition for which there was a corroborating witness."[9]

Could Matthew and Luke have drawn upon some common, if anonymous, witness to compose their nativities? If so, then we should find a great deal of agreement between the two, even if their accounts were composed independently. There are eleven overlapping points:

1. Mary and Joseph are legally engaged or married, but not yet cohabiting or sexually active (Mt 1:18; Lk 1:27-34).
2. Joseph is of Davidic descent (Mt 1:16, 20; Lk 1:27, 32; 2:4).

---

[7]The question "did the virginal conception take place?" has little to do with the theological manipulation of historical sources and more to do with whether one is predisposed to believing in miracles. Even if Matthew and Luke think that the virginal conception occurred in our time and space, this does not—indeed cannot—meet a skeptic's burden of proof that the miracle did in fact occur. Those who believe in miracles generally and in the miraculous conception of Jesus specifically will find support for so believing here; those who do not will not. If skeptics continue to seek a historical core behind the narratives, clarity would be better served by replacing the word *historical* with the more accurate *naturalistic* or *materialistic*. They have discounted a miraculous explanation at the level of presuppositions. One of the best is Jane Schaberg, *The Illegitimacy of Jesus: A Feminist Interpretation of the Infancy Narratives* (San Francisco: Harper & Row, 1987).

[8]Brown, *Birth of the Messiah*, p. 32.

[9]Ibid., p. 33.

3. There is an angelic announcement of the child's birth (Mt 1:20-23; Lk 1:30-35).
4. The child is conceived without intercourse (Mt 1:20, 23, 25; Lk 1:34).
5. The conception is through the Holy Spirit (Mt 1:18, 20; Lk 1:35).
6. The angel directs the child to be named Jesus (Mt 1:21; Lk 1:31).
7. An angel states that Jesus is the Savior (Mt 1:21; Lk 2:11).
8. The birth takes place after the parents start living together (Mt 1:24-25; Lk 2:5-6).
9. The birth takes place at Bethlehem (Mt 2:1; Lk 2:4-6).
10. The birth is chronologically related to the reign of Herod the Great (Mt 2:1; Lk 1:5).
11. The child is reared at Nazareth (Mt 2:23; Lk 2:39).[10]

These areas of agreement are not strong enough, however, to answer "the problem of conflicting details."[11] First are the differing details:[12]

1. The genealogies are different (Mt 1:1-17; Lk 3:23-28).
2. The annunciation to Joseph, the star, the magi, the massacre of the innocents, the flight to Egypt and the return to Nazareth (Mt 1:18—2:23) are without parallel in Luke.
3. Similarly the annunciation to Mary, the birth of John the Baptist, the census, the manger, the shepherds, the presentation of Jesus at the temple and the loss of the boy Jesus (Lk 2:1-52) are not in Matthew.

Then there are the contradicting details:[13]

1. In Luke, Mary lives in Nazareth (Lk 1:26), and Augustus's census is the motive for her move to Bethlehem (Lk 2:1-5). In Matthew, Joseph and Mary are already living in Bethlehem when the child is born (Mt 2:11).
2. Where Matthew presents Herod's homicidal order as the trigger for the move to Nazareth via Egypt (Mt 2:22-23), Luke depicts the holy family returning to Nazareth peacefully (Lk 2:22, 39).
3. Luke's Jesus is an infant upon arrival in Nazareth (Lk 2:21, 39); Matthew's is likely over two years old (Mt 2:16).

---

[10]Ibid., pp. 34-35.
[11]Ibid., pp. 33-37.
[12]Ibid., p. 35.
[13]Ibid., p. 36.

Attempts to harmonize two clearly different stories must, in the light of this evidence, fail.[14]

Nevertheless, Matthew and Luke did not simply create their nativities on the basis of a few overlapping details. Attention to detail shows not only that Matthew's and Luke's stories differ, but also that they rely on earlier sources. One should expect this from Luke. He is the latest of "many [who] have undertaken to set down an orderly account of the events" he is about to describe (Lk 1:1). Only after consulting "eyewitnesses" and "servants of the word" and "investigating everything carefully" did he compose his version (Lk 1:2-3). "Further, the way Matthew sometimes awkwardly works his formula citations into his narrative suggests he was working with one or several narrative sources to which he has added OT quotations."[15] If both Gospels were written within a few years of the temple's destruction,[16] then their sources had attained some authoritative status within six decades of the events themselves and within three decades of the beginning of the church. They are too close to living memory to be imaginative compositions.

How was the sources' authority attained? Brown presents three possibilities.[17] First, it is possible that the sources tailored pagan tales to suggest the divine origins of Jesus. Matthew and Luke, thinking them to be history, then adopted and adapted them further. This explanation proves to be dubious, for those Christians among whom the stories developed would have had little awareness of Greco-Roman and Egyptian legends.[18] And even if aware of them, Greek-speaking Jewish Christians most likely would have wanted to avoid impugning God with the gross sexual immorality often depicted in them. There is little resemblance between the nonsexual conception of Jesus

---

[14]The best harmonization remains J. Gresham Machen, *The Virgin Birth of Christ,* 2nd ed. (New York: Harper & Row, 1932), pp. 188-209.

[15]Ben Witherington III, "Birth of Jesus," in *Dictionary of Jesus and the Gospels,* ed. Joel B. Green and Scot McKnight (Downers Grove, Ill.: InterVarsity Press, 1992), p. 61.

[16]On the range of possibilities for the dating of Luke, see Darrell L. Bock, "Luke, Gospel of," in *Dictionary of Jesus and the Gospels,* ed. Joel B. Green and Scot McKnight (Downers Grove, Ill.: InterVarsity Press, 1992), pp. 498-500. Bock presents ca. 70 as the consensual position, but argues for a date around 65 or earlier. My position is not dependent on Bock's hypothesis, but works very well with both dates. John Maquarrie's date of A.D. 85 now reflects the upper end of New Testament scholarship and is unlikely; see *Mary for All Christians,* 2nd ed. (Edinburgh: T & T Clark, 2001), p. xx. Yet, even if one adopts the latest possible date, 95-100, the thrust of my argument still holds.

[17]Brown, *Birth of the Messiah,* pp. 521-28.

[18]The likelihood of such awareness holds best alongside late dates of composition, which would have allowed for greater Gentile influence in Matthean and Lukan communities. Scholarship over the last century has moved, however, in the opposite direction, dating the Gospels' composition earlier and earlier.

and the sexual conceptions of pagan heroes.[19]

It is also possible that the sources drew on stories of virginal conceptions in Judaism. But here, examples are even fewer. Isaiah 7:14 ("the virgin shall conceive"; NKJV) carried with it no hint of virginal conception among Hebrew- or Greek-speaking Jews before Matthew.[20] Based on the available evidence, it seems that the first—and to that point only—Jew to read Isaiah 7:14 that way was Matthew. His is a uniquely Christian interpretation and application of the prophecy. A second example, the supposed Hellenistic-Jewish myth of a Spirit-conceived Isaac (Gal 4:28-29), has already been examined and rejected.[21] There is no hard evidence that a first-century Jewish idea of a virginal conception influenced Christian communities to fashion their own.

With these alternatives lacking, the best explanation for the authority that both traditions so quickly acquired is that they testify to a widespread and early Christian belief that the virginal conception of Jesus happened. Various details in the stories make this possibility attractive. For what theological purpose, for example, did Luke include the name of Anna's father (Lk 2:36)? Similarly, why does Matthew proclaim that Jesus will be called Emmanuel (Mt 1:23) and then never use that title again in his Gospel? These anomalies suggest that these are more than theological constructions. Furthermore, if they are theological fictions, they create more problems than they solve. Whether articulated by Matthew or Luke, the virginal conception has from the second century left Jesus open to the devastating—at least in Jewish eyes—charge of illegitimacy.[22] It would seem odd, therefore, for Matthew or Luke to invent it.

The nativities of Matthew and Luke are not simple history, but theology mediated through narratives themselves rooted in a historical event. In terms of purely historical value, the infancy narratives offer very little. Ben Witherington III describes the infancy narratives as "theological history-writing."[23] And it is as theological-historical constructions that they are best approached.

Mary in the Birth Story

Following a seminal article by Krister Stendahl, Raymond Brown suggests that the first two chapters of Matthew answer four theological questions concerning

[19]Brown, *Birth of the Messiah,* pp. 522-23.

[20]Ibid., pp. 523-24; see also pp. 143-53.

[21]For more dubious examples than these, see ibid., p. 524 n. 21.

[22]Such charges may have been lodged much earlier. See the treatment of Matthew's genealogy below.

[23]Witherington, "Birth of Jesus," p. 61.

Jesus' "origins" (Mt 1:1, translated "genealogy" in the NRSV):[24]

1. Who? Through the device of genealogy, Matthew responds that Jesus is the Messiah, the heir of David and the descendent of Abraham (Mt 1:1-17).[25]
2. How? The story of Jesus' birth answers that Jesus the Son of God is also the son of David through legal adoption by Joseph, a Davidic descendant of righteous character.
3. Whence?[26] The magi and the star tell that Jesus was born in Bethlehem (Mt 2:1-12).
4. Whither?[27] The flight to Egypt and return to Nazareth says that the Davidic king will leave David's city, recapitulate Israel's journeys to and from Egypt, and return to the margins of social life in Galilee (Mt 2:13-23).[28]

Beverly Roberts Gaventa agrees with Brown's structure and shows how Matthew 1 and Matthew 2 parallel each other.[29] Her argument is persuasive.

1. Both narratives open with words derived from the same Greek root: *gennaō* or *genesis* (*geneseōs* in Mt 1:1 and *gennēthentos* in Mt 2:1).
2. Both narratives end with verbs derived from the same Greek root: *kaleō* (*ekalesen* in Mt 1:25 and *klēthēsetai* in Mt 2:23).
3. Both narratives are concerned with Jesus' origins and names.

Gaventa therefore clarifies Brown's four-question arrangement, proposing that

---

[24]Brown, *Birth of the Messiah*, pp. 52-54. See Krister Stendahl, "Quis et unde? An Analysis of Mt 1—2," in *Judentum, Urchristentum, Kirche: Festschrift für Joachim Jeremias*, ed. Walther Eltester, Beihefte zur Zeitschrift für die neutestamentliche Wissenschaft 26 (Berlin: Töpelman, 1964), pp. 94-105.

[25]The genealogy falls within the bounds of the "theological-historical construction" described above. It does not simply present the ancestry of Jesus but shows that Jesus, anchored as he is in the history of Israel (Mt 1:1-2) as the Davidic heir (Mt 1:1, 6) born at the right time (note the internal structure based on three collections of fourteen generations in Mt 1:6, 11-12, 17), could legitimately claim the title "Messiah" (Mt 1:1); see R. R. Wilson, *Genealogy in History and in the Biblical World*, Yale Near Eastern Researches 7 (New Haven: Yale University Press, 1977). I am indebted to Harrington, *Matthew*, p. 33, for this source.

[26]Brown uses "where?" *(ubi)* for the third question (*Birth of the Messiah*, p. 53). Beverly Roberts Gaventa opts for "whence?" in order to more clearly distinguish the third and fourth questions; see *Mary: Glimpses of the Mother of Jesus in the New Testament* (Philadelphia: Fortress, 1999), p. 31.

[27]Compare Brown, *Birth of the Messiah*, p. 54 ("whence?" *unde*), with Gaventa, *Mary*, p. 31. Again, I follow Gaventa.

[28]The rest of the Gospel may then be read as Jesus' journey from the margins of social life in Nazareth to the central power of David's throne. Although foreshadowed throughout the Gospel, it is only as the risen Lord that Jesus says, "All authority in heaven and on earth has been given to me" (Mt 28:18).

[29]Gaventa, *Mary*, p. 31.

the chapters be read as two parallel halves, each falling into two parts. Once this division is seen, a thematic structure of implied and actual threat emerges. The women in the genealogy personify the implied threats of part one, as does Herod's fear in part two. The righteousness of Joseph poses an actual threat in part one, as does the unrighteousness of Herod in part two.

In this arrangement Mary appears alongside Jesus as one who threatens and is threatened by the social, religious and political structures of the day.[30] This threatened/threatening dynamic has impact on the theological, social and political scandals that Mary and Jesus represented to those opposed to Matthew's community.

Mary and the scandalous women (Matthew 1:1-17). Theologically, the scandal resides in Jesus' lack of Davidic descent because of Mary's atypical pregnancy. Matthew addresses this apologetically through the women he includes in the genealogy:

> An account of the genealogy of Jesus the Messiah, the son of David, the son of Abraham. . . .
>
> And Judah the father of Perez and Zerah by Tamar, . . . and Salmon the father of Boaz by Rahab, and Boaz the father of Obed by Ruth, and Obed the father of Jesse, and Jesse the father of King David.
>
> And David was the father of Solomon by the wife of Uriah. . . .
>
> And Jacob the father of Joseph the husband of Mary, of whom Jesus was born, who is called the Messiah. (Mt 1:1, 3, 5-7, 16)

The obvious question is, why these women? Sarah, Rebecca, Rachel and Leah—the great matriarchs of the covenant promise, the wives of Abraham, Isaac and Jacob, who themselves were ancestors of our Lord—are better candidates. But not these women! Tamar played the prostitute with her father-in-law (Gen 38). Rahab was a foreigner and prostitute who lied to save the lives of Israelite spies (Josh 2; 6:22-25). Ruth's ancestral parents were Lot and his daughter (Gen 19:37-38); she was an enemy of God's people by birth. The wife of Uriah committed adultery with David and ended peace in his kingdom (2 Sam 11:1—12:24).

In order to answer this question, we begin by noting their deliberate presence in the genealogy. Matthew draws attention to these women by using them to break the patrilineal pattern, which is otherwise straightforward: A the father of B, B the father of C and so on. Matthew wants readers to notice these women. There remains significant disagreement, however, over just what their presence means and just what readers are to notice about them. Broadly speaking, three

---

[30]Ibid., pp. 29-48.

interpretations are offered, two of them not congenial to including Mary in their company.

Perhaps the most ancient explanation is that Tamar, Rahab, Ruth and the wife of Uriah are mentioned because they are all sinners, foreshadowing Jesus' saving role.[31] Espoused first by fourth-century church father Jerome, this view has defenders in the modern era.[32] The women have little to do with Mary beyond contrasting their sinfulness with her sanctity. This reading, however, is unsustainable. First, it is not clear that the women are sinners. Tamar seduces and becomes pregnant by her father-in-law Judah and is judged (by Judah himself!) to be "in the right" (Gen 38:26). His failure to care for her after the death of his son Er is sin. Rahab the prostitute (Josh 2:1) is the heroine of the story in which she appears. While an enemy of Israel by birth, Ruth the Moabite is a virtuous heroine. Her character in her dealings with Boaz is unquestioned by the narrator. Finally, Bathsheba's adultery with David is counted as David's sin, not hers (2 Sam 11:27). Second, in Jesus' time these women were not regarded as sinful: Tamar was esteemed as a convert who had faith in the messianic promise to Judah; Rahab was honored as a convert who helped the Israelite victory at Jericho (cf. Heb 11:31); even Bathsheba was praised as the mother of Solomon.[33]

More persuasive is the thesis that the women are included because they are foreigners. Rahab and Ruth are obviously Gentiles—one Canaanite, the other Moabite.[34] As far as Matthew is concerned, Bathsheba is a Gentile by marriage.[35] Tamar's case is much harder to judge; we cannot tell from the text whether she is a Gentile. Richard Bauckham, however, provides convincing evidence that "a Jewish exegete of the time of Matthew could consider Tamar to be of unequivocally Gentile origin."[36] These women thus stand alongside other Gentile char-

---

[31]Brown, *Birth of the Messiah,* p. 71.

[32]Ethelbert Stauffer, "Jeschu ben Mirjam: Kontroversgeschichtliche Anmerkungen zu Mk. 6:3," in *Neotestamentica et Semitica: Studies in Honour of Matthew Black,* ed. E. Earle Ellis and Max Wilcox (Edinburgh: T & T Clark, 1969), pp. 123-25.

[33]Brown, *Birth of the Messiah,* p. 72. Bathsheba's honor, however, was not universal (p. 72 n. 26).

[34]On the apparent chronological impossibility of the conquest's Rahab being the wife of Salmon, who lived at least two centuries later, see the fascinating and convincing explanation offered by Bauckham, *Gospel Women,* pp. 17-46, esp. 34-41.

[35]Gundry (*Matthew,* p. 15) persuasively argues that this explains why Matthew deviates from the genealogical material in the Septuagint version of 1 Chron 1-3, from which he otherwise draws extensively. There, Bathsheba is named Bersabey (cf. Bathshua in the Masoretic Text) and is listed as "the daughter of Ammiel," an Israelite. Matthew, however, omits her name and presents her as "the wife of Uriah." If, as seems most likely, Matthew has followed the designation in 2 Sam 11:26 and 2 Sam 12:10, 15 here, then readers are expected to assume that Uriah is a "Hittite."

[36]Bauckham, *Gospel Women,* p. 33.

acters in Matthew's Gospel—the magi (Mt 2:1-12), the centurion (Mt 8:5-13) and the Canaanite woman (Mt 15:21-28)[37]—foreshadowing the universal scope of Jesus' saving work (Mt 28:18-20).

This theory faces two criticisms. First, some challenge it because it excludes the Jewish Mary from the outset.[38] Elaine Wainwright argues that to tie the four women to Jesus and not to Mary betrays patriarchal prejudice.[39] Apart from a common sex, however, there is no textual ground to link them to Mary. Accordingly not seeing one does not necessarily betray patriarchal bias.[40] Matthew tells us that the genealogy is about "Jesus the Messiah, the son of David, the son of Abraham" (Mt 1:1). Would one not, therefore, expect the key elements of the genealogy—and the four women are certainly key—to refer primarily to him?[41] Mary's inclusion merely indicates that "Matthew cannot otherwise explain Joseph's relationship to Jesus."[42] This criticism does not threaten the viability of the theory.

The second criticism, however, poses more of a challenge. What if, as is the case with Rahab and Tamar, the women were regarded in postbiblical Judaism not as Gentiles but as converts to Judaism and therefore Jewish?[43] If, as most scholars agree, Matthew's audience was predominantly Jewish, then it is unclear just how they would see converts to Judaism (along with the magi, the centurion and the Canaanite woman) pointing to the eventual universal mission of the Jewish Messiah.[44] Further, if Matthew's predominantly Jewish audience included at least some Gentiles,[45] then the women's status as proselytes *to Judaism* would also be unclear to them for, as Brown puts it, "the Gentile Christians had *not* become Jewish proselytes in order to accept Jesus."[46] Thus, while in many ways more commendable than the first, the second theory is also not without difficulties.

---

[37]On the centurion and the Canaanite woman, see ibid., pp. 41-46. Bauckham argues that Matthew intends us to see the Canaanite woman as a new Rahab, with Jesus as the new Joshua (pp. 44-45).

[38]So Raymond Brown et al., *Mary in the New Testament: A Collaborative Assessment by Protestant and Roman Catholic Scholars* (Philadelphia: Fortress, 1978), p. 80.

[39]Wainwright, *Towards a Feminist Critical Reading,* p. 65.

[40]Bauckham, *Gospel Women,* pp. 19-23.

[41]Ibid., p. 19.

[42]Ibid., p. 21.

[43]Brown, *Birth of the Messiah,* p. 73 esp. n. 31.

[44]The inclusion of proselytes in the genealogy may signal that "in a community that had consisted predominantly of Jewish Christians, the Gentile Christians were looked on as proselytes not to Judaism but to Jewish Christianity" (Brown, *Birth of the Messiah,* p. 73). But if this is the case, of course, then they do not foreshadow the mission to the Gentiles, but display to Jewish Christians the *kind* of Gentiles that were welcome in the community.

[45]Gundry (*Matthew,* pp. 5-9) certainly suggests the plausibility of this notion.

[46]Brown, *Birth of the Messiah,* p. 73 (emphasis original).

Third, it could be that Rahab, Tamar, Ruth and Bathsheba each signal irregular marital unions that were vehicles of God's messianic plan. The similarity with the first theory is only apparent. The argument is not that the women were sinners, but that their marital unions themselves were extraordinary. Through Tamar's seduction the messianic line was preserved; through Rahab's courage Israel entered the land and Rahab became numbered among the people of God; through Ruth's initiative she and Boaz became David's great-grandparents; and, although an adulteress, it was through Bathsheba's strategic preparation that Solomon came to the throne. This third theory has the added advantage that it can be read in harmony with the second. That three of the women were non-Israelites while the other was married to one accentuates the irregularity of their unions further. Moreover, it comports well with the other occasions where Matthew breaks the simple "A was the father of B" pattern of the genealogy: "Jacob the father of Judah *and his brothers*" (Mt 1:2); "Judah the father of Perez *and Zerah*" (Mt 1:3); "Josiah the father of Jechoniah *and his brothers*" (Mt 1:11). In each of these cases Matthew highlights a providential selectivity in the preservation of the messianic line.[47] This is especially the case with Perez and Zerah, where the messianic line continues through the younger brother (cf. Gen 38:27-30).[48] Thus, these women prepare the reader for the next irregular union: "Joseph the husband of Mary, of whom Jesus was born, who is called the Messiah" (Mt 1:16).

Recently several authors have further developed this last theory. Wainwright argues that simple irregularity does not do full justice to the Old Testament women's stories. She refines irregularity to mean "outside of a patriarchal marriage or family structure":

> Each one's actions threatened this structure further. Tamar puts off her widow's garments and sits by the roadside awaiting Judah (Gen 38:14). Rahab, named harlot, dwells in her own home outside her patriarchal family structure (Josh 2:2). Ruth goes down to the threshing floor where she uncovers the feet of Boaz (Ruth 3:7); and the wife of Uriah comes to David, one of the few actions attributed to her in the entire story (2 Sam 11:4).[49]

Wainwright adds that each of these instances "encode aspects of women's power" through which God's messianic plan unfolds. There is merit to this refinement, but it is incomplete. Most troubling is Wainwright's characterization of

---

[47]Ibid.

[48]The reversal of primogeniture (i.e., the deliberate passing over of the older son to bless the younger) to highlight God's activity is a major theme in Genesis.

[49]Wainwright, *Towards a Feminist Critical Reading,* p. 68.

Bathsheba as an active character. Surely, her response to the king's summons (2 Sam 11:4) is an example of female passivity in the face of a powerful male aggressor.[50] Moreover, Matthew's Mary mirrors Bathsheba's compliance rather than showing the initiative of the others.[51]

For Gaventa the common irregularity is a dynamic fluctuation between threatening established social norms and being threatened by them.[52] Judah regards Tamar as a threat to his one remaining son (Gen 38:11), while Tamar is threatened both by her lack of a husband or son and by having to turn to prostitution to live. Rahab threatens Israel's entry into the land because she knows about the spies, and when Jericho falls she is threatened with destruction. Ruth threatens the accepted social norm by refusing to return to Moab with Orpah, choosing instead to stay with Naomi; her advances to Boaz, in turn, threaten to expose her to charges of harlotry if he does not marry her. Bathsheba's message of her pregnancy threatens both David and Uriah; she, in turn, "becomes the one who lives under the threat of having no father for the child she carries."[53] Each woman in her own way "threatens [the Davidic line] . . . and is in turn threatened. Each is delivered and the line preserved, although the circumstances of the women vary greatly."[54] The merit of this approach is its obvious applicability to Tamar, Ruth and Bathsheba. Once again, however, one story must be forced to fit. The threat/threatened dynamic in Rahab's case is called into question by the "crimson cord" (Josh 2:17-21) that guaranteed the safety of all in Rahab's household (Josh 6:22-25).

It seems then that, although the irregularity thesis is plausible, the two attempts to draw the circle smaller invariably end up excluding one of the women. Is there a way to refine the irregularity thesis without doing so? A way out may be suggested by previous discussions of Matthew's audience. If Matthew was engaged in an intra-Jewish struggle over the future of Jewish identity with the movement(s) that became rabbinic Judaism, then the genealogy is probably better read in the light of that larger polemic enterprise. In this reading, the scandal that would haunt these women because of their race or sexual situations is softened by their inclusion in the royal family line.

Marshall Johnson develops this argument, suggesting that Matthew accom-

---

[50]Schaberg, *Illegitimacy of Jesus*, pp. 29-32.

[51]Wainwright's footing would be more solid if she had accentuated Bathsheba's move from passive in the Uriah story to almost frighteningly active, conspiring with Nathan to secure the throne for her son Solomon (cf. 1 Kings 1:11-40).

[52]Gaventa, *Mary*, pp. 38-40.

[53]Ibid., p. 39.

[54]Ibid.

plished two objectives by mentioning these women. First, he aligned the Jesus movement of which he was a part with those rabbis defending a Davidic Messiah over against an Aaronic one. By so defending the rabbis, however, Matthew also removed a possible plank in their criticism of Jesus' messianic claim: his lack of a Davidic heritage. "Matthew wrote to show that in every respect the Pharisaic expectation of the Messiah had been fulfilled in Jesus of Nazareth, who was the son of David and therefore a descendant of the four women."[55] Unable to question Jesus' ancestry, critics had only one option left: to point to the irregularity of Jesus' conception. Then, however, Matthew could counter that sexual scandal was part of the Davidic line, touching not only the patriarch Judah but also the parentage and actions of David himself! Matthew's inclusion of Tamar, Rahab, Ruth and Bathsheba defends an awkward situation—Mary's atypical pregnancy.[56] If Tamar, Rahab, Ruth and Bathsheba could come to have the scandal that is associated with their biblical stories set aside and be presented as God's agents, why not Mary?

This reading is not without its critics. Brown presents it as a version of the first theory and therefore vulnerable to similar attacks.[57] But to say that the situations in which these women found themselves were scandalous is not necessarily to question their character. They may be daringly subversive daughters-in-law (Tamar), virtuous foreign prostitutes (Rahab), virtuous enemies of Israel (Ruth) or simply victims of unwanted male sexual aggression (Bathsheba) and still find themselves implicated in sexual scandal. In a slightly different vein, Gaventa counters that Ruth's marriage to Boaz is devoid of scandal.[58] I am not so sure. While Ruth's narrator suggests nothing sexually scandalous about her actions, she is a Moabite. That an Israelite like Boaz would marry a blood enemy is scandalous at the surface level at least. The strangest criticism, however, comes from Gundry, who alleges that this line of argument presents the genealogy as a rather poor version of "people in glass houses shouldn't throw stones—look at your own history!" As such, he insists that it would have only "deepened suspicions concerning the legitimacy of Jesus' birth"[59]—as though the story of a virgin miraculously conceiving a child would not have raised even first-century eyebrows on its own!

In spite of the critics, Matthew's presentation of Mary in the remainder of

---

[55]Marshall D. Johnson, *The Purpose of Biblical Genealogies: With Special Reference to the Setting of the Genealogies of Jesus,* 2nd ed. (Cambridge: Cambridge University Press, 1988), p. 178.

[56]In addition to Johnson, see also Edwin D. Freed, "The Women in Matthew's Genealogy," *Journal for the Study of the New Testament* 29 (1987): 3-19.

[57]Brown, *Birth of the Messiah,* p. 71. Cf. also pp. 142-43, where Brown seems to change his mind.

[58]Gaventa, *Mary,* p. 38.

[59]Gundry, *Matthew,* p. 15.

both the nativity narrative and the Gospel supports this reading. Because Jesus' conception is questionable, some sort of social scandal among righteous people is inevitable. This is true even of Jesus' legal father, Joseph. Therefore, God must intervene. Because Jesus' existence is considered to be a claim upon David's throne, he provokes a political scandal that culminates in a murderous directive from the court of Herod. Therefore, again, God must intervene. Scandal, however, must not be seen to arise from within the bounds of Jesus' family, for they have been granted revelatory insight that resolves the tension. Therefore, Matthew rewrites parts of Mark to remove that interpretive possibility.

Mary, Jesus and the righteous man (Matthew 1:18-25). Matthew's account of Jesus' birth of Jesus covers only eight verses. The main character is Joseph, with attention focused on his righteous character. But it is not clear that Joseph's moral rectitude is uncomplicated. Indeed, it causes the conflict that drives the story forward and provides for its resolution. It is because Joseph is righteous that he recognizes the social scandal of Mary's pregnancy; it is because he is righteous that he obeys God's command, marries Mary, adopts Jesus and accepts the scandal as his own:

> Now the birth of Jesus the Messiah took place in this way. When his mother Mary had been engaged to Joseph, but before they lived together, she was found to be with child from the Holy Spirit. Her husband Joseph, being a righteous man and unwilling to expose her to public disgrace, planned to dismiss her quietly. But just when he had resolved to do this, an angel of the Lord appeared to him in a dream and said, "Joseph, son of David, do not be afraid to take Mary as your wife, for the child conceived in her is from the Holy Spirit. She will bear a son, and you are to name him Jesus, for he will save his people from their sins." All this took place to fulfill what had been spoken by the Lord through the prophet:
>
> "Look, the virgin shall conceive and bear a son,
> and they shall name him Emmanuel,"
>
> which means "God is with us." When Joseph awoke from sleep, he did as the angel of the Lord commanded him; he took her as his wife, but had no marital relations with her until she had borne a son; and he named him Jesus. (Mt 1:18-25)

The connection with the genealogy is easily seen. Joseph appears briefly to signal Jesus' legal claim to Davidic descent. In Matthew 1:18-25 that legal claim is narrated. Thus "Joseph dominates the narrative as the one who has control over the destiny of Mary (v. 19), as the recipient of the divine message (v. 20), the one who can give legal paternity to Jesus . . . (vv. 20, 21), and as the one who is obedient to the divine command in this situation (vv. 24-25)."[60] Joseph

[60]Wainwright, *Towards a Feminist Critical Reading,* p. 172.

is the answer to the "how" of Jesus' Davidic descent.

Matthew describes Joseph's shameful situation. After he was betrothed to Mary (translated "engaged" in the NRSV) but before they were married, she became pregnant (Mt 1:18). A better understanding of betrothal in first-century Palestine may help modern readers span cultural differences and enter imaginatively into Joseph's thought process. As a legal arrangement, betrothal was the first formal step in a "property" exchange between the bride's father and her husband.[61] Once betrothed, Mary still lived with her parents; but she was regarded as Joseph's wife and would have been considered his widow if he died. Like a full-blown marriage, a betrothal could be broken only by death or divorce; similarly, sexual relations with someone other than the betrothed constituted adultery, which remained harshly sanctioned in Joseph's time. Matthew's announcement of Mary's pregnancy should therefore remind readers of Deuteronomy 22:23-27 and the penalty for such adulterous liaisons: if the liaison took place in a populated area, the punishment was death for both parties; if in the country, only the man was to be executed.[62] Clearly, Mary's pregnancy was a scandalous matter, threatening to bring disgrace on her family, on Joseph's and on their community. What would Joseph do?

Exploration of this question is interrupted as readers are immediately granted an omniscient perspective. Matthew discloses the source of Mary's pregnancy: "She was found to be with child from the Holy Spirit." Joseph is in no way Jesus' biological father and therefore not the genetic source of his Davidic descent. Matthew "is so careful on this point that he violates the normal pattern of angelic revelation whereby the reader should learn of God's action through the words addressed to the visionary."[63] Readers know ahead of anyone else the miracle that underlies Mary's pregnancy.[64]

Then, as abruptly as readers are wrenched from the story, they are returned to the question of Joseph's response to Mary's pregnancy. Matthew stresses that

---

[61]Joachim Jeremias, *Jerusalem at the Time of Jesus: An Investigation into Economic and Social Conditions During the New Testament Period,* trans. F. H. Cave and C. H. Cave (London: SCM Press, 1969), p. 367.

[62]The punishment for the latter is different because "in the open country, the engaged woman may have cried for help, but there was no one to rescue her" (Deut 22:27).

[63]Brown, *Birth of the Messiah,* p. 138.

[64]Schaberg, *Illegitimacy of Jesus,* pp. 62-68, argues that "from the Holy Spirit" need not be read to imply a miraculous conception, but rather simply as the Spirit's election of this naturally conceived child from the instant of his conception. This is a possible reading, but the story as a whole, including the citation of Is 7:14, mitigates against it. Although Schaberg offers plausible explanations at each difficult turn, the onus remains on her to explain why the simplest reading of the text is wrong. She cannot, but can only "suspect" (Schaberg's word; p. 66) that this is the case.

Joseph is a righteous man and will act accordingly. That his righteousness seems to lie in his careful observance of the law is an ancient Christian understanding of the phrase that remains probable.[65] It is clear that Joseph thinks that Mary is guilty of adultery. In order to discern whether this adultery was the result of seduction, prostitution or rape, a public trial would be required, in which witnesses would be called and evidence weighed (Deut 22:23-27). It seems, however, that Joseph has already drawn conclusions about what has happened: there will be no trial because in his eyes Mary is a victim of sexual violence. Instead, he will proceed with a quiet divorce.[66] It could not be a secret divorce for two reasons. First, a divorce required a "writ of repudiation" to be delivered before at least two witnesses.[67] Second, obviously, Mary's secret would not remain secret long.

Joseph's righteousness is scandalized by Mary's situation. While it prevents Joseph from pursuing a public and humiliating trial, it is menacing because it demands that Joseph "purge the evil from [the community's] midst" (Deut 22:24) by divorce. Even as his righteousness disposes him to be merciful in his judgment, he will act to meet his legal obligations. At no point is Joseph's righteousness questioned; throughout, his motives remain inviolate. As a righteous man, he is appalled by Mary's pregnancy and is therefore a threat to her, to her unborn child and ultimately to the plan of God. Readers alone know that Joseph's fault lies not at the level of intentions, but information.

In a providential reversal, however, Joseph's righteousness is not only the source of narrative conflict but also the source of its resolution. It is because he is righteous that he attends to God's intervention via an angelic message delivered in a dream. Joseph is addressed as son of David, highlighting again Jesus' messianic status as the Davidic heir. The heavenly command is simple: Joseph is not to fear the scandal that will result when Mary gives birth; he is to complete the marriage contract by taking Mary home. The heavenly explanation is breathtaking: Mary's child has been conceived by "the Holy Spirit." He is to be named "Jesus, for he will save his people from their sins." The narrator then resumes the story by presenting the pregnancy as fulfilled prophecy and informing readers of Joseph's immediate response to the angel's instructions.

While Mary's shame has evaporated for Joseph, it has not for the community.

---

[65] On other views and their weaknesses, see Brown, *Birth of the Messiah,* pp. 126-27.

[66] It is possible that the word translated "quietly" modifies Joseph's planning (i.e., "he planned quietly to dismiss her"). This rendering suggests a parallel between the righteous Joseph and the unrighteous Herod, who also plans in private (Mt 2:7). See Gaventa, *Mary,* pp. 41, 48 n. 16.

[67] Brown, *Birth of the Messiah,* p. 128.

Busybodies in Bethlehem will count the months from the completion of the marriage contract to the birth of Jesus, and then tongues will start wagging. The account of Joseph's righteousness is thus accentuated. By acting on a complete account of Mary's situation, the righteous Joseph absolves Mary of scandal; by embracing the child as his own in the eyes of the wider community, he confers status on Mary's child. All gossip aside, by taking Mary into his home, he has guaranteed that this child who is not his own will nevertheless be his heir, and if his heir then David's heir, and if David's heir then possibly the Davidic Messiah. This child who is God's son (Mt 1:18, 20, 23) will also be the son of David. In this way the threat to Mary and Jesus is removed and the true depth of Joseph's righteousness is revealed.[68]

Mary, Jesus and the unrighteous man (Matthew 2:1-23). In Matthew 1, Matthew answers the who and how questions concerning Jesus' origins. Who is he? He is Joseph's son and David's heir (Mt 1:1-17). How did he become the Davidic heir? Because Joseph was righteous, he completed the marriage contract with Mary's father, granting his Davidic lineage to Mary's son (Mt 1:18-25). In Matthew 2, Matthew turns to two more questions. Whence came Jesus? He was born in Bethlehem (Mt 2:1-12). Whither did he go? Because of Herod's murderous threats, he fled to Egypt and afterward lived in Nazareth (Mt 2:13-23). Matthew's story remains as theologically rich as its beginning. Explicit Old Testament citations include Micah 5:2, Hosea 11:1 and Jeremiah 31:15. Allusions are also present: Eastern magi come to Bethlehem bearing gifts (cf. Ps 72:10-11; Is 60:6); Gentiles recognize Jesus as God's son (Ps 72:1); the massacre of the innocents recalls the story of Moses (cf. Ex 1:22—2:4); and the sojourn in Egypt recapitulates the exodus. Although there is much grist for the mill here, none of it deals directly with our study. Our focus lies in the juxtaposition of righteous Joseph and unrighteous Herod.

Through the repeated phrase "the child and his mother" (Mt 2:13, 14, 20, 21), Matthew presents Herod, like Joseph, as politically scandalized by Mary and her child. Like Joseph, Herod resolves to act. Like Joseph, Herod endangers Mary and her child. Again, God must intervene through an angelic visitation to rescue Mary and the child from harm. These similarities mask deeper differences. Jo-

---

[68]In passing, I draw readers' attention to Mt 1:25, which states that Joseph did not have sex with Mary "until she had borne a son." In the light of passages concerning Jesus' brothers (Mt 12:46-50; 13:54-58), readers may infer that Mt 1:25 assumes that Joseph and Mary engaged in sexual intercourse after Jesus' birth, as a normal part of their marriage. However legitimate the inference, it is just that—an inference. Grammar and context both suggest that Matthew's point is not to allude to Mary and Joseph's assumption of a normal sexual relationship after Jesus' birth, but to explicitly affirm one of chastity prior to it. It thus reemphasizes that Jesus can in no way be biologically connected to Joseph.

seph is concerned for his community. Joseph resolves to act in a way that preserves Mary's dignity as much as possible. Joseph attends to a divine dream and changes his plans. Herod is different. He is scandalized out of concern for his throne. He resolves to act to preserve his dynasty no matter the bloody cost. Nothing can dissuade him; God intervenes not to change Herod's plans, but to rescue Jesus from them. If Mary scandalized the righteous man above, then she scandalizes the unrighteous man now.

This is not obvious at first. The magi trouble Herod and all Jerusalem with the news that the "king of the Jews" has been born (Mt 2:2). Herod then inquires of the religious leaders where "the Messiah" is to be born (Mt 2:4) and instructs them to search for "the child" (Mt 2:8). The magi follow the star to "the place where the child was" (Mt 2:10). The king, the Messiah, the child: Jesus has assumed the foreground dominated by Joseph earlier. He is the new center of the narrative's attention.

While the scene has shifted considerably—approximately two years have passed in the space of a few verses—the still-silent Mary remains almost completely hidden in the background. "The negative conclusion we might draw from this silence regarding Mary is that Matthew regards her as unimportant. She utters not a single word and takes not a single action. The actions of which she is the object are limited to being seen and being moved about."[69] This is premature, for while the magi and Herod, for very different reasons, are searching for a boy, the magi find "the child with Mary his mother" (Mt 2:11). Herod's search for "the child" (Mt 2:13) is frustrated. Joseph, acting on God's instruction, takes "the child and his mother" (Mt 2:13-14) to safety in Egypt. Those who search, search for Jesus. Those who find, find the child with his mother. Those who do not, do not because Joseph protects the child and his mother. Mary is always with Jesus.

For Joseph the scandal was associated with Mary. Preoccupied with her supposed adultery, he did not become conscious of her child's identity until his dream. Now Matthew reverses the positions of mother and Son. Now the scandal is associated with Jesus. As the true Davidic king, he threatens Herod's Idumean dynasty. But because of his youth, the scandal overtakes Mary too. Both must seek protection in a foreign land.

Mary in the Public Ministry of Jesus

True family of Jesus (Matthew 12:46-50). Matthew's birth story adds new depth to Mary's New Testament portrait through the social scandal caused by

[69]Gaventa, *Mary,* p. 43.

Mary's pregnancy and the political scandal caused by Jesus' Davidic ancestry. Mary and Joseph know, however, that the scandal is God's gracious intervention. Readers should therefore expect to find that Matthew treats Jesus' family more kindly than does Mark. This is confirmed in two final scenes.

> While he was still speaking to the crowds, his mother and his brothers were standing outside, wanting to speak to him. Someone told him, "Look, your mother and your brothers are standing outside, wanting to speak to you." But to the one who had told him this, Jesus replied, "Who is my mother, and who are my brothers?" And pointing to his disciples, he said, "Here are my mother and my brothers! For whoever does the will of my Father in heaven is my brother and sister and mother." (Mt 12:46-50)

The similarities with Mark 3:31-35 are obvious. Jesus is surrounded by the crowds; his mother and brothers are standing apart from him. Their call allows Jesus to teach about discipleship and separate himself from kinship privileges and responsibilities. It is unclear whether the family follows Jesus and whether his words are directed against them. That it is the fourth in a cycle of stories in which Jesus engages opponents (Mt 12:1-8; 12:9-14; 12:22-32) may indicate hostility on the part of Jesus' family, but hostility is certainly not as evident as it is in the previous three encounters.

Two significant differences suggest that more is going on. Matthew extracted this story from its Markan context, where the family is associated with those accusing Jesus of being the devil's ally. Matthew's version of the story (Mt 12:22-37) includes an even harsher indictment of the Pharisees. Then two new episodes, one concerning the signs by which Jesus' authority might be confirmed (Mt 12:38-42) and another concerning unclean spirits (Mt 12:43-45), separate Jesus' family from his enemies, erasing any connection that Mark once drew. Second, in Matthew the family members do not think Jesus is deranged or under demonic influence. Any explicit association with scandal has been removed.

Rejection of Jesus by his own (Matthew 13:54-58). A similar emendation is found in Matthew's version of the rejection of the synagogue:

> He came to his hometown and began to teach the people in their synagogue, so that they were astounded and said, "Where did this man get this wisdom and these deeds of power? Is not this the carpenter's son? Is not his mother called Mary? And are not his brothers James and Joseph and Simon and Judas? And are not all his sisters with us? Where then did this man get all this?" And they took offense at him. But Jesus said to them, "Prophets are not without honor except in their own country and in their own house." And he did not do many deeds of power there, because of their unbelief. (Mt 13:54-58)

Again the context is altered. Rather than completing a miracle cycle as in Mark 4:35—5:43, Matthew's version follows a string of parables (Mt 13:1-53). Matthew mentions Joseph through the identification of Jesus as "the carpenter's son" (cf. Mk 6:3). Most significant is Jesus' abbreviated response. Both Gospels acknowledge that prophets are without honor in their own hometowns and houses. But Matthew omits "and among their own kin" (Mk 6:4), thus distancing Jesus' family from scandal.

Conclusion

Theological scandal. Three conclusions may be drawn. First, Matthew recognizes that among his rabbinic opponents Mary's pregnancy invites theological scandal. He must respond if his claims for Jesus are to be taken seriously. While Matthew's story of the miraculous conception is not a simplistic reporting of events, neither is it a piece of fiction. Quite simply, it would have caused more problems than it solved. Surely the theological imagination behind the story could not have constructed a less scandalous tale. Two small alterations would have removed any notion of shame without changing any theological theme that the story conveys: the narrator could have introduced Mary as betrothed and childless; and the angelic messenger could have instructed Joseph to complete the marriage process because the child that he and Mary would conceive together would be from the Holy Spirit. In this way Jesus' Davidic ancestry would have been affirmed, his election to divine sonship would have been maintained and any notion of his mother's adultery would have been removed.[70]

But Matthew takes the harder route. The simplest explanation is that both he and his opponents agreed on a certain fact: Joseph was not Jesus' biological father. He acknowledges with his opponents that Mary's pregnancy is atypical. His apologetic strategy is threefold. First, he argues that analogous sexually scandalous situations have already occurred in the messianic line. The genealogy insists that Jesus' messianic claim cannot be dismissed on a charge of illegitimacy while ignoring the scandal of Perez (Tamar), Boaz (Rahab), Obed (Ruth) and Solomon (Bathsheba). Mary's morals cannot be questioned without doing the same to four of the Messiah's foremothers. Second, both the genealogy and the birth story aver that even if Joseph is not Jesus' father, he is the adoptive father. Jesus'

[70]"If the situation described in Matthew is not a factual one but is the product of Christian romantic imagination, one must deem it a great religious blunder; for it gave rise to the charge of illegitimacy against Jesus that was the mainstay of anti-Christian polemic for many centuries" (Brown, *Birth of the Messiah,* p. 143 n. 28).

Davidic claim is intact. Finally, Matthew shows that his opponents could not dispute Jesus' claim without also disputing those of the sons of his foremothers.

By using arguments with which his opponents would have been sympathetic, Matthew blunts any charge of illegitimacy brought against Jesus. Now Matthew goes on the offensive. He argues that Jesus' Davidic ancestry and messianic identity is devoid of scandal because throughout Joseph's dealings with Mary—both in the preempted decision to divorce her and in the final decision to marry her—Joseph remains righteous. It is new information, not a change of intention, that causes the about-face. He is given an explanation for the facts in evidence: the child conceived in the womb of Mary is "from the Holy Spirit."

Social scandal. Joseph's righteousness also authenticates and alleviates any concern for those of the synagogue community scandalized by the social breach that is Mary's pregnancy. He agrees that according to how things look, righteous people can, indeed should, be scandalized. Joseph is. Having assessed the situation according to all the information available, Joseph makes the decision to forego a public trial and instead quietly divorce his betrothed. In this decision Joseph is righteous. By presenting Joseph in this way Matthew disarms those opponents confused by the claims of those following a so-called illegitimate Messiah. He invites them to stand in Joseph's place, sharing the scandal that once confounded him.

After thus legitimating their anxiety, Matthew asks what might have caused Joseph, the righteous man, to change his mind. Joseph's righteousness demanded that he fulfill his social obligations. Only divine revelation concerning the true miraculous source of Mary's pregnancy could allow Joseph to look past the social breach and marry her. In this way Matthew invites all righteous people to absolve Mary. He invites them to stand with Joseph, who after receiving revelation chose to make Mary's scandal his own.

Political scandal. Finally, Jesus' Davidic ancestry is legitimated by the political scandal aroused in Herod's court. The magi rightly recognize that Jesus is the "king of the Jews." Herod rightly realizes that this king challenges his kingship. Even the Gentiles and the Idumean puppets of the Romans know who Jesus is. If Jesus is not David's heir, then he is no threat. Why then does Herod act like Pharaoh of old to destroy the child and his mother? Why then does God intervene in Joseph's life a second time in order that the child and his mother may find refuge in Egypt? Matthew thinks that the onus lies with his opponents.

The apologetic motif employed by Matthew is that of scandal. Theologically he argues that such scandal is part and parcel of salvation history, running through the royal line from Judah to David; he argues through the birth narrative that beneath the appearance of social and political scandal is to be found the miraculous work of God. Accordingly he adapts later Markan scenes to remove any notions of scandal arising within Jesus' family. Having already moved from Paul's bland anonymity to Mark's darker tones of opposition, Matthew now adds a tint of red. For him Mary is the scandalous mother of the Messiah.

4

Poor Prophet, Pondering Mother, Persistent Disciple

Mary in Luke/Acts

In Luke/Acts Mary emerges as a major character. She is not an afterthought, there by virtue of the accidents of birth—an "after all, *somebody* had to be Jesus' mother." Neither is she a plot device highlighting her husband's character. In the infancy narrative (Lk 1—2), she is the center of all narrative action. She stands ahead of Joseph (Lk 2:5). Joseph is named after her (Lk 2:16). Although Simeon blesses the family, he speaks directly to Mary (Lk 2:33-34). Mary even speaks for her husband (Lk 2:48). Luke names Mary twelve times and alludes to her two more. Once the birth narrative is finished, however, Luke hurries Mary offstage.[1] Still, careful readers know the important role she plays in Luke's Gospel.[2]

Biblical scholars summarize Mary's significance in a variety of related ways: "a model for all Christians," "the exemplary disciple, a Christian prototype," "the

---

[1]Beverly Roberts Gaventa, *Mary: Glimpses of the Mother of Jesus* (Philadelphia: Fortress, 1999), pp. 49-50.

[2]Some scholars think that Luke celebrates women's contributions to the early Christian community; e.g., Richard Bauckham, *Gospel Women: Studies of the Named Women in the Gospels* (Grand Rapids: Eerdmans, 2002), p. 47. Others counter that Luke seduces readers to accept traditional gender roles; e.g., Jane Schaberg, "Luke," in *Women's Bible Commentary,* ed. Carol A. Newsom and Sharon H. Ringe (Louisville: Westminster John Knox, 1998), p. 363. Both interpretations marshal exegetical evidence, often from the same passages. Amy Jill Levine's description of Luke as "a storm center concerning the question of women's roles" is apt; "Introduction," in *A Feminist Companion to Luke,* ed. Amy Jill Levine (London: Continuum Sheffield, 2002), p. 3. An appreciative feminist reading of Luke can be found in Elizabeth Johnson, *Truly Our Sister: A Theology of Mary in the Communion of Saints* (New York: Continuum, 2004), pp. 247-87.

first believer" or "the perfect Christian."[3] These titles stress just how positively Luke presents Mary; but they reduce her significance to her exemplary role. Beverly Roberts Gaventa delivers a more accurate description of Luke's Mary under the title "disciple, prophet and mother."[4]

As the title of this chapter indicates, I affirm Gaventa's description, altering her arrangement only to follow Luke's development of Mary's character more closely. When we first meet her, Mary is the prophetic voice of the poor who is called by God (Lk 1:26-38) and who proclaims God's saving will (Lk 1:39-56). Then, in Luke 2:1-20 the prophet becomes the mother of the Lord who ponders the strange events in which she has been caught up. A note of narrative tension introduced by the haunting prediction of the prophet Simeon in Luke 2:34-35 ought to leave the reader wondering whether Mary is one of those who will rise or fall because of Jesus. Most troubling is Simeon's image of Mary pierced through the soul by a sword. To what does it refer? Perhaps an answer begins to emerge in the next scene (Lk 2:41-52), where Mary's simple motherly concern is expressed as she searches frantically for Jesus while he confounds the sages at the temple. Perhaps Simeon's sword refers to a future in which Jesus' mission will be dictated by his Father, not by his mother. A strong conclusion cannot be drawn, for Mary now disappears. It is not at all clear that she will take up the mantle of disciple.

Unresolved throughout the Gospel, this tension surfaces in two remaining passages that mention Mary. The mother/son relationship hinted at in Luke 8:19-21 and Luke 11:27-28 is distant, even troubled, and is certainly not easily covered by the title "model disciple." Is Mary among those who "hear the word of God and do it" (Lk 8:21)? Is Mary among the blessed ones that "hear the word of God and obey it" (Lk 11:28)? Both cases are unclear. By so introducing elements of ambiguity in Jesus' relationship to Mary, Luke heightens the tension established by Simeon's prophecy. Luke's opacity invites the hypothesis that these instances are foreshadowed in Simeon's sword: Mary's soul is pierced by her failure to grasp and embrace her Son's mission even as she ponders the miracles surrounding Jesus' birth and childhood. It is impossible therefore to entertain a judgment on her discipleship by the Gospel's end. Only when Mary is found in the upper room with Jesus' other followers (Acts 1:14) is the question

---

[3]These phrases may be found, respectively, in John McHugh, *The Mother of Jesus in the New Testament* (Garden City, N.Y.: Doubleday, 1975), p. 347; Turid Karlsen Seim, *The Double Message: Patterns of Gender in Luke and Acts* (Nashville: Abingdon, 1994), p. 115; Joseph A. Fitzmyer, *Luke the Theologian: Aspects of His Teaching* (Mahwah: Paulist Press, 1989), p. 69; and Anthony Tambasco, *What Are They Saying About Mary?* (Mahwah: Paulist Press, 1984), p. 26.

[4]Gaventa, *Mary,* pp. 49-78.

answered. Because she has persevered, in addition to poor prophet and pondering mother, Mary is named persistent disciple.

A Marian Source for Luke's Nativity Story

Matthew and Luke used sources to construct their accounts of Jesus' conception and birth. Jesus' family members were unlikely sources for Matthew, but the hypothesis that Mary was a source for Luke needs to be tested. Luke admits that he was not a witness to the events he reports in his Gospel. He is dependent on "eyewitnesses and servants of the word" (Lk 1:2).[5] Scholarly consensus agrees that Luke's first book is not a Gospel per se, but ancient historiography or perhaps biography.[6] This is to say that Luke is not as consciously evangelistic as Mark, Matthew or John (cf. Mk 1:1; Mt 1:1; Jn 20:30-31). His is an ordered, investigated narrative aimed at convincing "Theophilus" of the reliability of the apostles' teaching (Lk 1:1-4).[7] Inquiring after Luke's sources may therefore be fruitful.

Unfortunately, this optimistic belief is undermined by the many source theories advanced by modern scholarship. With respect to the infancy narrative alone, questions concerning the nature of the sources (were they oral, written or both?), their number (are they one, a few or many?), their original languages (were they Hebrew/Aramaic or Greek?) and their content (where does the source end and Luke begin?) have yet to be definitively answered.[8] Three broad approaches are advanced. One extreme holds that Luke composed the narrative depending solely on oral tradition. The other believes that Luke relied on only one Hebrew/Aramaic document for both the Gospel and Acts. Most biblical scholars fall somewhere in between, arguing that Luke rewrites several sources into one narrative.[9]

Achieving agreement has proven difficult because of Luke's literary creativity.

---

[5]On whether "eyewitnesses and servants" designates one group or two, contrast Darrell L. Bock, *Luke 1:1—9:50,* Baker Exegetical Commentary on the New Testament 3A (Grand Rapids: Baker, 1994), p. 58; and Joseph A. Fitzmyer, *The Gospel According to Luke i-ix,* Anchor Bible 28 (Garden City: Doubleday, 1981), p. 294; with John Nolland, *Luke 1—9:20,* Word Biblical Commentary 35A (Dallas: Word, 1989), p. xxviii.

[6]Joel B. Green, *The Gospel of Luke,* New International Commentary on the New Testament (Grand Rapids: Eerdmans, 1997), pp. 1-6. Note also Fitzmyer, *Luke,* p. 290.

[7]On the question of Luke's reliability as a historian, compare Luke Timothy Johnson, *Luke,* Sacra Pagina 3 (Collegeville, Minn.: Liturgical Press, 1991), pp. 6-10; with Bock, *Luke,* pp. 66-67.

[8]I. Howard Marshall, *The Gospel of Luke: A Commentary on the Greek Text,* New International Greek Testament Commentary (Grand Rapids: Eerdmans, 1978), pp. 48-49.

[9]Although his commentary is older, Marshall (ibid., pp. 47-48) continues to offer a helpful snapshot of the various reconstructions posited by source critics.

Based on comparative analysis between the Gospel and one known source, Mark, it seems that Luke felt free to rewrite his sources.[10] Furthermore, he departs from his sources at some points and ignores them at others.[11] And it seems that Luke had an ability to write in a variety of styles.[12] As a result, any attempt to pinpoint the nature, number, language and contents of a given source will always be speculative.

Confining our speculations within the boundaries set by the problematic nature of the evidence, four comments may be made. First, Luke's use of Hebraisms and familiarity with the Old Testament may indicate one or more early Jewish-Christian traditions about the births of John and Jesus. Second, it is impossible to disentangle John from Jesus; Luke has written one seamless story.[13] Third, because some of the details of Luke's narrative could have been known only by Mary, parts of the(se) source(s) may have come from Jewish-Christian communities linked to Jesus' family. Finally, it is highly unlikely that Mary was a direct source. If we place the date of Jesus' birth as late as the evidence allows (ca. 4 B.C.), if we assume the age of Mary at that time to be as young as the evidence allows (fourteen years old), and if we adopt the earliest possible date for the completion of Luke/Acts (ca. 62), Mary would have been at least eighty years old—a remarkable achievement for a first-century Palestinian woman—when Luke picked up his quill. Even on the most generous reading of the evidence, the likelihood of direct contact between Luke and Mary is exceedingly remote. If Jesus was born earlier, if Mary was older or if Luke wrote later, the possibility recedes even more.

Luke's infancy narrative is theological history. Speculation about a Marian source is just that. Luke's text has resisted rigorous source-critical investigations. The very most to be claimed is that a Marian source passed through members of Jesus' extended family in early Jewish Christianity. The image of an aged Mary dictating to a much younger Luke belongs in the realm of pious imagination. "Beyond this it is difficult to go, and we must be content to keep an open mind on the problem of Luke's sources and hence on the historicity of the events recorded in them."[14] Our theological reflection therefore begins not in the history behind the text, but in the text itself.

---

[10]Johnson, *Luke,* p. 6.

[11]Luke omits Mk 6:45—8:27 entirely and mentions no appearances of Jesus in Galilee (cf. Mk 16:7; Mt 28:16). Acts presents Paul's arrival in Rome as the climax of the Great Commission (Acts 1:8; 28:15-16) even though Paul's letter to the Romans makes clear that a church existed there before he arrived.

[12]Johnson, *Luke,* p. 7.

[13]Marshall, *Luke,* p. 49.

[14]Ibid.

Mary in the Birth Narrative

Whatever its history, Luke's story of Jesus' beginnings resonates with the Gospel's dominant theme: those on the margins are not marginal in God's kingdom. Luke's descriptions of those who do not fit easily in proper Jewish society—Gentiles, women, children and the poor—are both central and uniformly sympathetic.[15] This reflects Luke's concern to establish rapport with his readers, who are embodied in the "God-lover" of Luke 1:1-4 and Acts 1:1. Theophilus is on the threshold: a God-fearing Gentile interested in Jewish Christianity.[16] Whether convert or interested outsider, his instruction in the faith has been minimal.[17] For him, Luke's deliberate focus on people in similarly ambiguous situations, whether within Judaism (e.g., the shepherds in Lk 2) or without (e.g., the faith-filled centurion of Lk 7), would have been appealing. Mary—a young, single, pregnant woman—is the most sharply drawn of all these characters.

Mary and the conception (Luke 1:26-38). As the story of Jesus' conception opens, Luke leaves the polished Greek of the prologue (Lk 1:1-4) behind, adopting the slower Semitic stylings of the Septuagint. Whether this indicates reliance on a Semitic source or the height to which Luke's artistic ability can reach in the service of the Gospel or both does not matter. The language is deeply infused with Old Testament and apocryphal imagery and deserves to be treated in its own right:

> In the sixth month the angel Gabriel was sent by God to a town in Galilee called Nazareth, to a virgin engaged to a man whose name was Joseph, of the house of David. The virgin's name was Mary. And he came to her and said, "Greetings, favored one! The Lord is with you." But she was much perplexed by his words and pondered what sort of greeting this might be. The angel said to her, "Do not be afraid, Mary, for you have found favor with God. And now, you will conceive in

---

[15]On Luke's audience, see Nolland, *Luke,* pp. xxxii-xxxiii; Marshall, *Luke,* p. 36; and Bock, *Luke,* pp. 14-15. On the need for modesty when describing Luke's readers, see Johnson, *Luke,* p. 3. On the positive, nontraditional roles of women in Luke/Acts, see Barbara E. Reid, *Choosing the Better Part: Women in the Gospel of Luke* (Collegeville, Minn.: Liturgical Press, 1996), pp. 21-54.

[16]Green (*Luke,* p. 44) reflects the consensus of contemporary scholarship that Theophilus was a real person for three reasons: "(1) Theophilus is a common name, found in the papyri and inscriptions as early as the third century B.C.; (2) the appellation 'most excellent' would then be pointless; and (3) a symbolic dedication of this sort would be unparalleled in Luke's literary culture."

[17]Nolland, *Luke,* p. xxxii. Whether Theophilus is understood to be a Christian hinges on the interpretation of "instructed" in Lk 1:4. Nolland contends that Theophilus is an interested outsider (*Luke,* p. 11). Johnson prefers a stronger understanding (*Luke,* p. 28). Others agree that it refers to minimal instruction: Green, *Luke,* pp. 45-46; Marshall, *Luke,* pp. 43-44; and Bock, *Luke,* p. 64.

> your womb and bear a son, and you will name him Jesus. He will be great, and will be called the Son of the Most High, and the Lord God will give to him the throne of his ancestor David. He will reign over the house of Jacob forever, and of his kingdom there will be no end." Mary said to the angel, "How can this be, since I am a virgin?" The angel said to her, "The Holy Spirit will come upon you, and the power of the Most High will overshadow you; therefore the child to be born will be holy; he will be called Son of God. And now, your relative Elizabeth in her old age has also conceived a son; and this is the sixth month for her who was said to be barren. For nothing will be impossible with God." Then Mary said, "Here am I, the servant of the Lord; let it be with me according to your word." Then the angel departed from her. (Lk 1:26-38)

This is Luke's second annunciation. The first is to Zechariah, father of John the Baptist (Lk 1:5-25). The Old Testament allusions in this first story are every bit as pervasive as those in the second. The opening phrase, translated literally, "it happened in the days of King Herod of Judea," looks very much like the opening verses of Jeremiah (Jer 1:2-3) and Amos (Amos 1:1). A mighty act of God reminiscent of the days of the kings and prophets is to be narrated.[18] Zechariah and Elizabeth's inability to conceive evokes memories of Manoah and his (unnamed) wife in Judges 13 and of Elkannah and Hannah in 1 Samuel 1. Their age calls to mind Abraham and Sarah as described in Genesis 18:11. Rebecca (Gen 25:21) and Rachel (Gen 29:31) also lurk in the background. Luke has placed Elizabeth in an honorable line of barren mothers and placed his characters in salvation history.[19]

The Old Testament allusions continue as the plot unfolds. The angelic encounter in the temple evokes images of Isaiah's commissioning (Is 6:1-6), and the announcement evokes images of the end time revealed to the prophet Daniel (Dan 9:20-21).[20] The parallels between the foretold son and Samson, Elijah and Elisha underscore his greatness.[21] Yet, being filled with the Spirit from before his birth, he will surpass them all. Zechariah, like Abraham in Genesis 15:5, grasps for certainty ahead of the angel's word. When dumbstruck Zechariah stumbles outside, all know that he has encountered God. After discovering that she is pregnant, Elizabeth echoes both Sarah (Gen 21:1) and Rachel (Gen 30:23). God has acted. The priest who by gender, family line and vocation should have understood is silenced—both to counter and to judge his unbelief.

---

[18]Nolland, *Luke,* p. 25.

[19]Raymond Brown, *The Birth of the Messiah: A Commentary on the Infancy Narratives in the Gospels of Matthew and Luke,* 2nd ed. (New York: Doubleday, 1993), pp. 268-69.

[20]Ibid., pp. 270-71.

[21]Ibid., pp. 272-74.

The barren woman who bears the signs of God's judgment in her sex, social standing and infertility understands and opens her mouth in praise. The tale is steeped in Old Testament imagery and rich in irony, but not unique.

Its significance lies in the second annunciation story, this time to Mary. The two annunciations are connected by the first phrase of Luke 1:26: "in the sixth month," which is specified in the context as the sixth month of Elizabeth's pregnancy.[22] When these stories are read together, striking parallels between Zechariah/Elizabeth and Mary are immediately observed:

Elizabeth is barren; Zechariah is old (Lk 1:7).	Mary is a virgin (Lk 1:27).
Zechariah encounters Gabriel (Lk 1:11, 19).	Mary encounters Gabriel (Lk 1:26, 28).
Zechariah is afraid (Lk 1:12).	Mary is perplexed (Lk 1:29).
Gabriel calls Zechariah by name (Lk 1:13).	Gabriel calls Mary by name (Lk 1:30).
A pregnancy is announced (Lk 1:13).	A pregnancy is announced (Lk 1:31).
The son's name is given (Lk 1:13).	The son's name is given (Lk 1:31).
The son's greatness is predicted (Lk 1:14-17).	The son's greatness is predicted (Lk 1:32-33).
Stature of the son is attributed to the Holy Spirit (Lk 1:15).	Stature of the son is attributed to the Holy Spirit (Lk 1:35).
Zechariah asks a question (Lk 1:18).	Mary asks a question (Lk 1:34).
A sign is given (Lk 1:19-20).	A sign is given (Lk 1:36-37).

The overlap is neither superficial nor accidental. Each story sounds out the other, disclosing a more powerful theme than either could alone. The God who opened the wombs of Sarah, Rachel, Rebecca, Manoah's wife and Hannah is acting again.

[22]Brigitte Kahl is convincing when she says that the "new way of dating, in which the beginning of God's time inscribes itself, bursts open every prevailing historical or religious chronology." Historical political time is measured in the lives of rulers; temple time, according to a male priesthood; "but now, the beginning of the time of God's promise is posited most dramatically in a time roster that is gynocentric"; "Reading Luke Against Luke: Non-Uniformity of Text, Hermeneutics of Conspiracy, and the 'Scriptural Principle' in Luke 1," in *A Feminist Companion to Luke,* ed. Amy Jill Levine (London: Continuum Sheffield, 2002), pp. 79-81.

Once pulled into the text by the overlapping plots, however, we notice that the commonalities are supplanted by a list of contrasts, highlighting the singularity of the second story. The contrasts between Zechariah/Elizabeth and Mary involve characters, conceptions and the children:

Contrasts Between Characters	
Zechariah and Elizabeth are old (Lk 1:7).	Mary is young (Lk 1:27).
Elizabeth is barren (Lk 1:7).	Mary is presumably fertile (Lk 1:27).
Zechariah and Elizabeth are pious and upright (Lk 1:5-6).	Mary's spirituality and morality are not described.
Zechariah is greeted by name (Lk 1:13).	Mary is greeted with the title "favored one" (Lk 1:28).
Contrasts Between Conceptions	
God responds to prayer (Lk 1:13).	God shows favor without explanation (Lk 1:28, 30).
Elizabeth's conception is unlikely.	Mary's conception is impossible (Lk 1:34).
Elizabeth's conception has biblical precedent.	Mary's conception is unprecedented.
Elizabeth's conception is a miracle of healing (Lk 1:25).	Mary's conception is a miracle of creation (Lk 1:35).
Contrasts Between the Children	
The son will be great before the Lord (Lk 1:15).	The son's greatness is unqualified (Lk 1:32).
The son is holy because of his vows (Lk 1:15).	The son is holy from his conception (Lk 1:35).
The son will prepare the people (Lk 1:17).	The son will reign on David's throne (Lk 1:32-33).
The son is filled with the Spirit in the womb (Lk 1:15).	The son's existence is from the Holy Spirit (Lk 1:35).
Zechariah doubted (Lk 1:18).	Mary believed (Lk 1:38, 45).

Luke's structure of the annunciation narratives highlights Jesus' superiority over John.[23] Also, the contrasting conceptions undermine the connection be-

[23]Raymond Brown et al., *Mary in the New Testament: A Collaborative Assessment by Protestant and Roman Catholic Scholars* (Philadelphia: Fortress, 1978), p. 108.

tween Mary, Elizabeth and the Old Testament barren-woman tradition. Against old, barren, pious and righteous Elizabeth, Mary is young, fertile,[24] and morally and spiritually unexceptional. Rather than praying for God's blessing, she is surprised and confused by a divine call. Rather than being addressed by name, she is given an exalted title. These contrasts distance Mary from Elizabeth. She does not stand with barren mothers. God is doing something different.

It is therefore with wonder that readers encounter Mary's acknowledgement of the angel's announcement and acceptance of God's call with the words: "Behold the slave of the Lord! May it be to me as you have spoken" (Lk 1:38).[25] Gaventa's translation of *doulē* is to be preferred to the NRSV's "servant," for two reasons. First, lexically "slave" is more accurate.[26] Translations of ancient literature apart from the New Testament are uniform. Gaventa is right to insist that "Mary recognizes with this statement God's selection of her and the compulsion under which that role is to be played. To translate 'servant' is to misconstrue Mary's role as that of one who has *chosen* to serve rather than one who has *been chosen*."[27] Second, Gaventa suggests that translation problems have arisen out of a desire to avoid the false stereotype of Mary (and all women) submitting to God (and all males). But, she warns, "misinterpretation of the text . . . does not give us license to make the text into what it is not."[28]

To avoid this eventuality, one should attend to the word's use elsewhere in Holy Scripture. In Luke/Acts *doulē* and related words describe all disciples: women and men (Acts 2:18), believers generally (Acts 4:29), and Paul and his companions (Acts 16:17). Paul speaks of himself as "a slave of Jesus Christ" (Rom 1:1 NRSV margin) and of all believers as "slaves of righteousness" (Rom 6:18). He announces how subversive "a slave of Christ" can be for socioeconomic norms

---

[24]There is no necessary connotation of virginity applied to *parthenos* in Lk 1:27, where it means "young woman." Mary is a young, engaged woman. Readers are to expect that marriage and sex would ensue in due course, followed by pregnancy and children. It is not until Lk 1:34, when Mary exclaims that she cannot conceive because she is a virgin, that biology becomes an issue. On whether a virginal conception is to be found in Luke's text itself or is only read into the text by readers familiar with Matthew's account, see Brown, *Birth of the Messiah,* pp. 298-309 (for the best defense of the traditional reading); and Joseph Fitzmyer, *To Advance the Gospel: New Testament Studies* (New York: Crossroad, 1981), p. 55 (for an alternative reading). Jane Schaberg offers a more sinister interpretation: Luke here and elsewhere alludes "to the seduction or rape of a betrothed virgin"; *The Illegitimacy of Jesus: A Feminist Theological Interpretation of the Infancy Narratives* (San Francisco: Harper and Row, 1987), pp. 84-101, esp. 89-100.

[25]Gaventa, *Mary,* p. 54.

[26]Walter Bauer, Frederick W. Danker, William F. Arndt, and F. Wilbur Gingrich, *A Greek-English Lexicon of the New Testament and Other Early Christian Literature,* 3rd ed. (Chicago: University of Chicago Press, 2000), p. 259.

[27]Gaventa, *Mary,* p. 54.

[28]Ibid.

(1 Cor 7:21-24). An alternative to sexist misinterpretation is emerging: believers, whether Jew or Gentile, male or female, are "slaves of the Lord."

It is the Old Testament and Apocrypha, however, that give "slave of the Lord" its full weight. By adopting the lowly status of this title, Mary places herself in powerful company—leaders and liberators of God's people: not only Abraham (Ps 105:42), Moses (Neh 9:14; Mal 4:4), Joshua (Josh 24:29; Judg 2:8), David (Ps 89:3), Daniel (Dan 6:20) and the Davidic Messiah (Ezek 34:23), but also women like Shiphrah and Puah, Deborah and Jael, Esther and Judith.[29] The women are striking. Shiphrah and Puah, both midwives, disobeyed Pharaoh's orders to kill the Israelite boys they delivered (Ex 1:15-21).[30] Deborah led Barak and his army to victory over the Canaanite King Jabin and General Sisera. In the same story Jael lured Sisera into her tent and killed him by driving a tent spike through his head (Judg 4—5).[31] Esther's actions saved the Jews from their enemies in Persia.[32] Judith rescued God's people from the pagan General Holofernes by beheading him.[33] These women comprise Mary's company. These biblical and extrabiblical analogues for Elizabeth and Mary provide the lenses through which to read their stories:

Barren Mothers of Promised Sons	***Female Liberators of God's People***
Sarah	Shiphrah and Puah
Rebecca	Deborah
Rachel	Jael
Manoah's wife	Esther
Hannah	Judith
Elizabeth	Mary

[29]Bauckham, *Gospel Women,* pp. 57, 66.

[30]For a feminist reading of women in Exodus, including Shiphrah and Puah, see Drorah O'Donnel Setel, "Exodus," in *Women's Bible Commentary,* ed. Carol A. Newsom and Sharon H. Ringe (Louisville: Westminster John Knox, 1998), pp. 32-34, esp. 34.

[31]For a feminist reading of the Deborah and Jael stories, see Danna Nolan Fewell, "Judges," in *Women's Bible Commentary,* ed. Carol A. Newsom and Sharon H. Ringe (Louisville: Westminster John Knox, 1998), pp. 74-76.

[32]For a feminist reading of Esther, see Sidnie Ann White Crawford, "Esther," in *Women's Bible Commentary,* ed. Carol A. Newsom and Sharon H. Ringe (Louisville: Westminster John Knox, 1998), pp. 131-37.

[33]For a feminist reading of Judith, see Denise Dombrowski Hopkins, "Judith," in *Women's Bible Commentary,* ed. Carol A. Newsom and Sharon H. Ringe (Louisville: Westminster John Knox, 1998), pp. 279-85.

When she embraces the title "slave of the Lord" as hers, Mary becomes "the active and responsible subject of her own story, when she acts as the Lord's servant, taking God at his word and taking responsibility for acting with trust in that word."[34] She is not an instrument in the designs of the divine patriarch. To so argue[35] is "to equate subservience to another human being with obedience to God in a crassly literalistic way, neglecting one of the central insights of biblical spirituality: that the service of God is the true liberation and fulfillment of the self."[36] This is a daring, subversive title. If Mary is *God's* slave then she is no one else's—not even her husband's. God calls, Mary assents, the redeemer is conceived and Joseph is not even a witness to the events.

"The slave of the Lord" is Mary's assent to God's plan and God's authority. It is a lowly status confident of divine vindication and exaltation. Mary's concluding words, "may it be to me as you have said" (NIV), underscore that she has not chosen this task for herself any more than Saul did, overwhelmed by the risen Lord on the road to Damascus. Like him, she has been chosen; like him, she freely assents to this choice. She will be the Lord's slave; she will conceive in social stigma, bear a son, name him Jesus and embark upon an uncertain future with an inauspicious beginning. It is God's plan.

Mary and Elizabeth (Luke 1:39-56). In the next scene, Mary continues as God's slave by journeying to Elizabeth's home to confirm the sign given by Gabriel:[37]

> In those days Mary set out and went with haste to a Judean town in the hill country, where she entered the house of Zechariah and greeted Elizabeth. When Elizabeth heard Mary's greeting, the child leaped in her womb. And Elizabeth was filled with the Holy Spirit and exclaimed with a loud cry, "Blessed are you among women, and blessed is the fruit of your womb. And why has this happened to

---

[34]Bauckham, *Gospel Women,* p. 66.

[35]V. K. Robbins, "Socio-Rhetorical Criticism: Mary, Elizabeth, and the Magnificat as a Test Case," in *The New Literary Criticism and the New Testament,* ed. E. Struthers Malbon and E. V. McKnight, Journal for the Study of the New Testament Supplement 109 (Sheffield: Sheffield Academic Press, 1994), pp. 196, 198.

[36]Bauckham, *Gospel Women,* p. 66.

[37]"As a young girl, Mary would not normally have left her home without accompaniment—either to browse in her own hometown or (especially!) to travel some seventy miles to the hill country around Jerusalem. Until she entered the bridal chamber, a girl lived in seclusion in her home. Moreover, Mary's journey is apparently unmotivated. She does not go in obedience to the angel, who gave her no such instructions" (Green, *Luke,* pp. 94-95). Slavery to the Lord apparently allows for initiative in the face of social convention! Marshall argues without evidence that seeing the fulfillment of the promised sign is a command implicit in Gabriel's announcement (*Luke,* p. 77).

> me, that the mother of my Lord comes to me? For as soon as I heard the sound of your greeting, the child in my womb leaped for joy. And blessed is she who believed that there would be a fulfillment of what was spoken to her by the Lord." (Lk 1:39-45)

This short encounter bridges angelic annunciation with songs of praise sung by Mary (Lk 1:46-55) and Zechariah (Lk 1:67-80). Because of this transitional purpose, these verses are easily passed over. To treat it merely as Luke's way of changing setting, however, is to miss three significant items.

First, Elizabeth dons the prophet's mantle. Mary is the focus, but apart from her initial greeting she is silent.[38] Elizabeth's Spirit-inspired utterance drives the story forward. Her opening exclamation, "blessed are you among women, and blessed is the fruit of your womb," reveals foreknowledge of Mary's pregnancy[39] and that conception has already occurred.

Second, the christological content in Elizabeth's description of Mary, "the mother of my Lord," is profound. Although *kyrios* can mean "sir" or "master," Luke intends a deeper meaning. He uses it seven times in the annunciation to Zechariah as a title for God:[40]

1. Elizabeth and Zechariah observed "all the commandments . . . of the Lord" (Lk 1:6).
2. Zechariah served in "the sanctuary of the Lord" (Lk 1:9).
3. "Then there appeared to him an angel of the Lord" (Lk 1:11).
4. Zechariah's son "will be great in the sight of the Lord" (Lk 1:15).
5. Zechariah's son "will turn many . . . to the Lord their God" (Lk 1:16).
6. Zechariah's son will "make ready a people prepared for the Lord" (Lk 1:17).
7. Elizabeth proclaims, "This is what the Lord has done for me" (Lk 1:25).

Moreover, Elizabeth knows Mary's son's identity because her unborn son leaped at Mary's voice. Also filled with the Holy Spirit, John's mission begins

---

[38]Green (*Luke,* p. 94) highlights the significance of Mary's greeting: "This is proper, for Elizabeth is clearly the superior, by normal canons at least. She is a daughter of Aaron, the wife of a priest, the elder of these two women. What is more, had she not received divine affirmation in the blessing of a child? What is surprising, then, is Elizabeth's greeting to Mary. . . . Suddenly the tables have turned, and we have from Elizabeth a second testimony to the favored status of Mary first proclaimed by Gabriel."

[39]Nolland, *Luke,* p. 75.

[40]*Kyrios* is employed in the same fashion in the Marian annunciation on three more occasions: Lk 1:28, 32, 38.

in utero, already going ahead of the Lord, preparing the people for his coming.[41] Luke thus implies that the meaning of "Lord" made clear above is also to be found here. While not likely a claim to divinity, "the mother of my Lord" asserts Jesus' intermediary role between God and God's people.[42]

Third, Elizabeth makes a twofold blessing of her younger cousin. Here English translations obscure a significant change in vocabulary. When Elizabeth first blesses Mary and her unborn child, the word used is *eulogēmenē* (Lk 1:42), meaning roughly "commended" or "adored." Social conventions are reversed. Though observed at the beginning, where the lesser Mary greets the greater Elizabeth, Elizabeth now embraces diminished status.[43] Mary's singular motherhood, however, is not the sole reason for her blessing. When Elizabeth blesses Mary a second time, *makaria* (Lk 1:45) connects Mary's blessedness with trust in God's promise.[44] The word can mean "happy," but this misses the depth of the biblical tradition, which uses it to denote divine favor. This is especially the case in the Greek translation of certain psalms (e.g., Ps 1:1; 2:12; 84:4; 94:12), with which a Greek-speaking Christian like Luke would have been familiar.[45] Thus Luke 1:45 may be translated as follows: "And favored by God is she who believed because what the Lord has said to her will be accomplished."[46] The word *because* rather than the NRSV's *that* avoids the false conclusion that Mary's belief was a precondition to God's action. While grammatically possible, the reading implied by the NRSV is not right. For Luke, Mary's blessedness is christological; it is centered on her child. "Because" correctly emphasizes that God's favor will be shown because what God has said will occur. Mary's trust is not the basis of the divine

[41]As the inspirer of Elizabeth's speech and John's leap, the Holy Spirit safeguards the veracity of both utterance and act. Against those who see the unborn John's identification of Jesus as contradicting other Gospel passages (e.g., Jn 1:31; Lk 7:18-22) in which John does not know or recognize Jesus (cf. Brown, *Birth of the Messiah,* p. 341 n. 7), Bock rightly observes that "Elizabeth interprets the significance of the movement. She functions as a prophetess, declaring the divine significance of an action" (*Luke,* p. 135). Bock underscores the Spirit's inspiration of John and his mother.

[42]Green, *Luke,* p. 95; and Johnson, *Luke,* p. 41. Nolland (*Luke,* p. 75) underplays this understanding in his description of "my Lord" as a "court expression" (cf. Dan 4:19) with messianic overtones (cf. Ps 110:1).

[43]In this way "the superiority of Jesus over John is thus again highlighted. . . . However, the *nature* and *exercise* of the superior status of Jesus is anticipated. With his coming, social conventions will be turned on their head; the greater will serve the lesser" (Green, *Luke,* p. 96). This theme will be seen again in Mary's song (Lk 1:51-53).

[44]Criticism of the doubting Zechariah may be implied here.

[45]Johnson, *Luke,* p. 41.

[46]Not only has the vocabulary changed, but so has the person: Elizabeth's first blessing is in the second person ("blessed are you") while her second is in the third person ("blessed is she"). Green sees in this change an invitation to readers "to respond, like Mary, with faith" (*Luke,* p. 97).

favor; rather, the fulfillment of the promise is the divine favor.[47]

Mary's unique place at the forefront of Luke's narrative is derivative. Blessed not because of her piety, Mary is adored because of God's dramatic action in Jesus' conception. The ground of Mary's twofold blessedness is the fulfillment of God's promise. Mary herself embraces this exalted status and takes up the role of prophet as she responds to Elizabeth's declaration in the words of the Magnificat:

> And Mary said,
> "My soul magnifies the Lord,
> and my spirit rejoices in God my Savior,
> for he has looked with favor on the lowliness of his servant.
> Surely, from now on all generations will call me blessed;
> for the Mighty One has done great things for me,
> and holy is his name.
> His mercy is for those who fear him
> from generation to generation.
> He has shown strength with his arm;
> he has scattered the proud in the thoughts of their hearts.
> He has brought down the powerful from their thrones,
> and lifted up the lowly;
> he has filled the hungry with good things,
> and sent the rich away empty.
> He has helped his servant Israel,
> in remembrance of his mercy,
> according to the promise he made to our ancestors,
> to Abraham and to his descendants forever."
> And Mary remained with her about three months and then returned to her home.
> (Lk 1:46-56)

One of the most beautiful passages of the New Testament, the Magnificat or Mary's song is Mary's first lengthy speech. It interprets the strange sequence of events into which Mary has been pulled and her role in the larger narrative. Two interpretive issues about the Magnificat need to be exposed and tested.

First, did Mary compose the Magnificat? This is Mary's only song as a character in Luke's Gospel. It becomes clear that Mary did not create it when two lines of evidence are considered: (a) analysis indicates careful poetic construction well beyond the capabilities of an illiterate first-century Palestinian teenager; and (b) the hymn's use of the past tense exclusively in Luke 1:51-55 does not fit Mary's context as much as it does that of one aware that God had raised Christ from the

---

[47]The connection of *makaria* with belief or trust is echoed in Lk 11:27-28, discussed below.

dead. This suggests that "this hymn originally dealt with salvation in retrospect (after the resurrection) rather than the inauguration of salvation."[48] The text makes it impossible to argue that it is a spontaneous Spirit-inspired speech.[49] Whatever its origins, the song allows us to see the miraculous conceptions of John and Jesus through Mary's eyes and to see Mary through Luke's.[50] In addition, the Magnificat contains many parallels with biblical and extrabiblical texts:[51]

Luke	***Biblical and Extrabiblical Parallels***
My soul magnifies the Lord, / and my spirit rejoices in God my Savior. (Lk 1:47)	My [Hannah's] heart exults in the LORD; / my strength is exalted in my God. . . . / I rejoice in my victory. (1 Sam 2:1-3) Then my soul shall rejoice in the LORD, / exulting in his deliverance. (Ps 35:9) Yet I will rejoice in the LORD; / I will exult in the God of my salvation. (Hab 3:18)
For he has looked with favor on the lowliness of his servant. (Lk 1:48a)	She [Hannah] made this vow: "O LORD of hosts, if only you will look on the misery of your servant, and remember me, and not forget your servant." (1 Sam 1:11) For [Leah] said, "Because the LORD has looked on my affliction." (Gen 29:32) God heard your servant, and looked upon my low estate, and considered my distress, and gave me a son. (4 Ezra 9.45; cf. 1 Macc 2:11)

[48]Brown et al., *Mary in the New Testament,* p. 140.

[49]It is possible to contend that the Holy Spirit uttered the song through Mary's lips. While this would account for the song's intertextual intricacy, the argument contradicts the classical Christian understanding of inspiration according to which the Spirit conveys his message without violating authors' capabilities.

[50]There are three possibilities regarding the origins not only of the Magnificat, but of all four of Luke's canticles (including the Benedictus [Lk 1:68-79], the Nunc Dimittis [Lk 2:29-32] and the Gloria [Lk 2:14]): (1) Luke authored them at the same time as he authored the Gospel; (2) Luke authored them at a later time and added them to his Gospel; or (3) Luke used canticles of Jewish or Jewish Christian origin to suit his own purposes. Bock offers a version of the third view that seeks nevertheless to treat the words as Mary's: "Mary composed the hymn later as a reflective response to Elizabeth's blessing (perhaps during her three-month stay). . . . In sum, Mary cannot be ruled out as the source for this material" (*Luke,* pp. 144-45). This is true; it is also true, however, that based on evidence found in the text itself, the likelihood is exceedingly remote. One wonders if Bock allowed his theology to determine his exegesis and whether, for an evangelical Protestant at least, it should not be the other way around. Brown, on the other hand, is quite confident that the canticles are drawn from the liturgical life of the *Anawim* ("poor ones"), that is, the Jerusalem Christian community (*Birth of the Messiah,* pp. 346-55). Marshall is more modest than either Bock or Brown, arguing that although it is obvious that the background to the hymns is Jewish "we have no means of distinguishing between tradition and redaction" (*Luke,* p. 79).

[51]Adapted from Brown, *Birth of the Messiah,* pp. 358-60.

Luke	***Biblical and Extrabiblical Parallels***
Surely, from now on all generations will call me blessed. (Lk 1:48b)	And Leah said, "Happy am I! For the women will call me happy." (Gen 30:13)
For the Mighty One has done great things for me. (Lk 1:49a)	He is your praise; he is your God, who has done for you these great and awesome things. (Deut 10:21) The LORD, your God, is in your midst, / a warrior who gives victory. (Zeph 3:17)
And holy is his name. (Lk 1:49b)	Holy and awesome is his name. (Ps 111:9)
His mercy is for those who fear him / from generation to generation. (Lk 1:50)	But the steadfast love of the LORD . . . is on those who fear him, / and his righteousness to children's children. (Ps 103:17) His mercy is upon those who fear him. (*Pss. Sol.* 13:12)
He has shown strength with his arm; / he has scattered the proud in the thoughts of their hearts. / He has brought down the powerful from their thrones, / and lifted up the lowly; / he has filled the hungry with good things, / and sent the rich away empty. (Lk 1:51-53)	The LORD makes poor and makes rich; / he brings low, he also exalts. / He raises up the poor from the dust; / he lifts the needy from the ash heap, / to make them sit with princes / and inherit a seat of honor. (1 Sam 2:7-8 [Hannah]) He leads priests away stripped, / and overthrows the mighty. (Job 12:19) Exalt that which is low, / abase that which is high. (Ezek 21:26) For he satisfies the thirsty, / and the hungry he fills with good things. (Ps 107:9) The Lord overthrows the thrones of the rulers, / and enthrones the lowly in their place. (Sir 10:14)
He has helped his servant Israel, / in remembrance of his mercy, / according to the promise he made to our ancestors, / to Abraham and to his descendants forever. (Lk 1:54-55)	But you, Israel, my servant, / Jacob, whom I have chosen, / the offspring of Abraham, my friend; / whom I took from the ends of the earth. (Is 41:8-9) He has remembered his steadfast love and faithfulness / to the house of Israel. (Ps 98:3) You will show faithfulness to Jacob / and unswerving loyalty to Abraham, / as you have sworn to our ancestors / from the days of old. (Mic 7:20) He . . . shows steadfast love to his anointed, / to David and his descendants forever. (2 Sam 22:51) And the Lord will remember his servants in mercy. (*Pss. Sol.* 10:4)

Second, did Luke intend Mary to sing the Magnificat? This assumption may be questioned for two reasons: (a) Although the vast majority of copies of Luke's Gospel agree that Luke 1:46 begins with "and Mary said," a variant textual tradition reads "and Elizabeth said."[52] The textual evidence is weak: where scholarship assumes that the earlier the text the greater the likelihood of its authenticity, this variant is generally late; where scholarship looks for broad support in terms of linguistic and geographical locations, this variant is found almost exclusively in Latin texts limited to Italy and the Balkans.[53] (b) More promising, the text seems to fit better with Elizabeth's story than with Mary's. The "lowliness" of the speaker, for example, is a more apt description of the elder woman's barrenness than of the younger's virginity.[54] Furthermore, the allusions to Hannah harmonize more with Elizabeth's pregnancy.

Even when taken together, however, the textual variant and the song's contents do not seriously challenge the traditional reading. Not only are the variant texts late and limited, the argument from the song's contents is not conclusive. Against the observations made above, the following items should be considered: (a) If "lowliness" is more fitted to Elizabeth, then "servant" is better suited to Mary (cf. Lk 1:38). (b) Although it is true that Mary's lowliness mirrors neither Elizabeth's nor Leah's nor the other women in the Old Testament's barren-mother motif, Mary is, "no less than they, to be identified with the poor and the powerless, as the rest of the Magnificat, and indeed the rest of the birth narrative, will demonstrate."[55] (c) It is only when sung by Mary that the Magnificat both parallels Zechariah's Benedictus (Lk 1:68-79) and responds to Elizabeth's praise (Lk 1:42, 45).[56] The stronger evidence and better argument lies with Mary as the speaker.

Although various structural proposals have been advanced, the simplest is a four-tier arrangement: introduction (Lk 1:46-47), first strophe (Lk 1:48-50), second strophe (Lk 1:51-53) and conclusion (Lk 1:54-55).[57] In the introduction words reminiscent of Hannah, the Psalms and Habakkuk praise the God of Mary's salvation, declaring the divine purpose behind the recent events. By so giving her a prophetic role, Luke makes a profound christological development. Having the pregnant Mary speak of God as her Savior moves salvation from its association with Jesus' death and resurrection in the earliest apostolic preaching (e.g., Acts 2:22-36; 3:11-26; 4:8-12) to his conception and birth (cf. Lk 1:69; 2:11, 30), thereby recasting the entire life of Jesus as God's saving act.[58] This serves

---

[52]Ibid., p. 334.
[53]Ibid., pp. 334-35.
[54]Ibid., p. 335.
[55]Gaventa, *Mary,* p. 57.
[56]Marshall, *Luke,* p. 78.
[57]Brown, *Birth of the Messiah,* pp. 358-60.
[58]Ibid., p. 360.

to exalt Mary as the vehicle through which this act will begin.

This exaltation is elaborated in the first of two strophes. While each gives the motivations for the praise that springs from Mary's soul, they do so in different ways. The first emphasizes God's mighty work specifically in Mary.[59] By stressing the divine initiative, Mary gives no indication that her status, rightly recognized by Elizabeth, is due to some capacity for righteousness. Rather, by calling to mind Hannah, Leah and the nation of Israel (and Judith; cf. Judith 13.18; 16.11), she declares her low position and reiterates her place as the Lord's slave. It is God's unanticipated favor that brings Mary—like Hannah, Leah, Israel and Judith—to greatness.[60] It is because of God's intervention that she will be the mother of him whose kingdom will have no end (Lk 1:33), who will establish God's mercy from generation to generation. Luke thus associates Mary with all those whom God has delivered and through whom God delivers his people and shows how she transcends them.[61] As a result, Mary predicts that Elizabeth's blessing will become a universal acknowledgement of the favor that God has lavished on her.

In the second strophe, Mary places God's work in her within the larger sweep of salvation history in which God acts mercifully toward those who fear him. God frustrates the designs of the proud, the mighty and the rich, while he raises the lowly and fills the hungry with good things. Mary draws on biblical and extrabiblical examples of divine reversals of fortune, showing that what the Mighty One has done in her is the culmination of a trajectory of previous acts.[62] The past tense of the verbs in this section (brought, lifted, filled, sent) suggests its pre-Lukan history. By singing a hymn about what God has done through the

---

[59]Both here and in the second strophe, two Old Testament divine motifs are held in tight balance. In the first God is the Mighty One who does great things, who shows his strength, who confounds the proud but lifts up the lowly. In the second God is the merciful rememberer of the Abrahamic covenant. "These two images of God are complementary, and coalesce in the theme of transposition: As a divine warrior, God acts dynamically against the proud and powerful; as the merciful God of the covenant, God's dynamic acts are for the sake of those who fear him, the object of his promise, Israel" (Green, *Luke,* p. 102).

[60]Bauckham, *Gospel Women,* pp. 69-76.

[61]Brown, *Birth of the Messiah,* p. 361. Like all Israel, Mary awaits God's saving intervention on their behalf. Unlike all Israel, she alone will bear in her body Israel's deliverer. See Nolland, *Luke,* p. 75; and Green, *Luke,* p. 103.

[62]This is, of course, one of Luke's favorite themes, running throughout his Gospel: "Luke places a special emphasis on those who are 'on the periphery,' the downtrodden, sinners, women, widows, Samaritans (7:11-17, 36, 50; 10:29-37; 17:11-19)" (Brown et al., *Mary in the New Testament,* p. 141). Green is therefore right to describe the Magnificat as "a foretaste of the salvific themes he will develop throughout Luke-Acts." He extensively documents the way in which Luke structured the song to parallel not only its Old Testament context but also the context of the surrounding narrative (*Luke,* p. 98).

death and resurrection of Jesus through the lips of Mary, Luke deepens his christological claim regarding the saving significance of Jesus' life and stresses Mary's prophetic office. In Jesus' conception, God displays strength, confounds the plans of the powerful and transforms the fortunes of the lowly.

Finally, Mary ties both strophes to the fulfillment of God's promise to Abraham and his descendents. The entire utterance is the fulfillment of the original covenant promise.[63] This is the capstone of Mary's self-understanding and Luke's understanding of her place in God's plan. She is the embodiment of the people of Israel, the one in whom Israel's vocation to be a light to the Gentiles will be fulfilled.[64] God remembers his covenant promise by frustrating the plans of the powerful and raising the lowly.[65] The pinnacle is the miraculous conception of the Son of God in the womb of the Virgin.[66] This is the message of Mary the prophet.

Mary and the birth (Luke 2:1-20). "In those days,"[67] so opens the familiar story, while Quirinius governed Syria, Caesar Augustus decreed an empirewide census that required all to return to the towns of their birth.[68] Joseph returns to Bethlehem with Mary because he was descended from David.[69] By using the

---

[63]Nolland, *Luke,* p. 76.

[64]Johnson, *Luke,* p. 43.

[65]Green, *Luke,* p. 105.

[66]Schaberg ("Luke," p. 373) is therefore right to observe that "Mary's song is precious to women and other oppressed people for its vision of their concrete freedom from systemic injustice—from oppression by political rulers on their 'thrones' and by the arrogant and rich. . . . The Magnificat is not the song of a victim but one that proclaims liberation with tough authority." "Indeed," adds Johnson, "at the annunciation Mary uttered her yes to the call of God's Spirit, a consent to adventure that has been used so abominably to promote the passive submission of women. Here her fiat finds its home in her defiant resistance to the powers of evil. She takes on as her own the divine no to what crushes the lowly, stands up fearlessly and sings out that it will be overturned. . . . Singing of her joy in God and God's victory over oppression, she becomes not a subjugated but a prophetic woman" (*Truly Our Sister,* pp. 271-72).

[67]The phrase may suggest "the narration of events of eschatological import (cf. [Luke] 4:2; 5:35; 9:36; Acts 2:18)" (Green, *Luke,* p. 125).

[68]Whether this census actually took place is debated. Johnson says that it did not: "Herod died in 4 B.C.E. and Augustus was emperor from 27 B.C.E. to 14 C.E. So far, so good. But Quirinius was governor in Syria from 6-7 C.E., and the gap can't be filled. Luke simply has the facts wrong." He adds that like all historians Luke depends upon sources, in this instance mistaken ones. Further, Luke stresses that Jesus was born in Bethlehem, not chronology (*Luke,* pp. 49, 51-52). According to Nolland, however, one could translate Lk 2:2 in a manner that removes the error: "This was the first census that took place *before* Quirinius was governor of Syria." The original grammar is awkward either way; this reading is as valid as the other (*Luke,* pp. 101-2).

[69]This is the first time that Joseph does anything. Even here, however, he is "introduced to us primarily in his relationship to Mary and in his inherited status as a Davidide (1:27)" (Green, *Luke,* p. 126).

emperor to further the divine plan, Luke situates Jesus' birth in world history and emphasizes the extent of God's providence.[70] Only after Luke has finished his explanation for Joseph's pilgrimage does Luke tell us that Mary had accompanied him to Bethlehem. Mary's pregnancy is overwhelmed by the everyday political affairs of life.

Once introduced so to emphasize her powerlessness, Luke immediately stresses Mary's activity: she gave birth; she swaddled her firstborn;[71] she laid him in a manger because there was no other place for him.[72] The irony "that emerges when the seemingly ordinary, insignificant Mary gives birth to her seemingly ordinary, insignificant baby within the confines of Caesar's attempt at control through counting" is clear.[73] Even local life does not stop to receive the Son of the Most High. He is swaddled—someone will care for him, but his bed is a trough—he has no place in the halls of power or the inns of the everyday.[74] God's promise comes hidden amid the principalities and powers who treat even descendents of David as pawns, bidding them come to be recorded and taxed.

A scene change in Luke 2:8 opens the second part of the story. Readers are transported from the stable to the shepherds' fields. Led by the "angel of the Lord,"[75] a celestial company shines with God's glory in its annunciation and praise, terrifying the shepherds. It is to shepherds, neither Caesar nor the temple elite, that

---

[70]Indeed, he may be going further, yet: "Luke might even be understood as providing evidence for a positive attitude toward imperial rule within the Christian movement or for the celebration of the rule of Augustus—who made one empire out of many nations and so created a suitable arena for the advent of God's Messiah" (Green, *Luke,* pp. 122-23). Green is skeptical of this reading because of the politically subversive themes in the Magnificat and Benedictus and the deliberate contrast of Augustus and Jesus (cf. Brown, *Birth of the Messiah,* pp. 415-16). In arguing for a simple disjunction between imperial support and imperial subversion, however, Green overreaches. Oliver O'Donovan convincingly argues both that the powers have been defeated and that under the rule of Christ they nevertheless continue to mediate God's justice (cf. Rom 13:1-7); *The Desire of the Nations: Re-discovering the Roots of Political Theology* (Cambridge: Cambridge University Press, 1996). I see no reason why support and subversion cannot cohabit under the victory of God in Christ.

[71]The Greek term translated "firstborn," *prōtotokos,* does not necessarily imply the births of subsequent children but means only that no children preceded Jesus. It "establishes for this child the status and privileges in Mosaic law of the firstborn child (Exod 13:2; Num 3:12-13; 18:15-16; Deut 21:15-17)" (Nolland, *Luke,* p. 105).

[72]There is a curious parallel between the threefold description of Jesus birth and his burial: "Wrapped it [Jesus' body] in a linen cloth, and laid it in a rock-hewn tomb where no one had ever been laid" (Lk 23:53).

[73]Gaventa, *Mary,* p. 60.

[74]Inns did not exist in Bethlehem at that time. Sermons on the innkeeper's heartlessness are baseless. Nor is the manger a sign of poverty. Mary and Joseph were likely guests of a family in a common room so crowded that her baby was placed in the animals' trough (Brown, *Birth of the Messiah,* p. 419).

[75]This probably describes God's messenger, Gabriel, whom we have already met.

God sends his angelic army to announce the fulfillment of his promise, the birth of his Son.[76] The shepherds' response moves the story to its concluding section:

> So they went with haste and found Mary and Joseph, and the child lying in a manger. When they saw this, they made known what had been told them about this child; and all who heard it were amazed at what the shepherds told them. But Mary treasured all these words and pondered them in her heart. The shepherds returned, glorifying and praising God for all they had heard and seen, as it had been told them. (Lk 2:16-20)

Readers return to the inn to begin the third segment of the narrative (Lk 2:16-20). Mary again is the center of the action. The image preserved in so many Christmas card nativities—with Mary as the focal point, Joseph in the background, the infant Jesus in the foreground and the shepherds and various animals looking on—is accurate. What they cannot capture, however, is just how noisy this scene is. The shepherds go with haste to find Mary, Joseph and the child and immediately begin to talk about it. But in the midst of the hubbub, Mary ponders all these things in her heart. At the center of the exuberance is silent reflection.[77] Here a different facet of Mary's character emerges. No longer a prophet, she silently weighs things that, while they include the shepherds' visit, are not limited to it. They may well embrace all that has happened over the last forty weeks.

What does Mary's silent pondering mean? Some early commentators suggest that in keeping these things (suggested by context, but never spelled out) Mary remembers them in order to pass them on to future generations.[78] This fails to reckon with Luke's near repetition of the phrase in Luke 1:51 at the conclusion of the temple story. There Luke says that although Jesus' parents did not understand his words, Mary kept them. The focus of Mary's retention is not the past (i.e., remembering them in order to record them later), but anticipation of what would come in the future (i.e., keeping her Son's words in hope that one day she would understand).

This is underscored by the vocabulary of the two passages. The Greek word

---

[76]The shepherds serve a dual purpose: they remind readers of the lowly whom God will exalt and also of David, the Messiah's ancestor, the shepherd-king. Some argue that the shepherds represent society's despised (Brown, *Birth of the Messiah,* p. 420 n. 38), but the evidence supporting this view is slight. Bock rightly points out that the New Testament tends to portray shepherds favorably (*Luke,* p. 213). The shepherds' social station is low, to be sure, but not hated.

[77]Gaventa goes further, saying that "the narrator makes clear that those who surround Mary respond with amazement and awe, but the verbs that describe Mary's response connote neither wonder nor praise but perhaps secrecy or even isolation" (*Mary,* p. 61).

[78]Bock, *Luke,* pp. 200-201. Fitzmyer (*Luke,* p. 398) argues that Lk 2:19 means that Mary kept these things to herself. She remained silent.

usually translated "pondered" in Luke 2:19 means combining or bringing different ideas together into a coherent whole.[79] It suggests that in silence Mary began to put together the details about the census, the trip to Bethlehem, the manger and the angelic appearance to the shepherds. Whether she saw God's plan for her and her child, however, is open to question. No resolution is indicated. In other ancient literature, the word refers to "an interpretation of dark or difficult matters, the right meaning of which is often ascertained only by means of divine help."[80] Thus Josephus (*Antiquities* 2.5.3 §72) describes Joseph interpreting the dream of the baker in prison by "pondering" it (cf. Gen 40:16). Mary's silence may be prophetic not in a predictive or proclamatory sense but in its dependence upon divine aid in order to interpret the events rightly.

The phrase "kept these things" (Lk 2:19, 51) is reminiscent of Jacob, who in the Septuagint version of the Joseph story (Gen 37:10-11) "kept this saying in mind" after Joseph aroused his brothers' jealousy by boasting about his dream. That is, Jacob regarded the saying with concern. Similarly, after experiencing terrifying night visions (Dan 7:2-28), Daniel "kept the words in his heart," concerned over what had been revealed and puzzled by what it meant.[81] When Luke combines notions of keeping and pondering, he hints that Mary has preserved the mysterious words and events surrounding Jesus' childhood, trying to interpret them. Mary "is trying to interpret her life. She is seeking to understand difficult matters concerning the lives of those she loves. She is hoping to fathom the meaning and keep on the right path. . . . Hers is a life in the process of becoming—no final answers yet available."[82]

This interpretation is supported by contrasting Mary's reaction with that of the shepherds and their audience in the birth story and that of the temple onlookers in the search story. The shepherds rush to the manger and immediately talk about their experience. Their hearers were amazed. The same is true of the witnesses to the temple dialogues: they, along with the parents of Jesus, are also amazed. But amazement is not necessarily faith. Only Mary held on to the words and puzzled over them. Mary is growing toward discipleship. She keeps in her heart all these things, including Jesus' seemingly insolent rebuke, words that she and Joseph do not yet understand.

Mary and the presentation at the temple (Luke 2:21-40). Beginning in Luke 2:21 yet another portrayal of Mary's character comes to the fore. She has

---

[79]Bock, *Luke,* p. 223; and Fitzmyer, *Luke,* p. 413.
[80]Brown et al., *Mary in the New Testament,* p. 150.
[81]Bock, *Luke,* pp. 222-23. See also Sir 39:2; Prov 3:1; Ps 119:11.
[82]Johnson, *Truly Our Sister,* p. 278.

assumed the roles of poor prophet and pondering mother with relative ease. She is not yet a full-blown disciple, but her willingness to keep an account of the events in which she has played so central a part, puzzling over them, trying to knit them into a single narrative, suggests that she is on her way. Now, however, outside the temple, tension is introduced:

> Now there was a man in Jerusalem whose name was Simeon; this man was righteous and devout, looking forward to the consolation of Israel, and the Holy Spirit rested on him. It had been revealed to him by the Holy Spirit that he would not see death before he had seen the Lord's Messiah. Guided by the Spirit, Simeon came into the temple; and when the parents brought in the child Jesus, to do for him what was customary under the law, Simeon took him in his arms and praised God, saying,
>
> "Master, now you are dismissing your servant in peace,
> according to your word;
> for my eyes have seen your salvation,
> which you have prepared in the presence of all peoples,
> a light for revelation to the Gentiles
> and for glory to your people Israel."
>
> And the child's father and mother were amazed at what was being said about him. Then Simeon blessed them and said to his mother Mary, "This child is destined for the falling and the rising of many in Israel, and to be a sign that will be opposed so that the inner thoughts of many will be revealed—and a sword will pierce your own soul too." (Lk 2:21-35)

The last weeks had been full of angelic announcements and prophetic proclamation. Now a hint of tragedy: this child will cause many to rise and fall. He will provoke opposition and disclose the thoughts of many. A sword will pierce Mary's soul before this is all over. What is this sword? Popular imagination tied Simeon's sword to the death of Jesus, and this cannot be ruled out as a possible partial referent for this poignant image, as seen in the moving words of the anonymous medieval author of *Stabat mater dolorosa:*[83]

Stabat mater dolorosa	The sorrowful mother stands
iuxta crucem lacrimosa	weeping beside the cross
dum pendebat filius;	where her Son was hanging;
cuius animam gementem	Through her weeping soul
contristantem et dolentem	compassionate and grieving
pertransivit gladius.	a sword passed.

[83]Quoted from Jaroslav Pelikan, *Mary Through the Centuries: Her Place in the History of Culture* (New Haven, Conn.: Yale University Press, 1996), p. 126.

This portrayal of Mary as *mater dolorosa* conflates Luke and John by explicitly tying Simeon's sword to the cross:

> And a sword will pierce your own soul too. (Lk 2:35)

> Meanwhile, standing near the cross of Jesus were his mother, and his mother's sister, Mary the wife of Clopas, and Mary Magdalene. (Jn 19:25)

Only John places Mary at the cross. If this alone is the sword's referent, why is Mary absent from Luke's account of the crucifixion (Lk 23:26-49)? While we cannot rule out the death of Jesus as one source of Mary's grief, it is not the one that Luke stresses. A better referent rooted both in the Old Testament and in Luke's text casts doubt on the thus-far positive image of Mary as emergent disciple.[84]

Let us begin with a wooden translation: "And Simeon blessed them and said to Mary his mother, 'Behold, this one is set for the falling and rising of many in Israel and a sign of opposition—and through your own soul will pass a sword—so that the thoughts of many hearts will be revealed.'" Luke ties the sword to the act of judgment (rising and falling) in Israel that Jesus will precipitate.[85] What is unclear is whether the sword refers to the sign of opposition or to the act of judgment itself. If it is the former, Simeon unites Mary and Jesus against common opponents. If the latter, Simeon implies that judgment will fall not only on Israel, but also on Mary.

John Nolland takes the former position: "Mary stands with her son as one opposed."[86] He understands the sword to refer to the death of Jesus, caused by the opposition he arouses. The metaphor draws upon Psalm 22:20 ("deliver my soul from the sword, / my life from the power of the dog!"), Zechariah 12:10 ("and I will pour out a spirit of compassion and supplication on the house of David and the inhabitants of Jerusalem, so that, when they look on the one whom they

---

[84]Another textually implausible interpretation sees "a reference to the 'protevangelium' of Gen 3:15 where there is enmity between the serpent and the woman, between his seed and her seed. This symbolic background catches some of the judgment motif of Luke 3:34c with its 'fall and rise'; but it also presupposes a messianic interpretation of Gen 3:15 for which we have no evidence in the pre-Lucan or Lucan tradition. Moreover, it does not do justice to the thrust of [Lk 2:]35a where Mary is not a positive figure opposed to the negative, but where the division seems to be brought into her own soul" (Brown, *Birth of the Messiah,* p. 463). This is cinematically portrayed in the juxtaposition of Mary with an effeminate Satan during the crucifixion in Mel Gibson's *Passion of the Christ* (2004).

[85]According to Johnson (*Luke,* p. 57), the falling and rising is meant to call to mind the image of the stone of stumbling in Is 8:14-15 (cf. Lk 20:17-18). It also echoes the conclusion of the Magnificat (Lk 1:51-53), "where God's mighty work exalts some, humbles others" (Green, *Luke,* p. 148).

[86]Nolland, *Luke,* p. 121.

have pierced, they shall mourn for him, as one mourns for an only child, and weep bitterly over him, as one weeps over a firstborn") and Zechariah 13:7 ("'awake, O sword, against my shepherd, / against the man who is my associate,' / says the LORD of hosts. / Strike the shepherd, that the sheep may be scattered; / I will turn my hand against the little ones").

This is unconvincing for two reasons. First, although the imagery is similar, the vocabulary is not. Psalm 22:20 includes a sword, but there is no mention of it "passing through" the psalmist's soul. Zechariah 13:7 suffers similarly: to strike is not to pass through. And in Zechariah 12:10 the sword is absent and the word translated "pierced" is another verb. There is thus no grammatical connection. Second, although Nolland concludes that the sword's referent is Jesus' death, he does not explain Mary's absence from Luke's crucifixion scene. Nor does he point to other passages in Luke's Gospel that would bolster his point. His position lacks both extratextual and intratextual support.

If the latter position—the sword of God's judgment divides not only Israel, but also Mary herself—is to hold, it must meet the same criteria. In terms of imagery and vocabulary, Ezekiel 14:17 is striking: "Or if I bring a sword upon that land and say, 'Let a sword pass through the land,' and I cut off human beings and animals from it." According to Brown, "The image is of a selective sword of judgment, destroying some and sparing others, a sword for discrimination and not merely for punishment."[87] This agrees both with the context of the Lukan passage and also with Jesus' own understanding of his ministry as presented in Luke 12:51-53:

> Do you think that I have come to bring peace to the earth? No, I tell you, but rather division! From now on five in one household will be divided, three against two and two against three; they will be divided:
>
> father against son
> and son against father,
> mother against daughter
> and daughter against mother,
> mother-in-law against her daughter-in-law
> and daughter-in-law against mother-in-law.

The extratextual and intratextual evidence supports the view that Simeon's sword is the eschatological divine judgment that will pass through not only Israel but also Mary's own soul.[88]

---

[87] Brown, *Birth of the Messiah*, p. 464.

[88] This may underscore Mary's role as the literary personification of Israel: "Israel will be divided, and so will Mary's life be run through by a sword" (Johnson, *Luke*, p. 57).

Mary and the boy Jesus at the temple (Luke 2:41-52). The first inkling of just what the sword of judgment entails comes in the next story. We have moved ahead only a few verses, but some twelve years have elapsed:

> Now every year his parents went to Jerusalem for the festival of the Passover. And when he was twelve years old, they went up as usual for the festival. When the festival was ended and they started to return, the boy Jesus stayed behind in Jerusalem, but his parents did not know it. Assuming that he was in the group of travelers, they went a day's journey. Then they started to look for him among their relatives and friends. When they did not find him, they returned to Jerusalem to search for him. After three days they found him in the temple, sitting among the teachers, listening to them and asking them questions. And all who heard him were amazed at his understanding and his answers. When his parents saw him they were astonished; and his mother said to him, "Child, why have you treated us like this? Look, your father and I have been searching for you in great anxiety." He said to them, "Why were you searching for me? Did you not know that I must be in my Father's house?" But they did not understand what he said to them. Then he went down with them and came to Nazareth, and was obedient to them. His mother treasured all these things in her heart.
>
> And Jesus increased in wisdom and in years, and in divine and human favor. (Lk 2:44-52)

Luke's second temple scene, whatever its history, has been rewritten to harmonize with the first.[89] Both open with a journey to Jerusalem (Lk 2:22, 41-42) and end with the return to Nazareth and a statement about Jesus' growth (Lk 2:39-40, 51-52). With Jesus now being twelve,[90] this is hardly a continuation of the infancy narrative; yet in its final form Luke clearly intends his audience to read the two temple encounters together.[91]

When read together, a clarification of the meaning of Simeon's sword takes place. To justify this hypothesis, we begin first with Mary's anguish. Having found her Son after days of searching, Mary expresses the worry of a frantic

---

[89]According to Brown, it is "an independent story of Jesus' youth added by Luke in a second stage of composition" (*Birth of the Messiah,* p. 479). See also Brown et al., *Mary in the New Testament,* p. 158. Nevertheless, "its location here is not at all artificial" (Green, *Luke,* p. 153).

[90]While it is possible that the "age is probably intended to mark Jesus' time to accept adult religious responsibility" (Johnson, *Luke,* p. 58), it more likely refers to a time of intense religious instruction before such responsibilities were assumed at thirteen. On this, see Bock, *Luke,* p. 264; and Fitzmyer, *Luke,* p. 440.

[91]Based on the similar descriptions of Mary's response to the revelation of Jesus' identity in Lk 2:19 and Lk 2:51, it is clear that this temple scene is also to be read alongside the birth story (Lk 2:1-20).

mother: "Child, why have you treated us like this? Look, your father and I have been searching for you in great anxiety."[92] Some may be embarrassed that the mother of Jesus—after having heard the angel's message and confirmed it with a sign, and having heard the testimonies of the shepherds and Simeon and Anna—should now erupt with such a worry-laden declaration. But this is not warranted. Although Jesus' identity and destiny are described in these instances, the timing and nature of his mission are not.[93] Further, the description of Mary trying to weave disparate events into a single narrative (Lk 2:19, 51) suggests that she did not fully understand God's revelation to her. Mary's anxiety is one that every parent experiences when a child goes missing.[94]

Far more troubling is Jesus' response: "Why were you searching for me? Did you not know that I must be in my Father's house?" Far from pacifying his worried mother, Jesus rejects her right to be worried by distinguishing himself from his parents by invoking his Father.[95] That neither Mary nor Joseph understood indicates that this incident created a barrier between Jesus and his family. When Luke adds that Mary included this among those treasured memories, it is clear that he does not intend to provide narrative resolution for two reasons. First, at this point Joseph drops from the story; he vanishes without indication that the conflict was ever mended. Second, Mary's willingness to continue to reflect on the events of Jesus' conception, birth and childhood only indicates struggle.[96] In his Gospel, Luke does not tell us whether Mary's struggle was ever clarified and resolved. In her last named appearance in Luke's Gospel, Mary's position is ambiguous. Jesus' understanding of family was radically different from hers. Even though he was her Son, she did not belong to him. His mission could not be constrained by natural bonds. This was going to be a source of great pain;

---

[92]Bock oddly calls this a "mild complaint" even though the surrounding language "refers to a reaction of being overwhelmed by events . . . and probably indicates both amazement and relief" (*Luke,* p. 268).

[93]Johnson is eloquent: "No matter how much they had been told of the child's special character, having the young man himself denominate God as his father would come as a shock" (*Luke,* p. 61).

[94]Gaventa, *Mary,* p. 68.

[95]Ibid. According to Brown et al., however, the rebuff is not sharp, but grieving (*Mary in the New Testament,* p. 161). Green adds that "the notion of 'household' in the Greco-Roman milieu was not only a designation of place but also authority. . . . [Jesus] must align himself with God's purpose, even if this appears to compromise his relationship with his parents" (*Luke,* p. 157).

[96]Bock, *Luke,* pp. 272-73. Turid Seim is right to conclude that the story demonstrates "both that Jesus is an alien in his parents' house and that his filial obedience is an act of willful subservience" ("The Virgin Mother: Mary and Ascetic Discipleship in Luke," in *A Feminist Companion to Luke,* ed. Amy Jill Levine [London: Continuum Sheffield, 2002], p. 103). This indicates that Jesus deliberately attempted to minimize his parents' pain.

it would be a sword passing through her very soul.[97]

Simeon's sword thus refers to Mary's apparent inability fully to understand and to identify with Jesus' mission. It was the recognition that, even from the time of the temple, Jesus' role and mission would sever the closest relationship in the human family—mother and child.[98] A declaration of Mary as a model disciple at this point is therefore premature. Two more times (Lk 8:19-21; 11:27-28) Mary will be mentioned by Luke. In each case, this ambiguity is raised. We do not know whether she is a disciple.

Mary in the Public Ministry of Jesus and the Church

Once Luke's infancy narrative is left behind, Mary, like Joseph, falls out of the text. There remain five interesting passages, four in the Gospel and one in Acts.

Genealogy (Luke 3:23-38). The first, Luke's genealogy, is only of indirect importance:

> Jesus was about thirty years old when he began his work. He was the son (as was thought) of Joseph son of Heli, son of Matthat, son of Levi, son of Melchi, son of Jannai, son of Joseph, son of Mattathias, son of Amos, son of Nahum, son of Esli, son of Naggai, son of Maath, son of Mattathias, son of Semein, son of Josech, son of Joda, son of Joanan, so of Rhesa, son of Zerubbabel, son of Shealtiel, son of Neri, son of Melchi, son of Addi, son of Cosam, son of Elmadam, son of Er, son of Joshua, son of Eliezer, son of Jorim, son of Matthat, son of Levi, son of Simeon, son of Judah, son of Joseph, son of Jonam, son of Eliakim, son of Melea, son of Menna, son of Mattatha, son of Nathan, son of David, son of Jesse, son of Obed, son of Boaz, son of Sala, son of Nahshon, son of Amminadab, son of Admin, son of Arni, son of Hezron, son of Perez, son of Judah, son of Jacob, son of Isaac, son of Abraham, son of Terah, son of Nahor, son of Serug, son of Reu, son of Peleg, son of Eber, son of Shelah, son of Cainan, son of Arphaxad, son of Shem, son of Noah, son of Lamech, son of Methuselah, son of Enoch, son of Jared, son of Mahalaleel, son of Cainan, son of Enos, son of Seth, son of Adam, son of God. (Lk 3:23-38)

One is immediately struck by the differences from Matthew's genealogy:

---

[97]For Johnson, this reading is possible, but not necessary (*Luke,* p. 59). He mistakenly treats the reading as a literal and immediate fulfillment of Simeon's prophecy (Lk 2:35). It is not. It is one indicator of the manner in which Simeon's prophecy will mark Mary's life. I concur with Bock: "This pericope, it would seem, is the fulfillment, or at least an initial fulfillment, of Simeon's prophecy. . . . Jesus' ministry will bring choices that will be hard for Mary to bear. . . . The passage emphasizes the division Jesus brings, not the nature of his suffering" (*Luke,* p. 250).

[98]"Presumably, by the imagery of a sword passing through Mary's soul, Luke describes the difficult process of learning that obedience to the Word of God transcends family ties. If thus far he has shown Mary as passing the test of obedience ([Lk] 1:38, 45), he has also hinted that the learning process is an ongoing one ([Lk] 2:19); here he insists that it is a process that is not without its perils and its suffering" (Brown et al., *Mary in the New Testament,* p. 157).

length (Luke's is longer), names (only two in common from David to Jesus; Matthew's includes women), purpose (Matthew's shows Jesus' descent from Abraham and David; Luke's show Jesus' descent from Adam and God) and citation formula (Matthew works from father to son, Luke works from son to father). While the two can be harmonized, it requires complex conjectures for which there is no evidence in either Luke or Matthew.[99] Fortunately, the debate is a distraction. It is enough to see that the evangelists have different theological purposes. Matthew uses genealogy to establish Jesus' Jewish and messianic bona fides. Luke uses the same technique to show that Jesus transcends these to embrace all people.

When considering Luke's genealogy alone, two facts emerge. First, it is not Mary's line. Although this position has been taken,[100] it does not conform to the most natural reading of the text. As far as Luke is concerned, this is Joseph's line. His use of the word *supposed* both harmonizes the genealogy with the birth narrative and reminds readers that Joseph is Jesus' father in name only.[101] Second, Jesus nevertheless inherits Joseph's paternity. This highlights again the family tension that arose at the temple. Although legally the son of Joseph, Jesus understood himself to have a different Father who alone could lay authoritative claim to the shape of the ministry to which he had been commissioned at his baptism (Lk 3:21-22) and which is about to begin (Lk 4:1).

Rejection of Jesus by his own (Luke 4:22, 24). Luke 4:24 recalls both Mark and Matthew. Although Luke has fleshed out the story by adding Jesus' sermon text (Is 61:1-2) and expanding his rebuke of the Nazarene synagogue congregation, only a small segment is germane to our study:

> And he said, "Truly I tell you, no prophet is accepted in the prophet's hometown." (Lk 4:24)
>
> But Jesus said to them, "Prophets are not without honor except in their own country *and in their own house*." (Mt 13:57)
>
> Then Jesus said to them, "Prophets are not without honor, except in their hometown, *and among their own kin, and in their own house*." (Mk 6:4)

As the juxtaposition of the three Synoptic texts make clear, we are dealing with the same story. The italicized segments show that Mark finds opposition to

---

[99]For a rehearsal of the various proposals and the inconclusive nature of the debate, see Bock, *Luke,* pp. 918-23.

[100]Ibid., pp. 919-20.

[101]On the possible pre-Lukan history of the genealogy, see Brown et al., *Mary in the New Testament,* pp. 163-64. The authors conclude that there is no way of settling the question: the genealogy may well be adapted by Luke, or it may have been composed by Luke.

Jesus not only in Nazareth, but also in Jesus' extended (house) and immediate (kin) families. Matthew softens Mark's charge, deleting any reference to Jesus' mother and siblings. Luke goes further yet, removing any indication that Jesus' relatives—whether near or distant—were to be found among his opponents. If Mary's purchase on discipleship is unclear, she is obviously not an enemy. She escapes categorization.[102]

Jesus' true family (Luke 8:19-21). This ambiguity is elaborated in the final two Gospel passages. The first tells us that Jesus' mother and brothers were prevented from seeing him because of the crush of the crowd. Like Matthew, Luke deletes Mark's intimation of hostility and willingness to use force. Jesus mother and brothers simply want to make contact. When their desire is brought to Jesus' attention, however, he responds ambiguously: "My mother and my brothers are those who hear the word of God and do it" (Lk 8:21). Does Jesus mean that his family is to be numbered among the disciples because of their hearing and obedience?[103] Or does Jesus mean that his true family is to be distinguished from his physical family, made up not by blood, but by obedience?[104] It is unclear. The former interpretation can claim textual support in Elizabeth's blessing of Mary as "she who believed" (Lk 1:45), while the second can call on Simeon's sword for assistance (Lk 2:35). Although most English translations give the grammar a negative cast, this is not demanded by the context. While Jesus' words indicate that his family relationships are not typical, they do not necessarily exclude Mary from Jesus' true family.[105]

True blessedness (Luke 11:27-28). This tension is found also in Luke 11:27-28. Mary does not appear here but is blessed by an unnamed woman who cried out to Jesus: "Blessed is the womb that bore you and the breasts that nursed you!" This recalls Mary's own prophetic words in the Magnificat: "From now on all generations will call me blessed" (Lk 1:48). Both the anonymous

---

[102]The categorization of the townspeople, however, is frighteningly clear: "The passage . . . announces the theme of prophetic rejection that had been adumbrated by the prophecy of Simeon ([Lk] 2:34). Jesus declares that no prophet is acceptable in his own country, and his townspeople's vivid rage and murderous intentions fulfill his prophecy" (Johnson, *Luke,* p. 81).

[103]So Brown et al., *Mary in the New Testament,* p. 168.

[104]So Nolland, *Luke,* pp. 394-95.

[105]Green captures the ambiguity nicely: "Luke does not present members of Jesus' family in any way that would mark them as 'outsiders' to his mission; their distance from him seems unavoidable in light of the magnitude of the gathered crowds and their own late arrival on the scene. On the other hand, neither does Luke at this point present his mother and brothers as exemplary disciples. . . . Jesus neither rejects nor praises his physical family; rather, he uses their arrival as a catalyst to redefine in the hearing of his disciples and the crowds the basis of kinship" (*Luke,* p. 330).

woman's utterance and Mary's own words focus attention on Jesus. Mary comes into view only as the recipient of God's gracious blessing. Again, Jesus' response is ambiguous. When he says "blessed rather are those who keep the word of God and obey it" does he mean that Mary is blessed not by biology but by her obedient discipleship?[106] Or is Jesus contrasting his physical and true families? Only those who hear and obey are blessed. It is difficult to know whether Mary is among the disciples, the blessed ones. At most, she is "a candidate for blessedness according to the criteria set forth by Jesus."[107] Jesus' understanding of family is broader than blood ties.[108]

Mary in the postresurrection community (Acts 1:14). It is only as Luke's second volume, Acts, opens that the question of Mary's discipleship may finally be put to rest. Finally he numbers her and Jesus' brothers among the disciples awaiting the advent of the Holy Spirit after Jesus' ascension: "All these were constantly devoting themselves to prayer, together with certain women, including Mary the mother of Jesus, as well as his brothers" (Acts 1:14). Having been the recipient of four divine disclosures concerning Jesus' identity, it may seem obvious for Luke to name Mary among the followers of Jesus. But it is not. Indeed, Mary's claim to be a disciple during Jesus' earthly ministry is tenuous at best. Now, without previous explanation or further elaboration, Luke places Mary in the upper room, a true disciple, a member of Jesus' eschatological family after all. What precipitated her entrance to the fellowship? Luke does not say. What subsequent career did she have among the apostles? Again Luke is silent. He is content to place her and her children "in one accord with those who would constitute the nascent church at Pentecost, engaged in prayer that would so mark the life of that church."[109]

For this reason we may claim the exalted descriptions of Mary's discipleship that were until now premature, for Luke's portrait of Mary is not as a disciple from first to last. Rather, it is one that mirrors the lives of many believers, with moments of intense spirituality interrupted by extended periods of ambiguity. She is rightly called "a model for all Christians," "the exemplary disciple, a Christian prototype," "the first believer" or "the perfect Christian," but not because of

---

[106]Brown et al., *Mary in the New Testament,* p. 172, take this position.

[107]Ibid., p. 461.

[108]"Jesus' response to the woman, then, should be understood as corrective. The issue for him is not so much the status that attaches to his mother on account of the status of her Son. Although the values represented in this way would have been understood among and attributed to women in Palestinian antiquity, this is precisely the sort of common wisdom Luke had begun to subvert in his narration of Gabriel's announcement to Mary regarding Jesus birth in [Lk] 1:26-38" (Green, *Luke,* p. 461).

[109]Brown et al., *Mary in the New Testament,* p. 177.

what happened to her. She is able to claim all of these titles, rather, for three reasons having nothing to do with maternity: (1) because Acts 1:14 testifies to her willingness to continue to ponder over the meaning of these events throughout her life; (2) because Simeon's sword pierced her soul, but it did not kill her faith; (3) because it is only here that Elizabeth's blessing achieves its full weight. Only now do readers understand "blessed is she who believed" (Lk 1:45), for only now do we understand that Mary's belief was not pious acceptance, but one of struggle, thought and doubt. If we affirm Mary as Luke's model disciple, it is only because we have come to know her first as Luke's persistent disciple.

Conclusion

Mary's three overlapping roles. By relocating the locus of God's salvation from the death and resurrection of Jesus to his miraculous conception and birth, Luke confers a new, higher status upon Jesus' mother. This status is reflected in Mary's three overlapping roles. The first role is that of the poor prophet. Mary's prophetic office begins with her call (Lk 1:26-38), one that aligns her not with Rebecca, Rachel, the wife of Manoah, Hannah and Elizabeth, but with Shiphrah, Puah, Deborah, Jael, Esther and Judith. She is the one through whom the judgment and salvation of Israel will take place because she bears in her womb Israel's judge and Savior. Her prophetic office is executed in the Magnificat (Lk 1:46-55) as she declares that the God who has been mindful of her has always cared for the lowly and, in such care, remembers and fulfills his promise to Abraham and the patriarchs.

The second role is that of the pondering mother. In Luke's account of the birth of Jesus and subsequent events, Mary does not fully understand all that is going on. Even though she is the unique recipient of divine revelation concerning Jesus' identity and destiny, the disclosure neither removes all ambiguity nor resolves all struggle. Rather, it comes in bits and pieces—from the angel, Elizabeth, the shepherds and even Jesus himself—and must be weighed and assembled over a long period of time. Her assent to the plan of God in the midst of all that is not understood is therefore to be commended.

It is only when Luke tells us that Mary was numbered among the first disciples awaiting Pentecost (Acts 1:14) that it becomes clear that Mary's willing assent persisted throughout her life. In the end she did not change her mind. She continued to ponder the events she treasured in her heart for some three decades. She models persistent discipleship that agrees to what is not yet understood because her confidence lies not in the revelation but the character of him who revealed.

Symbol of God's people. Do the three distinct yet overlapping narrative functions—prophet, mother, disciple—together testify to one overarching purpose for Mary within the Lukan narrative? I tentatively suggest that there is such a literary purpose for Mary: she is Luke's symbol for God's people, whether defined as Israel or as the church. In the roles of prophet and mother, Mary is the specially elected crucible in which the general election of the nation of Israel receives its fullest expression. In order to unpack this statement further, we begin with a rather pedantic observation: Mary was a Jew. As a poor Jewish woman in first-century, Roman-occupied Palestine, Mary could have occupied no lower rung on the social ladder. Nevertheless this same poor Jewish woman shared in God's election of Israel and in the purpose of that election: to be a blessing to "all the families of the earth" (Gen 12:3). She was a member of the people to whom belonged "the adoption, the glory, the covenants, the giving of the law, the worship, and the promises; to them belong the patriarchs" (Rom 9:4-5). In a general sense, divine election and its attendant gifts and responsibilities are hers as rights of birth.

Mary alone, however, from all the women of the nation whether at that time or before or since, was specially chosen by God to be the vessel through whom the divine promises to the patriarchs would be fulfilled. Luke's account of the annunciation (Lk 1:26-38) gives no explanation for the rationale of God's election of Mary other than God's graciousness. The favor bestowed on her (Lk 1:28) is not a thing, but a description of the quality of her relationship with God that God had initiated. Daniel Migliore is right to wonder why Reformed theologians especially have not thought more about Mary's gracious election, for it "serves the divine purpose whereby the eternal election of the Son of God is historically realized. As a daughter of the elect people of Israel, Mary is herself elected and called to a special vocation."[110] Indeed, we may go further. Mary is not elected to a special vocation, but as the mother of the Messiah of Israel and of the Savior of the world to a *singular* vocation. Mary's election uniquely discloses the purpose of God's general election of Israel: through her prophetic speech Luke's readers discover that it is through Mary's child that God's promises to Abraham and his descendents will be fulfilled (Lk 1:54-55).

Accordingly it ought not to surprise readers that the sword of judgment prophesied by Simeon (Lk 2:34-35) is both a sword of judgment passing through the land (Ezek 14:17), causing the falling and rising of many in Israel, and a sword of judgment passing through the soul of Mary, disclosing her thoughts

[110]Daniel L. Migliore, "Woman of Faith: Toward a Reformed Understanding of Mary," in *Blessed One: Protestant Perspectives on Mary,* ed. Beverly Roberts Gaventa and Cynthia L. Rigby (Louisville: Westminster John Knox, 2002), p. 123.

also. The winnowing visited upon Israel is the same as that visited upon the mother of Jesus. Just as the nation has been elected to bless the world, so has Mary. Just as the nation has been the recipient of divine disclosure, so has Mary. Just as the nation will be judged by that same revelation, so will Mary. She is the daughter of Zion: a symbolic portrayal of the nation as a whole.

At the same time Mary is a symbolic portrayal of the church. Here, however, she is not so much a type as an example of faith. Like all believers, Mary is the recipient of the good news of God's electing grace. Her confident assent to this sovereign choice is held up as an example, not of female acquiescence to the divine (male) Father, but as an example of the secure obedience that is to mark the lives of all disciples, whether male or female (cf. Gal 3:28). Her daring adoption of the title "slave of the Lord" signals that she has freely accepted her role in the plan of salvation, a role that links her to the great liberators of God's people. She bids all disciples to live in slavery to Christ, wherein is found true liberation and vocation. Her confident obedience and free acceptance, moreover, is given not because of the clarity of the revelation but because of her trust in him who revealed. With respect to the content of God's disclosure, it appears that her understanding is limited even as her will is determined to continue weighing matters until a coherent conclusion emerges. In the same way, all believers are to strive to trust in God even as they continue to ponder the meaning of the divine revelation entrusted to them.

Mary is now a person. So sharply drawn is she that it is possible to detect within Luke an emerging representative or symbolic role. It remains for the Johannine literature, however, to fully explore her symbolic significance.

5

Woman of the Hour

Mary in the Johannine Literature

The uniqueness of the Fourth Gospel is obvious from its first verses. Instead of Mark's abrupt account of John's ministry and Jesus' baptism or the infancy narratives of Matthew and Luke, John rewrites the Genesis creation story, presenting Jesus as the human manifestation of the Logos through whom all things were created. Although emphasizing the humanity of Jesus with the words "became flesh" (Jn 1:14), the fourth evangelist says nothing about just how he did so.[1] It is not surprising, therefore, to find that Jesus' mother is highly stylized. Where Matthew and Luke name her, John veils her in anonymity, referring to her only as "the mother of Jesus." Jesus calls her, simply, "woman." Her only scenes—the wedding (Jn 2:1-12) and the cross (Jn 19:25-27)—are themselves unique to John.

The Johannine literature continues the trajectory suggested in the previous chapter's conclusion. If Luke suggests a representative role for Mary as the daughter of Israel and the model Christian disciple, then John inimitably expands on this notion, which raises two sets of questions. The first is oriented around the two Gospel appearances of Jesus' mother: How does the mother of Jesus function in John's Gospel? At the wedding and the cross, is she merely an unnamed device, necessary provocation for the words and actions of her Son? Or does her portrayal actually suggest something symbolically and theologically significant? An answer lies in Jesus' reference to his "hour" in John 2:4 and John 12:23. The second set of questions revolves around the "great and wondrous sign" of Revelation 12:1-6, 13-17: Who is the heavenly woman of Revelation 12:1? Does the text disclose her identity? If so, what conclusions may be drawn?

---

[1]Furthermore, we do not know that the Logos that became flesh became a man (as opposed to a woman) until John the Baptist refers to a man (i.e., a male, Greek *anēr*) in Jn 1:30.

The Hour Is Not Yet (John 2:1-12)

John's view of Jesus' miracles is distinctive. Where the Synoptics use phrases such as "deed of power" (e.g., Mk 6:5) to denote Jesus' many miraculous acts, John uses the word *sign* and describes only seven.[2] It is not that John's accounts are totally different. Three—the healing of the official's son (Jn 4:46-54), the multiplication of loaves (Jn 6:1-15) and walking on the sea (Jn 6:16-21)—have Synoptic parallels. Three more—curing the paralytic (Jn 5:1-18), restoring the blind man (Jn 9:1-12) and raising Lazarus (Jn 11:38-44)—are similar to Synoptic stories. It is the purpose to which John puts them that is distinctive: they disclose the glory of God's "one and only" (Jn 1:14), eliciting thereby a variety of responses: belief (Jn 2:11; 4:53; 11:45), misunderstanding and confusion (Jn 6:14; 9:8-12), terror (Jn 6:19) or even opposition (Jn 5:15-18; 11:45-53). Turning water into wine was the first of Jesus' signs:[3]

> On the third day there was a wedding in Cana of Galilee, and the mother of Jesus was there. Jesus and his disciples had also been invited to the wedding. When the wine gave out, the mother of Jesus said to him, "They have no more wine." And Jesus said to her, "Woman, what concern is that to you and to me? My hour has not yet come." His mother said to the servants, "Do whatever he tells you." Now standing there were six stone water jars for the Jewish rites of purification, each holding twenty or thirty gallons. Jesus said to them, "Fill the jars with water." And they filled them up to the brim. He said to them, "Now draw some out, and take it to the chief steward." So they took it. When the steward tasted the water that had become wine, and did not know where it came from (though the servants who had drawn the water knew), the steward called the bridegroom and said to him, "Everyone serves the good wine first, and then the inferior wine after the guests have become drunk. But you have kept the good wine until now." Jesus did this, the first of his signs, in Cana of Galilee, and revealed his glory; and his disciples believed in him.
>
> After this he went down to Capernaum with his mother, his brothers, and his disciples; and they remained there a few days. (Jn 2:1-12)

To understand the literary function of Jesus' mother here, we must attend to (1) the immediate context provided by John 1 and the broader contexts provided by the status of this event (2) as a miracle story and (3) as one of the Gospel's seven signs. The first situates God's incarnate Logos (Jn 1:1-18) within fam-

---

[2]On whether John is drawing on a "sign source" that predates his Gospel at these points, see Raymond Brown et al., *Mary in the New Testament: A Collaborative Assessment by Protestant and Roman Catholic Scholars* (Philadelphia: Fortress, 1978), pp. 183-85.

[3]Two pieces of evidence hint that this first sign draws on a "preministry" source. First, it takes place in Cana where, according to the Synoptics, Jesus did no miracles. Second, his circle of associates seems still to include his mother and brothers, again contrary to the Synoptics.

ily and social relationships, underscoring humanity. The scene in John 2:1 is described sparsely: "On the third day there was a wedding in Cana." Each element is significant. The third day is the third day after the calling of Philip and Nathanael (Jn 1:43-51),[4] bringing Jesus' band of followers to five. There, Philip describes Jesus as "son of Joseph from Nazareth" (Jn 1:45; cf. Jn 6:42). Thus, the appearance of Jesus' mother in John 2:1 is not as abrupt as it first may appear to be. The Logos who assumed human flesh has both a mother and father and, as John 2:12 will later disclose, brothers.

It is as a member of an ordinary family that Jesus attends a typical social function, a wedding.[5] Jesus' mother provokes a conversation: "They have no [more] wine." Did she intend Jesus to perform a miracle?[6] It is far more likely that Jesus, an invited guest, was among those responsible for bringing wine to the feast. Because of the poverty of his family, however, he could not. Mary was not provoking a miracle, but desperately wanting to avoid family shame[7]—to the point of asking Jesus to leave.[8]

Although acknowledging the obligation that the request placed on him, Jesus' response is otherwise enigmatic: "What to you and to me, woman? My hour is not yet come" (Jn 2:4). The first half has been translated variously: "Woman, what concern is that to you and to me?" (NRSV); "Dear woman, why do you involve me?" (NIV); "Woman, what do you want from me?" (NJB); "Woman, how does this concern of yours involve me?" (NAB). The only point of agreement is Jesus' use of the word *woman*. John may have used this address, which was uncommon in Hebrew or Hellenistic culture, to downplay mother-

---

[4]Ben Witherington III, *John's Wisdom: A Commentary on the Fourth Gospel* (Louisville: Westminster John Knox, 1995), p. 77. Raymond Brown agrees but mentions an ancient tradition that counts this as the third day after Jesus' baptism (Jn 1:29-34); *The Gospel According to John,* 2 vols., Anchor Bible 29-29A (New York: Doubleday, 1966-1970), p. 97.

[5]Brown mentions a tradition dating to the early third century holding that Mary was the groom's aunt, who was John the son of Zebedee (*John,* p. 98). Witherington suggests that the wedding takes place in Nathanael's family (*John's Wisdom,* p. 77).

[6]This is bolstered by Jesus' response to his unbelieving brothers (Jn 7:1-9): "My time has not yet fully come" (Jn 7:8; cf. Jn 2:4). This reading is unlikely because of a change in vocabulary ("hour" to "time") and because, until now, John has given readers no clue about Jesus' ability to work wonders. See Brown, *John,* pp. 98-99, for details.

[7]The "disciple group invited with Jesus will have been viewed as his family, for whose contributions to the marriage feast he will have been responsible. It is a natural assumption that this motivated Mary's drawing the attention of Jesus to the lack of wine—not that she hoped for a miracle, but that his presence with the disciples, jointly embarked on a mendicant ministry which rendered them unable to fulfill the obligation of guests, contributed to the embarrassing situation" (G. R. Beasley-Murray, *John,* Word Biblical Commentary 36 [Waco: Word, 1987], p. 34).

[8]On "a pedestrian level, her words have been read as a suggestion that Jesus should leave" (Brown et al., *Mary in the New Testament,* p. 188).

hood as the key to her presence in the story.[9] The rest of the phrase is a Semitism and has Old Testament precedent. Unfortunately, that context suggests that it can mean either a rebuke (cf. Judg 11:12; 1 Kings 17:18; 2 Chron 35:21) or the rejection of a request (cf. 2 Kings 3:13; Hos 14:8). Here it is likely the latter. More than that cannot be said with certainty.

The second half of Jesus' response—"my hour has not yet come"—is more intriguing. Two readings are possible; both disassociate Jesus from his mother. On the one hand the phrase may be a question: "Has my hour not yet come?"[10] If so, then "hour" refers to the public ministry about to begin. Jesus thus explains that with the advent of his ministry, he can no longer be focused on family. Although internally consistent, this reading disagrees with those times when John speaks of Jesus' hour as having not yet come (Jn 8:20) or just arrived (Jn 12:23).[11] On the other hand reading the phrase as a statement has Jesus saying that his mother has no role in his public ministry until his hour. Not only does this reading agree with John 8:20 and John 12:23, it justifies the presence of Jesus' mother at the cross.

Oddly, after hearing her request refused, Jesus' mother then directs the wedding servants to her Son.[12] It can perhaps be explained with reference to Jesus' second sign, where a reluctant Jesus acts because of a persistent father (Jn 4:46-54).[13] Some Roman Catholic pious exegesis sees here the power of Mary's inter-

---

[9]"The context shows rather that [Jesus] wants to give Mary a role beyond that of simply physical motherhood" (Alain Blancy et al., *Mary in the Plan of God and in the Communion of Saints: Toward a Common Christian Understanding,* trans. Matthew J. O'Connell [New York: Paulist Press, 2002], p. 67); see also, Brown, *John,* p. 99. "On this reading, the form of address, while not denigrating her, would remind the reader that Jesus is the Word-made-flesh, whose principal relationship is not with any human being but with God" (Adele Reinhertz, "The Gospel of John," in *Searching the Scriptures: A Feminist Commentary,* ed. Elisabeth Schüssler Fiorenza [New York: Crossroad, 1994], p. 570).

[10]According to Brown (*John,* p. 99), this reading has an ancient heritage, being supported by Gregory of Nyssa and Theodore of Mopsuestia.

[11]Ibid., p. 100.

[12]Her command, "Do whatever he tells you," recalls Pharaoh's instructions to the Egyptians regarding Joseph: "Go to Joseph; what he says to you, do" (Gen 41:55). Francis J. Maloney suggests that it "is possible that the account of the gift of the Law at Sinai (Exodus 19; 24) and subsequent Jewish reflection on that foundational account may still be present to the narrative. On three occasions as the people of Israel receive the Law from the hands of Moses they commit themselves as a people of God by crying out: 'All that the Lord has spoken we will do' (Exod 19:8; see also Exod 24:3, 7). As one of the [words] of the Law offered life to a people, here the mother of Jesus trusts that the [word] of her son will do likewise" (*The Gospel of John,* Sacra Pagina 4 [Collegeville, Minn.: Liturgical Press, 1998], p. 72).

[13]Brown, *John,* p. 102. But Reinhertz observes that "a more whimsical, less reverent reading might recognize in this mother a rather natural appreciation of the abilities of her offspring. . . . Accordingly, her instruction to the servants to do as Jesus asks can be read as a refusal to respect his hesitation. This refusal would place pressure on her son to comply with her wishes, thereby giving her control of the situation" ("Gospel of John," p. 569).

cession.[14] It is far more likely that Mary is the first of three characters who, while having good intentions and some kind of faith, do not understand Jesus (cf. Nicodemus in Jn 3 and the Samaritan woman in Jn 4).[15] Finally taking action, Jesus instructs the servants to fill six stone jars used for purification rites with water and to present a cup to the headwaiter. Rather than water, however, he tastes the very best wine. The purpose of the story is straightforward: the Logos, without relinquishing his power as the agent of creation (Jn 1:3), is so thoroughly enmeshed in the social structures of first-century Palestine that he prevents the premature end of a wedding celebration and spares his family shame.[16] Jesus is a human being.

This simple reading is plausible and would be sufficient had not the evangelist concluded that "Jesus did this, the first of his signs, in Cana of Galilee, and revealed his glory; and his disciples believed in him" (Jn 2:11). It is not at all apparent that an anonymous, secret miracle reveals anything, let alone glory. Readers are therefore forced to ask just how this story functions as a sign. A possible answer may be found by comparing this story to miracles in the Synoptics. A cursory examination, however, shows this to be a cul-de-sac. The transformation of water into wine is utterly unique for two reasons.[17] First, it meets no human need. There is no misstep in creation to be undone, no life endangered by demonic influence or natural occurrence to be rescued. Second, the actual transformation of water into wine must be inferred. Only the servants who drew the water seem to know what has taken place (Jn 2:9).[18] While the disciples are at-

---

[14]The "first miracle worked by Jesus was at the behest of his mother, and this is meant to teach us to pray to Jesus through Mary" (Brown et al., *Mary in the New Testament,* p. 193).

[15]Ibid., p. 193.

[16]Brown (*John,* p. 100) observes that some moralistic commentators have difficulty with this reading because it affirms that Jesus transformed some 120 gallons of water into choice wine! Attempts to evade this conclusion, however, are unconvincing. On the so-called profane nature of the miracle, see Martin Hengel, "The Interpretation of the Wine Miracle at Cana: John 2:1-11," in *The Glory of Christ in the New Testament: Studies in Christology,* ed. L. D. Hurst and N. T. Wright (Oxford: Clarendon, 1987), pp. 84-86.

[17]The uniqueness of transforming water into wine leads some scholars to conclude that behind this sign story lies the pagan god of wine, Dionysius, whose temple fountains sprouted wine instead of water on his feast day, January 6. The Cana reading is part of the Epiphany liturgy celebrated on the same date. See Rudolf Bultmann, *The Gospel of John: A Commentary* (Oxford: Blackwell, 1971), pp. 118-19; and C. H. Dodd, *The Interpretation of the Fourth Gospel* (Cambridge: Cambridge University Press, 1953), p. 298. Craig R. Koester is right to say that the "legends of Dionysos . . . do help us understand how the story could *communicate* the significance of Jesus to Greeks as well as Jews. . . . Greeks would not have grasped the messianic significance of the sign, but they would have understood that the miraculous gift of wine revealed the presence of deity" (*Symbolism in the Fourth Gospel: Mystery, Meaning, Community,* 2nd ed. [Minneapolis: Fortress, 2003], p. 85).

[18]This leads Thomas L. Brodie to conclude that the sign is the transformation of the servants: "Thus the miracle is not in any juggling which Jesus does with the water, but in the acceptance

tuned to the significance of Jesus' actions, the text is unclear about when they understood. Did they understand and believe at the time? Or did such faith arise only when they remembered the event in the light of Jesus' hour? Attention to these broader contexts yields little direction.[19]

Fortunately, the story contains two other clues, directing us elsewhere in John: the presence of Jesus' mother and Jesus' declaration that his hour was still future. Jesus' "hour" arrives in John 12:20-36 when, after Jesus has been anointed at Bethany and has entered Jerusalem (cf. Zech 9:9), Philip and Andrew inform Jesus that "some Greeks" desired to meet him (Jn 12:20-22). Jesus' response is oddly disconnected. Neither granting nor rejecting the Grecian request, he says, "The hour has come for the Son of Man to be glorified" (Jn 12:23) and later adds cryptically:

> "Now my soul is troubled. And what should I say—'Father, save me from this hour'? No, it is for this reason that I have come to this hour. Father, glorify your name." Then a voice came from heaven, "I have glorified it, and I will glorify it again." The crowd standing there heard it and said that it was thunder. Others said, "An angel has spoken to him." Jesus answered, "This voice has come for your sake, not for mine. Now is the judgment of this world; now the ruler of this world will be driven out. And I, when I am lifted up from the earth, will draw all people to myself." (Jn 12:27-32)

John then interrupts to clarify Jesus' meaning: "He said this to indicate the kind of death he was to die" (Jn 12:33). The hour to which Jesus referred in John 2:4 is *both* the hour of his glory *and* the hour of his death. This is confirmed by Mary's presence at both places and nowhere else. By provoking the sign and witnessing the hour, her presence demands that the stories be read together.[20]

---

of his words by the servants. It is in them, and in the fact that they have listened sufficiently well to know the origin of the wine, that the miracle really happens" (*The Gospel According to John: A Literary and Theological Commentary* [New York: Oxford University Press, 1993], p. 173). It is more likely that the hidden nature of the gift's origins parallels those of the giver; see Maloney, *John,* p. 72.

[19]The closest context is the multiplication of the loaves (Jn 6:1-15). The textual parallel between the loaves and Elisha's similar miracle (2 Kings 4:42-44) leads Brown to find a background story not in the Dionysius cult but in the story's of Elijah's miraculous furnishing of a meal and oil in 1 Kings 17:1-16 and Elisha's supplying of oil in 2 Kings 4:1-7: "All of these are miracles which answer an unexpected physical need that in the particular circumstances cannot be satisfied by natural means" (*John,* p. 101).

[20]By tying my interpretation of the sign to the reality in this way, I hope to avoid "a bewildering array of interpretations, especially regarding Mary's place in the story" while at the same time doing justice to the nearly universally recognized Johannine symbolism (quotation from Beverly Roberts Gaventa, "Standing near the Cross: Mary and the Crucifixion of Jesus," in *Blessed One: Protestant Perspectives on Mary,* ed. Beverly Roberts Gaventa and Cynthia L. Rigby [Louisville: Westminster John Knox, 2002], p. 48). D. A. Carson helpfully observes that much in

When such a reading strategy is adopted, the first story is seen to be invested with many intriguing elements: its setting at a wedding on the third day, Jesus' apparent rejection of his mother's request, his as yet undeveloped reference to his coming hour, the six stone jars, the water, the choice wine. All point to the coming messianic days likened by Isaiah to a wedding. The third day may refer to the resurrection or the Sabbath[21] and therefore to the beginning of Jesus' messianic reign or to a renewal of creation. Either way, the dominant images are those of abundance and joy. Jesus rejects and then grants his mother's request to show that this sign was not performed to please Jesus' mother or to rescue Jesus' family from shame, but to show his glory to his disciples. In the coming hour, the very best of Jewish practice (symbolized by the stone jars) will be shown to be imperfect (expressed in their number: six), for they will be replaced by jars of choice wine.[22] All the symbols indicate messianic abundance, life and joy. The sign foreshadows the messianic times, the new dispensation wherein God would finally intervene.[23]

What is the role of Jesus' mother? She accomplishes four tasks. First, she is a functionary; producing the conflict that Jesus must resolve. Her statement, "they have no wine," initiates the action; her command, "do whatever he tells you," ensures its success. She presents her Son with a problem, confident in his ability to solve it. Second, alongside the allusion to Joseph (Jn 1:45), she reminds read-

---

terpretive diversity is due in part to the lack of explanatory discourse following the sign (*The Gospel According to John* [Grand Rapids: Eerdmans, 1991], p. 166). Koester offers two criteria that help interpreters of John's symbols: "One is that an interpretation must make disciplined use of the literary context in which the image appears. The symbol must be assessed in light of the immediate literary context, its development within the Gospel as a whole, and its relationship to other symbols in the Gospel. The other criterion is that an interpretation must give attention to the cultural and social setting in which the Gospel was composed" (*Symbolism in the Fourth Gospel,* p. 27).

[21]For the third day as resurrection, see Dodd, *Interpretation of the Fourth Gospel,* p. 300; for the third day as Sabbath, see Carson, *John,* pp. 167-68.

[22]Brown, *John,* pp. 104-5. Abundance of wine is a dominant figure for the joy of the last day in the Old Testament (Amos 9:13-14; Hos 14:7; Jer 31:12). As Witherington rightly says, "Just as the best wine has been served last at this banquet, so God's most powerful and life-giving force has only been unveiled at the end of the age. . . . God has saved the best revelation, the most life-giving One, for last" (*John's Wisdom,* p. 78). According to Dorothy Lee, the focus on wine leads to an undervaluing of the symbolic significance of the water (*Flesh and Glory: Symbolism, Gender, and Theology in the Gospel of John* [New York: Crossroad, 2002], pp. 66-71). She may well have a point, but it is not crucial to my argument.

[23]For this reason, Brown emphasizes that this story is from first to last about Jesus. Stress lies not on the "replacement" of Judaism or on the miraculous transformation. It does not even lie on Mary or her intercession. "The primary focus is, as in all Johannine stories, on Jesus as the one sent by the Father to bring salvation to the world. What shines through is *his glory,* and the only reaction that is emphasized is the *belief* of the disciples" (*John,* pp. 103-4 [emphasis original]).

ers of Jesus' humanity. Third, she connects this first reference to Jesus' hour to that hour itself. Fourth, she symbolizes corporate faith in God.[24] I am reluctant at this point, however, to specify the people as "church,"[25] even though this is a natural point of contemporary application. John's first readers, for whom church was not yet sharply distinguished from synagogue,[26] may well have seen in Jesus' refusal to act on his mother's request a reminder that the people through whom the Messiah was given for the world's sake cannot manipulate him. Like his mother, they have no role in Jesus' earthly ministry. It stems from the will of the Father, is designed to reveal the glory of the Son and is intended to produce belief in Jesus' followers. Like the Baptist, Jesus' mother has no direct involvement, but instead points always and only to him, commending the servants to heed and obey his commands.

The Hour Is at Hand (John 19:25-27)

John's crucifixion confronts us with the sharpest irony in the New Testament. The hour foreshadowed in the first of Jesus' signs, the hour of the messianic banquet when new wine would be provided as a gift of sheer divine generosity, is here—in the Place of the Skull, on a cross, where a Jewish man is suspended by ropes and nails. This is the hour to which the symbolic wedding wine had pointed all along. In the midst of suffering and humiliation, the one and only Son shines in messianic glory, full of grace and truth, completing his mission and securing for all who believe a new relationship with God.

And, near the cross stands the mother of Jesus. She was there at the beginning of his ministry; she is here at the end. Why? What role does she play? Is more going on here than a simple narration of history? We will unpack these questions in a moment, but first let us attend to the text itself:

> When Jesus saw his mother and the disciple whom he loved standing beside her, he said to his mother, "Woman, here is your son." Then he said to the disciple, "Here is your mother." And from that hour the disciple took her into his own home.

---

[24]Thus, for Brown, "both in Luke and in John Mariology is incipient and is expressed in terms of collective personality" (*John,* p. 109).

[25]Elisabeth Schüssler Fiorenza's suggestion that Mary is to be read as a reference to the Johannine community is much closer to the mark; see *In Memory of Her: A Feminist Theological Reconstruction of Christian Origins* (New York: Crossroad, 1983), p. 331.

[26]John's title for those who reject Jesus, "the Jews," probably reflects that the community to which he wrote was likely well into the process of the "parting of the ways" between what was to become Christianity and what was to become Judaism. At the time of his writing in the late first century, however, the community probably still contained many ethnically Jewish believers who remained committed to the faith of Israel. I therefore wish to avoid sharp distinctions between the communities, at least at this stage of interpretation.

After this . . . Jesus knew that all was now finished. (Jn 19:26-28)

While the soldiers gamble for what's left of Jesus' estate—his undershirt—four women stand transfixed by the horror before them.[27] John offers them in pairs. First are unnamed members of Jesus' family: his mother and his aunt. The second pair, which has no family relationship, is named: Mary of Clopas and Mary Magdalene. Neither Jesus' aunt nor Mary of Clopas appear anywhere else in this Gospel, though tradition has long maintained that the former is Salome and the latter is the wife of Cleopas (Lk 24:18). Mary Magdalene is introduced here and will figure prominently in the resurrection account (Jn 20).[28] John likely leaves the members of Jesus' family anonymous to underscore that what is important about them is contained not in their identities but in their relatedness to Jesus. Because Jesus has a mother and an aunt, we can say that he is no divine imposter. He is really human and really dying.[29]

Having introduced the four women, John again turns to Jesus, who speaks first to his mother and then to the disciple whom he loved. While the four women stand in opposition to the four soldiers, the beloved disciple seems utterly alone. When Jesus speaks, however, he turns first to his mother: "Woman." The designation reminds readers of the wedding. Having caught her attention, Jesus adds, "Here is your son." That Jesus' words are not an invitation to look for a last time on him is clear from his next speech, this time to his beloved disciple: "Here is your mother." Jesus establishes a new relationship, a perfectly natural thing to do. Jesus initiates an adoption by which his mother will be looked after.[30] "And from that hour," John tells us, "the disciple took her into his own home." It seems that, upon receiving Jesus' instruction, they then leave the

---

[27]That the presence and actions of the four soldiers is to be contrasted with the presence and actions of the four women is clear from John's use of a *men . . . de* construction in Jn 19:24-25, which is often translated as "on the one hand . . . but on the other hand." See Beasley-Murray, *John,* p. 348.

[28]The presence of these women again displays the relative independence of John *vis-à-vis* the Synoptic evangelists. Mark 15:40 and Mt 27:56 name only three women; Luke's women (Lk 23:49) are unnumbered and anonymous. Where the Synoptic Gospels agree that the women stood at a distance, John places them near the cross. For a detailed, fascinating, but ultimately distracting (for our purposes at least) account of the women and their relationships to Jesus, Jesus' family and to each other, see Brown, *John,* pp. 904-6; and idem, *The Death of the Messiah: From Gethsemane to the Grave: A Commentary on the Passion Narratives in the Four Gospels* (New York: Doubleday, 1994), pp. 1013-19. This liberty causes Witherington, with unconscious irony, to call this scene the "crux of the Johannine problem" (*John's Wisdom,* p. 309).

[29]At one level, Mary's role "has to do with Jesus' separation from his own earthly life" (Gaventa, "Standing near the Cross," p. 50).

[30]Brown (*John,* p. 907) observes that this does not resemble adoption formulas found in the Old Testament at 1 Sam 18:21; Ps 2:7; and Tob 7:12.

scene almost immediately. Having neither father nor mother, Jesus faces his hour alone.

On the surface this last of Jesus' actions is John's way of disclosing to us just how much Jesus loved his mother, "a picture of profound care, even in very difficult circumstances."[31] And as such, it is a sign of his humanity.[32] He saw her, he recognized her need and, as at the wedding, he met it. But this is an insufficient reading for at least two reasons. First is the vocabulary: Jesus' mother is not named, but addressed only as "woman"; the filial relationship between Jesus' mother and the beloved disciple is established "from that hour." The language that suffused the Cana miracle with symbolism appears again.[33] Second, if it is a simple narration of a last loving act, its odd construction provokes a series of questions unanswerable on these terms. For example, why does Jesus invite his mother to look not on him but on his beloved disciple? Why does Jesus speak to her at all? "Had the narrator wished simply to demonstrate that Jesus continued to exercise a child's obligation to care for his mother, he could have given only one construction," and that to the beloved disciple.[34] Why does the newly united pair leave Jesus to die alone and Joseph of Aramathea and Nicodemus to care for his corpse? There seems to be more to this story than the narration of a final act of affection.

The most likely candidate for a *primary* symbolic referent is straightforward. John re-presents a theme close to the heart of the Synoptic tradition and especially Mark: Jesus' family is created not by bloodlines, but by discipleship to the crucified and risen Lord (cf. Mk 3:31-35; Mt 12:46-50; Lk 8:19-21). He does so in his own fashion. With Matthew and Luke, but against Mark, John is clear that the mother of Jesus is not an opponent. With Matthew and Mark, but against Luke, John is dubious about other family members. The advent of Jesus' hour reveals that Jesus' true family can no longer be thought of as constituted by blood because of their unbelief (cf. Jn 7:1-9). Rather, Jesus' true family is created near the cross, composed of the beloved disciple, who in his position as an es-

---

[31]Brodie, *John,* p. 547.

[32]According to Brown, many church fathers, including Athanasius, Epiphanius and Hilary, used this interpretation as an argument to prove Mary's perpetual virginity: "If she had other sons, Jesus would not have entrusted her to John son of Zebedee, the Beloved Disciple. Indeed, a tradition still recalled on the hilltop of Panaya Kapulu in modern Turkey . . . maintains that Mary subsequently resided with John, even when he moved to Ephesus" (*John,* p. 923). The absence of Jesus' brothers is better explained geographically (they lived in Capernaum; Jn 2:12) or with respect to fidelity (they did not believe; Jn 7:5).

[33]Brown, *Death of the Messiah,* pp. 1020-21.

[34]Gaventa, *Mary,* p. 94. Brown (*John,* p. 907) notes that "ordinarily in antiquity a dying person commended his mother to another with a direct commission or charge: 'I leave to you my mother to be taken care of.'"

pecially loved nonrelative symbolizes the individual follower of Jesus, and Jesus' mother, who now invested with "a spiritual role as mother of the disciple par excellence"[35] reassumes her symbolic status as the people of God.[36] They are established in a relationship of mutual care that begins "from that hour." The Word "who came to what was his own" (Jn 1:11) but was not received has seen his mother received into his disciple's home.[37] Having been rejected by his family, he creates a new one.[38] Any further *secondary* symbolic referent will be more speculative.

Heavenly Woman (Revelation 12:1-6, 13-17)

The final stop in our Johannine journey is a strange territory mapped out in a strange way. Is the book of Revelation about the future, the past, the present or some combination? Scholars (sometimes sharply) disagree. Alongside questions of historical referent come questions of content (what is it saying?) and application (to whom is it being said? how may what is being said be applied in contemporary times?). Again, the answers are as numerous as commentators. Speaking broadly there are two schools of thought. One says that the book is an example of predictive prophecy. It describes what were to the author future events.[39] The other insists that Revelation is prophetic but not predictive, adding that the genre in which the author declares his prophecy is apocalyptic. Revelation, they say, stands alongside parts of Ezekiel, Zechariah, Daniel and Isaiah (Is 24—27; 34—35),[40] in which the author, through symbols, images, codes and so on, describes and comments on issues pertinent to him or his time.

That none of these problems are new complicates matters further. Revelation is the last book in the Bible for a reason. The early church was divided over it. The Western, Latin church favored it because of its connection with John the Apostle. The Eastern, Greek church distrusted it because its content was so unlike everything else in the New Testament.

Given the nature of this long-running dispute, I will disclose my biases at the

---

[35]Brown et al., *Mary in the New Testament,* p. 213.

[36]It is therefore absolutely right and necessary for all Christians, regardless of the divides of the Great Schism and the Reformation, to affirm the place of the church as the spiritual mother of the individual believer. This is, of course, distinct from the notion that Mary as an individual here becomes the mother of all Christians.

[37]Maloney, *John,* p. 504.

[38]This reading is advanced by Brown in *Death of the Messiah,* pp. 1025-26. It departs from the much more elaborate understanding advanced in Brown's *John,* pp. 107-9, 922-27.

[39]The predictive-prophecy group then subdivides over whether the events narrated, though future for the author, are now past, partially past and partially future, or entirely future.

[40]Many noncanonical works may also be listed, including 1 Enoch, 2 Baruch and 4 Ezra.

outset. It is my conviction that Revelation is apocalyptic prophecy.[41] The author was not interested in describing the future (whether his or ours), but his present. He is offering a message of hope to Christians in the seven churches of Asia Minor, who are (at the time of writing) suffering tremendous persecution under Roman Emperor Domitian (A.D. 81-96). Accordingly interpreters ought to search for the meaning(s) of this New Testament text in a manner similar to any other New Testament text: by finding out the necessary background information, by reading the text closely and by seeking possible insights from the text's world that apply to their own.

Developing full answers to those questions would take us well beyond the scope of this study. The following summary will therefore have to suffice. The book was written (at least in its final form) by a seer named John in the late first century, during or shortly after the persecution of Domitian.[42] There is no evidence to suggest, however, that this John is also the author of the rest of the Johannine corpus. Indeed, what indicators we have lead in the opposite direction.[43] The book itself falls into two parts. The first, Revelation 1—11, opens with an introductory vision (Rev 1—3) and then narrates a series of events that climax with the return of Jesus (Rev 4—11). The second, Revelation 12—22, narrates a series of events that climax with the return of Jesus (Rev 12—20), followed by a conclusion (Rev 21—22).[44] With these admittedly scant details in mind, we may ask the following questions of the text cited be-

---

[41]Richard Bauckham, *The Theology of the Book of Revelation* (Cambridge: Cambridge University Press, 1993), pp. 2-8.

[42]See David E. Aune, *Revelation,* 3 vols., Word Biblical Commentary 52A-C (Dallas: Word, 1997-1998), pp. lviii-lxx, who argues that although the final form of the book was completed somewhere between 81 and 96, segments include oral or written apocalyptic traditions dating from the 60s and even earlier.

[43]See the excellent discussion of authorship in Aune, *Revelation,* pp. xlviii-lvi. He judiciously concludes that while "the final author-editor of Revelation was named 'John,' it is not possible to identify him with any other early Christian figures of the same name, including John the son of Zebedee or the shadowy figure of John the Elder. The otherwise unknown author of Revelation in its final form was probably a Palestinian Jew who had emigrated to the Roman province of Asia, perhaps in connection with the first Jewish revolt in A.D. 66-70. He regarded himself as a Christian prophet and his composition as a prophetic book, and he was well acquainted with the Christian congregations in Roman Asia to which he addressed the final version of his book. Though Revelation has been linked with the other Johannine writings in the New Testament, there are in fact very few features that suggest that this author was part of the Johannine community in any meaningful sense" (p. lvi).

[44]This two-part construction is not universally agreed on, but is advocated by many leading scholars. There is, nevertheless, a surprising amount of agreement among divergent understandings that Rev 12 marks a major division in the book. See Aune, *Revelation,* pp. xc-cv; and Richard Bauckham, *The Climax of Prophecy: Studies in the Book of Revelation* (Edinburgh: T & T Clark, 1993), pp. 15-18.

low: (1) Who is the woman clothed with the sun? Specifically, is she Mary? (2) If she is Mary, what conclusions does this text invite that in turn will guide our investigations in parts two and three of this study? With these in mind, we turn to the text:

> A great portent appeared in heaven: a woman clothed with the sun, with the moon under her feet, and on her head a crown of twelve stars. She was pregnant and was crying out in birthpangs in the agony of giving birth. Then another portent appeared in heaven: a great red dragon, with seven heads and ten horns, and seven diadems on his heads. His tail swept down a third of the stars of heaven and threw them to the earth. Then the dragon stood before the woman about to bear a child, so that he might devour her child as soon as it was born. And she gave birth to a son, a male child, who is to rule all the nations with a rod of iron. But her child was snatched away and taken to God and to his throne; and the woman fled into the wilderness, where she has a place prepared by God, so that there she can be nourished for one thousand two hundred sixty days. . . .
>
> So when the dragon saw that he had been thrown down to the earth, he pursued the woman who had given birth to the male child. But the woman was given the two wings of the great eagle, so that she could fly from the serpent into the wilderness, to her place where she is nourished for a time, and times, and half a time. Then from his mouth the serpent poured water like a river after the woman, to sweep her away with the flood. But the earth came to the help of the woman; it opened its mouth and swallowed the river that the dragon had poured from his mouth. Then the dragon was angry with the woman, and went off to make war on the rest of her children, those who keep the commandments of God and hold to the testimony of Jesus. (Rev 12:1-6, 13-17)

Revelation 12 describes a vision in three scenes. The first scene (Rev 12:1-6) takes place in the heavens and introduces a woman, a dragon and a child.[45] The second scene (Rev 12:7-12) is transitional: it begins in heaven, where a cosmic war erupts between the dragon and his angels, and ends on earth, to which the defeated dragon has been cast by Michael. The last scene (Rev 12:13-17) takes place on earth and involves the woman, her other children and the dragon. Beyond the two locations (heaven and earth), the relationship between these scenes is difficult to work out. The events of scene one seem to lead readers to anticipate that the child snatched from God's throne will return in scene two, as an adult, to make war on the dragon. Instead, the archangel Michael leads God's army to victory. This leads some commentators to suspect, not unwisely, that scene two is in fact an insertion into a story that once consisted of only scenes

---

[45]The author is likely drawing upon ancient astrological imagery to describe two constellations of stars. See Aune, *Revelation,* p. 663.

one and three.[46] I follow this view: this was once a story about a woman and a dragon, with the angelic battle scene being a later insertion.

To determine the identity of the woman in scenes one and three, we begin by considering possible extrabiblical backgrounds for the story of a woman and her son fleeing a serpent monster.[47] David Aune documents several versions of the story:

> In Babylon the protagonist and antagonist were Marduk and Tiamat or Gilgamesh and Humbaba; in Canaan, Baal and Yamm (Sea) or Baal and Mot (Death); in Egypt Osiris and Set (or Typhon) or Rê (the Sun), to whom Pharaoh was assimilated, and Apophis (the serpent representing night). The Greek world knew many versions of the combat myth, often narrated as a succession myth: Ouranos and Kronos; Zeus and Kronos; Zeus and the Titans; . . . and Zeus and the Giants. . . . Other Greek variants included Zeus and Typoneus . . . Bellerophon and the Chimaera . . . Helios and Phaethon . . . and the Apollos and Python myth.[48]

All recapitulate the eventual vanquishing of night, chaos, sterility and disorder (the serpent) by conquering day, harmony, fecundity and order (the son). Further, to see the woman described as clothed with the sun, standing on the moon and wearing a crown of stars may well have reminded John's first readers of the goddesses Isis, the Egyptian queen of heaven, or Artemis/Diana, the virgin goddess of fertility associated with the city of Ephesus (cf. Acts 19:21-41), possibly John's home before his exile to Patmos.[49] John uses pagan images for his own purposes.

He has made wide and deep use of biblical imagery as well. The sun, moon and twelve stars call to readers' minds Joseph's dream in Genesis 37:9, where the sun represents Jacob/Israel, the moon Rachel and the twelve stars his sons.[50]

---

[46]Brown et al., *Mary in the New Testament,* p. 227; see also Aune, *Revelation,* pp. 663-64; and Wilfrid J. Harrington, *Revelation,* Sacra Pagina 16 (Collegeville, Minn.: Liturgical Press, 1993), p. 129.

[47]The story of a woman and her son fleeing a serpent monster is widespread throughout the ancient world, leading some folklorists in the mid-twentieth century to search for the archetypal version. See Joseph Eddy Fontenrose, *Python: A Study in Delphic Myth* (Berkeley: University of California, 1959), pp. 2-3. According to Aune (*Revelation,* p. 667), this quest was largely abandoned for the view "that a myth consists of all its versions."

[48]Aune, *Revelation,* p. 667. See also Bruce J. Malina, *On the Genre and Message of Revelation: Star Visions and Sky Journeys* (Peabody, Mass.: Hendrickson, 1995), pp. 155-60, 164-65; Harrington, *Revelation,* p. 129; and Frederick J. Murphy, *Fallen Is Babylon: The Revelation to John* (Harrisburg, Penn.: Trinity, 1998), pp. 278-86. Scholars debate the degree to which Rev 12 was influenced by one or more of these stories. The best analysis is offered by Adela Yarbro Collins, *The Combat Myth in the Book of Revelation* (Missoula, Mont.: Scholars Press, 1976).

[49]Aune, *Revelation,* pp. 680-81.

[50]Another possibility is suggested by the noncanonical *Testament of Naphtali* 5, in which a priestly figure, Levi, is associated with the sun while a royal figure, Judah, is associated the moon. See J. Massyngberde Ford, *Revelation,* Anchor Bible 38 (New York: Doubleday, 1975), pp. 196-97.

Similarly the description of the woman's labor pains would have reminded readers of the metaphor employed by Isaiah (Is 26:17; 54:1; 66:7-9) and Micah (Mic 4:9-10) that portrays Israel or Zion as a woman giving birth to the joys of the messianic age.[51] Her flight to the wilderness for protection is probably meant to recall the story of the exodus (cf. Ex 16:4-17; 19:4) and God's provision for the Israelites in the desert (cf. Deut 32:11-12). John's description of her male child as one "who is to rule all the nations with a rod of iron" employs the description of the Davidic king in Psalm 2:8-9, a psalm that other New Testament writers applied directly to Jesus (e.g., Lk 3:22). John applies the same description in Revelation 19:15 to "the Word of God," Jesus Christ.

Finally, the red dragon evokes memories not only of pagan monsters, but also of Tiamat/Leviathan/Rahab, the ancient sea monster who represented chaos in ancient Near Eastern mythology and who appears throughout the Old Testament, both as God's enemy and as God's plaything.[52] Further, the influence of the book of Daniel is evident in two ways. The dragon's seven heads, ten horns and seven crowns are drawn from Daniel's beastly vision (Dan 7:8, 20, 24). Therein, the dragon had a political referent: it was the fourth and worst of the world empires that persecuted the Jews, the Syrian or Seleucid kingdom descended from Alexander the Great. The political and religious implications, especially after the description of two more beasts in Revelation 13, would not have been lost on Revelation's first audience.[53] The mention of Michael may also allude to his struggle with the angelic guardian of Persia (Dan 10:13, 20; 12:1-2).

---

[51]"In the OT the image of a woman is a classical symbol for Zion, Jerusalem, and Israel" (ibid., p. 195). See also Harrington, *Revelation,* pp. 129-30.

[52]With reference to creation, see Ps 74:12; 89:9-14; 104:6-9; Job 26; 38:8-11; Prov 8:29. With reference to God's conquest over the monster, see Ps 74:13-14; 89:9-10; Job 7:12. The prophets employ similar images metaphorically to describe Israel's enemies (Is 14:10-15; Ezek 28:1-9)—especially Egypt (Is 51:9-11), Assyria (Is 8:5-8; 17:12-14) and Babylon (Hab 3:8-10, 15; Jer 51:34). Interestingly, in the prophets the notion of God's primordial victory over his enemies begins to develop into an eschatological one (cf. Is 27:1). See Aune, *Revelation,* pp. 667-68; John Day, *God's Conflict with the Dragon and the Sea* (Cambridge: Cambridge University Press, 1985), pp. 88-140; Ford, *Revelation,* pp. 198-99; and Harrington, *Revelation,* p. 130. Murphy helpfully observes that politics can also be found in the pagan imagery, but at an ironic level: "Allusions to the Apollo myth are appropriate in a work that sees Roman power as demonic. Several Roman emperors, including Augustus and Nero, identified with Apollo, interpreted as the ruler of a bygone golden age. Nero's appropriation of Apollo imagery for himself is especially important, for he was the first emperor who persecuted the Christians. Most see the sea-beast in Rev 13, at least partially, as representing Nero, and that beast contrasts with the Lamb in several ways. Thus Revelation's use of the Apollo myth is ironic, for it uses the myth to speak of Christ opposed by the sky-dragon, whereas Nero, who had pretensions to being Apollo, is a sea-monster who is the opposite of Christ" (*Fallen Is Babylon,* p. 280).

[53]Brown et al., *Mary in the New Testament,* p. 229.

The author further specifically identifies the dragon as "that ancient serpent"—a clear reference to Genesis 3 and containing possible allusions to 2 Corinthians 11:3 and Romans 16:20.[54]

John, it seems, is quite willing to mingle pagan and Jewish imagery for his own Christian purpose: namely, to assure readers of ultimate victory in times of persecution.[55] But who is the woman? Symbolically she functions at three levels. First, the designation of the dragon as "that ancient serpent" (Rev 12:9) ties the vision to the story of the Fall in Genesis 3. She is Eve. This is how the seed of the woman will triumph over the dragon (cf. Gen 3:15).[56] Second, John's use of the sun, moon and stars allows readers to infer that the woman is the daughter of Zion, the people of Israel who will, out of their travail, bring forth the Messiah to deliver God's people and rule the nations.[57] Third, as the context of Revelation as a whole makes plain, she is the New Testament people of God, who even as they face persecution on earth are already situated with Christ in the heavenly realms.[58] She is "the heavenly Jerusalem who is free and who is our mother" (Gal 4:26, my translation). The primary referents for the symbol end here. Nevertheless, the case can be made for a fourth secondary referent: Mary.

There are grounds to read the heavenly woman as Mary, the maiden of Nazareth through whom God's plan was realized not in heaven but in this world. But those grounds reside in Revelation only after it is placed in its context as Christian canon.[59] There are no indicators in John's text on its own terms or in the imagery he uses to suggest that he had Mary in mind. Having said that, "when Revelation was placed in the same canon of Scripture with the Gospel of Luke and the Fourth Gospel [in which Mary and the people of God seem to be symbolically related], the various images of the virgin, the woman at the cross, and the woman who gave birth to the Messiah would reinforce each other."[60] Set alongside the Gospels, in other words, it is virtually impossible for

---

[54]For a discussion of nonbiblical Jewish versions of the combat myth, see Aune, *Revelation,* pp. 668-69; and Bauckham, *Climax of Prophecy,* pp. 174-98. The wide variety of symbolic associations—both biblical and other—on which John draws leads me to endorse Bauckham's assessment: "The Dragon is a fine example of John's capacity to envision the figures of Old Testament texts and to raise them to new imaginative life by exploiting the vital symbolism of his readers' environment" (p. 198).

[55]Brown et al., *Mary in the New Testament,* p. 231.

[56]Bauckham, *Climax of Prophecy,* p. 284.

[57]This is the dominant image for both Collins, *Combat Myth,* pp. 104-7, and Ford, *Revelation,* pp. 194-205.

[58]This is the dominant image of the early church prior to the fourth century and continues to the present. See Harrington, *Revelation,* p. 136.

[59]Aune, *Revelation,* p. 712.

[60]Brown et al., *Mary in the New Testament,* p. 239.

a Christian reader to perform such a radical act of epoche that all thought of Mary is removed. It is not surprising, therefore, to find that Marian interpretation of Revelation 12 begins in the fifth century, after the New Testament canon is fixed.[61] As a part of the New Testament canon, Revelation's depiction of the heavenly woman completes the biblical Marian material.

Conclusion

Conclusion to chapter five. Our survey of the Johannine literature suggests two almost contradictory conclusions. First, the Fourth Gospel and Revelation, regardless of whether they are related beyond anything other than the common name of their (traditional) authors, treat Mary as a highly developed literary device. The representative image first suggested by Luke has been significantly developed. In the Gospel, Mary symbolizes God's people. In Revelation, at least in its canonical context, she retains her corporate referent and is exalted as the Queen of Heaven. The seer even describes images associated with pagan goddesses as the apocalyptic fulfillment of the mythologically expressed dreams of Gentiles.

There is tension here. On the one hand Mary has been portrayed in the pages of the New Testament in such a way as to become a symbol for the corporate faithful. On the other hand it is not at all clear that the exaltation rightly associated with the symbols—the Heavenly Queen, Eve, the faithful of both the Old and New Testaments and so on—may be abstracted from the obviously figurative contexts of these symbols in order to be applied in a more literalistic fashion to the handmaid of Nazareth. The legitimacy of such a move, which has surely taken place in the history of mariological developments, is not at all obvious. The symbolic exaltation, however, cannot be denied. Indeed, the symbol of corporate faith is drawn so sharply that Mary the individual is overwhelmed.

This leads to the second conclusion: the Johannine portrayal of Mary *as an individual* is not that far removed from that of Paul's, with which part one began. In both, they are anonymous. Whether she is Paul's mother of the heavenly man, John's mother of Jesus or the seer's heavenly woman, we simply do not know much more about her as an individual than we did at the beginning of this study. For both Paul and John, Mary's motherhood guarantees the humanity

---

[61]In her classic study, Hilda Graef records that Quodvultdeus, a disciple of Augustine, writing in the mid- to late fifth century, made the first overtly Marian identification of the woman of Rev 12. She adds that it is not until the first half of the sixth century that Oecumenius, in his commentary on Revelation (the earliest extant commentary on the whole book), read the woman exclusively as Mary; see *Mary: A History of Doctrine and Devotion,* vol. 1: *From the Beginnings to the Eve of the Reformation* (London: Sheed & Ward, 1963), pp. 131-32.

of him who entered existence from another, divine kind of life. When the evangelist and the seer add deeper symbolic dimensions, using the mother of Jesus to disclose the theological significance of corporate faith, the purpose is to exalt Jesus, the Savior of all who are his. Mary is submerged in the symbolism that they have attached to her.

Conclusion to part one. It has been said that to tie Mary too closely to the text of the New Testament is to end up with a minimal picture of a Nazarene housewife. At the conclusion of this investigation, it is evident that this statement is only partially true. Its truth lies in that the Mary-behind-the-text, the historical mother of the historical Jesus, is almost as unknown to us now at the end as she was in the beginning. The Mary-of-the-text, however, is another matter entirely. We have documented just how deeply she came to affect the Christian imagination as the apostolic witness was committed to writing in the first decades following the resurrection of Jesus. Of this affectation three final points may be made.

Diversity of New Testament views on Mary. The New Testament's portrayal of Mary is diverse. For Paul, she is no more than an anonymous mother. For Mark, she is a misguided, well-intended opponent. For Matthew, the scandal surrounding her pregnancy must be explained if the messianic credentials of her Son are to hold weight. For Luke, she is a prophet, a mother, a disciple and perhaps even a representative of Jesus' new community. For John, she is a symbol of corporate faith that has no role in the ministry of Jesus, but becomes the mother of believers at the advent of his hour. For the seer, she is the exalted Heavenly Queen who is Eve and the persecuted faithful all at once. The New Testament does not speak with one voice about this woman. It offers threads that future generations of Christians have, through their piety and theological reflection, woven into a tapestry that is at points theologically profound and at others, for this author at least, worrying. How best are we to think of the relationship among these diverse threads?

Development within the New Testament. The most helpful way to incorporate these threads is to see them in terms of development. The New Testament's witness regarding the mother of the Lord developed over time from the truly minimal obscurity of the Pauline writings, through the ambiguity and scandal of Mark and Matthew, to the highly sophisticated, representational imagery of Luke, John and the revelator. It seems that as Christian proclamation spread throughout the ancient world, for whatever reasons, greater emphasis was placed in the theological significance of Mary's singular motherhood. Furthermore, the New Testament gives no indication that such development stopped with the closure of the canon. Just as the first generations of believers pondered the significance of the mother of the Lord (as indeed they pondered the significance of her Son), so also will subsequent generations. This is inevitable as contemporary readers, along with those of the past, gather around the witness of Holy Scripture in order to discern not merely what Holy Scripture has said concerning her but what it says.

Development outside the New Testament. Consequently, the question around which our discussions in parts two and three should be oriented is not whether extrabiblical development is warranted, but what extrabiblical developments are legitimate. Doctrinal development—whether for Mary or for any other item of Christian belief—must affirmatively answer at least one of the following questions. Is this development, although overlooked by previous generations, explicitly taught in Holy Scripture? Is this development implicitly taught by Holy Scripture? Is this development logically related to other doctrines explicitly or implicitly taught by Holy Scripture? Thus, even as I affirm the inevitability of the development of doctrine, I continue to assert the priority of Scripture to guide it and to plot its trajectory. With that we turn to the history of Mary in the Christian theological imagination.

PART TWO

Mary in the History of Christian Thought

6

New Eve

Patristic Roots of Mariology

In her summary of the Marian biblical material, Hilda Graef writes that Mary remained hidden. She "emerged into the full light of day in the first chapters of Luke, only to retire again into comparative darkness during the ministry of her Son and to merge with the figure of the Church in the Apocalypse."[1] Part two of our study shows how this relative anonymity is lost as Mary's singular motherhood is increasingly emphasized by later Christians. It begins with two chapters devoted to the fathers of the church.

At first glance, this may seem to reflect a lack of balance. Why spend two large chapters on the church's first five centuries and only three chapters on the remaining fifteen centuries? First, the fathers are the heritage of the undivided church. They teach us how to read Scripture, and they carry a real, if secondary, authority for theological construction. They provide a touchstone from which Roman Catholic, Orthodox and Protestant Christians may work together to assemble the relevant data necessary to draw contemporary conclusions—even as we will likely continue to disagree over just what those implications and conclusions are. This is as true for Christian thought about Mary as it is for debates about the relationships among the Father, Son and Holy Spirit or about the relationship of deity to humanity in Jesus Christ. Still, these chapters are not exhaustive. Only the major players are considered.[2]

Second, the fathers established the infrastructure that later theologians would

---

[1]Hilda Graef, *Mary: A History of Doctrine and Devotion,* vol. 1: *From the Beginnings to the Eve of the Reformation* (London: Sheed & Ward, 1963), p. 32.

[2]I have set aside the deep mariological reflections of Syriac Christianity. I have also pursued a decidedly Western course. To any who feel that I have paid insufficient attention to the Byzantine mariological tradition, I beg patience. I and my readers must first get reacquainted with our heritage(s).

refine. The implications of the reality and singularity of Mary's motherhood, the nature of her role in the divine economy, her relationship to the rest of the church—these are not issues invented by theologians from the eighth to fifteenth centuries. These matters concern the earliest Christian writers. Whatever developments occur in the medieval era—and whatever legitimacy they may or may not have—they are not innovations. The period from Ignatius to John of Damascus sets the trend for all mariological thought.

Developments from the early second to the mid-fourth century may be divided into three sections. First, the modesty of Ignatius of Antioch is offset by the exuberance of early Christian devotional writings. Where Ignatius was content to mention Mary to defend Jesus' humanity, popular works freely speculated about the details of her life and the nature of her sanctity. Second, three figures—Justin, Irenaeus and Tertullian—and their writings dominate the first serious mariological development. For them Mary is the New Eve who undoes the sin of the first. Finally, in the theologians of Alexandria—Clement, Origen and Athanasius—we see Marian writings that prepare for the formalization of patristic Mariology, which will be taken up in chapter seven.

Early Trends

Ignatius of Antioch (died ca. 110). Even though the so-called apostolic fathers[3] were once criticized for departing from the purity of New Testament faith, their paucity of Marian reflection is strikingly similar. Only Ignatius of Antioch mentions her. His entire literary corpus was completed over a few weeks while en route from Antioch to Rome. For reasons unknown,[4] Ignatius was arrested and sent to Rome to be executed. Three of his seven letters were written to churches that he and his escort bypassed: Tralles, Magnesia and Ephesus. A fourth, sent ahead to the church in Rome, described Ignatius's situation, announced his arrival and instructed the Romans not to act for his release.[5] During a stopover in Troas, two letters were sent to churches already visited, Philadel-

[3]The term *apostolic fathers* covers a somewhat arbitrary collection of authors of early Christian writings, limited to the following: *1-2 Clement, Letters* of Ignatius of Antioch, *Letter* of Polycarp to the Philippians, *Didache, Epistle of Barnabas, Shepherd of Hermas, Epistle to Diognetus* and *Fragments of Papias.*

[4]Ignatius is traditionally presented as a model of selfless devotion, concerned only for the well-being of the churches; see William R. Schoedel, *Ignatius of Antioch: A Commentary on the Letters of Ignatius of Antioch,* ed. Helmut Koester, Hermeneia (Philadelphia: Fortress, 1985), p. 10. A close reading of the texts suggests that this picture is simplistic. See n. 8 below.

[5]Ignatius *Romans* 4, 7-8 (in Michael Holmes, ed., *The Apostolic Fathers: Greek Texts and English Translations* [Grand Rapids: Baker, 1999], pp. 171, 173, 175). Many readers seize upon Ignatius's willingness, while missing the relative prominence of the church of Rome.

phia and Smyrna, along with a personal letter to Bishop Polycarp of Smyrna. In a later letter Polycarp commends Ignatius, implying that his journey to martyrdom was completed.[6]

The letters are dominated by three interrelated worries: false teachers, church unity and Ignatius's own death. Beginning with the third topic, they sometimes seem to be infused with macabre glee.[7] At other times, they acknowledge the possibility of future moments of weakness and beg the church's resolve not to appeal for his release should such moments arise.[8] Whatever Ignatius's feelings toward journey's end, the letters display concern for the well-being of his church, left vulnerable without its bishop. He understands the episcopacy to be the sign of the church's unity[9] and the bishop to be God's representative to the community.[10] Those who threaten the bishop-oriented unity of believers—Ignatius specifically mentions Judaizers and docetists—are treated harshly.[11]

Although Ignatius believes in the unity of the divinity and the humanity in Jesus Christ, this belief is not worked out, for Ignatius does not write as a theologian, but as a pastor with particular concerns for particular congregations.[12] "His message of Christ speaks of an objective reality and a historical, cosmic event, and yet at the same time it is a message of man and his salvation."[13] Thus, his doctrinal statements are constructed neither carefully nor systematically.[14] With that in mind, we turn to the four texts.

The first text comes in the midst of a general warning about false teachers,[15] who are "carrying about the Name" maliciously. Moving from congregation to congregation they seek to convert people to their own (heretical) brand of

---

[6]Polycarp *Letter to the Philippians* 1.1; 9.1 (Holmes, *Apostolic Fathers*, pp. 207, 215).

[7]Ignatius *Romans* 5.3 (Holmes, *Apostolic Fathers*, p. 173).

[8]Ignatius *Romans* 7.2 (Holmes, *Apostolic Fathers*, p. 175). Schoedel plausibly suggests that Ignatius's preoccupation with martyrdom reflects a perceived failure as a bishop. His reaction to his arrest reveals "a person whose self-understanding had been threatened and who was seeking to reaffirm the value of his ministry by what he did and said as he was taken to Rome" (*Ignatius of Antioch*, p. 10).

[9]Ignatius *Ephesians* 4.1 (Holmes, *Apostolic Fathers*, p. 139).

[10]Ignatius contends that "we must regard the bishop as the Lord himself" (*Ephesians* 6.1 [Holmes, *Apostolic Fathers*, p. 141]). This is a theological rationale quite different from Clement's, which is based on apostolic succession; see, e.g., Clement of Rome *1 Clement* 44.1-3 (Holmes, *Apostolic Fathers*, pp. 77, 79).

[11]Ignatius *Ephesians* 9.1; *Smyrneans* 4.1; 7 (Holmes, *Apostolic Fathers*, pp. 143, 187, 189).

[12]Aloys Grillmeier, *Christ in Christian Tradition*, vol. 1: *From the Apostolic Age to Chalcedon (451)*, trans. John Bowen, rev. ed. (London: Mowbray, 1975), p. 87.

[13]Ibid., p. 86.

[14]That segments of Ignatius's writings were later claimed to support Antiochene, Monophysite and Chalcedonian positions in christological debates underscores this conclusion. See Schoedel, *Ignatius of Antioch*, pp. 1-2.

[15]Ignatius *Ephesians* 7-8 (Holmes, *Apostolic Fathers*, pp. 141, 143).

Christian faith. They are "dogs that bite by stealth," whose "bite is hard to heal."[16] The reference to dogs calls on "a widespread proverb that referred to a fawning behavior masking intent to do harm."[17] Ignatius is as worried about their pedagogy as he is their doctrines.[18] In this context, he writes that "there is only one physician, who is both flesh and spirit, born and unborn, God in man, true life in death, both from Mary and from God, first subject to suffering and then beyond it, Jesus Christ our Lord."[19] The series of christological declarations emphasizes that in the "one physician" true humanity and true divinity are united. The reference to Mary in no way hints at a supernatural birth, but is used to counter the docetic denial of the Lord's true humanity. The true faith holds that Jesus was a human male in part because he had a mother.

The second text comes at the conclusion of reflections on the passion of Christ symbolized in baptism. After alluding to Paul both directly (cf. 1 Cor 1:19, 20, 23) and possibly indirectly (cf. Rom 3:27), Ignatius writes that "our God, Jesus the Christ, was conceived by Mary according to God's plan, both from the seed of David and of the Holy Spirit. He was born and was baptized in order that by his suffering he might cleanse the water."[20] Although echoing Romans 1:3-4, Ignatius departs from the Pauline formula significantly: where Paul associates Christ's declaration as the divine Son with "the spirit of holiness by resurrection from the dead," Ignatius accentuates Mary's conception of Jesus. He stresses Christ's humanity. The human son of Mary, Christ our God, by his suffering, purified the waters of baptism for all.[21]

The third text places the birth of Christ in a cosmic framework and may reflect a hymn with gnostic roots.[22] Whether this is so, it clearly relocates the hymnic material in an orthodox context: "Now the virginity of Mary and her giving birth were hidden from the ruler of this age, as was also the death of the Lord—three mysteries to be loudly proclaimed, yet which were accomplished in the silence of God."[23] It is Ignatius's opinion that the fundamental events of salvation were hidden from the devil, a notion contained in the New Testament Apocrypha and developed by later Christian thinkers such as Justin Martyr and Ori-

---

[16]Ignatius *Ephesians* 7.1 (Holmes, *Apostolic Fathers,* p. 141).

[17]Schoedel, *Ignatius of Antioch,* p. 59.

[18]Ignatius *Ephesians* 9.1; 16; *Smyrneans* 4.1 (Holmes, *Apostolic Fathers,* pp. 143, 147, 187).

[19]Ignatius *Ephesians* 7.2 (Holmes, *Apostolic Fathers,* p. 141).

[20]Ignatius *Ephesians* 18.2 (Holmes, *Apostolic Fathers,* p. 149).

[21]According to Schoedel (*Ignatius of Antioch,* pp. 84-85), the tying together of Christ's passion with baptism calls on the same Near Eastern mythology as Rev 12—the ancient defeat of the dragon in the deep.

[22]See ibid., pp. 87-89, for arguments for and against gnostic influences for *Ephesians* 19.2-3.

[23]Ignatius *Ephesians* 19.1 (Holmes, *Apostolic Fathers,* p. 149).

gen.[24] The notion is a difficult one to unpack; fortunately it is sufficient to note the first extrabiblical allusion to Mary's virginity alongside a familiar Ignatian theme: the reality of her motherhood.

The final passage is found in the letter to the Trallians, at the beginning of a series of exhortations to avoid false teachers and their teachings.[25] Again, though the doctrinal contents are not spelled out, it is evident that Ignatius has docetists in view: "Be deaf, therefore, whenever anyone speaks to you apart from Jesus Christ, who was of the family of David, who was really the son of Mary; who really was born, who both ate and drank; who really was persecuted under Pontius Pilate, who really was crucified and died."[26] Mary, David and Pilate refute the notion that Christ did not stoop to the level of human being. Jesus' humanity is evident in his ancestry (David), his birth (Mary) and his suffering and death (Pilate). Family, bounded by birth and death, proved that the Son of God entered human existence as a human being.

Popular literature in the second century. In contrast to Ignatius's limited statements, popular hymnic and devotional literature of the second century was rife with accounts of the births and childhoods of both Jesus and Mary. The reason is simple: "Whenever biographical literature shows gaps, legend generally springs up, in the absence of reliable information, to supply the deficiency."[27] Dealing neither with Scripture nor the writings of those who succeeded the apostles, we are sifting through a genre that may be analogously linked to contemporary Christian fiction. When treated with care it discloses beliefs and attitudes held by the generation that produced it, even if it did not intend it to be theology.[28]

Three documents yield important pieces of information, shedding light on early Christian views of the Blessed Virgin, views that continue to exert influence. The earliest is the *Ascension of Isaiah*, "a Jewish-Christian apocalypse

---

[24]See *Ascension of Isaiah* 11.2-16 (trans. R. H. Charles and J. M. T. Barton, in *The Apocryphal Old Testament*, ed. H. F. D. Sparks [Oxford: Oxford University Press, 1984], pp. 809-10); Justin *Dialogue with Trypho* (*ANF* 1:212-13); and Origen *Homilies on Luke* 6.4-5 (FC 94:24-25).

[25]Ignatius *Trallians* 11.1 (Holmes, *Apostolic Fathers*, p. 165).

[26]Ignatius *Trallians* 9.2 (Holmes, *Apostolic Fathers*, p. 163). I have not included the reference to the virgin birth in *Smyrneans* 1.1 because the content is very similar to *Trallians* 9.1-2.

[27]Oscar Cullmann, quoted in J. K. Elliott, *The Apocryphal New Testament: A Collection of Apocryphal Christian Literature in an English Translation* (Oxford: Clarendon, 1993), p. 46. See also Bruce Metzger, *The Canon of the New Testament: Its Origin, Development, and Significance* (Oxford: Clarendon, 1987), pp. 186-87.

[28]Likewise, church historians will learn much more about the theological attitudes of North American evangelicalism in the late twentieth and early twenty-first centuries not by reading Wayne Grudem, Millard Erickson, Clark Pinnock or Stanley Hauerwas but by reading Tim LaHaye, Rick Warren, Bruce Wilkinson and Frank Peretti.

which was written (so far as we know) in Syria between about 112 and 138 CE."[29] The book details two visions: the first, set in the context of the prophet Isaiah's death, describes the last things (*Ascension of Isaiah* 1—5); and the second (*Ascension of Isaiah* 6—12) narrates the "Beloved One's" descent from heaven, victory over Beliar and ascent to God's right hand.[30]

The heart of the second vision describes the Beloved One's descent to Sheol from the seventh heaven through the firmament controlled by Beliar and his demons. *Ascension of Isaiah* 11.2-16 details the Beloved's coming to earth as Jesus:

> And I saw clearly a woman of the family of the prophet David, whose name was Mary, and she was a virgin; and she was betrothed to a man whose name was Joseph, a carpenter (and he too was of the stock and family of the righteous David, of Bethlehem in Judah; and he had received her as his wife by lot). And when she was betrothed she was found to be with child; and Joseph the carpenter was minded to repudiate her. But the angel of the Spirit appeared in this world; and after that Joseph did not repudiate her, but kept Mary and told no one anything about it. And he did not approach Mary but kept her as a holy virgin, though a child was in her womb. And he did not live with her *for* two months. And two months afterwards Joseph was in his house and Mary his wife; and they were alone together. And while they were alone, Mary looked up and saw a little child; and she was frightened. And at that very moment her womb was found as it had been before she had conceived. And when her husband Joseph said to her, What is it that has frightened you?, his eyes were opened and he saw the infant and praised the Lord, because *he realized that* God had come into what was his. And there came a voice to them, Tell no one about this vision. Yet the story of the infant spread through Bethlehem. There were some who said, Mary the virgin has borne a child less than two months after she was married. And many said, She has not borne a child, for no midwife has attended *her,* and we have heard no cries of *labour* pains. And they were all kept from recognizing who he was: they all knew about him; but they did not know where he came from. And they took him and went to Nazareth in Galilee.[31]

This vision clarifies early Christian traditions about Mary. For example, Mary, like Joseph, is reckoned to be of Davidic descent. She was Joseph's wife by lot, a reference to an account of Mary's childhood in the temple and "marriage" to the aged widower (this story will be expanded on by the *Protevangelium of James*). Mary delivers miraculously, with neither pain nor midwife, and with her

---

[29]Jonathan Knight, *The Ascension of Isaiah* (Sheffield: Sheffield Academic Press, 1995), p. 9.
[30]Ibid., p. 11.
[31]*Ascension of Isaiah* 11.2-16 (trans. Charles and Barton, pp. 809-10). Italic type identifies words inserted by the translators to improve the sense.

womb intact. This is the first recorded reference to Mary's virginity *in partu*—not only was Mary a virgin at the time of Jesus' conception, she remained a virgin in the act of giving birth.

Similar sentiments are expressed in the *Odes of Solomon,* probably written in Syriac, no later than A.D. 125.[32] Ode 19 opens with a rich trinitarian image of the Holy Spirit offering milk from the breasts of the Father to the world (*Odes of Solomon* 19.1-5). Those who receive it are "in the fulness of the right hand"—that is, in fellowship with the Father:

> The womb of the Virgin embraced *it,*
> And she conceived and bore;
> And the Virgin became a mother with great compassion;
> And she was in labour, and bore a Son without feeling pain,
> Because it did not happen without a reason;
> And she did not seek a midwife,
> Because he delivered her.
> She bore as it were a man by the will *of God,*
> And bore *him* and made him known,
> And obtained *him* in great power;
> And she loved *him* in deliverance,
> And guarded *him* in kindness,
> And made *him* known in greatness.
> Hallelujah.[33]

The similarity with the *Ascension of Isaiah* is clear: a painless delivery attended only by God. *Odes of Solomon* 19.10, however, contains translation difficulties most germane to our study, which may be highlighted by J. H. Charlesworth's rather wooden translation:

> She brought forth like a strong man with desire,
> And she bore according to the manifestation,
> And acquired with great power.[34]

---

[32]The *Odes of Solomon* are pseudonymously attributed to King Solomon (cf. 1 Kings 4:32), but James Charlesworth contends that a Jewish Christian who may well have been an Essene, but eventually came to live in the Johannine community, is the author; see *Critical Reflections on the Odes of Solomon,* vol. 1: *Literary Setting, Textual Studies, Gnosticism, the Dead Sea Scrolls and the Gospel of John,* Journal for the Study of the Pseudepigrapha Supplement 22 (Sheffield, U.K.: Sheffield Academic Press, 1998), pp. 14-15.

[33]*Odes of Solomon* 19.6-11 (trans. J. A. Emerton, in *The Apocryphal Old Testament,* ed. H. F. D. Sparks [Oxford: Oxford University Press, 1984], pp. 709-10). Italic type identifies words inserted by the translators to improve the sense.

[34]James Hamilton Charlesworth, *The Odes of Solomon* (Oxford: Oxford University Press, 1973), p. 82.

Literally rendered, this verse makes little sense in English. Accordingly translators interpret this text according to their understanding of its background. An earlier generation considered the *Odes of Solomon* to be rooted in Gnosticism. In this vein, Graef cites J. H. Bernard's 1912 rendering of *Odes of Solomon* 19.10: "She brought forth, As if she were a man, Of her own will, And she brought him forth openly, And acquired Him in great power." Graef is rightly concerned that this "seem[s] to fit the goddess Isis, the mother of Horus, rather than the wholly human Mother of Jesus."[35] Fortunately, the case for a gnostic background has weakened considerably since both Bernard's translation and Graef's study. Most recently, Charlesworth argued that the *Odes of Solomon* are Jewish-Christian.[36] Consequently, J. A. Emerton's translation cited above is more likely to be accurate. Obviously not gnostic, this translation fits with the Lukan account of Jesus' conception and birth even as it exalts Mary in a way and to a degree that Luke does not.[37]

The most important popular Marian document of this era is the *Protevangelium of James*.[38] Although the author purports to be James, the stepbrother of Jesus (*PJ* 25.1), and is identified elsewhere as James son of Alphaeus,[39] his ignorance of Palestinian geography and Jewish temple practices suggest otherwise. Most scholars date the earliest levels of the *Protevangelium of James* to sometime around A.D. 150.[40]

From first to last, the story is about Mary's purity, to the degree that Mary "herself is almost a function of that purity rather than the purity being a characteristic of Mary."[41] Mary's parents, Joachim and Anna, stand in the Old Testament tradition of barren parents: they are old, wealthy, devout and childless. When they conceive in the normal way (the *Protevangelium of James* does not denigrate sex) it is described as an answer to prayer. Once Mary is born, however, her purity dominates the drama, as it faces four challenges, each more serious than the last.

The first two challenges have to do with location. For fear that Mary may be-

---

[35]Graef, *Mary,* 1:35.

[36]Charlesworth, *Critical Reflections on the Odes of Solomon,* pp. 176-260.

[37]Charlesworth suggests that the Lukan annunciation may be in the background as the "manifestation" mentioned in the second line of *Odes of Solomon* 19.10; see *Odes of Solomon,* p. 84 n. 16; and *Critical Reflections on the Odes of Solomon,* pp. 157-58.

[38]Quotations of *Protevangelium of James* are from J. K. Elliot's translation in *Apocryphal New Testament,* pp. 57-67 (cited by section number).

[39]Ibid., p. 49.

[40]Ibid., p. 51.

[41]Beverly Roberts Gaventa, *Mary: Glimpses of the Mother of Jesus* (Philadelphia: Fortress, 1999), p. 120.

come ritually unclean simply by being an inquisitive, mobile baby, Anna "made a sanctuary in her bedroom and did not permit anything common or unclean to pass through it. And she summoned the undefiled daughters of the Hebrews, and they served her" (*PJ* 6.1). After three years, the toddler was then moved by a torchlight procession of Hebrew virgins to the temple in order that her undefiled existence might continue (*PJ* 7). There, she abandons her parents for a childhood devoted to God; her existence is so rarified that she must receive "food from the hand of an angel" (*PJ* 8.1). The onset of puberty transforms her temple sanctuary into another opportunity for ritual impurity. When she was twelve, a council of priests implored the high priest Zacharias to ask God what to do with Mary lest her menstruation defile the temple (cf. Lev 15:19-24). God then instructs Zacharias to assemble the widowers of the people, one of whom God will choose to "marry" Mary (*PJ* 8.2). Joseph is miraculously selected from the group (*PJ* 9.1). He accepts Mary as his ward but promptly abandons her to "build my buildings" (*PJ* 9.2) for a period of four years (cf. *PJ* 13.1).

The last two challenges have to do with Mary's virginity: Jesus' conception and birth. The risk posed by the questionable circumstances surrounding the conception is serious, removed only after an angelic annunciation (*PJ* 10—11), further confirmation by a priest and Elizabeth (*PJ* 12), and a public trial of both Mary and Joseph (*PJ* 13—16). Although the author draws on Luke 1:5-80 and Matthew 1:18-19 for inspiration, no angel visits Joseph. Like the people, he is pacified by the test of the "bitter waters" (*PJ* 16; cf. Num 5:11-31). Finally, the greatest danger to Mary's virginal purity is Jesus' delivery. Mary's labor begins while en route to Bethlehem, in the wilderness (*PJ* 17). After sheltering Mary, Joseph searches for and miraculously finds a Hebrew midwife (*PJ* 18.1—19.1). They return to find the cave overshadowed with cloud (*PJ* 19.2; e.g., Ex 16:10; 19:9; 1 Kings 8:10-11; Ps 18:11) and then a dazzling light (*PJ* 19.2; e.g., Ps 4:6; Is 2:5). Blinded by it, no one witnesses the delivery. Mary is seen suckling the infant Jesus when the light dims. Emerging from the cave, the midwife exclaims to Salome that she has just seen a virgin give birth. Skeptical, Salome declares, "As the Lord my God lives, unless I insert my finger and test her condition, I will not believe that a virgin has given birth" (*PJ* 19.3; cf. Jn 20:25). Salome's hand is consumed by fire and restored only after she touches the infant Jesus (*PJ* 20.4).

The *Protevangelium of James* influenced other infancy Gospels and a great deal of Marian thought and devotion of future generations.[42] From it we "know" the names of Mary's parents and of Mary's childhood. From it comes the portrayal of Joseph as an elderly widower whose marriage to Mary is in name only

[42]Elliott, *Apocryphal New Testament,* p. 48.

(as it was in the *Ascension of Isaiah*).[43] From it we "know" that Jesus' brothers and sisters were Joseph's children from his first wife. Most importantly, from it we have the first complete description of the perpetual virginity of Mary.[44] Mary was and remained a virgin before, during and after Jesus' birth.

Although later generations of ascetics would use the *Protevangelium of James's* portrayal of Mary as an example of chastity, its point, rather, seems to be the opposite. It insists that Mary's purity was protected throughout her life.[45] Whatever the hazard, Mary's virginal purity is preserved by miraculous means: food from angels, protection from Joseph, vindication by trial and a delivery that leaves her womb closed. Mary is not an example to be emulated, but a great exception to be adored.

Although rejected by Saint Jerome and accordingly condemned by popes Damasus, Innocent I and Gelasius,[46] the *Protevangelium of James* was especially popular in the eastern regions of the empire where "the 'mother goddess' image was more intense and where Christians were more under the influence of female divinities than in the west."[47] The author's elevation of Mary over the great virgin mother goddesses of the Greco-Roman world was so well achieved that even the resistance of Rome waned. It is therefore vitally important to observe that the author of the *Protevangelium of James* was not inventing new notions; the popularity of his work suggests that he was merely compiling the oral traditions of popular piety dating from the first third of the second century.[48] This, in turn, suggests that the development of such forms of Marian doctrine and devotion arose very early as the gospel penetrated the eastern empire.

Apologists and Theologians

Justin Martyr (ca. 100-ca. 165). Writing around the same time as the author of the *Protevangelium of James*,[49] Justin was a Palestinian trained in Roman and

---

[43]According to Elliot, it is impossible to prove the dependence of the *Ascension of Isaiah* on the *Protevangelium of James* or vice versa. The most that can be claimed is a common Syrian provenance (ibid., p. 49).

[44]Jaroslav Pelikan, "Exemplar of the Development of Christian Doctrine," in *Mary: Images of the Mother of Jesus in Jewish and Christian Perspective,* ed. Jaroslav Pelikan and David Flusser (Philadelphia: Fortress, 1986), p. 86.

[45]Gaventa, *Mary,* p. 121.

[46]Joseph A. Grassi, *Mary, Mother and Disciple: From the Scriptures to the Council of Ephesus* (Wilmington, Del.: Glazier, 1988), p. 98.

[47]Stephen Benko, *The Virgin Goddess: Studies in the Pagan and Christian Roots of Mariology,* Studies in the History of Religions 59 (Leiden: Brill, 1993), p. 200.

[48]Ibid., p. 203.

[49]In his own words, "we say that Christ was born 150 years ago under Cyrenius [Quirinius; cf. Lk 2:2]"; Justin *First Apology* (*ANF* 1:178).

Greek philosophy before becoming a Christian. His account of his conversion indicates that Justin's quest for truth was satisfied only by Christ.[50] Consequently Justin is concerned to show that Christianity brings the highest and best of Greek philosophy to its natural fulfillment. He argues that the persecution of Christians is a crime against reason, which is none other than the Logos incarnate in Jesus Christ.[51] He is "the first ecclesiastical writer who attempts to build a bridge between Christianity and pagan philosophy."[52] As his title indicates, he bore final witness to the true philosophy with his life around 165.

His remarks about Mary are reminiscent of those of Ignatius in their christological emphasis. For example, Justin stresses the virgin birth of Jesus as a legitimate fulfillment of Isaiah 7:14[53] and denies that Jesus' conception by the Holy Spirit in Mary's womb resembles Greek stories of divine impregnation.[54] Justin is not content, however, to use Mary merely to guarantee of the humanity of the divine Savior. His writings contain the earliest comparison between Mary and Eve thus far discovered:

> He became man by the Virgin, in order that the disobedience which proceeded from the serpent might receive its destruction in the same manner in which it derived its origin. For Eve, who was a virgin and undefiled, having conceived the word of the serpent, brought forth disobedience and death. But the Virgin Mary received faith and joy, when the angel Gabriel announced the good tidings to her that the Spirit of the Lord would come upon her, and the power of the Highest would overshadow her: wherefore the Holy Thing begotten of her is the Son of God; and she replied, "Be it unto me according to your word." And by her has he been born, to whom we have proved so may Scriptures refer, and by whom God destroys both the serpent and those angels and men who are like him; but works deliverance from death to those who repent of their wickedness and believe upon him.[55]

Mary is contrasted with Eve: while both were virgins, the latter disobeyed God and conceived sin and death at hearing the serpent's word, and the former obeyed God and conceived life at hearing the angel's word. Justin, however, did not develop the parallel any further. That was left for Irenaeus of Lyons.

Irenaeus of Lyons (ca. 140-ca. 202). Irenaeus is claimed as a father by both

---

[50]Justin *Dialogue with Trypho* 2-8 (*ANF* 1:195-99).

[51]At this point, Justin betrays Stoic, Platonic and Middle Platonic influences. See Grillmeier, *Christ in Christian Tradition,* 1:91-93.

[52]Johannes Quasten, *Patrology,* vol. 1: *The Beginnings of Patristic Literature* (Westminster, Md.: Newman, 1950), p. 198.

[53]Justin *Dialogue with Trypho* 63-67 (*ANF* 1:228-32).

[54]Justin *First Apology* 33; *Dialogue with Trypho* 67 (*ANF* 1:174, 232).

[55]Justin *Dialogue with Trypho* 100 (*ANF* 1:248-49).

East and West because of his close associations with regions in modern Turkey and France. While we know little about the date and place of his birth, we do know that as a young man or boy he saw and heard Bishop Polycarp of Smyrna.[56] At some point, however, Irenaeus left the eastern empire, traveling west via Rome to Celtic Gaul, perhaps to assume the bishopric of the city of Vienne. Around 177, Bishop Pothinus of the neighboring city of Lyons was martyred, and Irenaeus assumed his place. Here Irenaeus wrote his most famous work, *Against Heresies*.[57] Although the manner of his death is uncertain, tradition holds that he was martyred in 202 under the persecution of Septimius Severus.

To understand Irenaeus's development of the Mary-Eve typology, it must be set within a broader understanding of his doctrine of recapitulation, which is in turn a working out of Paul's "philosophy of history"[58] as it is set out in Romans 5 (and to a lesser degree in 1 Cor 15). As the fifth chapter of Romans opens, Paul has already described Jews and Gentiles alike as condemned before God (Rom 1—3); he has also offered his solution, justification by faith, the model of which is Abraham (Rom 4). The ground of that justification, for Jew and Gentile, is the death of Jesus, providing present reconciliation with God and future hope for resurrection through the Holy Spirit (Rom 5:1-11). What follows is a summary of history as the transition from one phase marked by sin, death and the law to another marked by gift, life and grace. Both eras are personified, the latter as Christ and the former as Adam, "who is a type of the one who was to come" (Rom 5:14). Both Adam and Christ represent the race and must be understood together. Through the disobedience of Adam, sin and death came to define the human race. Through the obedience of Christ, justification and life replace them. Irenaeus's word for this Pauline theology of redemption is "recapitulation," the gathering of all creation again under one head (cf. Eph 1:22; Col 1:20).

As Irenaeus develops the idea, recapitulation corrects and perfects human beings and inaugurates and consummates a new creation.[59] It is a setting to right of what has gone wrong. Adam's disobedience enslaved human beings to the devil, corrupted their bodies and alienated them from God. But God himself has acted in Christ, the second Adam, in order that his obedience might liberate, purify and reconcile. He "returns to the point of error and replaces the wrong deed

---

[56]Ancient church historian Eusebius quotes a letter of Irenaeus to Florinius, which recalls Polycarp's teachings (*Church History* 5.20.5-7 [*NPNF*^{2} 1:238-39]).

[57]Irenaeus *Against Heresies* (*ANF* 1:315-567).

[58]I owe this apt description to Benko, *Virgin Goddess,* p. 237.

[59]Eric Osborn, *Irenaeus of Lyons* (Cambridge: Cambridge University Press, 2001), p. 97. I follow his excellent summary of the doctrine in what follows.

with the right deed, thereby rectifying the ancient fault."[60] It is a bringing to completion of all things under Christ. Where Adam's disobedience thwarted the perfection into which all Adam's children were to grow, Christ's obedience has made that possible again.[61] By correcting and perfecting humanity, God in Christ inaugurates a new humanity and a new creation in which all things are restored and set free. As freed and restored, this new humanity will, under the reign of Christ, fulfill the purpose for which it was created in the beginning.

In this context, Irenaeus develops Justin's casual description of Eve-Mary. Three passages warrant attention. The first is as follows:

> In accordance with this design, in Mary the Virgin is found obedience, saying, "Behold the handmaid of the Lord; be it unto me according to your word." But Eve was disobedient; for she did not obey when as yet she was a virgin. And even as she, having indeed a husband, Adam, but being nevertheless as yet a virgin, having become disobedient, was made the cause of death, both to herself and to the entire human race; so did Mary, having a man betrothed [to her], and being nevertheless a virgin, by yielding obedience, become the cause of salvation, both to herself and the whole human race. . . . And thus also it was that the knot of Eve's disobedience was loosed by the obedience of Mary. For what the virgin Eve had bound fast through unbelief, this did the Virgin Mary set free through faith.[62]

The Eve-Mary parallel established by Justin is extended by the Pauline imagery of Adam-Christ. Although both were married, both were virgins. Where Eve by her disobedience became the cause of death, Mary by her obedience has become the cause of salvation. What Eve's disobedience had bound, Mary's obedience has set free.

The second passage moves from an implicit use of Pauline themes to an explicit union of Paul's Adam-Christ to Eve-Mary:

> That the Lord then was manifestly coming to his own things, and was sustaining them by means of that creation which is supported by himself, and was making a recapitulation of that disobedience which had occurred in connection with a tree, through the disobedience which was [exhibited by himself when he hung] upon a tree, [the effects] also of that deception being done away with, but which that virgin Eve, who was already espoused to a man, was unhappily misled—was happily announced, through means of the truth [spoken] by the angel to the Virgin Mary, who was [also espoused] to a man. For just as the former was led astray by the word of an angel, so that she fled from God when she had transgressed his word; so did

---

[60]Ibid., p. 100.
[61]Ibid., p. 106.
[62]Irenaeus *Against Heresies* 3.22.4 (*ANF* 1:455).

> the latter, by an angelic communication, receive the glad tidings that she should sustain . . . God, being obedient to his word. And if the former did disobey God, yet the latter was persuaded to be obedient to God, in order that the Virgin Mary might become the patroness . . . of the virgin Eve. And thus, as the human race fell into bondage to death by means of a virgin, so it is rescued by a virgin; virginal disobedience having been balanced in the opposite scale by virginal obedience. For in the same way the sin of the first created man . . . receives amendment by the correction of the first-begotten, and the coming of the serpent is conquered by the harmlessness of the dove, those bonds being unloosed by which we had been fast bound to death.[63]

Irenaeus both expands the role of the Virgin Mary in the economy of salvation and subordinates it to the work of Christ. She is called the "cause of salvation" precisely because of her recapitulation of the work of Eve, the "cause of death." Mary's obedience and faith actively undoes Eve's disobedience and doubt. Mary is now Eve's "patroness."

This word is difficult. Although Irenaeus wrote in Greek, his work has been preserved only in translation. The Latin text employs the word *advocata* ("advocate") to translate the original. An Armenian translation indicates that the Greek word may well have been *paraklētos* (cf. Jn 14:26). Notoriously difficult to define, the word carries connotations of defending, counseling or teaching and interceding for another. Here, it seems synonymous with recapitulation. Mary is Eve's patroness insofar as she "did the opposite of what Eve had done; that is, she obeyed, and thus removed the deplorable consequences of Eve's disobedience."[64]

That this is no mere matter of literary flourish is made plain by the third passage:

> And just as it was through a virgin who disobeyed that man was stricken and fell and died, so too it was through the Virgin, who obeyed the word of God, that man resuscitated by life received life. For the Lord came to seek back the lost sheep, and it was man who was lost; and therefore he did not become some other formation, but he likewise, of her that was descended from Adam, preserved the likeness of formation; for Adam had necessarily to be restored in Christ, that mortality be absorbed in immortality, and Eve in Mary, that a virgin, become the advocate of a virgin, should undo and destroy virginal disobedience by virginal obedience.[65]

Irenaeus contends that recapitulation—and Mary's role therein—is a step-by-

---

[63]Irenaeus *Against Heresies* 5.19.1 (*ANF* 1:547).

[64]Luigi Gambero, *Mary and the Fathers of the Church: The Blessed Virgin Mary in Patristic Thought,* trans. Thomas Buffer (San Francisco: Ignatius, 1999), p. 56.

[65]Irenaeus *Proof of the Apostolic Preaching* 33 (Ancient Christian Writers 16:69).

step undoing of the Fall in order that God's original plan for the cosmos may be fulfilled.[66] In Christ humankind receives a new representative in place of Adam. Since, however, the first woman, Eve, was implicated in the Fall by her disobedience, it is necessary that the healing process should begin with the obedience of another woman, Mary.[67] Recapitulation is thus a development of the Pauline philosophy of history in which the New Testament continues the story begun in the Old Testament. The perfection of humans-in-creation, derailed by the disobedience of Adam and Eve, is recovered and completed by the obedience of Christ and Mary.

Irenaeus evidently believes that the language of New Testament has set the precedent for his own. Unlike the gnostics against whom he wrote, he is no innovator. He stands in the tradition of the apostles, having been trained by their first students.[68] Nevertheless it is equally clear that he takes the exalted Marian language of the Gospel of Luke to a new level, granting the Blessed Virgin a spiritual maternity over all believers by calling her "that pure womb which regenerates men unto God, and which he [Jesus] himself made pure."[69] He does not mean that she saves alongside and perhaps independently of Christ. Rather, like Eve, she is a thoroughly human vessel who is not without her faults. One of them, for example, is impatience.[70] Nevertheless the trend seems toward greater degrees of exaltation seems well established. In the third century only Tertullian stands as the exception to this rule.

Tertullian (ca. 155-ca. 220). Alive when a thriving North African church looked across the Mediterranean at an unconverted Europe, Tertullian, a native of Carthage, embraced Christianity around 193. Unlike Justin, his conversion did not follow after inquiry into various philosophical systems but was due to the heroism that Christian martyrs demonstrated during persecution—common in North Africa at this time.[71] Apart from Saint Augustine, Tertullian is the most important Latin church father; although known primarily as an apologist, his works

---

[66]Quasten, *Patrology,* 1:298.

[67]The use of "necessary" is deliberate. I follow M. C. Steenberg, who challenges the previous consensus by arguing that Mary's subordinate role as corecapitulator is essential. Irenaeus's anthropology "provides for a distinction between the individual or essential aspect of human nature and that of humanity as social creature, typified separately and distinctly in the persons of Adam and Eve." Within this context, "a socially recapitulative 'new Eve' is in fact a soteriological necessity" ("The Role of Mary as Co-recapitulator in St. Irenaeus of Lyons," *Vigilae christianae* 58 [2004]: 117-37, esp. 118).

[68]Irenaeus *Against Heresies* 4.27.1 (*ANF* 1:498).

[69]Irenaeus *Against Heresies* 4.33.11 (*ANF* 1:509).

[70]Irenaeus *Against Heresies* 3.16.7 (*ANF* 1:443).

[71]Johannes Quasten, *Patrology,* vol. 2: *The Ante-Nicene Literature After Irenaeus* (Westminster, Md.: Newman, 1953), p. 247.

continue to exert a profound if hidden influence on the theological vocabulary of both East and West. In our study Tertullian stands in a unique position: on the one hand his Marian writings fall within the patristic tradition begun by Ignatius; on the other hand their resistance to the general trend of increasing Marian exaltation is exceptional.

Continuity with previous writers may be demonstrated in two areas, the first being Tertullian's reiteration of the Eve-Mary motif:

> For it was while Eve was yet a virgin, that the ensnaring word had crept into her ear which was to build the edifice of death. Into a virgin's soul, in like manner, must be introduced that Word of God which was to raise the fabric of life; so that what had been reduced to ruin by this sex, might by the selfsame sex be recovered to salvation. As Eve had believed the serpent, so Mary believed the angel. The delinquency which the one occasioned by believing, the other by believing effaced. But (it will be said) Eve did not at the devil's word conceive in her womb. Well, she at all events conceived; for the devil's word afterwards became as seed for her that she should conceive an outcast, and bring forth in sorrow. Indeed she gave birth to a fratricidal devil; while Mary, on the contrary, bare one who was one day to secure salvation to Israel, his own brother after the flesh, and the murder of himself. God therefore sent down into the Virgin's womb his Word, as the good brother, who should blot out the memory of the evil brother. Hence it was necessary that Christ should come forth for the salvation of man, in that condition *of flesh* into which man had entered ever since his condemnation.[72]

Although resembling both Justin and Irenaeus on this account, Tertullian added his own emphases. Where the former authors tended to contrast Eve's unbelief and disobedience with Mary's faith and obedience, Tertullian contrasts the content and source of what is believed. The problem is not that Eve disbelieved God, but that she believed the devil; just so, the solution is found in Mary's belief in God. Tertullian also reflects at greater length on the parallel conceptions of the two mothers. While he admits that Eve did not literally conceive as a result of believing the devil's lie, he insists that the conception and birth of Cain, who murdered Abel his brother, was the outcome. Mary, on the other hand, conceived Christ, who standing in the tradition of Abel undoes the sin of Israel.

---

[72]Tertullian *On the Flesh of Christ* 17 (*ANF* 3:536). The close connection between hearing the word of the angel and the conception (in Eve's case, the conception of sin and eventually Cain, and in Mary's, the conception of Jesus) was an image especially developed in Syriac Christianity, which came to see the ear as the route for the Word's entry into Mary, thus guaranteeing her *ante partum* virginity. See Robert Murray, "Mary: The Second Eve in the Early Syriac Fathers," *Eastern Churches Review* 3 (1971): 374-75.

Second, like Ignatius, Tertullian uses Mary to defend the humanity of Christ against those who denied it. Although a staunch defender of the virginal conception as a sign and guarantee of Christ's divine nature,[73] he would not allow the absence of a human father as evidence for an apparently human Christ. His argument is simple: if Christ is really Mary's son, then he shares her humanity.[74] Tertullian, however, does not write as a dispassionate systematic theologian, and his arguments are seldom constructive. He is a polemicist. Accordingly his line of reasoning is constructed controversially: if Christ is other than human or if his humanity is of his own making rather than that of his mother's, then Mary is unnecessary. The Bible, however, portrays Mary as Christ's mother. He must therefore be her Son, and if her Son, then human.

Three examples display his concern for Christ's humanity. First, Tertullian comments on his opponents' rather ingenious use of Matthew 1:20 to deny that Mary's humanity was communicated to her Son:

> [They] say that he was born *through* a virgin, not *of* a virgin, and *in* a womb, not *of* a womb, because the angel in the dream said to Joseph, "That which is born in her" (not of her) "is of the Holy Spirit." But the fact is, if he had meant "of her," he must have said "in her"; for that which was of her was also in her. The expression, therefore, "in her," has precisely the same meaning as the phrase "of her." . . . He was *born* of a virgin's flesh.[75]

A similar concern animates the rebuttal of his antagonists' understanding of Matthew's use of Isaiah 7:14 in Matthew 1:22-23:

> If . . . the Word became flesh of himself, then he both conceived and brought forth of himself, and the prophecy is stultified. For in that case a virgin did *not* conceive, and did *not* bring forth; since whatever she brought forth from the conception of the word is not her own flesh. . . . No flesh can speak of a mother's womb but that which is itself the offspring of that womb; nor can any be the offspring of the said womb if it owe its birth solely to itself.[76]

Third, Tertullian affirms the reality of the apparent relationship between Mary and Christ as he asks, "What can we more suitably suppose that the Word became flesh than from that flesh in which it submitted to the dispen-

---

[73]Thus, e.g., Tertullian writes: "It was not fit that the Son of God should be born of a human father's seed, lest, if he were wholly the son of a man, he should fail to be the also the Son of God. . . . For as much, therefore, as he is of the Spirit he is God the Spirit and is born of God; just as he is also born of the flesh of man, being generated in the flesh as man" (*On the Flesh of Christ* 18, 20 [*ANF* 3:537]).

[74]Tertullian *On the Flesh of Christ* 17 (*ANF* 3:536).

[75]Tertullian *On the Flesh of Christ* 20 (*ANF* 3:538).

[76]Tertullian *On the Flesh of Christ* 21 (*ANF* 3:538-39).

sation?"[77] Mary *appears* to be the mother of Christ, quite simply, because she *is* the mother of Christ.[78]

What marks Tertullian among the church fathers is, first, his insistence that Mary neither understood nor accepted the claim of discipleship that Jesus exerted over her, at least before the resurrection, and therefore stood under his judgment. Commenting on the Synoptic story of Jesus' mother and brothers (Mk 3:31-35; Mt 12:46-50; cf. Lk 4:14-30), Tertullian writes that

> he was justly indignant, that persons so very near to him "stood *without*," while strangers were *within* hanging on his words, especially as they wanted to call him away from the solemn work he had in hand. He did not so much deny as disavow them. . . . That he adopted others only confirmed those in their relationship to him whom he refused because of their offence, and for whom he substituted the others, not as being truer relatives, but worthier ones. Finally, it was no great matter if he did prefer to kindred (that) faith which it [the kindred] did not possess.[79]

Where Irenaeus allows that Mary may have been impatient, Tertullian holds her to be an example of unbelief, whose blessedness had been taken from her and given to the disciples.[80]

Second, Tertullian's understanding of Mary is remarkable because of its explicit denial of Mary's *in partu* virginity:

> She who bare (really) bare; and although she was a virgin when she conceived, she was a wife when she brought forth *her Son*. Now, as a wife, she was under the very law of "opening the womb," wherein it was quite immaterial whether the birth of the male was by virtue of a husband's cooperation or not; it was the same sex that opened her womb. . . . *The Virgin's womb,* therefore, was especially opened, because it was especially closed. . . . It was in this sense that the apostle declared that the Son of God was born not of a virgin, but "of a woman."[81]

Mary's womb was opened by the very real, very human birth of Christ. As a result, although she conceived as a virgin, she gave birth, in Tertullian's words, as a woman.

Tertullian's rejection of Mary's *post partum* virginity is more complicated. It stems from his passionate protection of Christ's true humanity. Where he saw in

---

[77]Tertullian *On the Flesh of Christ* 18 (*ANF* 3:537).

[78]Tertullian also holds the common patristic view that Mary was herself of the line of David such that the fully human Christ is indeed David's son, even if he is not Joseph's. See Tertullian *On the Flesh of Christ* 21 (*ANF* 3:539). According to Murray ("Mary," p. 374), this is a Syriac Christian tradition rooted in Syriac versions of Lk 2:5.

[79]Tertullian *Against Marcion* 4.19 (*ANF* 3:378).

[80]Tertullian *On the Flesh of Christ* 7 (*ANF* 3:530).

[81]Tertullian *On the Flesh of Christ* 23 (*ANF* 3:541).

the story of Jesus' mother and brothers Jesus' turn from his blood family to his disciples, his opponents apparently imagined it to be about Jesus' disavowal of human beings altogether. On their reading, he who relayed the message that Jesus' mother and brothers were outside thereby allowed Jesus to deny that he had either and to assert instead his "inhumanity." Tertullian, however, would have none of it. Again insisting on a commonsense approach to the biblical text, he countered that "nobody would have told him that his mother and brothers were standing outside, if he were not certain both that he had a mother and brothers."[82] For Tertullian, in other words, "brothers" means just that: Joseph and Mary had other children. Perhaps as importantly, he also discerned a moral quality to Mary's participation in a regular sex life with Joseph. He acknowledges Mary as first virgin and then wife to have distinctively hallowed both celibacy and monogamy as worthy Christian callings.[83]

School of Alexandria

While previous generations of Christian leaders certainly produced writings that continue to ground and guide inquiry, they were more immediate and local. Although Justin's Logos Christology, for example, remains one of the key steps toward the Nicene definition of Christ's person, it was developed as part of an apologetic argument directed against the persecution of Christians. Similarly, Irenaeus—who is the most systematic among the early fathers—directs his theology against heretics. Whether aimed at non-Christian or Christian audiences, "the works of that period were characterized by defense and attack; they were apologetic and anti-heretical."[84] As the second century gave way to the third, however, a new genre of Christian literature arose: theology. And it was centered in the great Egyptian port of Alexandria.

Long before Christianity, Alexandria was a vibrant, artistic, intellectual and religious cultural center. Founded by Alexander the Great in 331 B.C., Alexandria mingled Asian, Egyptian and Greek cultures, producing the Hellenism that influenced both Jewish and, later, Christian minds. It was the Jewish community at Alexandria that produced the Septuagint, which became the first Christian Old Testament. It was the Jewish community of Alexandria that produced Philo, who synthesized the Old Testament and Greek speculation in a way later developed by Christian theologians. It was the Christian community of Alexandria whose debates about Mary defined Mariology for succeeding generations, whether

---

[82]Tertullian *On the Flesh of Christ* 7 (*ANF* 3:527-28). See also *Against Marcion* 4.19 (*ANF* 3:378).
[83]Tertullian *On Monogamy* (*ANF* 4:65).
[84]Quasten, *Patrology,* 2:1.

Latin or Greek. It was at Alexandria that the most significant Marian development to date and for all time emerged: the title "*Theotokos,* Mother of God."

Clement of Alexandria (ca. 150-ca. 215). Clement was a Christian convert who began his instruction in Christian faith in Athens. After visiting Italy, Syria and Palestine, Clement settled in Alexandria where he came under the instruction of Christian theologian and former Stoic philosopher Pantaenus. Because of persecution initiated by Septimius Severus and implemented by the Roman government of Egypt, Clement fled Alexandria for Cappadocia, where he remained until his death around 215. He theorized that the coherent integration of biblical and nonbiblical learning was the best way to overcome Gnosticism. Although little more is known about him, subsequent generations "owe it above all to him if scholarly thinking and research are recognized in the Church."[85]

Although he stands with previous writers in affirming the reality of Mary's motherhood and Christ's humanity,[86] he apparently goes beyond them in his affirmation of Mary's perpetual virginity:

> But, as appears, many even down to our own time regard Mary, on account of the birth of her child, as having been in the puerperal state [i.e., the state of having given birth], although she was not. For some say that, after she brought forth, she was found, when examined, to be a virgin.
>
> Now such to us are the Scriptures of the Lord, which gave birth to the truth and continue virgin, in the concealment of the mysteries of the truth. "And she brought forth, and yet brought not forth," says the Scripture; as having conceived of herself, and not from conjunction.[87]

This quotation is striking for three reasons. First, the affirmation of Mary's perpetual virginity is the earliest in extant *theological* literature. Although second-century devotional literature demonstrates its widespread acceptance (as discussed above), only in the early third century does it attract theological attention. Where Tertullian rejects perpetual virginity as a gnostic dismissal of Christ's humanity, Clement, in a document also concerned with Gnosticism, takes it to be a matter of biblical fact. Second, Clement's espousal shows that the canon is not yet set. He alludes to the *Protevangelium of James* and quotes *Pseudo-Ezekiel.* Both are granted the status of Holy Scripture.[88] Third, Mary starts to emerge as a theological ideal. She is a model for the right understanding of the Holy Scriptures, which themselves remain virginally pure even as they give birth to the truth.

---

[85]Ibid., 2:7.
[86]Clement *Stromata* 6.15 (*ANF* 2:511-12).
[87]Clement *Stromata* 7.16 (*ANF* 1:551).
[88]Gambero, *Mary and the Fathers,* p. 70 n. 5.

It is also in Clement's works that we find the first extensive application of Marian imagery to the church:

> But the Lord Christ, the fruit of the Virgin, did not pronounce the breasts of women blessed, nor selected them to give nourishment; but when the kind and loving Father had rained down the Word, himself became spiritual nourishment to the good. O mystic marvel! The universal Father is one, and one the universal word; and the Holy Spirit is one and the same everywhere, and one is the only virgin mother. I love to call her the church. This mother, when alone, had not milk because she was not a woman. But she is once virgin and mother—pure as a virgin, loving as a mother. And calling her children to her, she nurses them with holy milk, viz., with the Word for childhood. Therefore she had not milk; for the milk was this child fair and comely, the body of Christ.[89]

Like Mary, Clement's church is both a virgin and a mother. She is a virgin insofar as her faith is pure and intact. She is a mother insofar as she brings forth children and nourishes them on the milk of the Word.

Origen (ca. 185-ca. 253). It was under Clement's most famous pupil and successor, Origen, that the Alexandrian school reached its apex.[90] Born during the reign of Commodus and reared in a Christian home, Origen was educated in subjects both Hellenic and biblical. After the martyrdom of his father, Leonidas, in 202,[91] the theological school was in dire straits until Bishop Demetrius appointed Origen, then only eighteen, as master. During his tenure from 203 to 231, the school prospered, offering courses in a wide variety of disciplines. His success, however, was not always well received. It seems to have aroused Demetrius's jealousy and led to Origen's excommunication from the Alexandrian church, forcing Origen to relocate to Caesarea in Palestine. He died in Tyre around 253 as a result of injuries sustained during the Decian persecution.

Theologically Origen is a contradiction;[92] he is rightly described as both "the

---

[89]Clement *Instructor* 1.6 (*ANF* 1:220).

[90]This is the traditional view espoused by Eusebius. Henri Couzel observes contrarily that Origen never quotes Clement and at most seems only familiar with his work. See Henri Couzel, *Origen,* trans. A. S. Worrall (Edinburgh: T & T Clark, 1989), p. 7.

[91]According to Couzel, "Leonidas was certainly an important man. The fact that he was beheaded seems to show that he was a Roman citizen. . . . [The] prosecution of Leonidas shows that he must have played a certain part in the training of catechumens in the Church of Alexandria. Furthermore the education that he gave to his son shows that he was an intellectual who, in addition to the common Hellenic curriculum, had assiduously studied the Bible. Perhaps he was a teacher of grammar, that is of literature: it was that profession his son took up, after the father's death, to support the family" (ibid., pp. 5-6).

[92]See ibid., pp. xi-xii, for an indication of just how much controversy Origen caused, especially after his death. For a detailed account of his theology, consult pp. 153-266.

Father of the Fathers and the Father of the Heretics." The influence of Neoplatonic philosophy led to views now regarded as heterodox: the preexistence of the soul, reincarnation, universal salvation and so on. Fortunately these difficulties may be set aside, for his Marian thought is quite conservative. While maintaining the Mary-Eve typology[93] and defending the reality of Mary's motherhood,[94] Origen tends to focus on Mary's virginity.

He insists that Mary's *ante partum* virginity is an indispensable part of the deposit of faith such that to deny it is tantamount to denying the faith altogether.[95] He defends Matthew's use of Isaiah 7:14 as predictive prophecy and argues from it that Jesus' virginal conception is absolutely unique[96]—so exceptional, in fact, that it challenges then-received notions of human reproduction, which held that the material that became a child was contained in the father's semen alone. Mary's *ante partum* virginity necessitated that Christ's humanity be derived solely from Mary.[97] Origen defended Mary's *ante partum* virginity against all opponents, whether Jewish Christians, pagan philosophers or even biological facts.

Unlike Clement, however, he is not so definitive about virginity *in partu*. While commenting on Luke 2:22, Origen indicates that Mary needed purification after giving birth.[98] Later writings, however, suggest that he did come to adopt the notion. It may be assumed in this passage from his commentary on Matthew:

> Now Mary, after giving birth to the Savior, went to worship and stood in the place of the virgins. And when those who knew she had given birth were preventing her, Zachariah said to them that she was worthy of the place of the virgins, because she was a virgin. Therefore, as he was evidently transgressing the Law and allowed a woman to take her place among the virgins, they killed him between the temple and the altar.[99]

Origen's eighth homily on Leviticus removes all doubt: "There is a mystical exception, which separated Mary along from the rest of women whose birth was

---

[93]Origen *Homily on Matthew* 1.5 (Graef, *Mary,* 1:45).

[94]In a possible challenge to Jewish Christians who denied the virginal conception of Jesus, Origen writes, "Consider if it is possible that someone believe in the same person so far as some particular aspect is concerned, but not believe so far as another is concerned. Take, as an example, those who believe in the Jesus crucified in Judea in the time of Pontius Pilate, but who do not believe in the one born of the Virgin Mary. These believe and disbelieve in the same one" (*Commentary on John* 20.269 [FC 89:261]).

[95]Origen *Commentary on John* 32.191 (FC 89:378).

[96]Origen *Against Celsus* 1.34 (*ANF* 4:410-11).

[97]Origen *Epistle to the Romans* 3.10(5) (FC 103:232-33).

[98]Origen *Homilies on Luke, Fragments on Luke* 14.6 (FC 94:59).

[99]Cited in Graef, *Mary,* 1:44.

not by the conception of seed but by the presence 'of the Holy Spirit and the power of the Most High.'"[100]

Finally, Origen defends Mary's *post partum* virginity as an ancient tradition, "fitting" according to theological reason:

> [Mary's *post partum* virginity is based] on a tradition in the Gospel according to Peter, as it is titled, or "The Book of James" [i.e., the *Protevangelium of James*] that the brothers of Jesus were sons of Joseph by a former wife, whom he married before Mary. Now those who say so wish to preserve the honor of Mary in virginity to the end, so that that body of hers which was appointed to minister to the Word . . . might not know intercourse with a man after that the Holy Spirit came into her and the power from on high overshadowed her. And I think it in harmony with reason that Jesus was the first fruit among men of the purity which consists in chastity, and Mary among women; for it were not pious to ascribe any other than to her the first fruit of virginity.[101]

Like Tertullian, Origen finds a moral rationale in Mary's virginity. But where Tertullian averred that Mary's life demonstrated the sanctification of both celibacy and monogamy, Origen has only virginity in view: just as Jesus is a model for all chaste men, so Mary is a model for all chaste women.

This stress on Mary's virginity throughout her life may cause some to wonder why God's plan included a *betrothed* virgin. After all, defending Mary's virginity in the light of her marriage to Joseph is difficult. To any with such wonders, Origen cites Ignatius to argue that God shrouded Mary's virginity in mystery in order that the economy of salvation might proceed without satanic opposition until the appropriate time.[102]

Origen follows Irenaeus and Tertullian in attributing fault to Mary. A relatively minor matter is his early view of Mary's need for purification after Jesus' birth.[103] More significantly Origen held that Simeon's sword described the scandal and uncertainty that Mary experienced during her Son's passion. Although a virgin from first to last, Origen does not remove Mary from the realm of human experience. As far as he is concerned, alongside all human beings, Mary stands in need of the redemption accomplished on the cross and offered by her Son.

Finally, the most intriguing aspect of Origen's reflections on Mary comes not

---

[100]Origen *Homilies on Leviticus* 8.2(6) (FC 83:155).

[101]Origen *Commentary on Matthew* 17 (in *Ante-Nicene Christian Library*, additional volume, *Containing Early Christian Works Discovered Since the Completion of the Series, and Selections from the Commentaries of Origen*, ed. Allan Menzies [Edinburgh: T & T Clark, 1897], p. 424).

[102]Origen *Homilies on Luke* 6.4-5 (FC 94:24-25).

[103]Origen *Homilies on Luke, Fragments on Luke* 14.6 (FC 94:59).

from him but from Christian historian Socrates, who when recounting the Nestorian controversy claimed that Origen defended the term *Theotokos.*[104] If Socrates' historiography is correct, then Alexandrian Christians were heralding Mary as bearer or Mother of God in the third century. Socrates' account does resonate with the earliest Marian prayer thus far discovered: "Under your wings we take refuge, O Mother of God. Do not reject our supplications in necessity, but deliver us from danger, [O you] alone pure and alone blessed."[105] Known as the *sub tuum praesidium,* from its opening words in Latin translation, this originally Greek prayer has been found on a manuscript dating from third-century Egypt. Unfortunately, however, Socrates' account cannot be verified. The surviving versions of Origen's commentary on Romans do not contain this word or anything like it. The reference is lost.[106]

Athanasius (ca. 295-373). The earliest undisputed use of *Theotokos* is found in an encyclical letter written in 319 by Bishop Alexander of Alexandria,[107] whose successor, Athanasius, is perhaps the greatest of all Alexandrian theologians. Becoming bishop in 328, Athanasius is best known for his insisting that the Son of God was God, but few recall that his so-called victory came at a high price. His Arian and semi-Arian opponents retained considerable political influence and used it to depose Athanasius from his see in 335, 339 and 355. After suffering two more exiles, one in 362 and another in 365, Athanasius was finally restored to his diocese in 366, where he remained until his death in 373.

Athanasius's writings on Mary arise in theological treatises, personal letters and ascetical exhortations. The focus of the first group is always the reality of the incarnation. Mary is invoked to defend the humanity, divinity and unity of Christ.[108] All three elements are found here: "Now the scope and character of Holy Scripture, as we have often said, is this—it contains a double account of the Savior; that he was ever God, and is the Son, being the Father's Word and Radiance and Wisdom; and that afterward for us he took flesh of a virgin, Mary

---

[104]Socrates Scholasticus *Ecclesiastical History* 7.32 (*NPNF*[2] 2:171).

[105]Cited in Gambero, *Mary and the Fathers,* p. 79.

[106]Thomas P. Scheck, "Introduction," in *Origen: Commentary on the Epistle to the Romans Books 1-5,* trans. Thomas P. Scheck, FC 103 (Washington: Catholic University Press of America, 2001), p. 17.

[107]"After this we know the resurrection of the dead, the first fruit of which was our Lord Jesus Christ who in very deed, and not in appearance merely, carries a body of Mary, Mother of God [ἐκ τῆς θεοτόκου Μαρίας]" (cited in Johannes Quasten, *Patrology,* vol. 3: *The Golden Age of Greek Patristic Literature from the Council of Nicaea to the Council of Chalcedon* [Westminster, Md.: Newman, 1960], p. 19).

[108]This is not to attribute anachronously to Athanasius a full-blown Chalcedonian Christology, which would not be articulated until the first half of the fifth century.

bearer of God *[theotokou]*, and was made man."[109] The one Savior is both God from all eternity and a human being, born of Mary. Similar statements can be found throughout the Athanasian corpus.[110]

The theological writings of Athanasius also leave Mary's perpetual virginity alone. When *On the Incarnation of the Word* asserts that "not even when the Virgin bore him did he suffer any change . . . by being in the body,"[111] it implies that the Virgin did. Jaroslav Pelikan's translation better captures this implication: "When the Virgin was giving birth to him, it was not he *[autos]* who suffered or was stained by being in the body."[112] Athanasius appears to affirm Mary's normal, painful labor and delivery. Pelikan helpfully adds that every instance of the term *ever-virgin (aeiparthenos)* in Athanasius's works is "either fragmentary or dubious or both."[113] The theological writings focus on Christ. Even the ascription of *Theotokos* to Mary is intended to convey an anti-Arian point: the man who was born of the Virgin is God.

Moving to his letters, we find that Athanasius instinctively worked from the principle *lex orandi lex credendi.* Literally translated "the law of prayer [leads] the law of belief," this principle teaches that theological content is implicit in Christian worship practices and is evident of those letters in which Mary is described as an object of Christian devotion. The most important of these is the *Letter to Epictetus,*[114] a defense of the Nicene faith against neo-docetists, holding that Jesus' body is not human, and neo-adoptionists, contending that Jesus and the Word of God are distinct persons.[115] These, he insists, "have gone further in impiety than any heresy"[116] not only because they have so obviously departed from the teachings of the Scriptures and the Nicene fathers, but also because they render "the commemoration and the work of Mary . . . superfluous."[117] Here Mary functions as she did for Ignatius some three centuries before: a guarantee of Christ's humanity.

---

[109]Athanasius *Four Discourses Against the Arians* 3.29 (*NPNF*^{2} 4:409).

[110]Athanasius *Four Discourses Against the Arians* 3.31 (*NPNF*^{2} 4:410); *On the Incarnation of the Word* 8.2-3; 19.5; 37.3 (*NPNF*^{2} 4:40, 46, 56).

[111]Athanasius *On the Incarnation of the Word* 17.5 (*NPNF*^{2} 4:45).

[112]Jaroslav Pelikan, *Development of Christian Doctrine: Some Historical Prolegomena* (New Haven: Yale University Press, 1969), p. 99.

[113]Ibid.

[114]Athanasius *Letter to Epictetus* (*NPNF*^{2} 4:570-74).

[115]Athanasius *Letter to Epictetus* 2 (*NPNF*^{2} 4:571).

[116]Athanasius *Letter to Epictetus* 4 (*NPNF*^{2} 4:571).

[117]Athanasius *Letter to Epictetus* 4 (*NPNF*^{2} 4:571). A very similar remark is found the *Letter to Maximus,* where those holding that the Word became incarnate as a consequence of his nature are told that "if this were so, the commemoration of Mary would be superfluous" (*Letter to Maximus* 3 [*NPNF*^{2} 4:579]).

Far more interesting is the perceived necessity and normativity of a church practice, the commemoration of Mary, in determining correct theology. Pelikan suggests that the commemoration is an early mariological festival that may well have developed into the Commemoration of Mary, celebrated the Sunday before Christmas.[118] This festival apparently honored Mary's role in the salvation of humanity. She was the vehicle through and in whom the Word became flesh to save the world. The Scriptures, the Nicene fathers and the practices of the church coalesce to attest to the humanity of Christ.

Such a theological method may ring oddly in Protestant ears. It is therefore important to observe just how it mirrors one of Athanasius's classical arguments for the deity of the Son of God. Christians implicitly know that the Son of God is God insofar as they worship the Son of God as God: "While he is adored, because he is Son of the adorable Father, we adore, confessing him Lord and God, because we are creatures and other than he."[119]

Finally, the core of Athanasius's Mariology lies in his exhortations on the Christian ascetic life. *The Letter to the Virgins*[120] commends Mary as an example of consecrated virginity.[121] The nuns to whom he wrote should "know [themselves] through her [Mary] as though through a mirror."[122] Mary's virginity *post partum* makes an ethical point: just as Mary had no other children after Jesus, so the nuns to whom he writes should follow in her footsteps, taking a vow of lifelong chastity.[123]

This is an admirable admonition, to be sure, but on its face Athanasius's strategy seems to suffer a serious drawback: the lack of biblical material concerning Mary's character and actions. And yet, chastity is merely the beginning of a long list of virginal qualities that the nuns are expected to embody. When Athanasius declares that "the life of Mary, who bore God, should be to you all the image to which each should conform her virginity" and urges on that basis that they return to "the good works which [they] have neglected . . . progressing until

---

[118]Pelikan, *Development of Christian Doctrine,* p. 111; see also Graef, *Mary,* 1:133-38.

[119]Athanasius *Defense of the Nicene Definition* 11 (*NPNF*^{2} 4:157).

[120]Traversing the terrain of this text is notoriously difficult for two reasons. First, it has not been preserved in Greek, but must be reconstructed from fragments of Coptic copies and from parallels between these and a similarly titled treatise by Ambrose of Milan (see Pelikan, *Development of Christian Doctrine,* p. 100). Second, a text claiming Athanasian provenance with a nearly identical title, *On Virginity,* has been shown decisively to be pseudonymous (see David Brakke, "Introduction," in *Pseudo-Athanasius On Virginity,* ed. David Brakke, Corpus scriptorum christianorum orientalium 592 (Louvain: Peeters, 2002), pp. xi-xii.

[121]Athanasius "Lettre aux Vierges," in *Lettres festales et pastorales en copte* (trans. L.-T. Lefort, Corpus scriptorum christianorum orientalium 151 [Louvain: Durbecq, 1955], p. 59).

[122]Athanasius "Lettre aux Vierges" (*Lettres festales et pastorales,* p. 59 [my translation]).

[123]Athanasius "Lettre aux Vierges" (*Lettres festales et pastorales,* p. 59).

[their] life will one day be an example of virginity to others,"[124] he has very specific attitudes and actions in mind. Like Mary, nuns are to be hard-working, generous, devout, modest, humble, progressing in sanctification and yearning for eternity with God. None of these virtues, as Athanasius well knew, are found in the New Testament.[125] On what basis does he say such things? According to Pelikan, he does so by "what might be called development of doctrine by extrapolation"[126] or a reapplication of the hermeneutic of "prophecy-fulfillment," from the Old Testament to the New Testament to the church.

This move requires a brief explanation. The prophecy-fulfillment hermeneutic allowed the church fathers to find in the Old Testament statements about Christ that were not explicitly reaffirmed in the New. For example, in his second oration against the Arians, the most detailed biblical exegesis through which Athanasius argued for what he understood to be a right understanding of the relationship of the Son of God to the rest of creation comes not, as a modern reader might think, from the opening chapters of John or Ephesians or Colossians but from Proverbs 8:22-31. In an oration consisting of nine chapters, his christological reading of the personification of wisdom as the agent of creation in Proverbs comprises seven.[127] Similarly, in his teachings on Mary as the model nun, this same method permitted him "to amplify the teachings of the New Testament on the basis of what had become explicit in the history of salvation since the New Testament."[128] The extended description of Mary's life should therefore be seen as a summary of the ideal Eastern Christian ascetic, an ideal that Athanasius had explored fully elsewhere in his hagiographic *Life of Antony*.[129] He felt free to extrapolate from this ideal back to Mary because the evidence provided by the lives of fourth-century Egyptian monks and nuns had, he believed, taught him the deep meaning of the Bible's portrayal of the Mother of God. The ongoing life of the church, in other words, continued to illumine the Scriptures by disclosing a meaning not explicit in the biblical text alone.

The Mother of God, commemorated in the church's memory for her role in the divine economy, the ascetic ideal, the best of Egyptian monasticism—Athanasius clearly has a high view of Mary. But even in such an exalted state Athanasius's Mary remains one of us: "That then which was born of Mary was according to the divine Scriptures human by nature, and the body of the Lord

---

[124]Athanasius "Lettre aux Vierges" (*Lettres festales et pastorales,* pp. 59-60 [my translation]).
[125]Athanasius "Lettre aux Vierges" (*Lettres festales et pastorales,* p. 60).
[126]Pelikan, *Development of Christian Doctrine,* p. 101.
[127]Athanasius *Four Discourses Against the Arians* 3.16-22 (*NPNF*^{2} 4:357-93).
[128]Pelikan, *Development of Christian Doctrine,* p. 102.
[129]Athanasius *Life of Antony* (*NPNF*^{2} 4:195-221).

was a true one; but it was this, because it was the same as our body, for Mary was our sister inasmuch as we all are from Adam."[130] His logic is simple: if Mary is not one of us, then her Son is not human. If her Son is not human, then we are not saved. And if Mary is our sister, sharing fully in our descent from Adam, then monastics (and others) may appeal to her example, for she can be imitated. It is not until the (Eastern) language of Marian elevation is synthesized with the (Western) language of original sin that the impulse somehow to segregate Mary from the rest of humanity is given freer theological reign. But that is to anticipate a theme in the next chapter.

Conclusion

Three conclusions may be drawn. First, for the ante-Nicene fathers Mary's motherhood was both real and unique. By the end of the fourth century, theologians had largely accepted the popular trend to fill in the blanks of Mary's life, for example, the names of her parents and her virginity *ante partum, in partu* and *post partum*. But the major contention of the *Protevangelium of James,* namely, that Mary's humanity was of a rarefied, exceptional kind was resisted. For the church fathers from Ignatius to Athanasius, Mary was a human being who erred by demonstrating impatience, lack of faith and doubt. She needed salvation. She needed to progress in sanctification. Even the theological appropriation of the pious title *"Theotokos"* did not exalt Mary as much as it grounded the feet of her divine Son securely on this earth. Mary was the fully human mother of the fully human Savior.

At the same time Mary played a unique role in the divine economy that extended beyond that of guarantor of the humanity of Jesus. Her early and widespread acclamation as the New Eve accentuates that in the mind of the early church Mary played a (secondary) part in the salvation of the human race just as Eve played a (secondary) part in its fall. She is Eve's "patroness," whose obedience to the Word of God given through the angel undoes the disobedience of her foremother. She is honored with a feast day because that same obedience ensured the salvation of us all. Alexandrian piety, at least, was willing to push this conclusion further to find for the Mother of God a continuing role as the protector and intercessor of the faithful.

Later generations will explore that role more fully. The ante-Nicene fathers were content to discuss Mary's role as an ideal or example. Her virginal conception of the Word of God mirrors the Scriptures, which themselves speak God's Word. As virgin and mother she typifies the church, the virgin bride who is

[130]Athanasius *Letter to Epictetus* 7 (*NPNF*[2] 4:573).

mother to many children. And she is an example of the ascetic life, whose piety, chastity, hard work and generosity are to be emulated by all who wish spend their lives in pursuit of the ideal of Egyptian monasticism. These trends are deepened even as they are formalized in the fifth century, at which time the Council of Ephesus will issue the first Marian dogmatic pronouncement.

7

Mother of God

Formalizing the Patristic Heritage

Two dominant themes emerged in the last chapter: the reality of Mary's motherhood (she was the fully human mother of the fully human Savior) and the uniqueness of this same motherhood (fully expressed in the Alexandrian term of devotion: *Theotokos,* Mother of God). Although apparently difficult to reconcile, both themes are summarized in the first widespread Marian title, New Eve, the former in the common humanity of both women, the latter in their representative function. As thought progressed, Mary's relatively undefined role as "Eve's patroness" was clarified. As the fully human mother of the Savior, Mary was an example of the ascetic life. As *Theotokos,* her obedience to the Word of God undid the disobedience of her foremother, and she was honored with a feast day because that same obedience ensured the salvation of us all.

Such views continued to be developed. First, the Cappadocians and John Chrysostom both exalted Mary and acknowledged her errors and lapses. Second, Ambrose, Jerome and Augustine, under pressures created by Jovinian, Helvidius and Pelagius, were both more modest in their adoration and more reticent to admit the possibility of sin. Last, three capstones of Marian thought in the patristic era—the Council of Ephesus and John of Damascus in the East and Leo the Great in the West—established the trends to be developed in the medieval era and challenged by the Reformation.

Eastern Church Fathers

The Arian crisis of the fourth century is often presented as ending with the Athanasian party's victory at the Council of Nicea in 325. In fact, not only did his more powerful Arian opponents exile Athanasius three times after Nicea, but also the Eastern church continued to be dogged by Arian Christologies until well into the late fourth century. It was the brilliant and persistent theological, ecclesiastical and political work of the Cappadocian fathers—Basil the Great (330-379), his brother Gregory of Nyssa (ca. 335-394) and his companion Gregory of Nazianzus (ca. 330-ca. 390)—that finally vindicated the Athanasian position at the Council of Constantinople in 381. Thus, although named for their home region in the Roman province of Asia Minor, the Cappadocians continued to develop Alexandrian theology. And this applies not only to their Christology, but also (and derivatively) to their Mariology.

Reality of the incarnation. For the Cappadocians, Mary safeguards the union of human and divine in the incarnate Lord in two ways. First, she is a reminder of Jesus' humanity by being his mother. Thus, when commenting on Galatians 4:4, Basil contends that "the apostle . . . corrects . . . the error of those who supposed that the body of the Lord was a spiritual body, and, to show that the God-bearing flesh was formed out of the common lump of human nature. . . . The nature was shared by the mother and the offspring."[1] The true assumption of a true human nature is of vital importance to the Cappadocians. Following Athanasius, they insist that salvation is to be found not so much in the cross and resurrection of Jesus, as in his incarnation and life. As a result, Mary's real humanity and its assumption by God the Son in her womb cannot be overemphasized. Basil asks rhetorically, "If the God-bearing flesh was not ordained to be assumed of the lump of Adam, what need was there of the Holy Virgin?"[2]

The reality of the Son's humanity, however, does not deny the reality of his divinity. If Mary's motherhood proves Jesus' humanity, then her virginity is a sign of his deity. Basil puts it this way: "He exists neither from Mary nor from her time. But then, from whence? 'In the beginning was the Word and the Word was with God and the Word was God': existence from eternity, generation without passion, consubstantiality with the Father."[3] Gregory of Nazianzus goes further: "He was born—but he had been begotten: he was born of a woman—but she was a virgin. The first is human the second divine. In his human nature he had no father, but also in his divine nature no mother. Both these belong to Godhead."[4]

Because she guarantees Christ's humanity and signs his divinity, Mary is a

---

[1]Basil *On the Spirit* 5.12 (*NPNF*[2] 8:7-8).

[2]Basil *To the Sozopolitans* (*NPNF*[2] 8:300).

[3]Basil *Contre eunome: suivi de eunome apologie* 2.15 (trans. Bernard Sesboüé et al., Sources chrétiennes 305 [Paris: Cerf, 1983], p. 59 [my translation]).

[4]Gregory of Nazianzus *On the Son* (*NPNF*[2] 7:308).

sign of human salvation.[5] As a result, to deny Mary is to deny the faith:

> If anyone does not believe that Holy Mary is the Mother of God, he is severed from the Godhead. If anyone should assert that he passed through the Virgin as through a channel, and was not at once divinely and humanly formed in her (divinely, because without the intervention of a man; humanly, because in accordance with the laws of gestation), he is in like manner godless. . . . For both natures [divine and human] are one by the combination, the deity being made man, and the manhood being deified or however one should express it.[6]

Gregory of Nazianzus binds the uniqueness and reality of Mary's motherhood together: both are necessary for a right understanding of the incarnation, in and through which is found the salvation of the human race. Because of her relation to Christ, Mary is a guarantor of orthodoxy.

Reality of Mary's virginity. It is in these christological and soteriological contexts that Mary's virginity—whether *ante partum, in partu* or *post partum*—arises. *Ante partum* virginity is a fact. Against continuing Jewish criticism of the Christian exegesis of Isaiah 7:14, Basil insists that the Hebrew word *'almah* must mean "virgin," otherwise the pregnancy of which it speaks could not function as a sign of God's presence with his people.[7] Other than that, it is simply taken as a matter of record that, at the time of the conception of Jesus, Mary was a virgin.

Much the same can be said for Mary's virginity after Jesus' birth. Basil, for example, is aware that Matthew 1:25 could be seen to say that Mary and Joseph had a normal sexual relationship after Jesus' birth. He concludes, however, that a true lover of Christ would reject such exegesis and continue to affirm "that the Theotokos never ceased to be a virgin."[8] Mary's marriage to Joseph, although never physically consummated, was a deliberate part of the divine plan, for through it Joseph would witness Mary's purity and the devil would be tricked into ignoring Mary's pregnancy.[9] The rationale for such exegesis is supplied by Gregory of Nyssa's understanding of Luke 1:34, according to which Mary had taken a lifelong vow of virginity.[10] Mary's continued virginity was again a matter of biblical record and therefore needed little defense. Only an explanation of

---

[5]Gregory of Nazianzus *On the Testaments and the Coming of Christ* (in *Poemata arcana,* ed. C. Moreschini, trans. D. A. Sykes [Oxford: Oxford University Press, 1997], p. 45).

[6]Gregory of Nazianzus *To Cledonius the Priest Against Apollinarius* (*NPNF*[2] 7:439-40).

[7]Basil *Homilia in sanctam christi generationem* 5 (Patrologia graeca 31:1468).

[8]Basil *Homilia in sanctam christi generationem* 5 (Patrologia graeca 31:1468).

[9]Basil *Homilia in sanctam christi generationem* 3 (Patrologia graeca 31:1463).

[10]Luigi Gambero, *Mary and the Fathers of the Church: The Blessed Virgin Mary in Patristic Thought,* trans. Thomas Buffer (San Francisco: Ignatius, 1999), p. 157.

those texts that seemed to contradict the claim was necessary.

Considerably more energy is spent on Mary's *in partu* virginity. Reflecting the current state of biological studies, Basil contends that it is analogous to conception and birth in various species of birds and is surprised that some refuse to believe it is possible. He admonishes his readers that "if ever you see anyone laugh at our mystery, as if it were impossible and contrary to nature that a virgin should become a mother without losing the purity of her virginity, bethink you that he who would save the faithful by the foolishness of preaching, has given us beforehand in nature a thousand reasons for believing in the marvelous."[11] He further bolsters this claim by repeating Origen's apocryphal story of the murder of Zechariah between the altar and the temple for allowing Mary to worship with the virgins after the birth of Jesus.[12] The appeal to apocryphal legends for support is hardly shocking given the doctrine's origins in the popular devotional literature of the second century.

Gregory of Nyssa, more subtle than Basil in his defense of the doctrine, calls on the Old Testament. Bringing to mind Mary/Eve, Gregory argues that the pain of a normal delivery is part of the curse (cf. Gen 3:16). It would not be fitting for the birth of the Savior to be marked by anything but delight. Mary "did not know how the divine body was produced in her body and did not undergo birth pangs. . . . Because woman brought death to human nature through sin, she was condemned to give birth in pain and labor. . . . It was indeed necessary that the mother of life conceive her child with joy and to perfect her act of giving birth in joy."[13] He also finds biblical support for virginity *in partu* from Moses' encounter with God in Exodus 3:1-6: "we learn also the mystery of the Virgin: The light of divinity which through birth shone from her into human life did not consume the burning bush, even as the flower of her virginity was not consumed by giving birth."[14] Just as Christ, the light of the world, shone through the burning bush without consuming it, so he came into this world through the Virgin without need of a regular delivery.

Role of Mary in the divine economy. The Cappadocians follow Athanasius in presenting Mary as an ascetic exemplar. Gregory of Nazianzus is convinced that although the glories of virginity were once hidden, "after Christ was born of a chaste and Virgin Mother, . . . virginity began to sanctify women and drive

---

[11]Basil *Hexaemeron* 8.6 (*NPNF*^{2} 8:99).

[12]Basil *Homilia in sanctam christi generationem* 5 (Patrologia graeca 31:1469).

[13]Gregory of Nyssa *Commentary on the Song of Songs* (trans. Casimir McCambley [Brookline: Hellenic College Press, 1987], p. 237).

[14]Gregory of Nyssa *The Life of Moses* (trans. Abraham J. Malherbe and Everett Ferguson, Classics of Western Spirituality [Mahwah: Paulist Press, 1978], p. 59).

away the bitter Eve. It took away the laws of the flesh, and, through the preaching of the gospel, the letter gave way to the spirit, and grace entered in."[15] Employing terminology more at home in Platonism, Gregory insists that with the incarnation of God "virginity shone out clearly before mortals; it appeared in the world freely, as the liberator of a helpless world. It is as superior to matrimony and to the conditions of life as the soul is superior to the body and as the wide heavens are superior to earth, as the lasting life of the blessed is superior to the fleeting life of earth, as God is superior to man."[16]

Mary is also a protector, especially for those whose virginity is threatened. Gregory of Nazianzus relates the story of Justina, who, although extraordinarily beautiful and of noble birth, chose a life of virginity over the seductive overtures of Cyprian. So greedy and grasping was he that he became a satanic attack on Justina's "holy soul and virtuous body." This, says Gregory, is a recapitulation of the temptation in the Garden of Eden, save only that this time Satan used an "absolute devil" of a man rather than one of those "who are old hands at the trade" of temptation, that is, a woman. Following the examples of Susanna and Thecla, Justina resisted Cyprian's (and Satan's) invitations, trusting that her true husband, Christ, would deliver her as he had Daniel from the lions, Jonah from the whale and the Hebrew children from the furnace. Gregory continues, "Recalling these and other circumstances and imploring the Virgin Mary to bring her assistance, since she, too, was a virgin and had been in danger, she [Justina] entrusted herself to the remedy of fasting and sleeping on the ground."[17]

Faults in Mary. Sign and guardian of the incarnation, example to and special protector of consecrated virgins—this Cappadocian understanding of Mary stands squarely in the Alexandrian tradition of Athanasius, whose roots lie in Origen. And following Origen, they point out that on at least one occasion, while standing at the foot of the cross, Mary's faith lapsed.[18] When confronted by the cross, Mary doubted. She was a daughter of Adam and Eve who themselves had doubted and then disobeyed.

Far from being chosen because of her virginal purity, God's choice of Mary required an extraordinary gracious act of purification in order that she might be made a vessel fit for the Son of God. In a short description of the incarnation, Gregory of Nazianzus states the matter simply: "Conceived by the Virgin, *who first in body and soul was purified by the Holy Spirit* (for it was needful both that

---

[15]Gregory of Nazianzus *Moral Poems* 1 (Gambero, *Mary and the Fathers,* p. 163).
[16]Gregory of Nazianzus *Moral Poems* 1 (Gambero, *Mary and the Fathers,* p. 163).
[17]Gregory of Nazianzus *Sermon* 24 9-11 (Gambero, *Mary and the Fathers,* pp. 166-67).
[18]Basil *To Optimus the Bishop* 9 (*NPNF*^{2} 8:299).

childbearing should be honored and that virginity should receive a higher honor), he came forth then as God with that which he had assumed, one person in two natures, flesh and spirit, of which the latter deified the former."[19] Far from being an exception to the rule that all have sinned and fallen short of God's glory, Mary's exceptional status is the result of a gift of purifying grace at or before the incarnation.[20]

Although the Western concept of original guilt is absent, there is a notion of original sin in which Adam left the entire human race condemned to death. Naturally Mary shares in this condemnation. In and of herself, she is one of us. It is only through the extraordinary working of the Holy Spirit that she was delivered from corruption such that the Son of God could assume her full humanity without thereby becoming contaminated by the disease of sin universally present after the Fall of Adam.

John Chrysostom (ca. 344-407). Until now, we have focused exclusively on those three of the four Eastern church fathers known collectively as the Cappadocians. The fourth, John Chrysostom, deserves to be treated singly for three reasons. First, unlike the Cappadocians, John represents the Antiochene school of theology.[21] Although John the Golden Mouth defends the Nicene Creed, he resists speculation, focusing on literalistic exegesis and moral exhortation. Second, for these reasons he is the only Greek father extensively quoted by the Reformers. Indeed, he is second only to Augustine. He thus may represent a point of access to Eastern theology for Protestant readers. Third, John is willing to ascribe faults to Mary to a degree beyond what we have seen thus far, including Tertullian.[22]

As fervently as the Cappadocians, John asserts the reality of the incarnation, insists upon the Davidic descent of Mary and makes use of the Eve-Mary motif.[23] He is especially concerned to defend Mary's perpetual virginity, arguing that virginity *ante partum* is both foreshadowed by the barren women and predicted

---

[19]Gregory of Nazianzus *On the Theophany* 13 (*NPNF*[2] 7:349 [emphasis added]).

[20]Gregory of Nyssa *To Eustathia, Ambrosia, and Basilissa* (*NPNF*[2] 5:543-44).

[21]A rival to the theology of Alexandria, Antioch is in many ways its antithesis. With respect to hermeneutics, where the former heavily relied on allegorical interpretations of the Old Testament, the latter stressed the plain meaning of the text. In Christology, where the former emphasized the divine assumption of human nature in the incarnation, the latter stressed the humanity of Jesus Christ. In preaching and writing, where the former tended toward mysticism and speculation, the latter emphasized practical Christian living.

[22]Ambrose Agius, "The Problem of Mary's Holiness in the First Christian Centuries," *Marian Studies* 14 (1963): 49.

[23]For these three points, see John Chrysostom *Commentary on the Psalms* (trans. Robert Charles Hill [Brookline: Holy Cross Orthodox Press, 1998], 1:260-61); "Homily II" 7 (*NPNF*[1] 10:11); and *Commentary on the Psalms* 1:271.

by the Old Testament prophets.[24] Virginity *post partum* is inferred from Joseph's righteous character confronting the miracle of Jesus' birth and Jesus' command to John from the cross.[25] Mary's marriage served to protect her from Jewish wrath.[26] His description of Jesus' birth as "a new sort of travail, and a childbearing so strange" likely alludes to virginity *in partu*.[27]

John's defense of the central Marian claims is matched by his ascription of fault to her. First, Chrysostom advances a minor criticism. Mary was unaware of Jesus' identity: "Even the pregnant Virgin did not know the ineffable truth of the divine plan, his brethren did not believe in him, and the man who passed for his father imagined nothing particular about him. And why mention human beings? He escaped notice of the devil himself."[28] Much more serious is Chrysostom's understanding of Mary's request at Cana: "For in fact that which she had essayed to do [i.e., provoke a miracle], was of superfluous vanity; in that she wanted to show the people that she hath power and authority over her Son, imagining not as yet anything great concerning him; whence also her unseasonable approach."[29] Mary's conduct at Cana was deceitful manipulation: "She desired both to do them a favor and through her Son to render herself more conspicuous; perhaps too she had some human feelings like his brothers, when they said, 'Show yourself to the world' [cf. Jn 7:4], desiring to gain credit from his miracles."[30]

Chrysostom's motives for such harsh words lie in the tendency in the Antiochene school generally, and in his homilies specifically, toward moral exhortation. It seems that John is taking advantage of Matthean and Johannine silence about Mary's motives in order to apply the text to listeners in Constantinople. Apparently, he felt it necessary to remind them that she herself is human, that she herself stands in need of salvation and that like her so do they. This much is made plain:

> Her having borne him would have nothing availed her, had she not been very good and faithful. Now if, setting aside the excellence of her soul, it profited Mary noth-

[24]On barren women, see John Chrysostom "Quarante-neuvième homélie sur la Genèse" (in *Oeuvres complètes de S. Jean Chrysostome*, trans. M. L'Abbé Joly [Paris: Bordes Frères, 1864], 3:443). On the prophets, see John Chrysostom "Commentair sur Isaie" 7 (in *Oeuvres complètes de S. Jean Chrysostome*, trans. M. L'Abbé Joly [Paris: Bordes Frères, 1867], 8:60). See also "Homily V" 4 (*NPNF*[1] 10:33).

[25]John Chrysostom "Homily V" 5 (*NPNF*[1] 10:33).

[26]John Chrysostom "Homily II" 1 (*NPNF*[1] 10:15). See also "Homily IV" 5 (*NPNF*[1] 10:22).

[27]John Chrysostom "Homily V" 5 (*NPNF*[1] 10:33).

[28]John Chrysostom *Commentary on the Psalms* 1:351.

[29]John Chrysostom "Homily XLIV" 1 (*NPNF*[1] 10:278-79). Though the reference is to Jn 2, Chrysostom is actually expounding on Mt 12:46-50.

[30]John Chrysostom "Homily on St. John XXI" 2 (*NPNF*[1] 14:74).

> ing that the Christ was born of her, much less will it be able to avail us to have a father or a brother, or a child of virtuous and noble disposition, if we ourselves be far from his virtue. . . . We must place our hopes of salvation in nothing else, but only in our own righteous deeds (done) after the grace of God.[31]

For John, Mary's feet remain firmly on the ground, and because of that her conduct can serve both as a caution and an example to future generations of believers.[32]

Latin Doctors

Ambrose of Milan (ca. 337-397). Moving from East to West, writings on Mary become more circumspect in two almost contradictory ways. On the one hand the Latin church fathers hesitate to embrace the East's exalted language. On the other hand, however, the Latin fathers recoil from speculation about Mary's supposed lapses. Both trends are evident in the works of Ambrose of Milan. Although he "spoke of the Virgin Mary with a frequency and to a degree that were unusual up until then,"[33] he rarely uses the Latin translation of *Theotokos: Mater Dei*. In his extant writings it is found only twice, while phrases like *the Lord's mother* are more numerous.[34] He did affirm the doctrinal implications of the title in Cappadocian terms.[35] Ambrose's reluctance stems not so much from the title itself as it does from the desire to avoid any appearance of a regression to the *Magna Mater* cult of pre-Christian Rome.[36]

At the same time Ambrose represents the beginning of Western reluctance to ascribe any fault or sin, not because the dignity of Mary's motherhood had separated her from the human race, but because she was the mother of Christ's (sinless) humanity.[37] Christ's humanity was Mary's humanity. Because Christ's humanity was a full humanity, Mary must be one of us. Because Christ's humanity was free from sin, preserving grace must have been operative in Mary's life in a unique way to preserve her also.[38] Nowhere is this grace more evident than

---

[31]John Chrysostom "Homily on St. John XXI" 2 (*NPNF*[1] 14:75).

[32]Hilda Graef, *Mary: A History of Doctrine and Devotion*, vol. 1: *From the Beginnings to the Eve of the Reformation* (London: Sheed & Ward, 1963), p. 76.

[33]Brian Ramsey, *Ambrose*, The Early Church Fathers (London: Routledge, 1997), p. 51.

[34]Graef, *Mary*, 1:78. Compare Ambrose of Milan's "Duties of the Clergy" 1.69 (*NPNF*[2] 10:13) and "Concerning Virgins" 2.3.21 (*NPNF*[2] 10:376) with his "Concerning Virgins" 2.2.7 (*NPNF*[2] 10:374).

[35]Ambrose "On the Decease of Satyrus" 1.12 (*NPNF*[2] 10:163). See also "Of the Christian Faith" 1.12.77-78 (*NPNF*[2] 10:214); and "Concerning Virgins" 1.5.21 (*NPNF*[2] 10:366).

[36]Graef, *Mary*, 1:77.

[37]Ambrose "The Sacrament of the Incarnation of Our Lord" 9.104 (FC 44:257).

[38]Ambrose "The Sacrament of the Incarnation of Our Lord" 9.104 (FC 44:257).

in Mary's *ante partum* virginity.[39] She was uniquely sanctified by the Spirit of her Son;[40] sinless indeed, but sinless only by grace.[41] As a result, from the time of Jesus' conception, Mary committed no sin, but was an example of zeal and devotion. So firm was her faith that not even the cross, which was an occasion for scandal for the disciples, could shake it. In words that seem consciously to challenge the East, Ambrose contends that

> when the apostles fled, she stood at the cross, and with pious eyes beheld her Son's wounds, for she did not look for the death of her offspring, but the salvation of the world. Or perchance, because that "royal hall" [a title for the Virgin found elsewhere in Ambrose] knew that the redemption of the world would be through the death of her Son, she thought that by her death also she might add something to the public weal. But Jesus did not need a helper for the redemption of all, who saved all without a helper. . . . He received indeed the affection of his mother, but sought not another's help.[42]

Given Ambrose's high view of Mary, the second half of this citation merits closer inspection. Whatever role Mary plays, it is not coredeemer, for such would impugn the sufficiency of Christ's work. Ambrose is aware of the danger that adoration of Mary may blur into worship: "Mary was the temple of God, not the God of the temple. And therefore he alone is to be worshiped who was working in his temple."[43]

Ambrose thus represents Western reluctance. Yet he is also more. His Mariology also includes three new elements. The first new element is his presentation of Mary as the ascetic ideal. The principal text, *Concerning Virgins,* was assembled in response to a request from his sister, Marcellina, for definite teaching on virginity. Its three books praise virginity as a form of Christian life superior to marriage and widowhood;[44] offer examples of virginal conduct, the chief of whom is the Virgin Mary; and give advice. The second book, where our attention is drawn, reflects on Mary's life before the annunciation, describes her conduct during Gabriel's visit, speaks of her pious life with Joseph and considers her heavenly role as the representative of all consecrated virgins. "This

---

[39]Charles William Neumann, *The Virgin Mary in the Works of Saint Ambrose,* Paradosis 17 (Fribourg: University Press, 1962), p. 78.

[40]Ambrose "On the Christian Faith" 4.9.114 (*NPNF*^{2} 10:277).

[41]Agius, "Problem of Mary's Holiness," p. 57.

[42]Ambrose "Letter LXIII" 110 (*NPNF*^{2} 10:473).

[43]Ambrose "Of the Holy Spirit" 3.11.80 (*NPNF*^{2} 10:146).

[44]Ambrose clearly believes virginity to be a holier form of life than either marriage or widowhood. What is unclear is whether he means thereby to denigrate the latter two. "Concerning Widows" 4.23-24 (*NPNF*^{2} 10:395) contains remarks that seem to indicate that he does not wish to deny the goodness of marriage.

whole development is envisaged as a rule of life illustrating how virgins should conduct themselves; to show them the courage with which they should defend their virginity unto death."[45]

Ambrose writes with such passion that he leaves himself open to two misinterpretations: either that Mary had always been a model for consecrated virginity or that he invented the notion.[46] With respect to the latter, *Concerning Virgins* is deeply dependent upon Athanasius's *Letter to the Virgins* to the point of textual transposition: "Let, then, the life of Mary be as it were virginity itself, set forth in a likeness, from which, as from a mirror, the appearance of chastity and the form of virtue is reflected. From this you may take your pattern of life, showing, as an example, the clear rules of virtue: what you have to correct, to effect, and to hold fast."[47] Ambrose is not an innovator. Rather, his uniqueness lies in his desire to bring what he believes to be the glory of Egyptian asceticism to the West and especially to his sister.

Not only is Ambrose the first Western theologian to make this case, but he also does so distinctively by associating Mary's exemplary conduct with her *ante partum* virginity. Although Ambrose affirms Mary's virginity *in partu* and *post partum* in the strongest way, these are treated as miracles unique to mother of the Savior. They are doctrinal matters. Contrarily Ambrose believed Mary's virginity *ante partum* to be so obvious that doctrinal apology was unnecessary;[48] its significance lay in its moral force and may be seen in this description of the Virgin's youth:

> She was unaccustomed to go from home, except for divine service, and this with parents or kinsfolk. Busy in private at home, accompanied by others abroad, yet with no better guardian than herself, as she, inspiring respect by her gait and address, progressed not so much by the motion of her feet as by step upon step of virtue. But though the Virgin had other persons who were protectors of her body, she alone guarded her character; she can learn many points if she be her own teacher, who possesses the perfection of all virtues, for whatever she did is a lesson. Mary attended to everything as though she were warned by many, and fulfilled every obligation of virtue as though she were teaching rather than learning.
>
> Such has the Evangelist [Luke] shown her, such did the angel find her, such did the Holy Spirit choose her. Why delay about details? How her parents loved her, strangers praised her, how worthy she was that the Son of God should be born of her. She, when the angel entered, was found at home in privacy, without a com-

---

[45]Neumann, *Virgin Mary,* p. 45.
[46]Ibid., p. 3.
[47]Ambrose "Concerning Virgins" 2.2.6 (*NPNF*^{2} 10:374).
[48]Neumann, *Virgin Mary,* p. 67.

> panion, that no one might interrupt her attention or disturb her; and she did not desire any women as companions, who had the companionship of good thoughts. Moreover, she seemed to herself to be less alone when she was alone. For how should she be alone, who had with her so many books, so many archangels, so many prophets?
>
> And so, too, when Gabriel visited her, did he find her, and Mary trembled, being disturbed, as though at the form of a man, but on hearing his name recognized him as one not unknown to her. And so she was a stranger as to men, but not as to the angel; that we might know that her ears were modest and her eyes bashful. Then when saluted she kept silence, and when addressed she answered, and she whose feelings were first troubled afterward promised obedience.[49]

The pattern that consecrated virgins are to emulate is drawn exclusively from Mary's life before and during the annunciation, because it is here that she most resembles those to whom Ambrose writes.[50]

The second new element of Ambrose's Mariology is his extensive defense of Mary's *in partu* and *post partum* virginity against Jovinian and Helvidius, respectively. Jovinian reacted against a wave of asceticism spreading through the Western church for some time by challenging it. While such challenges were not lacking,[51] Jovinian's were uniquely theological. Directed against the denial of the goodness of creation evident in much of the early ascetic movement, Jovinian defended the authenticity of Christ's humanity, promoted the earthiness of the Old Testament and the goodness of marriage and challenged an overemphasis on the authority of the devil in the created world. He did so by arguing that Christ's birth was a fully human one and accordingly that Mary lost her virginity in the act of giving birth.[52] Marriage and virginity were equally worthy vocations; the baptized were invincible against the malice of the devil.

While Jovinian's "primary concern is not to attack virginity or abstinence as legitimate Christian practices, but to reject the view that asceticism was a higher and truer form of the Christian life, a view which he believed led inevitably to Manicheism,"[53] the manner in which he did so set himself in opposition not only to those ascetics who were world-denying Manicheists but also to those who

---

[49]Ambrose "Concerning Virgins" 2.2.9-11 (*NPNF*^{2} 10:375).

[50]Neumann, *Virgin Mary,* p. 69.

[51]According to David Hunter, fourth-century "parents objected to losing their children to the monastic life; emperors opposed the flight of citizens who were escaping curial duties; even slaves objected to their masters' ascetic renunciation for fear of being sold on the open market" ("Resistance to the Virginal Ideal in Late-Fourth-Century Rome: The Case of Jovinian," *Theological Studies* 48 [1987]: 45-46).

[52]Ibid., p. 51.

[53]Ibid., pp. 49-50.

wished to channel the enthusiasm in Christian ways. Their champion, Ambrose, mounted the most extended and powerful defense of Mary's virginity *in partu* seen thus far: Mary's *in partu* virginity is a matter of biblical record, one that does not deny Christ's humanity, but affirms the uniqueness of the incarnation.

While Matthew and Luke clearly teach Mary's *ante partum* virginity, the same cannot be said for her virginity *in partu*. As a result Ambrose's consideration of New Testament material is very short. He notes simply that both evangelists cite Isaiah 7:14 (Mt 1:23; Lk 1:31) and observes that the prophetic utterance predicts both. He reads "the virgin will be with child" (Is 7:14) as a straightforward prediction of Christ's virginal conception and accordingly Mary's virginity *ante partum*. The phrase "and will bring forth a son" is a further prediction of her virginity *in partu*.[54] Old Testament material, however, abounds. According to Ambrose, *in partu* virginity can be inferred when the story of Miriam is read as a foreshadowing of the story of Mary: "In the Old Testament, a Hebrew virgin [Miriam] led an army through the sea; in the New Testament a king's [David's] daughter was chosen to be the heavenly entrance to salvation."[55] As well, Ambrose contends that Isaiah (cf. Is 11:1-5) and Ezekiel (cf. Ezek 44:20) foresaw the miracle.[56] Jovinian's denial of the miraculous preservation of Mary's virginity in the act of giving birth is a denial of Holy Scripture, worthy of censure.

What of Jovinian's contention that virginity *in partu* ultimately denies the reality of the incarnation and the authenticity of Christ's humanity? Ambrose answers that the miracle is a further sign of his deity by removing from the incarnation any possibility of the taint of original sin. Charles Neumann summarizes Ambrose well at this point:

> Christ chose to come into the world by an *unused* way, an altogether *new* one including *also* a birth which, like his conception, was *immaculate*. Ambrose's thought here attains Mary only through Christ, and it is not centered on her *immaculateness* (whatever sense the word would have here if it applied to Mary) but on her corporal integrity. He does not want to assert that Mary was kept immaculate because she was to give birth to Christ, but rather that for Christ to be immaculate (i.e., sinless) he had to be born from one who remained a virgin—a virgin in conception and even in birth.[57]

It is very difficult to avoid the conclusion that Ambrose not only holds virginity to be superior to marriage, but is indeed suspicious of human sexuality alto-

---

[54]Ibid., pp. 105-6.

[55]Ambrose "Synodal Letters" 44 (FC 26:228).

[56]Ambrose "On the Holy Spirit" 2.5.38 (*NPNF*[2] 10:119). See also "Patriarchs" 4.19 (FC 65:252-53).

[57]Neumann, *Virgin Mary,* p. 161.

gether. That sexuality even within marriage is the occasion for the generation of original sin is inferred from a married couple having fallen.[58] The sinlessness of Christ's humanity accordingly demanded that Mary remain a virgin in the strongest possible sense of the word. And as the Virgin Mother, Mary uniquely possesses the greatest joys of womanhood—virginity and birth—while lacking the usual means of moving from one to the other—sex.

Like Jovinian, Helvidius also wanted to affirm the goodness of creation and human sexuality within marriage. Unlike Jovinian, he did so by denying virginity *post partum*. His revival of Tertullian's notion that Mary sanctified virginity and marriage as Christian vocations clashed with those who, while affirming marriage, held virginity to be superior. Although Helvidius's most famous opponent is Jerome, he also provoked Ambrose to write. Helvidius "implied a weakness of will in Mary who was unable to keep a virginity already miraculously secured."[59] As a result, if Helvidius's argument was correct, the presentation of Mary as model virgin was not. Ambrose had to respond.

Ambrose did not marshal an argument similar to that employed earlier by Gregory of Nyssa, who insisted that Mary's words in Luke 1:34 implied a lifelong vow of virginity. He understood her words to apply only to her past. In saying "how can this be, since I know I am a virgin?" Mary meant simply that to that point in her life, she had remained a virgin. There was no vow to exclude sexual relations in the future.[60] Rather, Ambrose develops an alternative sixfold explanation for the necessity of Mary's unconsummated marriage to Joseph: (1) Such a marriage would preserve Mary's reputation and prevent any possible punishment for the crime of adultery. (2) It would legitimate Jesus in the eyes of the Jews and remove any justification for killing him. (3) It would permit Joseph to be a constant witness to her purity. (4) Without it Mary would have been forced to act dishonestly to shield her pregnancy from others. (5) It would allow Jesus to mature under the nose of the devil, awaiting his revelation in the fullness of time.[61]

A sixth argument warrants closer attention. Ambrose follows Athanasius in reading John 19:25-27 as proof that Mary had remained a virgin. Why, they both reasoned, would Jesus entrust his mother to John if she had other children to care for her needs? Ambrose's unique twist to this position was his conviction that Joseph remained alive at the time of Jesus' death. If so, Jesus' action, at least in Ambrose's eyes, clearly proves that Joseph's marriage to Mary was never con-

---

[58]Ambrose "Letters to Priests" 59 (FC 26:332-33).
[59]Neumann, *Virgin Mary,* p. 221.
[60]Ibid., p. 101.
[61]Ibid., pp. 82-84. See the full discussion on pp. 184-235.

summated[62] and that after Jesus' death she did not "seek the consolation of being able to bear another son."[63]

The third new element of Ambrose's Mariology is his articulation of an ongoing role for Mary in the divine economy. Although the points of comparison vary with the circumstances (virginity in general, virginal motherhood, virginity *in partu* or spousal relation to Christ), she is the type and image of the church:[64]

> Well [does the Gospel say]: married but a virgin; because she is the type of the Church, which is also married but remains immaculate. The Virgin [Church] conceived us by the Holy Spirit and, as a virgin, gave birth to us without pain. And perhaps this is why holy Mary, married to one man, is made fruitful by another [the Holy Spirit], to show that individual churches are filled with the Spirit and with grace, even as they are united to the person of a temporal priest.[65]

Both Mary and the church are virgin mothers whose fertility depends on the Holy Spirit. Mary personifies the church, for when Christ was conceived in her womb, so were all who where his.[66] Now in heaven, she is the "royal" or "heavenly" palace, whose pondering of God's Word and works has rendered her the storehouse of those divine mysteries.[67]

Jerome (331-419). Like Ambrose, Jerome follows in the Western tradition in two ways.[68] First, Mary exemplifies Christian holiness in Jerome's homilies,[69] letters and doctrinal treatises. Like Ambrose, Jerome insists that believers emulate Mary's surpassing purity: "Set before you the blessed Mary, whose surpassing purity made her meet to be the mother of the Lord."[70] The emergence of Pelagianism (the view that humans can earn salvation through their own obedience to God's law) in the Western church, however, compels Jerome to insist more strongly that the purity for which God selects Mary is itself God's gracious gift.[71] Since Mary even in her exalted state needs grace, and precisely for that reason, she can be held up for emulation.

Second, Jerome's exaltation of consecrated virginity to a position superior to

---

[62]Ibid., p. 189.

[63]Ambrose "Letter LXIII" 111 (*NPNF*² 10:473).

[64]Neumann, *Virgin Mary,* p. 76.

[65]Ambrose *Epositio in Lucam* 2.7 (trans. Gambero, *Mary and the Fathers,* p. 198).

[66]Graef, *Mary,* 1:86.

[67]Neumann, *Virgin Mary,* pp. 195-96.

[68]The similarity is partly caused because both Jovinian and Helvidius were reckoned to be opponents.

[69]See, e.g., Jerome "Homily 93: On Easter Sunday" (FC 57:247); "Homily 88: On the Nativity of the Lord" (FC 57:225).

[70]Jerome "To Eustochium" 38 (*NPNF*² 6:39).

[71]Jerome "Against the Pelagians" 1.16 (*NPNF*² 6:457).

that of Christian marriage all too easily slips into the view that sexuality within marriage is evil. Consequently Mary's virginity is sometimes presented as a necessary step in the creation of Christ's sinless humanity:

> To show that virginity is natural while wedlock only follows guilt, what is born of wedlock is virgin flesh, and it gives back in fruit what in root it has lost. "There shall come forth a rod out of the stem of Jesse, and a flower shall grow out of his roots" [Is 11:1 Septuagint]. The rod is the mother of the Lord—simple, pure, unsullied; drawing no germ of life from without but fruitful in singleness like God himself. The flower of the rod is Christ.[72]

In both Jerome and Ambrose, although the connection between Christ's sinless humanity and Mary's virginity is unclear, it is established.

And yet Jerome does not merely plow in Ambrose's furrows; he shows his uniqueness first by using the Bible exclusively to establish his claims. While the *Protevangelium of James* was popular in the empire (especially in the East), Jerome rejects it because it contradicts the canonical accounts of Jesus birth:

> No midwife assisted at his birth; no women's officiousness intervened. With her own hands she wrapped him in the swaddling clothes, herself both mother and midwife, "and laid him," we are told, "in a manger, because there was no room for them in the inn"; a statement which . . . refutes the ravings of the apocryphal accounts, for Mary herself wrapped him in the swaddling clothes.[73]

While the *Protevangelium of James* is not directly named, the references to "midwife" and "women's officiousness" leave little doubt that it is at least included in the "ravings" that Jerome refutes. He insists that the limits of his Mariology be strictly biblical. To speculate is to invite error. This minimalist hermeneutic is nicely summarized in this way: "As we do not deny what is written, so we do reject what is not written."[74]

Jerome's highly developed understanding of the Blessed Virgin draws the bulk of its material from the Old Testament. He avoids allegory, choosing instead more textually based strategies. He presents an argument for understanding *'almah* to mean "virgin" in Isaiah 7:14, for example, not by arguing for what counts as a miracle or a sign but by examining how the word is used elsewhere in the Bible.[75] More common, however, is his insistence that the

---

[72]Jerome "To Eustochium" 19 (*NPNF*^{2} 6:29). See also "Commentaire abrégé sur les Psaumes" 77 (in *Oeuvres complètes de Saint Jérome, prêtre et docteur de l'église,* trans. L'Abbé Bareille [Paris: Vivès, 1884], 11:558).

[73]Jerome "Perpetual Virginity of Blessed Mary: Against Helvidius" 10 (*NPNF*^{2} 6:339).

[74]Jerome "Perpetual Virginity of Blessed Mary: Against Helvidius" 21 (*NPNF*^{2} 6:344).

[75]Jerome "Against Jovinian" 1.32 (*NPNF*^{2} 6:370).

meaning of the Old Testament is found in the New:

> Jesus has entered in through the closed doors, and in his sepulcher—a new one hewn out of the hardest rock—no man is laid either before him or after him. Mary is "a garden enclosed . . . a fountain sealed" [Song 4:12], and from that fountain flows, according to Joel, the river which waters the torrent bed either of cords or of thorns [Joel 3:18 Septuagint]. . . . She is the east gate, spoken of by the prophet Ezekiel, always shut and always shining, and either concealing or revealing the holy of holies [Ezek 44:2-3]; and through her "the sun of righteousness" [Mal 4:2], our "high priest after the order of Melchizedek" [Heb 5:10], goes in and out. Let my critics explain to me how Jesus can have entered in through closed doors when he allowed his hands and his side to be handled, and showed that he had bones and flesh, thus proving that his was a true body and no mere phantom of one, and I will explain how the holy Mary can be at once a mother and a virgin. A mother before she was wedded, she remained a virgin after bearing her Son.[76]

> The title-superscription of this psalm is: "When his land was restored to him." Since it says, "was restored," it is evident that the land had been his before, was afterwards lost, then recovered again. What land is this that was restored to David? David's land is holy Mary, the mother of the Savior: "who was born to him according to the flesh of the offspring of David." The promise made to David was fulfilled in the virginity of Mary and in her childbearing, when a virgin was born of a virgin. The announcement of the Gospel: "The Word was made flesh, and dwelt among us," thus came to pass, so that what had been promised to David was restored to us through holy Mary.[77]

In the first quotation, Jerome justifies his rereading of the prophets and wisdom literature by alluding to New Testament accounts of Christ's postresurrection appearances. Similarly, Psalm 96 is understood to be prophetic, finding its fulfillment in the Gospel.

While such allusions to Mary may be found throughout Jerome's commentaries, homilies, letters and doctrinal treatises, he is justly famous for the first Western work devoted to the Virgin Mary. Titled *Against Helvidius,* it is a sarcastic apologetic against Helvidius's ideas. For example, where Helvidius alleges that Matthew 1:25 challenges those who advocate that Mary and Joseph remained only betrothed, Jerome is scornful:

> I know not whether to grieve or laugh. Shall I convict him of ignorance, or accuse him of rashness? . . . If I choose to say . . . (as I certainly might) "Helvidius, before he repented, was cut off by death," . . . must Helvidius repent after death, although the Scripture says "in sheol who shall give you thanks?" Must we not rather under-

---

[76] Jerome "To Pammachius" 21 (*NPNF*[2] 6:78-79).
[77] Jerome "Homily 73: On Psalm 96 (97)" (FC 57:109).

> stand that the preposition *before,* although it frequently denotes order in time, yet sometimes refers only to order in thought? So that there is no necessity, if sufficient cause intervened to prevent it, for our thoughts to be realized. When, then, the Evangelist says *before they came together,* he indicates the time immediately preceding marriage, and shows that matters were so far advanced that she who had been betrothed was on the point of becoming a wife. . . . It does not follow . . . that he had intercourse with Mary after her delivery, when his desires had been quenched by the fact that she had already conceived.[78]

Should Helvidius then appeal to human experience, observing that to become betrothed but forego a proper marriage is truly exceptional, Jerome agrees and offers three reasons that warrant such an exceptional arrangement:

> If anyone feels a doubt as to why the Virgin conceived after she was betrothed rather than when she had no one betrothed to her . . . let me explain that there were three reasons. First, that by the genealogy of Joseph, whose kinswoman Mary was, Mary's origin might also be shown. Second, that she might not in accordance with the law of Moses be stoned as an adulteress. Third, that in her flight to Egypt she might have some solace, though it was that of a guardian rather than a husband.[79]

Indeed, Joseph himself is to be regarded as a consecrated virgin because, contrary to the claims of the *Protevangelium of James,* there is no biblical account of Joseph's first marriage; because there is no biblical indication that Joseph's "marriage" to Mary moved past betrothal; and because only a truly righteous man—that is, one uncontaminated by sex—would be a truly fit partner for the Virgin.[80] The "brothers" of Jesus—following the legitimately loose meaning of *adelphoi*—are Jesus' cousins: sons of Mary's sister.

Jerome's seeming denial of Mary's virginity *in partu* is therefore striking. Where Ambrose was convinced that the doctrine was biblical and bolstered belief in the uniqueness of the incarnation, Jerome—although he (wisely) does not deny it outright—does not affirm it, presumably because of its origins outside the biblical canon. When Helvidius objects that those who affirm Mary's virginity

---

[78]Jerome "Perpetual Virginity of Blessed Mary: Against Helvidius" 4 (*NPNF*^{2} 6:335-36). A similar argument, probably with Helvidius in mind, is advanced regarding the word *firstborn* in Mt 1:25: "From this passage, some perverse spirits have concluded that Mary had other children; 'Is he not called *firstborn,* they ask, to indicate that he had brothers?' But the Holy Scriptures always use *firstborn* not to indicate that one has siblings, but that he is born first" (Jerome "Commentaires sur l'évangile du saint Matthieu" [in *Oeuvres complètes de Saint Jérome, prètre et docteur de l'église* 9, trans. L'Abbé Bareille (Paris: Vivès, 1881), p. 533 (my translation)]).

[79]Jerome "Perpetual Virginity of Blessed Mary: Against Helvidius" 4 (*NPNF*^{2} 6:336). See also "Homily 88: On the Nativity of the Lord" (FC 57:224).

[80]Jerome "Perpetual Virginity of Blessed Mary: Against Helvidius" 21 (*NPNF*^{2} 6:344).

post partum should also affirm her virginity *in partu,* since both are ashamed and fearful of the human realities of sex and birth, Jerome does not reply directly. Rather, he seems to say that the natural birth of the Son of God is part of the humiliation he accepted in the incarnation:

> Add, if you like, Helvidius, the other humiliations of nature, the womb for nine months growing larger, the sickness, the delivery, the blood, the swaddling clothes. Picture to yourself the infant in the enveloping membranes. Introduce into your picture the hard manger, the wailing of the infant, the circumcision on the eighth day, the time of purification, so that he may be proved to be unclean. We do not blush, we are not put to silence. The greater the humiliations he endured for me, the more I owe him. And when you have given every detail, you will be able to produce nothing more shameful than the cross, which we confess, in which we believe, and by which we triumph over our enemies.[81]

The most that can be argued is that Jerome regards Mary's virginity *in partu* as an attempt to speculate beyond what the Bible reveals about Mary's virginity, namely, that she was a virgin before Christ was conceived and remained a virgin afterward. Whatever happened in between is a mystery akin to the risen Lord's entry into the house though the doors were locked (cf. Jn 20:19, 26).[82]

Augustine of Hippo (354-430). Augustine of Hippo continues to influence Western disciplines as diverse as philosophy, political theory, psychology and spirituality. The trained ear can still hear Augustinian themes buried in the many variations that have accrued over fifteen centuries. Much the same can be said about his Mariology. As he draws on the wealth of Christian teaching and adds his own distinctives, Augustine gives Western Mariology its modern shape. In future debates—whether about the immaculate conception in the medieval era or the bodily assumption and the reforms of Vatican II in the modern era—the form of Western Mariology remained unchanged.

Regarding Mary's perpetual virginity, Augustine holds that she is "a virgin in conceiving, a virgin in giving birth, a virgin when with child, a virgin on being delivered, a virgin forever."[83] This robust understanding stresses Mary's *ante partum* virginity; it then grounds virginity *in partu* and *post partum*. Augustine understands Mary to have taken a lifelong vow of virginity, a vow to be emulated by later generations of monastics.[84] If this vow were to have been broken at any-

---

[81]Jerome "Perpetual Virginity of Blessed Mary: Against Helvidius" 20 (*NPNF*^{2} 6:344).

[82]See Jerome "Homily 87: On the Gospel of John 1.1-14" (FC 57:217-18).

[83]Augustine "Sermon 186: On Christmas Day" 1 (in *Sermons III/6 [184-229Z] on the Liturgical Seasons,* trans. Edmund Hill, Works of Saint Augustine: A Translation for the 21st Century [Hyde Park, N.Y.: New City Press, 1993], p. 24).

[84]Augustine "Of Holy Virginity" 4 (*NPNF*^{1} 3:418).

time, its moral force and Mary's exemplary status would have been lost; therefore, it must have been miraculously preserved, even as Mary delivered Jesus, and maintained throughout her life. As a result, "Joseph might be called the husband of Mary, though she was his wife only in affection, and in the intercourse of the mind, which is more intimate than that of the body."[85] Through Mary's vow Augustine binds together all three stages of Mary's perpetual virginity and emphasizes the primacy of her virginity at the time of her conception. So plainly taught in Holy Scripture, Mary's virginity needs no further argument to establish it.[86] In fact, Augustine cautions against anything less than a full-blooded affirmation: "No one could say without violation of the Christian faith, that perhaps Christ was born of a virgin."[87]

An inconsistency then emerges. On the one hand Augustine acknowledges that Mary's virginity is neither logically nor theologically necessary for the incarnation to have taken place: "The reason for our believing him to have been born of the Virgin Mary is not that he could not otherwise have appeared among men in a true body, but because it is so written in the Scripture, which we must believe in order to be Christians, or to be saved."[88] God did not need the Virgin for the incarnation, but found it fitting to choose her in order to provide hope for salvation for both men and women through a work of recapitulation.[89]

On the other hand Augustine attributes necessity to Mary's virginity. Against the Pelagians, he argued that the sin of concupiscence—which is often understandably and inaccurately reduced to sexual lust, but is better termed disordered desire—lies at the root of original sin. The Fall of humanity is the corruption of the desires of Adam and his wife. Eating the forbidden fruit is but the sign of a Fall that has already happened. This disordered desire—and its consequences: guilt and death—is then passed on from parent to child, like a genetic disease, corrupting all of Adam and Eve's children. Although concupiscence lies behind every sin, it is so present in the sexual act that it is passed from parent to child at the instant of conception. Accordingly Christ must be conceived in a way that prevents this concupiscence from being passed to his humanity:[90] "He came of this flesh, but he came not as other men. For the Virgin conceived him not by lust, but by faith."[91]

---

[85]Augustine "Reply to Faustus the Manichean" 23.8 (*NPNF*[1] 4:315). See also "Sermon I" 26 (*NPNF*[1] 6:255) for similar remarks.

[86]Augustine "Reply to Faustus the Manichean" 26.7 (*NPNF*[1] 4:323).

[87]Augustine "On the Trinity" 8.5.7 (*NPNF*[1] 3:119).

[88]Augustine "Reply to Faustus the Manichean" 26.7 (*NPNF*[1] 4:323).

[89]Augustine "Sermon I" 3 (*NPNF*[1] 6:246).

[90]Augustine "On Marriage and Concupiscence" 13 (*NPNF*[1] 5:269).

[91]Augustine "Sermon XIX" 4 (*NPNF*[1] 6:316). See also "Sermon 214: On the Handing Over of the Creed" 6 (in *Sermons III/6 [184-229Z] on the Liturgical Seasons,* p. 154) for similar remarks.

The inconsistency remains unresolved. Moreover, it creates a new dilemma concerning the nature of Christ's humanity. If Mary is conceived such that her humanity is infected with original sin and Mary really is Jesus' mother, such that her humanity is his, how does even a virginal conception preserve Christ's humanity from the effects of the Fall? Augustine's answer is not worked out systematically, but combines notions of both salvation and predestination:

> [Christ] never had any sin, nor did he assume a flesh of sin, though born of a maternal flesh of sin. For what he then took of flesh, he either cleansed in order to take it, or cleansed by taking it. His Virgin Mother, therefore, whose conception was not according to the law of sinful flesh (in other words, not by the excitement of carnal concupiscence), but who merited by her faith that the holy seed should be framed within her, he formed in order to choose her, and chose her in order to be formed from her.[92]

This gracious act ensured that Mary would be a fit vessel for the Son of God, first in her heart and then in her body,[93] to the degree that Augustine thought Mary never actually sinned.[94] Mary, like all human beings, stands in need of redemption but, because of God's predestining and saving grace, her redemption is uniquely worked out in relation to her singular motherhood. Thus Augustine sets the stage for the famous medieval debates about the immaculate conception (see chap. 8).

Augustine draws a close connection between Mary and the church. Prima facie, there is an obvious resemblance in that both Mary and the church are virgin mothers.[95] The relationship, however, goes much deeper than that. Because she is a believer she is the sister of all disciples, and at the same time because she is Christ's physical mother she is linked in a mysterious yet maternal way to all those who are members of his body, the church:

> And on this account, that one female, not only in the Spirit, but also in the flesh, is both a mother and a virgin. And a mother indeed in the Spirit, not of our head, which is the Savior himself, of whom rather she was born after the Spirit: forasmuch as all, who have believed in him, among whom is herself also, are rightly

---

[92]Augustine "Treatise on the Merits and Forgiveness of Sins and on the Baptism of Infants" 38 (*NPNF*[1] 5:60). See also "On the Gospel of St. John" 8.9 (*NPNF*[1] 9:61) and "Sermon XIX" 4 (*NPNF*[1] 6:316) for similar remarks.

[93]Indeed, Augustine asserts that Mary's motherhood in itself is not sufficient for her salvation: "What profit was there in that being of kin? Thus also her nearness as a Mother would have been of no profit to Mary, had she not borne Christ in her heart after a more blessed manner than in her flesh" ("Of Holy Virginity" 3 [*NPNF*[1] 3:418]).

[94]Augustine "On Nature and Grace" 41 (*NPNF*[1] 5:135).

[95]Augustine "Of Holy Virginity" 2 (*NPNF*[1] 3:417). See also "Sermon 192: On Christmas Day" 1 (in *Sermons III/6 [184-229Z] on the Liturgical Seasons,* p. 47).

> called "children of the bridegroom": but clearly the mother of his members, which are we: in that she wrought together by charity, that faithful ones should be born in the church, who are members of that head: but in the flesh, the mother of the head himself.[96]

With Augustine, Western Mariology comes into its mature form. Mary is regarded as the perpetual Virgin who, even as she stood uniquely in need of the salvation accomplished by her Son, was his sinless mother. Furthermore, she is intimately connected to the church both as its prototype and as the mystical mother of all members of Christ's body. Whatever medieval (and indeed modern) developments take place, this fundamental shape will remain unaltered.

Capstones East and West

With the form (and a great deal of the content) of Mariology now securely in place, it remains only to mention three capstones that will cement the arguments above: the Council of Ephesus, John of Damascus[97] and Leo the Great.

Council of Ephesus (431). The Council of Ephesus is the first to deal expressly with Mary. Unfortunately, the debate is clouded by factors such as the rivalry of Alexandria and Constantinople, the competing theologies of Alexandria and Antioch, the combative personalities of Cyril and Nestorius and imperial intervention.[98] The controversy began when Proclus, a priest with Alexandrian tendencies, on December 23, 428, in the cathedral of Constantinople with his patriarch, the Antiochene Nestorius, present, proclaimed that

> we have been assembled by the holy Mary, the stainless jewel of virginity, the rational paradise of the second Adam, the workshop of the unity of the natures [scil., of Christ], the scene of the saving contract, the bridal chamber, in which the Word espoused the flesh, the living bush, which was not burnt by the fire of the divine birth [cf. Exod. 3.2ff.], the truly light cloud that bore him who is above the cherubim together with his body, the fleece cleansed by the dew from heaven [cf. Judges 6.37ff.], from which the shepherd put on [the garment of] the lamb, servant and mother, virgin and heaven, the only bridge between God and men [a metaphor frequently used by the later Fathers], the awesome loom of the "economy" on which

---

[96]Augustine "Of Holy Virginity" 5-6 (*NPNF*[1] 3:418-19).

[97]John of Damascus, who is "out of date" by some three centuries, is included in this discussion for two reasons. First, in the East, the patristic era lasted much longer than it did in the West because of the security provided by the Byzantine Empire, which itself lasted until the fifteenth century. Second, after the Eastern church fathers, John is the most influential Eastern theologian on Western developments, not only in Mariology, but in theology generally.

[98]A full account of the controversy may be found in Susan Wessel, "Nestorius, Mary, and Controversy in Cyril of Alexandria's *Homily IV* (*De Maria deipara in Nestorium*, cpg 5248)," *Annuarium historiae conciliorum* 31 (1999): 1-49.

> the garment of union [of Christ's two natures] was woven in ineffable manner, the weaver of which is the Holy Spirit, the spinner the overshadowing power from on high, the wool Adam's ancient fleece, the woof the stainless flesh of the Virgin, the comb the measureless grace of the bearer [of that flesh] the artist the Word that went in through the ear. . . .
>
> I see the miracles and proclaim the Godhead; I see the sufferings and do not deny the manhood. Emmanuel has, indeed, opened the gates of nature, because he was man, but he did not break the seals of virginity, because he was God. As he had entered through the hearing, so he went out from the womb [i.e., without violating it]; he was born as he was conceived; he had entered without passion, he went forth without corruption. . . . Behold, an exact description of the holy Theotokos Mary![99]

With our survey of the Greek and Latin church fathers completed, we should not be surprised at such extravagant language. The same cannot be said for Nestorius, whose immediate and public response inveighed against those who called Mary *Theotokos*. The term confused a right notion (the Word is indissolubly united to the one born from Mary) with a wrong one (the ascription to the eternal Son of a measured period of time).[100] He proposed instead the term *Christotokos* in order to clarify that while Mary was indeed the mother of that to which the Word was joined, she was in no way the mother of the deity.

Nestorius failed for historical and practical reasons. Historically *Theotokos* was too well established in Constantinopolitan piety to be overturned even by a bishop's decree (worship wars, it seems, are not a twentieth-century evangelical Protestant invention). Furthermore the term had been given a christological formulation by the Cappadocians in the previous century with Gregory of Nazianzus's rejection of one who denies that *Theotokos* is thoroughly christological. Such a view invariably denies either Christ's humanity or divinity and is thereby excluded from orthodoxy. Practically Nestorius faced an opponent as theologically brilliant as he was politically and ecclesiastically ruthless: Cyril.

For Nestorius, the matter was one of piety: *Theotokos* resembled pre-Christian paganism, portraying Mary as a thinly veiled mother goddess. For Cyril, on the other hand, the issues were christological and soteriological:

> They grant the word *"Theotokos,"* which the holy fathers who preceded us devised and applied to the holy Virgin, an illegitimate and inept term, or rather one that goes beyond all reasonable language. They bisect the one Lord Jesus Christ, dividing him into two separate sons, and remove from God the Word the sufferings of

---

[99]Quoted in Graef, *Mary,* 1:102-3.

[100]Wessel, "Nestorius, Mary, and Controversy," p. 18, quoting Nestorius "Sermono xxvii: In commemorationem sanctae Mariae, cum prious concionatus esset Proclus."

> the flesh, even though we have certainly not said that he suffered in his own nature, by which we conceive of him as god, but rather have attributed to him along with the flesh the sufferings that befell the flesh, so that he too should be acknowledged as the Savior.[101]

Cyril thought the Nestorian position advanced two sons: Son of God and son of Mary, the former impassible and immortal while the latter suffered and died. Remaining true to the Alexandrian linkage of salvation with assumption, Cyril countered that this denied the taking up of human nature by God the Son, leading invariably to the conclusion that God the Son was not born, did not grow, did not suffer, did not die and did not rise again as a human being. In his mind, if God the Son did not fully enter into human experience in these ways, then he was not the Savior.

The Cyrillian position affirmed the opposite: that from the instant of his conception, God the Son assumed a human nature and in that human nature was born, grew, suffered, died and rose again. Only the term *Theotokos* could affirm the unity of the natures in one person. Accordingly he writes: "We confess One Christ, One Son, One Lord. And it is with reference to this notion of a union without confusion that we proclaim the holy Virgin to be the mother of God, because God the Word was made flesh and became man, and by the act of conception united to himself the temple that he received from her."[102] Far from reviving the mother goddess, *Theotokos* directs believers to the mysterious union of human and divine in the one person.[103] In the end Cyril insists that Mary is not the mother of a nature—whether divine or human. She is mother of a person, and that person is the Son of God incarnate.

This is not to say that *Theotokos* says nothing about Mary. As Proclus's sermon indicates, there was a well-established devotion to Mary, which continues to cause concern among those Christians who, like Nestorius before them, find it to resemble goddess worship. There is much in Cyril's victory sermon that appears to justify such concerns:

> Hail from us, Mary, Mother of God, the venerable treasure of all the world, the inextinguishable flame, the crown of virginity, the sceptre of orthodoxy, the indissoluble temple, the place for the infinite, the Mother and Virgin; . . . Hail, the one who contains the uncontainable in the holy virginal womb, through whom the holy

---

[101]Cyril of Alexandria "Against Nestorius" (quoted from Norman Russell, *Cyril of Alexandria* [London: Routledge, 2000], pp. 131-32).

[102]Cyril of Alexandria *Commentary upon the Gospel According to S. Luke by S. Cyril, Patriarch of Alexandria* (trans. R. Payne Smith [Oxford: Oxford University Press, 1849], 1:8).

[103]Cyril of Alexandria "Second Letter to Nestorius" (in *Cyril of Alexandria: Select Letters,* ed. and trans. Lionel R. Wickham [Oxford: Oxford University Press, 1983], pp. 9-11).

> Trinity is glorified and venerated throughout the world, through whom heaven is exalted, through whom angels and archangels are delighted, through whom demons are banished, through whom the tempting devil fell from heaven, through whom fallen human nature is assumed into heaven, through whom all of creation, possessed by the madness of idolatry, came to the full knowledge of truth, through whom holy baptism came into being for all the faithful, through whom is the oil of exultation, through whom the churches have been founded for all the world, through whom the nations are brought to repentance. . . . Through whom the only begotten Son of God shined light for *those that sit in the darkness of the shadow of death;* through whom the prophets prophesied; through whom the apostles proclaim salvation to the nations; through whom the dead were revived; through whom kings reign, through the Holy Trinity. . . . The virginal womb; O thing of wonder! The marvel strikes me with awe! Who ever heard of a builder who, after he constructed his own temple, was prevented from dwelling in it? Who is insulted for having summoned his own servant into motherhood?[104]

Marian praise is consistently raised in the context of the mystery of the incarnation and is subservient to the worship of the Trinity. Mary is adored as the vessel through whom the second person of the blessed Trinity assumed a human nature.

Alongside such exuberant expressions of devotion, Cyril continues in the Eastern tradition of ascribing ignorance and doubt to the Mother of God.[105] Cyril's Mary may have been scandalized by the cross because of "the bitterness of Our Lord's death, the mockery of the Jews, the ribaldry of the soldiers, tossing up his clothes and laughing at the hanging figure in the very presence of his mother."[106] He exalts Mary and attributes fault to her because, lacking an Augustinian doctrine of original guilt, he does not need to exempt Mary from questionable conduct. Cyril simply does not understand the human condition in this way. For him, human beings were created good but imperfect. They are subject to physical and spiritual death because of Adam, but the guilt of Adam's sin is his own alone. In the Eastern view an imperfect Mary is granted a singular motherhood, and becomes worthy of all veneration appropriate to a created being. Perhaps those who are offended by Cyril's language are reading him through an Augustinian hermeneutic.

John of Damascus (died 750). While Cyril's intent was christological, his victory also legitimated and extended Alexandrian Marian piety. "In the East,

---

[104]Cyril of Alexandria "Homily IV" (trans. Wessel, "Nestorius, Mary, and Controversy," pp. 42-49; quotations at pp. 43, 45).

[105]Cyril of Alexandria *Commentary on Luke* 27-28.

[106]Agius, "Problem of Mary's Holiness," p. 54.

feasts multiply and devotion becomes even more fervent," writes Hilda Graef; "the death and decomposition of her body seem no longer compatible with the dignity of the Mother of God; both the feast of her passing and the affirmations of contemporary apocryphal writings lead the preachers to think out the implications."[107] The implications revolve around Mary's relationship to original sin—whether conceived in Eastern or Western terms.

Although raised from at least 377,[108] it is only after the Council of Ephesus that these questions are worked out by preachers in homilies based on the invocation and adoration of *Theotokos*.[109] But even here, the preachers of the East, of which John of Damascus is the greatest example, are not innovators. They find a vocabulary: that of Arianism.

Arius taught that Christ mediated God's salvation by providing humans with a perfect example of obedience to God.[110] The Athanasian party countered that the Savior could truly mediate between God and humans only if he were God. In so doing, the Athanasian party established that the mediatorial office of the Son of God was uncreated and hence beyond imitation.[111] But the language of example and exaltation, of *created* mediation, did not wither. It was reinvigorated by a transplanting of subjects. It was increasingly applied to Mary, first among the saints to be imitated and adored. Thus "what the Arians had taught about Christ, the orthodox now taught about Mary."[112]

This is evident in the homilies of John of Damascus, where Mary is a created mediator of the grace of God, first by being Jesus' mother. Or, as John of Damascus puts it in his homily on the nativity, she is the ladder that joins earth to

---

[107]Graef, *Mary,* 1:160-61.

[108]The date refers to the completion of the *Panarion,* a heresy-hunting handbook written by Epiphanius of Salamis, in which he admonished caution with regard to speculation about Mary's earthly end: "One will neither find the death of Mary, nor whether she died or did not die, whether she was buried or was not buried. . . . Scripture is simply silent because of the exceeding greatness of the Mystery, so as not to overpower people's minds with wonder. . . . If the holy Virgin died and was buried, her falling-asleep was honorable and her end holy; her crown consisted in her virginity. Or if she was put to death . . . her fame is among the martyrs and her holy body should be an object of our veneration, since through it light came into the world. Or else she remained alive; for it is not impossible for God to do whatever he wills. In fact, no one knows her end" (*Panarion* 78.11, trans. Brian E. Daley, *On the Dormition of Mary: Early Patristic Homilies* [Crestwood: St. Vladimir's Seminary Press, 1998], pp. 5-6).

[109]John Samaha, "Is There a Byzantine Mariology?" *Ephemerides mariologicae* 47 (1997): 103.

[110]Jaroslav Pelikan, *Mary Through the Centuries: Her Place in the History of Culture* (New Haven, Conn.: Yale University Press, 1996), p. 63.

[111]Ibid., p. 64.

[112]Adolf von Harnack, *Lehrbuch der Dogmengeschichte,* 5th ed. (Tübingen: Mohr, 1931), 2:477, quoted in Pelikan, *Mary Through the Centuries,* p. 64.

heaven, the mediator by which God comes to us.[113] As the vehicle through whom God entered his creation, Mary is worthy of a miraculous beginning and end. Anna had to be a barren mother because of the glory to be bestowed on her one daughter.[114] Indeed, both Joachim and Anna seem to have been the beneficiaries of a grace that preserved his semen and her womb from the effect of sin (i.e., spiritual corruption) in order that their daughter may be similarly protected.[115]

Of course, because John understands Mary to have been exempted from corruption from the instant of her conception, he finds it baffling that any would believe that she would undergo corruption's consequence—physical death.[116] If she did die, her death was as unique as her conception, with her body being placed by God beyond the reach of corruption.[117] The reasons that John advances are not so much dogmatic (and certainly not biblical) as they are reasons of "fittingness":

> It is fitting that she whose virginity remained intact while giving birth should have her body preserved from corruption even after death.
>
> It is fitting that she who carried her Creator as an infant in her womb should live in the tabernacles of heaven. . . .
>
> It is fitting that she who contemplated her Son on the Cross and received in her heart the sword of suffering which she had avoided while giving birth should contemplate him reigning with the Father.
>
> It is fitting that the Mother of God share in all that belongs to her Son, and be honored as the Mother and servant of God by all of creation.[118]

John simply cannot conceive that Mary was not in some way preserved from the wages of sin such that the redemption of her body either prevented or immediately followed upon her "falling asleep."

In heaven, finally, Mary continues in her mediatorial role, now as a queen.[119] Indeed, John goes so far as to pray

> We also, today, we remain in your presence, O Sovereign Lady, yes, I will repeat, Sovereign Lady, Mother of God and Virgin: We bind our souls to the hope that you

---

[113]John of Damascus "Sur la nativité" 3 (in *Homélies sur la nativité et la dormition,* trans. Pierre Boulet, Sources chrétiennes 80 [Paris: Cerf, 1998], p. 53). See also "Sur la dormition" 1.8 (*Homélies sur la nativité,* p. 105).

[114]John of Damascus "Sur la nativité" 2 (*Homélies sur la nativité,* p. 49).

[115]John of Damascus "Sur la nativité" 2 (*Homélies sur la nativité,* p. 49).

[116]John of Damascus "Sur la dormition" 1.10 (*Homélies sur la nativité,* p. 107).

[117]John of Damascus "Sur la dormition" 1.10 (*Homélies sur la nativité,* p. 109).

[118]John of Damascus "Sur la dormition" 2.14 (*Homélies sur la nativité,* p. 159).

[119]John of Damascus "Sur la nativité" 9 (*Homélies sur la nativité,* pp. 71, 73).

> are for us, like an absolutely firm and immovable anchor, to you we consecrate our spirit, our soul, our body, each of us wholly: we wish to honor you with those psalms, hymns and spiritual songs as are in us.[120]

John's praise is so lavish that the line between created and uncreated mediation blurs:

> Through her our worldly hostilities with the Creator have been brought to an end. Through her, our reconciliation with him is proclaimed, peace and grace were given, humans united their choirs with those of angels, and we became children of God who once were objects of wrath! Through her we have harvested the grape of life; from her we have received the seed of incorruptibility. All that is good has come to us through the mediatrix. In her God became man and humans become God.[121]

The last sentence is particularly interesting for it is a clear allusion to the Athanasian summary of the uncreated mediation of Christ: "He became human in order that humans might become God."

Leo the Great (ca. 400-461). If it is true that Augustine shaped Western Mariology, it is so because his position became the Western position when Leo the Great adopted and advanced it. The perpetual virginity of Mary (in its incarnational context), for instance, is affirmed in a letter to the bishop of Constantinople:

> He was truly conceived of the Holy Spirit within the womb of his Virgin Mother, who bore him while preserving her virginity just as, preserving her virginity, she conceived him. . . . Fecundity was given to the Virgin by the Holy Spirit, but the reality of the body was taken from her body. . . . He was born in a "new type of birth" in that undefiled virginity experienced no concupiscence, yet supplied the material for the flesh. From the Mother the Lord took his nature, but no fault; and the Lord Jesus Christ, born from a virgin's womb, does not have a nature different from ours just because his birth was an unusual one.[122]

This intervention was in fact predestined in the light of the Fall, from the beginning of the world.[123] Accordingly Mary's marriage to Joseph is to be regarded as divine sleight of hand, a means of hiding Christ's true identity from the devil.[124] From creation, Mary was predestined to be Virgin Mother of the fully divine, fully human Jesus Christ.

---

[120]John of Damascus "Sur la dormition" 1.14 (*Homélies sur la nativité,* p. 119 [my translation]).
[121]John of Damascus "Sur la dormition" 2.16 (*Homélies sur la nativité,* p. 165 [my translation]).
[122]Leo the Great "To His Dearly Beloved Brother, Flavian, Bishop of Constantinople (June 13, 449)" (FC 34:95, 97).
[123]Leo the Great "Sermon 22: 25 December 441 (Recension A)" (FC 93:80).
[124]Leo the Great "Sermon 22: 25 December 441 (Recension B)" (FC 93:82).

Leo closely associates human sexuality with the transmission of original sin, such that Mary's virginity is now regarded as a necessary to Christ's sinless humanity.[125] This in turn leads Leo and the Western tradition to depart from the East's view that Mary—even in her exalted state—remains one with the rest of humanity. Rather, she is the great exception over whom sin has no dominion. By remaining a virgin throughout her life, she remained aloof from all corruption.[126] Indeed, such was her confidence of her place in the divine plan that her faith never wavered.[127]

Finally, for Leo there is a natural affinity between the Virgin Mother of God and the virgin mother of all believers to the degree that the distinction between Mary and the church is obscured. This affinity is effected by the Holy Spirit: "By the same Spirit through whom Christ was born form the body of an undefiled mother, Christians are reborn from the womb of the Holy Church."[128] It is also inherent in the sacraments: "To every human being who is 'reborn' the water of Baptism is an image of the Virgin's womb—as the same Holy Spirit fills the font who also filled the Virgin, so that the mystical washing cancels in our case the sin which the holy Conception lacked entirely in theirs."[129]

Conclusion

We have spent the last two chapters surveying the first five centuries of the church (with the anachronistic but defensible inclusion of John of Damascus). In so doing, we have seen the two biblical themes of the reality and uniqueness of Mary's motherhood become so intertwined that it is now impossible to pry them apart. Whereas for the apostolic fathers the reality of Mary's motherhood was a means to assert the humanity of Jesus, by the time of the later fathers it has become a means to divinize Mary so that by the time of John of Damascus she is coming to be regarded as the sinlessly conceived Virgin Mother, Queen of Heaven, exempt from the consequences of sin, who continues to offer heavenly mediation for the sake of all her Son's brothers and sisters, for all her spiritual children. This is an important observation for a growing number of evangelicals who wish to leap over the near millennium of "medieval darkness" that separates the recovered theology of the Reformers from the so-called pristine theology of the patristic era. The medieval rationalists were not doctrinal inven-

---

[125]Leo the Great "Sermon 22: 25 December 441 (Recension B)" (FC 93:81-82). See "Sermon 24: 25 December 443" (FC 93:93) for similar remarks.

[126]Leo the Great "Sermon 21: 25 December 440" (FC 93:78).

[127]Leo the Great "Sermon 21: 25 December 440" (FC 93:77-78).

[128]Leo the Great "Sermon 29: 25 December 453" (FC 93:122).

[129]Leo the Great "Sermon 24: 25 December 443" (FC 93:95).

tors. They rigorously applied their minds to exploring the implications of a doctrinal structure already in place. They are neither to be faulted nor credited for the edifice that they inherited.

A disturbing undercurrent is the deep-seated suspicion of human sexuality (even as expressed within marriage) in the Western tradition as expressed by Ambrose and Jerome (though remarkably this theme is muted in Augustine). It is difficult at this point not to sympathize with the aims (at least) of Jovinian and Helvidius, who rightly sought to oppose the dualistic views of certain ascetics that ended up denying the goodness not only of sexuality but ultimately the goodness of creation. It is unclear whether the strategy of Ambrose and Jerome—namely, to channel the Manichean ascetic tendencies—succeeded in curbing them or in fact allowed the mainstream tradition regarding the goodness of creation to be subverted. Any modern attempt to recover Mary will have to face squarely the way in which the model-disciple motif has led to an inappropriate denigration of the goodness of marriage.

8

Queen Mother

Mary and the Medieval Imagination

Mariological infrastructure was set in the patristic period and filled out in Latin Christianity from the seventh to the fourteenth centuries. First, the Venerable Bede sets a baseline against which developments can be measured, while Peter Damian charts their direction from simplicity to complexity, from humble handmaid to courtly queen. Turning to early scholastic discussions, two themes emerge. The more dominant is Mary's purity as debates over the immaculate conception begin. The contributions of Anselm, Eadmer, Bernard of Clairvaux, Nicholas of St. Albans and Peter of Celle show that it was unfitting for the king's mother to commit any actual sins and, for some, to have been tainted by sin at all. A minor theme for all five writers is Mary's intercessory power before God. At points, Mary intercedes according to God's will; at others, she intercedes to bend it to her own. Both themes—purity and power—are also found in high Scholasticism in the work of Saint Thomas Aquinas, preceded by his teacher Albert the Great and succeeded by his Franciscan rivals: Bonaventure, William of Ware and John Duns Scotus. Emphasis again falls on Mary's purity as the immaculate conception debate moves into its mature form.

Early Middle Ages

Venerable Bede (ca. 672-735). The Venerable Bede was the first great English historian. He was also a biblical copyist, commentator, preacher, and preserver and transmitter of the patristic heritage.[1] What weaves these disparate tasks into

[1]These roles are explored more fully in Benedicta Ward, "Bede the Theologian," in *The Medieval Theologians: An Introduction to Theology in the Medieval Period,* ed. G. R. Evans (Oxford: Blackwell, 2001), pp. 57-64.

the fabric of one life is Bede's commitment to the evangelization of the English. Even his so-called secular works (i.e., biographies and histories) were to aid in the conversion of the tribes of the British Isles.[2] In the bull canonizing him, Pope Leo XIII in 1899 acknowledged Bede's efforts by placing him alongside the four Latin doctors of the church and giving him the title "Doctor Anglorum."[3]

Bede's remarks about Mary often echo patristic themes, concerns and even language, as seen in four examples. First, Bede repeats the ancient Eve/Mary motif: both were women, both were virgins, both had an angelic experience, both listened and obeyed the words of the angel who appeared to them. But where the proud actions of Eve introduced sin and death into the human family, Mary's humble acceptance led to the Savior's conception.[4] Second, Mary's virginity is the result of a vow,[5] necessary for the incarnation of the Son of God,[6] and perpetual.[7] Although not Joseph's son, Jesus is David's descendant through Mary.[8] Third, relatedly, their marriage, which is both real and chaste,[9] has nothing to do with Jesus' parentage, legal or otherwise, but providentially ensures Jesus' physical well-being and Mary's reputation.[10] Fourth, Simeon's sword prophesies Jesus' passion and Mary's grief, though Bede contradicts the Eastern tradition that such grief led to doubt or scandal.[11] He even reproduces patristic mistakes, such as an earlier copyist's misprint of Jerome's definition of the name Mary as *stella maris* ("star of the sea") rather than the original *stilla maris* ("drop of the sea").[12] Bede is intent on preserving a heritage on the verge of being forever lost.

Bede's unique contributions exalt Mary in muted language. His Marian piety is simple and biblically anchored. Mary is praised for her virginity, her mother-

---

[2]Ibid., p. 61.
[3]Ibid., p. 57.
[4]Bede "Homily I.3 on the Gospels" (*HG* 1:19-20, 30, 33).
[5]Bede "Homily I.3 on the Gospels" (*HG* 1:24).
[6]Bede "Homily I.5 on the Gospels" (*HG* 1:44); see also "Homily I.3 on the Gospels" (*HG* 1:22); "Homily I.6 on the Gospels" (*HG* 1:52-53); and "Homily I.14 on the Gospels" (*HG* 1:134).
[7]Bede "Homily I.5 on the Gospels" (*HG* 1:48); see also "Homily I.14 on the Gospels" (*HG* 1:135); and "Homily II.7 on the Gospels" (*HG* 2:61).
[8]Bede "Homily I.3 on the Gospels" (*HG* 1:20); see also "Homily I.6 on the Gospels" (*HG* 1:55).
[9]Bede "Homily I.5 on the Gospels" (*HG* 1:45-46); see also "Homily I.5 on the Gospels" (*HG* 1:48).
[10]Bede "Homily I.3 on the Gospels" (*HG* 1:21); see also "Homily I.19 on the Gospels" (*HG* 1:192); and "Homily II.1 on the Gospels" (*HG* 2:1).
[11]Bede "Homily I.18 on the Gospels" (*HG* 1:184).
[12]Bede "Homily I.3 on the Gospels" (*HG* 1:21). See also Hilda Graef, *Mary: A History of Doctrine and Devotion,* vol. 1: *From the Beginnings to the Eve of the Reformation* (New York: Sheed & Ward, 1963), pp. 162-63. In so doing, Bede introduced "Star of the Sea" into the Western Marian imagination, where its roots continue to run deep.

hood and her holiness.[13] When reflecting on the Magnificat, Bede concludes that Mary was the recipient of unique spiritual gifts that enabled her to wholly devote her interior life to God's praise and her exterior life to obedience to God's commands: "Her spirit exults in God her Savior since nothing among earthly things is pleasing to her, no superfluity of perishable things soothes her, nor does adversity break her down; but she takes delight only in the memory of her Maker, from whom she hopes for her eternal salvation."[14] Although true of all saints, it is especially so with Mary because of her motherhood. Only for her would Jesus be both Son and Lord. Bede deals only with Mary's earthly life. On her heavenly reign—by now a familiar Eastern idea—he is silent.

Standing generally within the Augustinian tradition, Bede has a strong sense of the universality and weight of human sinfulness. Only Jesus is untouched.[15] He freely speaks of Mary's need of purification to fulfill her role as the Mother of God: "In coming upon the Virgin, the Holy Spirit revealed in her the efficacy of his divine power in two ways: he purified her mind of all stain of vices, to the extent that [her] human weakness had suffered [them], so that she might be worthy of a heavenly child-bearing, and, by his operation alone he created in her womb the holy and venerable body of our Redeemer."[16] Mary stands with us in sin, freed from it only to bear the Son of God. Of course, such a gracious action freed Mary from the demands of the law. She, however, chose to forego such privileges for the sake of following Jesus' example.[17] This juxtaposition of divine exaltation and exemplary personal humility is the core of Bede's Mariology.[18] Mary's willingness to forego her privileges for our sakes[19] models religious devotion and physical chastity that, if followed, will lead people to the "heavenly fatherland."[20]

Chief among Mary's virtues is her acknowledgment of the primacy of grace in her life.[21] Although she can claim much, she chooses instead to defer to those of lower position, as she did with Elizabeth, treating her with the same humility as she did Gabriel.[22] Although granted insight into the events surrounding her, Mary does not utter a word, but waits for Jesus to reveal himself

---

[13]Bede "Homily I.3 on the Gospels" (*HG* 1:21-22).
[14]Bede "Homily I.4 on the Gospels" (*HG* 1:36).
[15]Bede "Homily I.3 on the Gospels" (*HG* 1:25).
[16]Bede "Homily I.3 on the Gospels" (*HG* 1:24).
[17]Bede "Homily I.18 on the Gospels" (*HG* 1:181).
[18]Bede "Homily I.3 on the Gospels" (*HG* 1:27).
[19]Bede "Homily I.4 on the Gospels" (*HG* 1:36-37).
[20]Bede "Homily I.4 on the Gospels" (*HG* 1:30-31).
[21]Bede "Homily I.4 on the Gospels" (*HG* 1:37).
[22]Bede "Homily I.4 on the Gospels" (*HG* 1:31).

at the appropriate time.[23] Only after Pentecost did Mary become an instructor, explaining everything that had taken place to those who wished to know.[24] In all this, Mary teaches Bede and his fellow monks how best to resist temptation: "Let us too, my brothers, imitate the Lord's holy mother; and by keeping all of our Lord and Savior's words and deeds in a steadfast heart, let us also, by meditating on them day and night, drive away the troublesome assaults of empty and harmful thoughts."[25]

This is not to say that the notion of Mary as a heavenly intercessor is unfamiliar to Bede. In his *Ecclesiastical History of the English People,* for instance, he recounts a conversation between Saint Wilfrid and a priest named Acca in which Wilfrid said that his life had been spared by the prayers and tears of Mary's intercession.[26] The notion of Mary interceding alongside and on behalf of the faithful was part of the piety in which Bede was raised. But it is not a major part. When placed over against the Marian praise of Saint John of Damascus—his Eastern contemporary—Bede's Mariology is modest indeed.

Peter Damian (1007-1072). Peter Damian hovers between the preservation of Christian civilization that marked Bede's era and the first stirrings of its renaissance in the twelfth and thirteenth centuries. Born in Ravenna, Italy, in 1007, very little is known about his early life. Historians place his entry into monastic life around 1035 at Fonte Avella. In 1043 he was elected prior of his congregation and in 1057 became cardinal. His life is marked by attempts to reform both his monastery and the larger church. In 1072, while returning to Fonte Avella from his hometown, Peter died in Faenza, at the monastery of Saint Mary. In 1828 he was canonized and declared a doctor of the church.

Peter Damian's Marian thought, found mainly in his letters, fits squarely within the doctrine of the incarnation. In what is a primer on Catholic Christianity, Peter insists to a new monk, Ambrose, that Mary was the mother of Jesus and, as such, the Mother of God.[27] He is also an avid defender of Mary's *ante partum* and *post partum* virginity, appealing to the patristic interpretation of Ezekiel 44:20 to prove that "both before and after giving birth she remained always inviolate."[28] He is equally certain of her *in partu* virginity, insisting that it is well within the redeemer's omnipotence to be born of Mary without opening

---

[23]Bede "Homily I.7 on the Gospels" (*HG* 1:69-70).
[24]Bede "Homily I.19 on the Gospels" (*HG* 1:193).
[25]Bede "Homily I.19 on the Gospels" (*HG* 1:193).
[26]Bede *Ecclesiastical History of the English People* 5.19 (ed. Bertram Colgrave and R. A. B. Mynors [Oxford: Oxford University Press, 1969], pp. 527, 529).
[27]Peter Damian "Letter 81" (FCMC 3:208, 220).
[28]Peter Damian "Letter 1" (FCMC 1:73).

her womb just as a ray of sunlight penetrates a glass pane without breaking it.[29] Mary's marriage to Joseph is a chaste one, a fact that Peter ingeniously uses to increase the number of generations from Jeconiah to Christ in Matthew's genealogy from thirteen to fourteen, resolving a textual difficulty.[30] His Mariology, moreover, is not simply theoretical. In "Letter 17" Peter stresses that a Ravenna nobleman should include the Magnificat in his evening prayers for the whole church in order to magnify the Lord at evening just as Mary did.[31]

So far Peter is in lockstep with Bede and the church fathers. We do, however, note a significant departure in two areas. The first has to do with Marian exaltation. For Bede, Mary was an example of humility; Peter's praise is far more fulsome. Using the title "Star of the Sea," Peter draws on the Western patristic emphasis on Mary's predestination: "Let the Gentiles be glad and the Jews exult; for the Sun has shone forth from the star, and the Maker of the Virgin has been formed in the Virgin his creature. The man who was formed in her was also the Highest Himself who established her."[32] He then employs decidedly Eastern images to describe just how the Virgin resembles a star. A star, he says, is fiery, is bright and clear, emits rays and shines in the night. Similarly, Mary burned with the presence of God in her womb. She is bright like the morning, fair as the moon and clear as the sun. She emits a ray, the Word of God, and as starlight leaves the star without destroying its integrity, so Jesus' birth did not compromise Mary's virginity. Last, she shines in the darkness, enlightening everyone and destroying heresies.[33]

In the same sermon Peter avers that Mary's gifts eclipsed those offered to Jesus by the magi. Where they offered gold, she gave Jesus "the gold of royal majesty," that is, Davidic ancestry. She also gave her own, superior, versions of frankincense and myrrh: the devotion of her pure spirit and the integrity of her pure body. She was so filled with the gifts of the Holy Spirit that she deserved the title "full of grace."[34] In all of this she serves as the pristine example in the

---

[29]Peter Damian "Letter 81" (FCMC 3:210-11).

[30]Matthew's genealogy is arranged as three paragraphs of fourteen generations (Mt 1:17). The last cycle, however, has only thirteen generations—a fact that Matthew apparently misses. Peter counters that because Joseph and Mary did not have sex, Mary counts as a generation in herself, thereby yielding the required fourteen generations and creating a symmetrical relationship with previous paragraphs ("Letter 36" [FCMC 2:67-69]). Ingenious exegesis, but whether it is good exegesis is another question entirely.

[31]Peter Damian "Letter 17" (FCMC 1:152).

[32]Peter Damian "Sermon for the Feast of Epiphany" (in *St. Peter Damian: Selected Writings on the Spiritual Life,* trans. Patricia McNulty [London: Faber & Faber, 1959], pp. 148-49).

[33]Peter Damian "Sermon for the Feast of Epiphany" (*Selected Writings on the Spiritual Life,* pp. 149-50).

[34]Peter Damian "Sermon for the Feast of Epiphany" (*Selected Writings on the Spiritual Life,* p. 153).

monastic pursuit of holiness. Peter even rewrites Scripture, applying words that once referred to Christ to his mother: "Such is our star, brethren, such is the Virgin Mary, the star of the sea, and because she has left us an example, that we should follow her steps [cf. 1 Pet 2:21], of such kind should our souls be."[35] Of course, this is a sermon, not technical theology. Nevertheless it suggests that the humble handmaid is, by the eleventh century, being replaced by the Heavenly Queen in Western Christianity.

This tentative conclusion is bolstered when we examine Peter's view of Mary's intercessions. "Letter 50" includes a prayer to Mary to be said morning and evening:

> I, miserable and unhappy man, confess to God and to you, holy and glorious Virgin Mary, and to all the saints of God, that through my own fault I have sinned grievously by pride, suggestion, pleasure, consent, in thought, word, and deed. Wherefore, I beseech you, most loving mother of God, and all you saints and chosen ones of God, in your goodness to pray for me, a miserable sinner. With all your intercession may almighty God have mercy on me, forgive all my sins, deliver me from all evil, preserve, encourage, and strengthen me in every good work, and may God free me from the chains of all my sins, and may Christ, the Son of God, bring me to life everlasting.[36]

This careful construction distinguishes between the roles of Mary as intercessor and Christ as Savior. Prayers such as these were no doubt familiar to Bede as well, as they were to the church fathers before him.

Peter, however, is not content to remain with this simple expression of piety. In "Letter 17" he relates a legendary tale that, even if false, conveys—so he believes—a deep theological truth. There was a cleric guilty of great sin. Sick, aware of his imminent death and fearing divine judgment, he turned to Mary for her help with a desperate plea:

> I know very well, O blessed Queen of Heaven . . . that in many ways I have offended you, and in my body have violated the seal of chastity and virginity, of which you are the mother. I have also involved myself in countless kinds of sin, and am not worthy to call on you, the sovereign of all purity, with my polluted lips. But, O gate of heaven, window of paradise, and true Mother of God and man, you are my witness that "seven times a day I praised you," and although I am a sinner, although I am unworthy, I did not cheat you any of the canonical hours in your honor.[37]

---

[35]Peter Damian "Sermon for the Feast of Epiphany" (*Selected Writings on the Spiritual Life,* pp. 149-50).

[36]Peter Damian "Letter 50" (FCMC 3:321).

[37]Peter Damian "Letter 17" (FCMC 1:157-58).

As the penitent finished his prayer, Mary appeared to him, comforted him and declared that God had forgiven him. Peter cannot vouch for the story's truth, but he still concludes that whoever perseveres in daily Marian observances, no matter how notorious his conduct, "will have the mother of the Judge as his helper and advocate in his day of need."[38]

What are we to make of this clear departure from the plain piety that had marked Bede's faith? Just this: Peter is not inventing doctrine (even as he may be telling a tall tale). He is merely catching up to expressions that had marked Eastern Christianity from before the time of John of Damascus. The most likely explanation for this Eastern infiltration is twofold. Geographically Peter in Italy was closer to Eastern Christianity than was Bede in Britain. Indeed, Byzantine monasteries had been established in Italy for centuries by Eastern monks fleeing the persecution of iconoclastic emperors. Culturally eleventh-century Italy was very different from eighth-century Britain. Political stability based on a landed aristocracy allowed Peter to voice an intuition transplanted from the Byzantine Empire, namely, the Queen Mother can influence her Son the king.[39]

A second conclusion needs also to be drawn. The association of Christ with justice and of Mary with mercy—a hallmark of the Marian piety against which the Reformers would react—is also present. If one fears the reaction of the righteous judge, says Peter, one must appeal to his merciful mother. Provided that Marian devotions have been maintained, the penitent will find in Mary's intercessions the ability to move Christ's heart from just wrath to forgiving love.

Even as Peter represents Western Marian piety coming alongside that of the East, however, Western theology continues to lag behind. It is only in the twelfth century, as monasteries add theological speculation to their task of cultural preservation, as universities emerge and as new monastic orders arise, that truly systematic theologians attempt to make sense of the Marian piety that defined the medieval era and indeed their own Christian lives.

Emergent Scholasticism

Anselm of Canterbury (ca. 1033-1109). Anselm of Canterbury embodied an uneasy combination of passionate Marian devotion and theological precision. Born in Aosta, Lombardy, around 1033, Saint Anselm is truly remarkable figure, rising during his lifetime from monk to prior to abbot to archbishop. While serving at the Abbey Bec, Anselm wrote two of his most famous works in philo-

---

[38]Peter Damian "Letter 17" (FCMC 1:158).

[39]See Jean Leclerq, "The Queen Mother in the Xth-XIIIth Centuries," *Word and Spirit* 10 (1988): 57-77.

sophical theology: the *Monologium,* a treatise on the nature of God, and the *Proslogium,* a prayer that contemplates the existence of God. Both works continue to invite study and inspire debate among contemporary theologians and philosophers of religion. In 1093 he was elected—tradition says by force—Archbishop of Canterbury. His tenure was marked by conflict with Norman Kings William Rufus and Henry I—and subsequent periods of exile. He died on April 21, 1109.

Our examination starts with three prayers to the Blessed Virgin Mary. Anselm informs us that one prayer became three because the first did not satisfy its unnamed petitioner and the second failed to satisfy Anselm himself. The third only "seems satisfactory for the moment."[40] The prayers debase the one who prays, exalt the Blessed Virgin and plead for her intercessions. They are deliberately constructed and vary in length. The first prayer, "when the mind is weighed down with heaviness,"[41] has five stanzas; the second prayer, "when the mind is anxious with fear,"[42] seven; and the third prayer, "to ask [Mary] for her and Christ's love,"[43] twenty. Both their length and contents are intended to produce contrition and love for Mary.[44] The first opens with Marian praise reminiscent of Peter Damian:

> Mary, holy Mary, among the holy ones the most holy after God. . . . Lady, shining before all others with such sanctity, preeminent with such dignity, it is very sure that you are not least in power and in honour. Life-bearer, mother of salvation, shrine of goodness and mercy, I long to come before you in my misery, sick with the sickness of vice, putrid with the ulcers of sin. . . . I look to you to convert me.[45]

Stanzas two and three follow in quick succession, with an ever bleaker description of the author's sinfulness and an ever more glorious description of the Blessed Virgin. The author wants the glorious lady, who surpasses angels in purity and saints in goodness, to cure his sins.[46] Yet, in stanza four he admits that his need to confess his sins is countered by his fear of exposure. Finally, in stanza five, however, true repentance takes place, and the Virgin is asked for her healing.[47]

The second prayer follows the same pattern and adds a new image: Mary and

---

[40]Anselm "To the Monk Gundulf" (in *The Letters of Saint Anselm of Canterbury,* 2 vols., trans. Walter Frölich, Cistercian Studies Series 96-97 [Kalamazoo: Cistercian, 1990], 1:121).

[41]Anselm "Prayer to St. Mary (1)" (in *The Prayers and Meditations of Saint Anselm,* trans. Benedicta Ward [New York: Penguin, 1973], p. 107).

[42]Anselm "Prayer to St. Mary (2)" (*Prayers and Meditations,* pp. 110-14).

[43]Anselm "Prayer to St. Mary (3)" (*Prayers and Meditations,* pp. 115-26).

[44]Anselm "To the Monk Gundulf" (*Letters of Saint Anselm,* 1:121).

[45]Anselm "Prayer to St. Mary (1)" (*Prayers and Meditations,* p. 107).

[46]Anselm "Prayer to St. Mary (1)" (*Prayers and Meditations,* p. 108).

[47]Anselm "Prayer to St. Mary (1)" (*Prayers and Meditations,* p. 109).

Jesus working together to save sinners. In the first stanza Mary is praised as a merciful refuge for saints and sinners whom the author approaches in great distress.[48] The second stanza then clarifies the nature of the refuge that Mary offers: she is a mediator who intercedes before "the all-powerful justice of the stern judge" and "the intolerable vehemence of his wrath." This image, however, is quickly set aside for one less threatening. If Jesus came to seek and save the lost, how can the "good mother of the man" despise and repel those who pray to her?[49] Both images coalesce to fuel the remainder of the prayer. In stanzas three to six mother and Son together overcome sin and save sinners, but sinners can find protection in the "kind mother" if they have offended the "good Son." Anselm seems unsure whether Jesus is merciful or wrathful, certain only that Mary is a sanctuary for all.[50] Finally, in stanza seven Anselm the rational theologian overpowers Anselm the Marian devotee just enough to conclude that while mother and Son save sinners together, they do so differently: "God, who was made the son of a woman out of mercy; woman who was made mother of God out of mercy; have mercy upon this wretch, you [Jesus] forgiving, you [Mary] interceding."[51]

Anselm was most satisfied by the final prayer, its twenty stanzas working out Mary's roles as intercessor and protector with greater theological precision. As an intercessor she is "exalted above all, after the highest of all, your Son, through your omnipotent Son, with your glorious Son, by your blessed Son."[52] Her power to protect exists only by virtue of "the salvation born of your [her] fruitfulness."[53] She is praised only insofar as she is a servant of Christ.[54] As such, she is our mother: "Blessed assurance, safe refuge, the mother of God is our mother. The mother of him in whom alone we have hope, whom alone we fear, is our mother. The mother of him who alone saves and condemns is our mother."[55] In stanzas fourteen to nineteen Anselm returns to the motif of Mary and Christ accomplishing salvation together according to their own roles. Christ saves while Mary intercedes with the Savior for her children. Both mother and Son are to be adored and served both in this life and the next.[56]

This close reading suggests three conclusions. First, in Anselm's Marian piety

---

[48]Anselm "Prayer to St. Mary (2)" (*Prayers and Meditations,* p. 110).
[49]Anselm "Prayer to St. Mary (2)" (*Prayers and Meditations,* p. 111).
[50]Anselm "Prayer to St. Mary (2)" (*Prayers and Meditations,* p. 112).
[51]Anselm "Prayer to St. Mary (2)" (*Prayers and Meditations,* p. 113).
[52]Anselm "Prayer to St. Mary (3)" (*Prayers and Meditations,* p. 116).
[53]Anselm "Prayer to St. Mary (3)" (*Prayers and Meditations,* p. 117).
[54]Anselm "Prayer to St. Mary (3)" (*Prayers and Meditations,* p. 120).
[55]Anselm "Prayer to St. Mary (3)" (*Prayers and Meditations,* p. 122).
[56]Anselm "Prayer to St. Mary (3)" (*Prayers and Meditations,* p. 126).

Mary is his lady. She is his mistress and the mother of his Lord, and he is her devoted servant and knight.[57] The image of the Queen Mother, once a Byzantine empress, has now become the thoroughly Westernized lady at the king's court. If the king is remote and terrifying, Anselm's lady can intercede on his behalf.[58] Second, while Mary is involved in salvation, she is not the Savior. She is to be exalted above all other creatures, only as a result of the one whom she bore and not her own achievements. Third, just how Mary exerts intercessory influence over her Son remains unclear. At points, it looks as though the merciful mother of the kind Son acts in accordance with his will. At others, it looks like the merciful mother of the just Son intercedes in order to soothe his wrath. Far from unique to Anselm, this confusion is a hallmark of medieval Marian spirituality.

Anselm's theology reins in his devotion at some points and lags behind it at others. Written between 1092 and 1094, *Cur deus homo* ("Why Did God Become Human?"), his best-known work, was Anselm's attempt to construct a doctrine of incarnation and atonement without recourse to Scripture in order to counter the objections of unbelievers—presumably Jews.[59] It presents itself as a dialogue between Anselm and Boso. At one point Boso asks how Christ can be sinless if his mother was conceived in concupiscence and therefore born with original sin.[60] Anselm answers that although Christ's humanity must have been sinless, he cannot say how. He speculates that Mary received the benefits of Christ's redemption before the incarnation in a manner similar to Old Testament saints and concludes that Mary's pure humanity from which Christ assumed his own is itself the gracious gift of her Son.[61]

This point is developed in *De conceptu virginali* ("The Virgin Conception"), written around 1098-1099. Anselm's Augustinian account understands original sin to be transmitted in procreation, not because sex is intrinsically evil but because fallen human parents have fallen human children.[62] Jesus' miraculous conception, freed from the laws of natural propagation,[63] preserves him from con-

---

[57]Graef, *Mary,* 1:213.

[58]Similar sentiments can also be found in Anselm's letters. See, e.g., "To Richard and Rohais" (*Letters of Saint Anselm,* 1:237); and "To Prior Baldric and the Other Monks of Bec" (*Letters of Saint Anselm,* 2:34).

[59]G. R. Evans, *Anselm,* Outstanding Christian Thinkers Series (Wilton: Morehouse-Barlow, 1989), p. 71.

[60]Anselm *Cur deus homo* 2.16 (in *Anselm of Canterbury,* trans and ed. Jasper Hopkins and Herbert Richardson [Toronto: Edwin Mellen, 1976], 3:118-19).

[61]Anselm *Cur deus homo* 2.16 (*Anselm of Canterbury,* 3:121-22).

[62]Anselm "Virgin Conception and Original Sin" 2 (*Anselm of Canterbury,* 3:145). To speak of original sin as a "something" is both unavoidable and incorrect. "It" is not an addition to human nature, but denotes the absence of "original justice."

[63]Anselm "Virgin Conception and Original Sin" 11-12 (*Anselm of Canterbury,* 3:159-60).

tracting original sin. Accordingly Mary's holiness is not necessary. It is, however, fitting. What is more pleasing than that the conception of the most pure man should have taken place in a most pure virgin?[64] God the Father gave her his only Son. God the Son chose her. God the Holy Spirit worked in her to accomplish the incarnation. As the beneficiary of this act of the triune God, Anselm cannot conceive that Mary would have sinned.

With respect to Mary's purity or holiness, Anselm's theology is modest. Like us, she was conceived in sin. Unlike us, she was graciously rendered sinless from birth. It is easy to miss that Anselm has taken a decisive step toward the immaculate conception: Mary was purified, he says, *in anticipation* of Christ's work on the cross.

Eadmer (ca. 1064-ca. 1124). The association of the immaculate conception with Britain is dated much earlier than the late medieval scholastic theologians. In perhaps what is one of the strangest quirks of history, the immaculate conception—with deep roots in Eastern Christianity—originates far from the Byzantine Empire, in England. Although it seems that Peter Damian had been influenced by Eastern monks, it is Eadmer, an Anglo-Saxon, who makes the first theological case for the doctrine that, by a singular work of grace, Mary was preserved from original sin. The historical evidence suggests a plausible narrative of this development.

The doctrine emerged to defend the feast of the conception of the Blessed Virgin Mary celebrated on December 8 or 9. While the feast of Mary's nativity (celebrating her holiness from birth) had long been observed in the West, in the eleventh century the feast of her conception was limited to the East's liturgical life. In addition to geographical, linguistic and political factors, this ignorance reflects the influence of Saint Augustine's writings on original sin, except in southern England where pre-Norman liturgical texts show that "the feast of the Conception was being celebrated from *c.* 1030 onwards."[65] That England, cut off from the rest of Europe, became the first Latin church to celebrate the holiness of Mary from the instant of her conception is due to several factors: revival of Eastern forms of monasticism throughout Europe around the year 1000, the emigration of Greek monks to cities along the Rhone Valley and eventually England and the pilgrimages of English celebrities to Rome from 1020 to 1030.[66]

After 1066 Lanfranc, the first Norman Archbishop of Canterbury, removed the

---

[64]Anselm "Virgin Conception and Original Sin" 17 (*Anselm of Canterbury,* 3:164-65).

[65]David Knowles, *The Monastic Order in England: A History of Its Development from the Times of St. Dunstan to the Fourth Lateran Council, 940-1216,* 2nd ed. (Cambridge: Cambridge University Press, 1963), p. 510.

[66]Ibid., pp. 510-11.

feast and those celebrating Anglo-Saxon saints from his liturgical calendar. Anselm followed suit. The suppression, however, did not last long. The feast of the conception was revived by Anselm's nephew (also named Anselm), the Abbot of Bury, around 1121. It soon spread to other southern monasteries and abbeys. Officially reinstated in 1129,[67] the feast's observance began to proliferate throughout England.

The first attempt to give the feast theological credence is Eadmer's tract "On the Holy Conception of Mary."[68] Eadmer, an Anglo-Saxon monk, defends the poor English who celebrated the feast prior to its abolition.[69] He acknowledges Scripture's silence on the matter and articulates the doctrine as one to be inferred from other, already accepted beliefs. Drawing on the piety that regarded Mary as a coworker with Christ in the work of redemption, he asserts that it is only proper for such a creature to have never been enslaved by sin.[70] Further, if Jeremiah could be known by God and if John the Baptist could be filled with the Spirit while in the womb, who dares to say that the "singular propitiation of the whole world and unique resting-place of the only Son of God"—that is, Mary—must lack the sanctifying grace of the Holy Spirit from her conception?[71] A sinless conception is appropriate to Mary's stature and in accord with biblical precedent.

But is it possible? Eadmer contends that it is. Just as it is possible for God to allow a chestnut to be formed surrounded by thorns but without being pricked by them, so it is possible for God to render a person naturally conceived immune to original sin.[72] And possibility is enough. For Eadmer—as for most medieval theologians—there was no sharp distinction to be drawn between God's power, God's will and God's act. If God could do something, he would. And if he would, then he did. "He has sufficient power," concludes Eadmer; "if, therefore, he willed it, he did it."[73]

It is on the basis of her immaculate conception that Eadmer regards Mary as queen of the entire universe,[74] standing between God and all that is not God.[75] Indeed, he conceives the relationship between her and her Son, or between her

---

[67]Ibid., p. 512.

[68]Eadmer *De conceptione santae mariae* (ed. H. Thurston and T. Slater [Herder: Freiburg, 1904]).

[69]Eadmer *De conceptione santae mariae* §1.

[70]Eadmer *De conceptione santae mariae* §9.

[71]Eadmer *De conceptione santae mariae* §9.

[72]Eadmer *De conceptione santae mariae* §10.

[73]Eadmer *De conceptione santae mariae* §10.

[74]Eadmer *De conceptione santae mariae* §11.

[75]Eadmer *De conceptione santae mariae* §14.

and God, in terms almost of rivalry. When Eadmer turns to the matter of intercession, he insists that Mary intercedes for sinners because Christ has died for them and that, just as Christ desires our salvation, so does she. At the same time, however, he begs Mary not to love God's justice too much, for that would deprive sinners of hope. He even asks her to free him from hell should Christ condemn him to it.[76] The careful lines drawn in the patristic era and affirmed by Anselm between created and uncreated mediation are obliterated. The result is well put by Hilda Graef: "It is never quite clear whether Mary always acts in accordance with the will of God or whether she is capable of bending it to her own."[77]

Many of Eadmer's contemporaries found his argument to be persuasive. The feast of the conception of Mary—along with Eadmer's defense thereof—spread across the channel to Normandy and eventually to Lyons, where it was pounced on by Saint Bernard of Clairvaux.

Bernard of Clairvaux (1090-1153). Born to Burgundian nobility at the end of the eleventh century, Bernard is an anomaly. A contemplative monk and abbot involved in politics (including leading a preaching tour to create support for what became the disastrous Second Crusade), a Roman Catholic saint admired by Reformers, a committed traditionalist and innovative theologian associated with the abbey at Clairvaux (he directly founded 163 monasteries and oversaw their expansion to 343), and an ardent Marian devotee—Bernard was a fierce opponent of the feast of the conception and its defense offered by Eadmer.

Bernard's Marian devotion is straightforward and unoriginal. To explore it in detail would be repetitive. He left four sermons on the feast of the assumption that praise the power of Mary's intercessions but never say whether the Virgin is, body and soul, in heaven. They do not deal with doctrinal speculation but with simple piety, with Mary as an intercessor—even mediator—between the faithful and her Son. In one sermon, he goes so far as to call her the "aqueduct" that carries the waters of divine grace to earth and the "neck" that connects the head (Christ) to the body (the church).[78] Her only biblical intercession, "they have no wine," models prayerful boldness tempered by simplicity and modesty.[79] Bernard's Marian devotion is well established.

His Marian devotion is not, however, uncritical. When word that a new feast had been established in Lyons, a baffled Bernard wrote a scathing letter to that

---

[76]Eadmer *De conceptione santae mariae* §§35-41.

[77]Graef, *Mary,* 1:220. See also Leclerq, "Queen Mother," pp. 68-72.

[78]Graef, *Mary,* 1:238.

[79]Bernard "The Steps of Humility and Pride" 22.53 (in *The Words of Bernard of Clairvaux,* vol. 5: *Treatises II,* trans. M. Ambrose Conway, Cistercian Fathers Series 13 [Washington: Cistercian/Consortium, 1974], pp. 79-80).

church's leadership, charging that this was to innovate "a rite of which the church knows nothing, of which reason cannot approve, and for which there is no authority in tradition." The feast was unknown, irrational and ungrounded. To institute it, therefore, smacks of hubris. "Are we more learned or more devout than the fathers?" he asks. "To introduce something which they, with all their prudence in such matters passed over in silence, is a most dangerous presumption."[80] Even if it was innocently introduced, the feast actually denigrates Mary by attributing to her a privilege she neither needs nor wants.[81] Furthermore, there is already a feast that celebrates Mary's purity. The feast of her nativity recalls that Mary "entered the world already holy because she had been sanctified in the womb."[82] In this she resembles and surpasses both Jeremiah and John the Baptist.[83] If such as these were sanctified before their birth, then it is certainly the case that God would have granted Mary a surpassing gift. Mary's sanctification, received before she was born, both commissioned and preserved her as sinless throughout her life.[84]

Not only is the feast of the conception of Mary unknown and unnecessary, the doctrine it invokes—the immaculate conception—is impossible. The issue is a straightforward matter of logic. All sides agree that Mary was holy before she was born. What remains to be resolved is the timing of her sanctification. Mary could not have been sanctified before her conception because before her conception she did not exist; Mary could not have been sanctified as she was conceived because all who are naturally conceived are conceived in sin. There remains only one option: Mary was sanctified at some point between her conception and birth. This sanctification both healed her of original sin and preserved her from actual sin, thereby rendering her birth holy.[85]

There is only one whose conception has been preserved from original sin—he whom the Blessed Virgin bore.[86] As a result, Mary—were she able—would abjure this feast: "Gladly will the mother of God forgo an honour by which either sin is honoured or by which a false holiness seems to be implied."[87]

Nicholas of St. Albans (died ca. 1174) and Peter of Celle (died ca. 1183). Bernard's opposition instigated a debate that would define the remain-

---

[80]Bernard "To the Canons of the Church of Lyons" (in *The Letters of St. Bernard of Clairvaux,* trans. Bruno Scott James [Kalamazoo: Cistercian, 1998], pp. 289-90).
[81]Bernard "To the Canons of the Church of Lyons" (*Letters of St. Bernard,* p. 290).
[82]Bernard "To the Canons of the Church of Lyons" (*Letters of St. Bernard,* p. 290).
[83]Bernard "To the Canons of the Church of Lyons" (*Letters of St. Bernard,* p. 291).
[84]Bernard "To the Canons of the Church of Lyons" (*Letters of St. Bernard,* p. 291).
[85]Bernard "To the Canons of the Church of Lyons" (*Letters of St. Bernard,* p. 293).
[86]Bernard "To the Canons of the Church of Lyons" (*Letters of St. Bernard,* p. 293).
[87]Bernard "To the Canons of the Church of Lyons" (*Letters of St. Bernard,* p. 293).

der of the medieval era. Unfortunately, although it often captured Eadmer's and Bernard's passion for their respective causes, it was seldom conducted with precision. Written about twenty years after Bernard's death, a correspondence between Nicholas of St. Albans and Peter of Celle demonstrates just how confused it could become. Nicholas (an Englishman) supports the English tradition while Peter (a Frenchman) opposes it. It is difficult to tell whether their rivalry is mainly theological or nationalistic.

In "On Celebrating the Conception of Blessed Mary, Against Blessed Bernard"[88] Nicholas declares that he cannot understand how opponents of the feast can allow that John the Baptist was filled with the Spirit before his birth and deny that Mary was conceived without original sin.[89] To the response that the former is a matter of biblical fact while the latter is attested by neither Scripture nor tradition, he counters that the church has the right to institute new feasts and doctrines and—quoting Bernard for support—insists that instituting something unknown to tradition need not subvert it.[90] Furthermore, the feast of the nativity of Mary is incomplete, affirming the sanctity of Mary from her birth, but leaving open the timing of the act. The feast of the conception answers this question. He further observes that Bernard rationally established the impossibility of a miraculous, immaculate conception and, drawing on a distinction between "natural conception" (which was possible only before the Fall) and "carnal desire" (which has marked human sexuality ever since),[91] argues against the Western tradition from Ambrose onward, that there is nothing necessarily sinful about sex. Mary could have been conceived naturally and yet preserved from original sin.[92]

A response has been preserved in a series of letters from Peter of Celle, "a monk of the Cluny reform and Abbot of St. Remy, who became Bishop of Chartres in 1181."[93] It seems that an initial epistolary debate has been lost, for when we take up the story, Peter writes that he is glad to hear that Nicholas is alive and wonders whether he has had time to correct "that error which arose not from hatred but from the highest, or more than highest, favour shown to the Virgin of virgins."[94] Nicholas's now-lost reply apparently made it clear that he

[88]The Latin edition of this treatise was first published by C. H. Talbot, "Nicholas of St. Albans and Saint Bernard," *Revue bénédictine* 64 (1954): 83-117.

[89]Nicholas "Incipit liber magistri nicolai de celebranda concepcione beate marie contra beatum bernardum" (quoted in Talbott, "Nicholas of Saint Albans," pp. 92-93).

[90]Nicholas "Incipit liber magistri nicolai," p. 95.

[91]Nicholas "Incipit liber magistri nicolai," p. 94.

[92]Nicholas "Incipit liber magistri nicolai," p. 115.

[93]Graef, *Mary,* 1:251.

[94]Peter "To Nicholas of St. Albans" (in *The Letters of Peter Celle,* trans. and ed. Julian Haseldine [Oxford: Oxford University Press, 2001], p. 577).

had not repented, and the friendly tone of Peter's initial letter vanishes. Now the defender of Saint Bernard,[95] Peter charges that Nicholas's fantasies lack a scriptural foundation. But he will not judge Nicholas too harshly. What more could one expect from an Englishman whose brain—made moist by the surrounding water—is given to fancy?[96] Peter will use his Gallic stability to lay out the truth. There is little content worthy of comment in a letter that amounts to page after page of nationalistic bombast. Its so-called argument boils down to two points: (1) by so exalting the Virgin, Nicholas has denied her her victory over sin. (2) To so demean Bernard, because of Bernard's own Marian devotion, is to attack Mary herself.

Nicholas's reply is only somewhat milder, and much of it may be safely ignored. With respect to Peter's second point, Nicholas observes that Bernard was canonized "so that we should not doubt his glory, but not so that we should dispute less about his sayings." Nicholas claims to "venerate the blessed confessor Bernard . . . [and] to praise and love his sanctity" even as he will "neither love nor praise his presumption concerning the mother of the Lord."[97] He follows with a tale in which, after his death, Bernard appeared to a fellow monk, his garments gleaming save for one dark spot. This, says the saint, was a sign of punishment for denying Mary's sinless conception.[98] As for the first point, Nicholas clearly scores. Bernard and Peter acknowledge the feast of Mary's nativity, affirming that Mary was sanctified before her birth and never sinned thereafter. How, then, did the Virgin conquer sin? Nicholas attempts several interpretations of Peter's point, but finds all to be nonsensical. He concludes that Mary "conquered every sin not by vanquishing all but by feeling absolutely none."[99]

In his final reply, Peter insists that he follows Jerome, Augustine and Mary herself, who professed that she was but the Lord's handmaid. Nicholas errs neither in his praise of the Virgin nor in the proclamation of her holiness, her position as Heavenly Queen, her sinlessness, her maternity or her intercessory power before God. On all these points Peter and Nicholas agree. But in the end Nicholas fashions a new teaching, and there Peter will not go: "I halt and do not cross the established limits. . . . I believe in the Gospel not in dreams about her, and if I am otherwise minded, God shall reveal this too."[100] Peter appears to be the picture of Marian modesty. It is therefore important to note that his Marian

[95]Peter "To Nicholas of St. Albans" (*Letters of Peter Celle,* p. 579).
[96]Peter "To Nicholas of St. Albans" (*Letters of Peter Celle,* p. 579).
[97]Nicholas "From Nicholas of St. Albans" (*Letters of Peter Celle,* p. 603).
[98]Nicholas "From Nicholas of St. Albans" (*Letters of Peter Celle,* p. 603).
[99]Nicholas "From Nicholas of St. Albans" (*Letters of Peter Celle,* p. 615).
[100]Nicholas "From Nicholas of St. Albans" (*Letters of Peter Celle,* p. 627).

praise would likely have incurred Bernard's wrath as well. In a sermon on Luke, Peter almost ascribes to her the attribute of transcendence by rewriting the biblical text with her in view: "In like manner it can also be said of the Mother: No-one knows the Mother except the Son, and to whom the Son will reveal her."[101] He even says that, were it possible, Mary could be assumed into the Trinity to create an "external quaternity."[102]

Peter and Nicholas show that while speculation and sharp disagreement about Mary's conception had begun, it was still very muddled. While theologians of stature such as Anselm, Eadmer and Bernard could think theologically and critically about the issues involved, most, like Peter and Nicholas, contented themselves with name calling. It is only in the High Middle Ages that the debate sharpens, especially in the classic medieval debate between the great Dominicans Albert the Great and Thomas Aquinas and their Franciscan equals: Bonaventure, William of Ware and John Duns Scotus.

High Scholasticism

Dominican school. Albert the Great (ca. 1193-1280). Study of Albert the Great's Mariology has been hampered for centuries by the mistaken attribution to him of the *Mariale.*[103] This thirteenth-century work reflects concerns similar to Albert's, chiefly, its denial of the immaculate conception.[104] At other points, however, the work explicitly departs from Albert's claims to affirm Mary's coredemptive role in salvation.[105] The value of the *Mariale* lies in its presentation of the medieval Marian imagination. Not only does it speculate on the sex, age and clothes of Gabriel, but argues from Mary's fullness of grace that she possessed all spiritual gifts, received six of the seven sacraments (all save ordination)[106] and had full knowledge of the Scriptures and of the doctrines of the Trinity, incarnation and her own predestination. She could "see" the immaterial world—angels, demons, souls and so on—and had full knowledge of

---

[101]Peter "Sermon 73" (Graef, *Mary,* 1:253).

[102]Peter "Sermon 13" (Graef, *Mary,* 1:253).

[103]The *Mariale* can be found in Albert *Opera omnia,* ed. Auguste Borgnet and Émile Borgnet (Paris: Vivès, 1890-1899), 37:1-362.

[104]Albert *Opera omnia,* 37:179-80 Q. 127.

[105]Albert *Opera omnia,* 37:219 Q. 150. Mary is the *adjutrix redemtionem* ("the helper of redemption").

[106]This is not to say that the medieval imagination denied Mary a priestly role. On the contrary, Anne L. Clark observes that Mary is often "a model for priestly purity, an analogy to priestly confection of the Eucharist, or as a sacrificial officiant at the presentation of her son at the Temple" ("The Priesthood of the Virgin Mary: Gender Trouble in the Twelfth Century," *Journal of Feminist Studies in Religion* 18 [2002]: 5. See also John M. Samaha, "Mary's Sacerdotal Role," *Homiletic and Pastoral Review* 100 [1999]: 10-17).

creation, including canon law, geography and astronomy.[107]

Albert's legitimate works are both more modest and more precise. Both qualities are evident in three theological treatises: "On the Incarnation," "On the Resurrection" and his "Commentary on the Sentences" of Peter Lombard. The first denies the immaculate conception and affirms Mary's sanctification before birth and personal sinlessness.[108] The second carefully distinguishes Mary's assumption from Christ's ascension. Mary was the passive object of the former act, Christ was the active subject of the latter.[109] The "Commentary on the Sentences," finally, ranks Mary higher than angels, but beneath God.[110] Mary is to be venerated as "the mother of the King," but not worshiped, for with respect to his divine nature he is begotten only of God.[111] Furthermore, whatever her intercessory role, Mary does not share in work of redemption.[112]

Apart from the desire to rein in the more extravagant claims of Marian piety, there is nothing remarkable about any of Albert's conclusions. Mary is Christ's sinless mother; she is assumed by her already-ascended son; however exalted, she is a creature beneath him. She intercedes, but he alone saves. Mary, for Albert, stands with her Son.

Albert's exegesis continues this christological orientation. In his commentary on Isaiah, for instance, Albert's description of Mary's sorrow at the cross says nothing of her helping Christ accomplish salvation.[113] If Mary helps at all, it is by providing an example of holy living to believers and acting as their (most effective) intercessor.[114] In his commentary on Luke, Albert rejects "apocryphal tales."[115] While he follows the medieval practice of reapplying Scripture that refers to Christ to Mary, he does so in a qualified and sensible way. For example, Colossians 2:9 applies to Mary, for the fullness of the Godhead did indeed dwell in her bodily while she carried the unborn Christ.[116] References to Mary as a container or aqueduct of grace or as a fountain of mercy are legitimate only because of her motherhood. Albert's notions concerning mercy and motherhood are still medieval.

---

[107]Albert *Opera omnia,* 37:280 Q. 193.

[108]Albert *Opera omnia,* 26:183-84.

[109]Albert *Opera omnia,* 26:287-88 Q. 9, arts. 4-5.

[110]Albert *Opera omnia,* 26:397 distinctio 44, art. 5.

[111]Albert *Opera omnia,* 28:181-82 distinctio 9, art. 9.

[112]Albert *Opera omnia,* 28:45 distinctio 3, art. 3.

[113]Albert *Opera omnia,* 19:110.

[114]Albert *Opera omnia,* 19:165. Mary is mother of believers, not because she experienced birth pains at the cross, but because "she conceived us in her heart at the same time as she conceived the divine Word in her womb" (trans. Graef, *Mary,* 1:277, citing Albert *Opera omnia,* 23:90).

[115]Albert *Opera omnia,* 22:5.

[116]Albert *Opera omnia,* 22:61.

With respect to the latter, Albert insisted that Christ was formed from Mary's blood[117] and that he was her Son and metaphorically her spouse.[118] As for the former, Mary's goodness extends to hell, where she invites sinners to repent.[119]

This final claim shows just how deeply the notion of the influential Queen Mother had penetrated even the most subtle and theologically proficient minds of the time. Albert will not ascribe to Mary anything beyond what can be vouchsafed by Scripture or patristic tradition. He subsumes his remarks under broadly christological categories. His acceptance of the pious notion that Mary has influence even on behalf of those in hell is inconsistent with such a method. If Mary can rescue those on whom Christ's judgment has been passed, then her influence can even rescind his judgment. If hell has an escape route in the Blessed Virgin, then Mary is no longer a channel of Christ's grace, but is an alternate redeemer capable of changing his will. This runs counter to Albert's otherwise fairly thorough christological orientation.

Thomas Aquinas (1225-1274). Albert's student, Saint Thomas Aquinas, is the greatest theologian of the medieval era and perhaps of all time. His writings on Mary are anything but controversial. If anything, he is more reticent than his teacher to venture beyond Scripture and tradition. If he does innovate, it is with an eye to explaining what the church already teaches rather than to developing new doctrine.

The first statement of Thomas's Mariology occurs in his "Commentary on Peter Lombard's Sentences" (written between 1254 and 1256), in which he treats her sanctification, pregnancy, annunciation and motherhood. Mary's sanctification took place in three steps. First, after her animation and before her birth Mary was cleansed from original sin and granted the ability not to sin.[120] A second sanctification at Christ's conception rendered her unable to sin. A third at her assumption completed the first two in heavenly glory.[121] Concerning her pregnancy, Thomas teaches that God compensated for the male seed, that is, the active principle by which the mother's passive matter is formed into a new human being,[122] thus ensuring that Christ would be conceived without original sin.[123] Third, Thomas contends that the annunciation was unnecessary but fitting. It allowed Mary to accept Christ with her mind before conceiving him in her body, granting her certainty

---

[117]Albert *Opera omnia,* 22:102.
[118]Albert *Opera omnia,* 22:103-4.
[119]Albert *Opera omnia,* 22:130.
[120]Thomas Aquinas *Opera omnia* (Paris: Vivès, 1871-1880), 9:49-52 §3.1.1.
[121]Thomas Aquinas *Opera omnia,* 9:52-56 §3.1.2.
[122]Thomas Aquinas *Opera omnia,* 9:56-60 §3.2.1-2.
[123]Thomas Aquinas *Opera omnia,* 9:65-70 §3.4.1-3.

about the events in which she was involved. It was fitting that Gabriel, a being of the same angelic rank as the devil, announced the conception of him who would undo the Fall and that an archangel, who is usually sent to groups of people, made the announcement because Mary's consent would affect the entire human race.[124] Finally, Thomas concludes that Mary is both the mother of Jesus and the Mother of God: the former because she contributed to him as much as any mother does to a child[125] and the latter because she is the mother of him who is God (not because she is the mother of the divine nature).[126]

Turning to the *Summa contra Gentiles,* written between 1261 and 1264, matters are stated more concisely. Thomas again insists on Mary's true motherhood and that, consequently, Mother of the Word and Mother of God are appropriate titles.[127] Displaying his dependence on Aristotelian biology, he contends that the male seed actively forms the new human being from the mother's passive material. If Christ is God, this active principle must have been divine, and therefore a virginal conception was necessary.[128] A virgin *birth,* moreover, properly highlights that Jesus Christ is the incarnate Word; for as a speaker conceives and speaks a word without diminishing himself, so the Virgin conceived and bore the Word without losing her virginity.[129]

Mary also arises in two exegetical works composed between 1269 and 1272. In the *Exposition of the Gospel of Matthew,* Thomas affirms Mary's personal sinlessness and sharply criticizes Chrysostom for implying that Mary wanted to share in Christ's glory. Accordingly Matthew 12:46-50 is not to be read as a rebuke, but as the elevation of spiritual generation over the physical.[130] More surprisingly Thomas also demurs from Jerome's insistence that Mary and Joseph never moved past betrothal. He counters that the couple were truly married because they enjoyed the three blessings of marriage: children, fidelity and sacrament.[131] The *Commentary on John* stresses that although the Blessed Virgin has a "superabundance" of grace that overflows to us, she is not the author of that grace. Christ alone is "full of grace and truth" and therefore the sole source of the grace that saves us.[132] Furthermore, the context of the remark suggests that the Marian over-

---

[124]Thomas Aquinas *Opera omnia,* 9:60-64 §3.3.1-2.
[125]Thomas Aquinas *Opera omnia,* 9:82-85 §4.2.1.
[126]Thomas Aquinas *Opera omnia,* 9:85-86 §4.2.2.
[127]Thomas Aquinas *Opera omnia,* 9:155 §30.6-7; 9:160 §32.7; 9:169-70 §34.15-21.
[128]Thomas Aquinas *Opera omnia,* 9:202-3 §45.2-3.
[129]Thomas Aquinas *Opera omnia,* 9:204 §45.4.
[130]Thomas Aquinas *Opera omnia,* 19:422-23.
[131]Thomas Aquinas *Opera omnia,* 19:243.
[132]Thomas Aquinas *Commentary on the Gospel of Saint John,* Aquinas Scripture Series 4, trans. and ed. James A. Weisheipl and Fabian R. Larcher (Albany: Magi, 1980), 1:98.

flow of grace is none other than Christ himself.[133] Similarly Thomas presents Mary's intercessions as exemplary because she draws no attention to herself but rather to her Son. Finally, when commenting on the words from the cross, Thomas observes not coredemptive suffering but exemplary care for a parent.

Last, in the *Summa theologiae,* Mary is almost wholly subsumed by Christology, appearing only twice outside it. The first of these arises as Thomas weighs whether God could make things better than he does. His answer is yes, but with three qualifications: "Christ's humanity, from being united with God, heaven, from being the enjoyment of God, and the blessed Virgin, from being the mother of God, have a certain infinite dignity deriving from the infinite good, which is God; in this respect there can be nothing better, just as there can be nothing better than God."[134] In this his most famous Marian passage, Thomas still reflects on Mary within Christology, affirming that Mary's dignity—however great—is not her own but derived from her motherhood.

The second, arising in Thomas's discussion of the transmission of original sin, also (indirectly) reflects christological concerns. Had Eve sinned alone, would her children have contracted original sin? Thomas sketches two possibilities. On the one hand if only Eve had disobeyed the divine command, then original sin would still have contaminated the race, for all maternal matter would be infected from then on. Thomas cites Saint John of Damascus, who understood the Holy Spirit's descent on the Blessed Virgin (Lk 1:35) to have purified her, for support. On the other hand Paul teaches that sin entered through one *man* (Rom 5:12). Accordingly original sin is found in the active seed of the father. Therefore, had only Eve sinned, original sin would not exist.

Thomas's resolution of the dilemma contains the Marian remark that concerns us. The father donates active principle to the formation of a human being and it is corrupt. Because maternal matter is passive, it can be neither good nor evil. Original sin is passed through the union of male (active) seed and female (passive) matter. Were a human being to be conceived without such a union, then, she or he would not have original sin. It is his virginal conception that ensures Christ's sinlessness. But, this does not mean that Saint John of Damascus was entirely wrong. In Thomas's view, Mary was sanctified by the coming of the Holy Spirit on her as a matter not of necessity but propriety.[135]

---

[133]Thomas R. Heath, "Appendix I: Historical Survey," in Thomas Aquinas *Summa theologiae,* vol. 51: *Our Lady,* trans. Thomas R. Heath (New York: McGraw-Hill, 1969), p. 93.

[134]Thomas Aquinas *Summa theologiae,* vol. 5: *God's Will and Providence,* trans. Thomas Gilby (New York: McGraw-Hill, 1967), p. 175 §25.6.4.

[135]Thomas Aquinas *Summa theologiae,* vol. 26: *Original Sin,* trans. T. C. O'Brien (New York: McGraw-Hill, 1965), p. 27 §81.5.3.

The remainder of Thomas's Mariology is found in the *Summa theologiae's* Christology. When discussing whether the incarnation was merited, Thomas counts as positive evidence (1) Psalm 33:22, which speaks of God's covenant love resting on those who hope in him, (2) Gregory the Great's indication that those who died before Christ merited the eternal life they received and, most important, (3) the Blessed Virgin Mary who, in Dominican worship, is said to have merited the privilege of being the mother of the Savior. Contrary evidence is supplied by Augustine's avowal that merits do not precede rebirth and Paul's claim that salvation is accomplished not by the works of justice but according to God's mercy (Tit 3:5). Thomas finds the contrary evidence to be overwhelming and concludes that merits did not precede the incarnation of our Lord in any way. The patriarchs, according to both Psalm 33:22 and Gregory the Great, certainly desired the incarnation, but desire and merit are not synonymous. Furthermore, Mary's merits—themselves gifts of grace—did not earn the incarnation as much as they earned that further grace by which she would become the Lord's mother.[136]

Just how we are to think of the grace that infuses Mary is Thomas's next problem. When working through his understanding of Christ's grace, Thomas asks whether the fullness of grace is found only in him. Again, evidence supports opposing answers. Negatively Mary (Lk 1:28) and Stephen (Acts 6:8) are also "full of grace"; Paul teaches that Christ passes grace on to others (Eph 3:19); and Gregory the Great suggests that each believer has the fullness of grace appropriate to him or her. However, Christ alone is the only begotten, full of grace and truth (Jn 1:14). The resolution lies in different understandings of "fullness." If by "full of grace" we mean "possesses grace to the maximal degree possible," then it is clear that Christ alone is full of grace. If, following Gregory, we understand it to mean "grace according to the requirements of a person's vocation," then many people—the Blessed Virgin, Stephen and others—may rightly be said to be "full of grace." The Blessed Virgin is, nevertheless, first in this group because she "had enough grace to fill the position for which she had been chosen by God, that of being mother of his only begotten Son."[137]

The next four questions are exclusively Marian; the first of these concerns Mary's sanctification. Thomas contends that, like Jeremiah and John the Baptist, Mary was sanctified before her birth. That she surpasses them as the mother of

[136]Thomas Aquinas *Summa theologiae,* vol. 48: *The Incarnate Word,* trans. R. J. Hennessey (New York: McGraw-Hill, 1976), p. 83 §2.11.3.

[137]Thomas Aquinas *Summa theologiae,* vol. 49: *The Grace of Christ,* trans. Liam G. Walsh (New York: McGraw-Hill, 1974), p. 37 §7.10.1.

the Lord is indicated by the feast of her nativity.[138] In this first sanctification, Mary was cleansed from original sin but not from original guilt. That would have removed her need for Christ's salvation. It did not occur before animation (i.e., the infusion of her soul into her body), for until then she would not have been a rational creature and only a rational creature can be guilty of (and therefore cleansed from) original sin. Thus, Thomas concludes that Mary did indeed contract original sin but was cleansed before her birth. This initial sanctification removed her desire to sin.[139] A second sanctification freed Mary from all actual sin, making her fit for the office of Mother of God.[140] Simeon's sword does indeed refer to doubt; not, however, one of faith, but one of wonder that tried to reconcile the humiliation of Christ on the cross with his power. This sanctification justifies Mary's title "full of grace," signifying as it does that "it was her due to receive a fuller intensity of grace than others"[141] because only she would be Jesus' mother. Thomas then concludes that Mary uniquely experienced three infusions of grace—*in utero*, at Jesus' conception and in glory: "In her sanctification she was cleared of original sin; then, in the conception of the Son of God, she was entirely cleared of sin's indisposition; and lastly, in her glorification she was liberated from every sort of suffering."[142] That is to say, the first inclined her goodness; the second confirmed her in goodness; and the third enabled her to enjoy all goodness.

The second question concerns Mary's virginity[143] and deals first with her virginity *ante partum*, which revealed the dignity of Christ's Father, disclosed his identity as the Word,[144] preserved him from sin and modeled the rebirth of Christians (Jn 1:13). Virginity *in partu* is a matter of biblical record (the Virgin shall conceive *and bear* a son [Mt 1:23; cf. Is 7:14]), again discloses that Christ is God's Word,[145] underscores the nature of Christ's healing mission and shows the extent to which he will obey the sixth commandment (cf. Ex 20:12). Most importantly, it points to Christ's two natures: that he was born shows humanity; that he was born of a virgin shows divinity. Thomas does not speculate about the signifi-

---

[138]Thomas Aquinas *Summa theologiae,* vol. 51: *Our Lady,* trans. Thomas R. Heath (New York: McGraw-Hill, 1969), pp. 13-15 §27.2.3.

[139]Thomas Aquinas *Summa theologiae,* 51:21 §27.3.3.

[140]Thomas Aquinas *Summa theologiae,* 51:23 §27.4.

[141]Thomas Aquinas *Summa theologiae,* 51:27 §27.5.

[142]Thomas Aquinas *Summa theologiae,* 51:29 §27.5.2.

[143]Thomas Aquinas *Summa theologiae,* 51:34-55 §28.1-4.

[144]Just as a word is conceived in the mind without diminishing the thinker, so the Word was conceived in the womb without diminishing his mother.

[145]Just as a word is spoken without damaging the integrity of the speaker, so the Word is born without damaging the virginity of his mother.

cance of Mary's virginity *post partum,* but merely assembles arguments from Jerome, Ambrose and Augustine to buttress it. Last, Thomas concludes that Mary's virginity was indeed the result of a personal vow, but one that took place only after her betrothal to Joseph. It was a vow of mutual chastity.

This introduces the third question: Mary's betrothal and marriage to Joseph.[146] Thomas first discusses the rationale for the relationship. He observes that, for Christ, it forestalled charges of illegitimacy, allowed his genealogy to be traced through David, prevented the devil from recognizing him prematurely and provided him and his mother with a caregiver. Thomas then adds that, for Mary, it prevented accusations of and punishment for adultery, provided a witness to Mary's virginity (being truly married, neither Mary nor Joseph would have motivation to lie) and made Mary an example to virgins tempted to sin. Finally, through this relationship God displays the goodness of both virginity and marriage, for it was a marriage, complete in form as the genuine union of two souls and complete in purpose, for it resulted in the birth and raising of a child.

The final question concerns the annunciation.[147] Gabriel's announcement was fitting for four reasons: it was proper to enlighten Mary before she conceived; it made her a witness to the mystery of the incarnation; it gave her the opportunity of free obedience (as Thomas puts it, "even though our wills do not cause a prophecy to come about, our consent is still needed");[148] and it disclosed that the union of the two natures in the person of Christ was analogous to a marriage between God and humanity, with Mary's consent standing for the consent of the race.

Thomas then considers whether an angel was a worthy messenger. God—who alone has full knowledge of the incarnation—could have done so directly; a man could have done so following the Pauline injunction in 1 Corinthians 14:34-35; even an angel of higher rank would, on the face of it, have been a better messenger. Nonetheless, God's choice of Gabriel was deliberate and proper. God did not intervene directly because in the Bible divine news is brought to humans by angels. Further, it is becoming to Mary's angelic virginity and dignity that she was instructed by an angel rather than a man. And finally, it fits the story of salvation that an angel of the same rank as he who precipitated the Fall should announce the Fall's undoing (moreover, Gabriel, while not the highest of all angels, is the highest of all archangels and his name, Power of God, is suited to this task).

Thomas also wonders whether the angel should have appeared bodily. Contrary to Augustine's rule that intellectual vision is superior to physical vision,

[146]Thomas Aquinas *Summa theologiae,* 51:56-67 §29.1-2.
[147]Thomas Aquinas *Summa theologiae,* 51:68-83 §30.1-4.
[148]Thomas Aquinas *Summa theologiae,* 51:71 §30.1.1.

Thomas holds that it was fitting that an angel came visibly to announce the incarnation of the invisible God. In so doing God increased Mary's certainty. Human beings—and Mary is no exception—trust their eyes more than their imaginations. Last, Thomas considers whether the angel's message was well organized. It seems that it was not for two reasons: the angel's words announced Mary's worth ("full of grace") before the reason for it ("you have found favor with God), and the conception of a barren woman (which is rare) is an insufficient sign to guarantee the conception of a virgin (which is impossible). And yet, the messenger called attention to strange news by greeting Mary in a strange way, made the announcement and then appealed to God's power. Thomas decides in the end that this arrangement focused the Blessed Virgin Mary on the mystery of the incarnation and therefore ought not to be gainsaid.

Although the bulk of his mariological work is now completed, Thomas raises Marian issues at two further points in the *Summa theologiae.* When speaking of Christ's childhood, Thomas again affirms the reality of Mary's motherhood[149] and the propriety of the title "Mother of God"[150] and stresses that in the act of giving birth Mary suffered no pain but experienced only the purest joy.[151] Moreover, Mary's purification at the temple (Lk 2:22) was undertaken not out of any necessity, but to follow the example of Jesus in humility and obedience.[152] The last reference to Mary occurs in Thomas's discussion of the Lord's passion. Christ suffered, he says, in every bodily sense—touch, taste, smell, hearing and sight—"because he saw there *his mother and the disciples whom he loved,* weeping."[153] In the *Summa theologiae* as elsewhere, there is no mention of Mary as a coredeemer who cosuffered with Christ on the cross.

To this point, Thomas has been a dispassionate and thorough theologian. In our final stop,[154] the "Exposition of the Angelic Salutation,"[155] completed in 1273,

---

[149]Thomas Aquinas *Summa theologiae,* vol. 52: *The Childhood of Christ,* trans. Roland Potter (New York: McGraw-Hill, 1972), pp. 51-55 §32.4.

[150]Thomas Aquinas *Summa theologiae,* 52:91-95 §35.4.

[151]Thomas Aquinas *Summa theologiae,* 52:101-3 §35.6.

[152]Thomas Aquinas *Summa theologiae,* 52:155-57 §37.4.

[153]Thomas Aquinas *Summa theologiae,* vol. 54: *The Passion of Christ,* trans. Richard T. A. Murphy (New York: McGraw-Hill, 1965), p. 23 §46.5.

[154]I have passed over the material in the *Compendium of Theology* written in 1272-1273 entirely because it treats much the same material, only in a compressed manner and different order. The only matters of note have to do with missing material. In the *Compendium of Theology,* Thomas says nothing about the annunciation, and the notion of Mary as mediatrix (even in Thomas's limited sense) is also entirely absent. See *Compendium of Theology,* trans. Cyril Vollert (St. Louis: Herder, 1949), pp. 258-68.

[155]Thomas Aquinas "Exposition of the Angelic Salutation (Ave Maria) (1273)," in *Thomas Aquinas: Selected Writings,* trans. and ed. Ralph McInerny (London: Penguin, 1998), pp. 822-27.

we encounter Thomas the preacher and Marian devotee. The sermons on the annunciation were preached in Naples, shortly before his death. They are simple expressions of adoration that show the compatibility—in Saint Thomas's mind—between theological reticence and exuberant piety. Thomas begins with the opening words of the greeting: "Hail [Mary], full of grace." Angels never used such an exalted title before in Holy Scripture. This demonstrates Mary's superiority to angels. She is full of grace in soul, says Thomas, enabled to act well and to avoid evil. She was conceived in sin, but not born in it. This grace then overflowed from her soul to her body, preparing it to receive the Son of God. From Mary, it overflows yet again to all humanity such that "in any peril you can obtain salvation from this glorious Virgin."[156]

Not only is Mary exalted above angels by God's grace, but also of all creatures, she is the closest to God. The next phrase in Gabriel's greeting makes this plain: "The Lord is with you." The whole Trinity is with Mary. God is her Father, her Son, and she conceived by the Holy Spirit. As a result, Mary is both pure in herself and obtains purity for others. Specifically she undoes the three curses of the Fall. Where conceptions and births were to be marked by sin, heaviness and pain, Mary conceived without sin, bore in comfort and gave birth in joy. Where humans were to labor for their food, Mary was concerned only with the things of God (cf. 1 Cor 7:32). Where the wages of sin for all is death, Mary was bodily assumed into heaven (Ps 132:8).

Finally, Thomas reflects on Elizabeth's words of blessing. "Blessed are you among women" highlights Mary's uniqueness. She alone was immune to the curse of sin, she alone ended it and she alone bore the blessing and opened the door of paradise. He concludes that "the name Mary becomes her, which is interpreted Star of the Sea, because just as sailors are directed to port by the star of the sea, so Christians are directed by Mary to glory."[157]

Thomas's exposition concludes with Elizabeth's second blessing: "Blessed is the fruit of your womb." Eve ate the fruit because she desired to become as a god knowing good and evil, sought pleasure from eating it and wanted to enjoy its beauty. Instead of these, she discovered that she was naked, was expelled from paradise and prevented from enjoying the fruit's beauty forever. Mary's fruit, on the other hand, provides Eve—and all human beings—with what they truly desire. Through Jesus the Blessed Virgin and all Christians are united to God; by eating his flesh (Jn 6:55) they find sweetness and salvation; and when gazing on him they gaze upon true beauty. Thomas concludes: "Eve could not

---

[156]Thomas Aquinas "Exposition of the Angelic Salutation," p. 825.
[157]Thomas Aquinas "Exposition of the Angelic Salutation," p. 826.

find in her fruit what no sinner can find in his sin. Therefore, what we desire, we should seek in the fruit of the Virgin. . . . So therefore is the Virgin blessed, but far more blessed is the fruit of her womb."[158]

Franciscan school. Bonaventure (1221-1274). Thomas has been emphasized in this chapter because of his significance for theology generally and for medieval views of Mary in particular. This is borne out when one compares the great Dominican with his Franciscan colleague Bonaventure. Although belonging to a rival order and although his theology is often noted for its departures from Thomas, with respect to Mary the two are very similar. Like Thomas, Bonaventure opposed the immaculate conception. Indeed, he cites Bernard of Clairvaux as an authority.[159] With Bernard, Bonaventure affirms that she was sanctified in the womb immediately after her animation and was kept pure from all actual sin.[160] Perhaps the only difference is a matter of nuance, which indicates that Bonaventure's opposition is not as strident. Where all humanity needed rescue after the Fall, he says, Mary was kept "as it were" from falling.[161] The qualification "as it were" is all that separates Bonaventure from later Franciscan theologians William of Ware and John Duns Scotus.

Bonaventure believes that such sanctification is fitting for the advocate of the human race, the spouse of God and the resting place of the Trinity. He understands it to have taken place in two stages. In the womb Mary was granted the ability not to sin; at the moment of the incarnation, the ability to sin was removed.[162] With Thomas, he acknowledges that this purity merited (in a qualified way) the reconciliation of the race[163] and is the basis for our devotion to her.[164] He labels such devotion *hyperdouleia* and clearly distinguishes it from both *latreia* ("worship offered to God alone") and *douleia* ("veneration offered to the saints"). Although he believed that Mary had been granted a measure of divine authority as an intercessor, he hesitated to present it in terms that would rival the authority of her Son. Specifically, he resisted the medieval axiom that every honor given to the Son should also be attributed to Mary; to predicate Christ's honor to another dishonors him.[165] Mary is an exalted creature and is honored as such.[166]

---

[158]Thomas Aquinas "Exposition of the Angelic Salutation," p. 827.
[159]Bonaventure *Opera omnia,* vol. 4: *In tertium librum sententiarum* (Paris: Vivès, 1865), pp. 58-62 §3.1.1.1.
[160]Bonaventure *Opera omnia,* 4:66-68 §3.(1.)1.3.
[161]Bonaventure *Opera omnia,* 4:62-66 §3.(1.)1.2.
[162]Bonaventure *Opera omnia,* 4:66-74 §3.(1.)2.1-3.
[163]Bonaventure *Opera omnia,* 4:102-3 §4.2.2.
[164]Bonaventure *Opera omnia,* 4:103-5 §4.2.3.
[165]Bonaventure *Opera omnia,* 4:65-66 §3.(1.)1.2.
[166]Bonaventure *Opera omnia,* 4:204-6 §9.1.3.

Mary's freedom from original sin establishes her as "mediatrix."[167] Bonaventure expands on just what this means in a work titled "The Seven Gifts of the Holy Spirit."[168] The priestly images that he employs to elaborate on Mary's intercessory role are especially striking. As our intercessor, she is our example whom we should follow;[169] whereas Eve sells us into sin, Mary buys us back.[170] In her consent to be Christ's mother, Mary agreed to offer him as a sacrifice for the world.[171] When reflecting on the passion, unlike Thomas, Bonaventure presents Mary's suffering at the cross as redemptive. While Christ's birth was painless, because of Mary's compassion for her Son and for us, she also suffered at the cross—even as she was glad to do so, for she knew the salvation it would bring.[172] Again, however, where Christ actively saves, Mary does so passively, participating in the acceptance of the divine will and accomplishing not only the salvation of others, but her own as well.[173]

William of Ware (1267-1300) and John Duns Scotus (1265-1308). The influence of Augustine's doctrine of original sin on medieval theologians such as Bernard, Thomas and Bonaventure inhibited the development and spread of the doctrine of the immaculate conception for over two centuries after Eadmer's death. But the popularity of the feast of Mary's conception grew among the faithful, and the question of the nature and timing of Mary's purification did not abate. Its leading defenders were British Franciscans: William of Ware and John Duns Scotus.

It does not tax the evidence to suggest that their common nationality and order provided deep motivation for continuing this debate. As Britishmen, William and John wished to defend the feast that held so many British hearts; as Franciscans, they were eager to attack the views of Thomas, *the* theologian of their rivals the Dominicans.

Ware notes that to the question "whether the blessed Virgin was conceived in original sin"[174] there currently exist three possible answers. The first is that of Henry of Ghent: Mary was conceived in sin and sanctified in the same instant.[175] The second is that of Thomas and Bonaventure: Mary was conceived in sin and

[167]Bonaventure *Opera omnia,* 4:63 §3.(1.)1.2. This is the only time that the word *mediatrix* occurs in Bonaventure's writings.
[168]Bonaventure *Les sept dons du saint-esprit* (trans. Marc Ozilou [Paris: Cerf, 1997]).
[169]Bonaventure *Les sept dons du saint-esprit,* p. 133.
[170]Bonaventure *Les sept dons du saint-esprit,* p. 135.
[171]Bonaventure *Les sept dons du saint-esprit,* pp. 136-37.
[172]Bonaventure *Les sept dons du saint-esprit,* pp. 137-40.
[173]Bonaventure *Les sept dons du saint-esprit,* pp. 135-36, 142.
[174]William of Ware, John Duns Scotus, and Peter Oriol, *Bibliotheca franciscana scholastics medii aevi,* vol. 3: *Quaestiones disputatae de immaculata conceptione beatae mariae virginis* (Florence: Ad Claras Aquas, 1904), p. 1.
[175]Ibid., p. 2.

cleansed at a later time.[176] William will defend the third: God graciously preserved Mary from original sin altogether.[177] He begins by securing the possibility of such a divine action.[178] He agrees with Augustine that the transmission of original sin is coterminous with insemination. He counters, however, that while Mary's parents were infected it is possible that she could have been purified at the moment of conception.

But possibility is not enough; the doctrine must also be suitable or fitting.[179] It is fitting that the Son—who is purity in himself—should give his mother as much purity as possible. To do so, he would not simply have to liberate her from sin but preserve her from sin altogether. If it is possible for God to create a sinless being (and it is) and if Mary were tainted with sin, she would be inferior to this hypothetical being. Such inferiority is not fitting. If it is possible and suitable, William avers, then it is a fact.[180] He concludes: "What he could do, it was appropriate that he should do, and from this it follows that he did it; for the Son should honor the Mother."[181]

William then sets about to counter the classical objection: if Mary were preserved from original sin, she would diminish the saving role of Christ. William disagrees. The immaculate conception does not render Mary above redemption, but recasts her redemption in a unique way. Mary needed Christ not for actual sin, but for the sin that would have been present had he not preserved her.[182] The feast of the immaculate conception should be continued because, he believes, it affirms this doctrinal truth.[183] He is smart enough, however, to leave himself an escape. Even if his argument should fail, if Mary did contract original sin, she was not merely pure at the time of her birth, but purified before her birth and this ought to be celebrated.[184]

It remains, finally, for him whom tradition names both the Subtle Doctor and the Marian Doctor to take the structure offered by William of Ware and cast it in its final form. John Duns Scotus is guided by three principles: (1) God was able to preserve Mary from original sin,[185] for anything that is not self-contradictory

---

[176]Ibid., p. 3.
[177]Ibid., p. 4.
[178]Ibid., pp. 5-6.
[179]Ibid., p. 6.
[180]Ibid., pp. 6-7.
[181]Ibid.
[182]Ibid., p. 10.
[183]Ibid., p. 8.
[184]Ibid.
[185]John Duns Scotus "Textus de immaculata conceptione b. virginis mariae" 3.3.1, in *Bibliotheca mariana medii aevii,* vol. 2: *Ioannis Duns Scoti doctoris mariani: theologiae marianae elementa,* ed. Carlo Balić (Sibenici: Instituti Theologici Marakrskensis, 1933), p. 28.

or does not lead to contradiction is possible for God;[186] (2) as in medieval Marian piety, it is better to err by ascribing too much to Mary than too little;[187] and (3) the ascription of the more excellent prerogative to Mary, provided it does not contradict church and Scripture, is likely true.[188]

Scotus begins, however, where William ends—by responding to objections. To the first, that it was not fitting for the Blessed Virgin Mary to be sanctified before or at the instant of animation for to do so would deny her humanity, Scotus counters by arguing that natural humanity is defined not by sinfulness. Sin, rather, is an intrusion on nature or, better, an absence of original justice present in the truly natural human being.[189] The second objection, that the immaculate conception renders Christ's work superfluous, is also misguided. Mary needed Christ all the more, for to be preserved from sin is a greater redemption than deliverance from it.[190] Scotus thus turns the charge on its head. Denying the immaculate conception diminishes Christ because a redeemer who only rescues is not as perfect as a redeemer who both rescues and preserves. Therefore, in order to be the redeemer whom Scripture presents, he ought to have saved one in this way. And he did—his mother.[191] Scotus may thus be seen as taking the argument of William and refining and reversing it. Where William moved from possibility to suitability to factuality, Scotus assumes that the doctrine is true and then shows how it is both suitable and possible.

We leave the Middle Ages with the question of Mary's purification officially unresolved. Unofficially, support for the doctrine of the immaculate conception, after being carefully articulated by Scotus, consolidated. The Franciscan order, not surprisingly, followed its theologian almost immediately.[192] Newer mendicant orders such as the Carmelites and the Servites of Mary soon followed.[193] The Council of Basel approved both the feast and the doctrine on September 15, 1438, but after the council had been officially dissolved and no longer had binding authority.[194] Later popes tended to steer clear of the debate while tacitly

---

[186]Carlo Balić, "The Mediaeval Controversy over the Immaculate Conception up to the Death of Scotus," in *The Dogma of the Immaculate Conception: History and Significance,* ed. Edward Dennis O'Connor (Notre Dame: University of Notre Dame Press, 1958), p. 204.

[187]John Duns Scotus "Textus de immaculata conceptione" 3.3.1, p. 31.

[188]John Duns Scotus "Textus de immaculata conceptione" 3.3.1, p. 31.

[189]John Duns Scotus "Textus de immaculata conceptione" 3.3.1, p. 18.

[190]John Duns Scotus "Textus de immaculata conceptione" 3.3.1, pp. 35-36.

[191]John Duns Scotus "Textus de immaculata conceptione" 3.3.1, p. 22.

[192]The definitive Franciscan stamp on the matter was given by Duns Scotus's student, Peter Oriol, around 1315. See Peter Oriol, "Tractatus Petri Aureoli," in *Quaestiones disputatae de immaculata conceptione,* pp. 23-94.

[193]Graef, *Mary,* 1:304-8.

[194]Ibid., 1:314-15.

supporting the doctrine's proponents. Sixtus IV, for example, prohibited each side from accusing the other of heresy even as he permitted the acknowledgement of Mary's conception in the Roman Catholic Church's liturgy.[195] The Dominicans, bound by an oath to teach only the theology of Saint Thomas, were the doctrine's most dogged opponents (even as they remained fervent in their devotion to the Blessed Virgin), withdrawing their opposition only in 1843 at the invitation of Pope Gregory XVI. At last the stage was set for an official recognition, but that is a story for the next chapter.

Conclusion

For now, it is time to draw conclusions. Although much of the material of this chapter is dense, three themes run through the entire presentation.

Catch-up of West to East. First, the Middle Ages may be rightly characterized in part as a catch-up of West to East. This may seem to be an odd conclusion to some, for the doctrine of the immaculate conception is a peculiarly Western invention, without Eastern counterpart. And yet, it is the sermons and festival of the Eastern church that first enthused about Mary's holiness from the womb. It is only as Greek monks move west that the idea penetrates Western consciousness. The West surpasses the East not in its affirmation of Mary's sanctification before her birth, but in the precision with which it seeks to articulate its understanding of the timing of that holiness.

Much the same can be said for the image of Mary as the Queen Mother. It was the political infrastructure of Byzantium that allowed Mary as *Theotokos* to become conflated with Mary the powerful intercessor in the heavenly court. As long as such a stable political infrastructure did not exist in Western Europe the notion of Mary as Heavenly Queen or the lady at court could not take hold. Bede's portrayal of Mary as a humble handmaid exemplifies the simplicity of the Marian piety of the early Middle Ages. As we move from Bede to Peter Damian and Anselm, however, the humble handmaid was supplanted by the courtly queen. There can be no doubt that this development can be attributed to the gradual stabilization of a social arrangement in which such a figure would make perfect sense. Thereafter, the idea that Mary could influence God was expressed in moderate and extreme forms. Moderately Mary was seen as an intercessor or created mediator who, by her intercessions, helped to accomplish the will of God. More extremely her intercessions were also sometimes presented as changing God's mind, as having the power to alter God's plan, even to amend

[195]E. D. O'Connor, "Immaculate Conception," in the *New Catholic Encyclopedia,* 2nd ed. (Washington, D.C.: Catholic University of America Press, 2003), 7:334.

God's judgment. That such confusion could occur within the devotion of one person—for example, the prayers of Saint Anselm—shows just how closely intertwined the two views had become in the medieval imagination.

Catch-up of theology to piety. Second, medieval Marian thought may also be thought of as the catch-up of theology to piety. This is especially evident in the relationship between the feast of Mary's conception and the doctrine of the immaculate conception. The feast came first. For reasons not entirely clear, it became popular among the Angle and Saxon tribes more easily than it did among the peoples of the European Continent. At the time of the Norman conquest, it was officially removed from the English church calendar, and yet it persisted and its suppression was eventually overturned. It was the celebration of the feast that prompted Eadmer to attempt to theologically defend the notion that Mary was not only holy at the time of her birth, but indeed holy from the instant of her conception. Even William of Ware—the first real theological defender of the doctrine—does so not as a matter of theological debate or mental exercise but out of concern for the continuation of the feast. The leadership of piety, furthermore, is true not only of the feast's defenders. Bernard of Clairvaux's opposition was itself oriented to the institution of the feast of Mary's conception in the church at Lyons. Piety set the theological agenda.

Restraining of piety by theology. Finally, the converse is also true. The Marian theology of the medieval era may also be legitimately presented as attempting to place restraints on popular piety in important ways. Certainly, Augustine's doctrine of original sin—especially as expressed through such powerful exponents as Bernard and Thomas—at least slowed the official acceptance of the immaculate conception. Likewise, where Anselm the devotee entrusted himself to Mary's care, Anselm the theologian carefully delimited the nature of that care, distinguishing her role as intercessor from Christ's role as Savior. Of course, it is true that more often than not such attempts failed. The image of Mary as the Mother of Mercy whose influence over her Son the wrathful judge rescues those in hell is one mild example of theology's failure to apprehend certain Marian expressions of piety that ultimately portrayed her as one who works to bend the will of God to her own.

It was this portrayal of Mary by medieval Christian piety—far more than any specific Marian doctrine—that the Reformers, beginning in the sixteenth century, rejected. The next chapter documents the parting of the ways in Latin Christianity in which Mary is gradually but nonetheless entirely eclipsed in Protestant theology even as she is dogmatically defined as being preserved from the stain of original sin in Roman Catholic theology.

9

Decline and Exaltation

Mary from the Reformation to the Nineteenth Century

The previous chapter sought to show, among other things, the centrality of piety in medieval debates about Mary. The medieval era was in part a time for theology to catch up to Marian piety and in part a time for theology to restrain it. By the close of the fifteenth century, it was clear to many that the restraints had failed too often. Marian devotion needed to be brought within the scope of Holy Scripture rightly interpreted. Among those voices calling for reform was Desiderius Erasmus, whose work in Bible translation led him to question Marian practices even as he retained a deep Marian devotion and remained loyal to the Roman Catholic Church.

This chapter plots two parallel attempts at reform: decline and exaltation. The first term summarizes the Protestant side of the Reformation, in which Marian devotion diminished and Marian theological reflection dwindled. From Luther to Schleiermacher, the trajectory moves toward silence, until Mary is irrelevant to Christian commitment and theological thought. The second term focuses on Roman Catholicism. Although Mary did not dominate discussions at the Council of Trent, after the Reformation, Roman Catholic Marian thought was gradually formalized and systematized both to respond to the Reformers and to rein in extreme forms of Marian devotion against which the Reformers reacted. Unlike their Protestant counterparts, however, Roman theologians sought to direct Marian devotion in orthodox ways. Thus, from Canisius and Suárez to Pius IX, the trend toward exaltation culminates in the dogmatic definition of the immaculate conception.

Decline: Protestant Theology to the Nineteenth Century

Desiderius Erasmus (1467-1536). Desiderius Erasmus demonstrates that loyalty to Rome—to Mary, in fact—and criticism of devotional excess were not necessarily mutually exclusive. Further, he sets the context for this chapter by showing that criticism of extremes was not a Protestant invention. Both claims are supported by Erasmus's devotional, doctrinal and polemical writings.

References to the Blessed Virgin Mary's intercessions are scattered throughout Erasmus's letters,[1] as are acknowledgements of his Marian devotional writings[2] and his approval of Marian pilgrimages.[3] His Marian piety was, however, truly committed to paper in only three works. The first two were composed in 1499, at an early stage in his career. Nevertheless, Erasmus never disowned them and often cited them when he felt his devotion was being unfairly attacked.

The "Paean in Honour of the Virgin Mother" praises the "singular glory of heaven, earth's surest safeguard" (*CWE* 69:17-38, quotation at 20). As a channel of grace (*CWE* 69:20), Mary is the "mistress of the world" (*CWE* 69:21) whom the "highest ranks of the heavenly court" esteem (*CWE* 69:22). When calling upon her to accept his prayer for Christ's sake (*CWE* 69:22-23), Erasmus employs pagan imagery: Mary is the true goddess of justice (*CWE* 69:25), the true Diana, virgin and mother (*CWE* 69:25) and the true Lucina, goddess of childbirth (*CWE* 69:25). Biblically she is also the New Eve, Jael, Judith and Esther (*CWE* 69:29). Allegorically she is also a mountain, cornerstone, rose bush of Jericho, sealed fountain, divinely protected garden, holy city of Zion, mirror of life, new earth, cedar of Lebanon, olive tree, dawn, sister of the church, matchless woman, bride, concubine (cf. Song 6:8-9) and beloved (*CWE* 69:29-32). At one point, erotic and devotional metaphors blur: "You are love, you are fire, you are the special delight of the one who is fairest of the sons of men. You are the precious lover uniquely desired by the Son of God. So passionate that you fainted with love for the one you desired, so beautiful that the lustre of your eyes caused the Word of God to fly from the bosom of his Father into your own womb" (*CWE* 69:33). All can call on Mary—young and old, great and least, sick, prisoners, pregnant women, sailors, merchants, farmers, soldiers, those oppressed by guilty consciences, orphans (*CWE* 69:34-37). Erasmus even praises Mary's intercessory power in language that he later criticizes: the Mother of Mercy mollifies Christ the judge (*CWE* 69:37-38). She is the Star of the Sea (*CWE* 69:38).

That last metaphor controls the "Prayer to the Virgin Mary in Time of Trouble" (*CWE* 69:41-54). Evil is a sea full of monsters: flatterers, false advisers,

---

[1]Erasmus "145/To Anna van Borssele 1501" (*CWE* 2:17).
[2]Erasmus "167/To Louis 1501" (*CWE* 2:55).
[3]Erasmus "262/To Andrea Ammonio 1512" (*CWE* 2:230).

open and hidden enemies and ignorance. Mary, who intervenes to help those tossed upon this sea, is both Ursa Major (the constellation of the North Star) who guides sailors without touching saltwater and the Moon, who faces the sun and reflects its light to earth. The poetic language rivals Anselm's when Erasmus calls Mary "my savior, my salvation, my sole and certain refuge" and implores her in these words: "Sweet glory of mine, save my soul; insignificant though it be, it dedicates itself to you" (*CWE* 69:45). Mary is the sinless ever-virgin whose virtues both impelled the Son of God to come to earth "like a suitor, drunk with love" (*CWE* 69:46) and culminated in her cosuffering for the redemption of the world (*CWE* 69:51). To her and to her Son, Erasmus entrusts himself in order that he may reach port, the heavenly Jerusalem (*CWE* 69:54).

The third text, a full mass titled the "Liturgy of the Virgin Mother Venerated at Loreto," was published in a shorter edition in 1523 and a longer one in 1525, with the addition of a homily and a commendation from the Archbishop of Besançon (*CWE* 69:86-108). Although prepared to honor the Loreto shrine, to which—according to legend—Mary's house had been miraculously transported from Nazareth in the 1200s, Erasmus makes no reference to it, focusing rather on Christ's miracles and his relationship to his mother. The Gospel text is the wedding at Cana. The homily extols Mary's purity, humility, prudence and strength (*CWE* 69:91-104). Traditionalists welcomed the liturgy, enabling Erasmus to rebut the charge that he lacked appropriate Marian devotion (*CWE* 69:81).

Coupled with a well-developed Marian devotion is Erasmus's overall Marian orthodoxy. Although he replaced the Vulgate's rendering of Greek *kecharitōmenē* as *gratia plena* ("full of grace") with *gratiosa* ("favored one"), giving rise to charges of lessening Marian devotion and attacking Mary's person,[4] Erasmus saved his salvos for expressions of devotion that, however widespread, had not been officially endorsed by the Roman Catholic Church. In doctrine he remained completely orthodox.

He preferred to keep the question of Mary's origins open. While he personally favored the immaculate conception,[5] he ridiculed attempts to set the terms of the debate as orthodoxy versus heresy. To do so, he wrote, was to impugn

[4]This charge continues to be repeated even though subsequent biblical language studies by both Roman Catholic and Protestant exegetes have thoroughly vindicated Erasmus's argument. See Michael O'Carroll, *Theotokos: A Theological Encyclopedia of the Blessed Virgin Mary* (Dublin: Dominican Publications, 1982), p. 137.

[5]Erasmus "1127/To Hermannus Buschius 1520" (*CWE* 8:16, 357 n. 40); see also "1196/To Vincentius Theoderici 1521" (*CWE* 8:178) and "1304/To Adrian VI 1522" (*CWE* 9:153).

the faith.[6] Until this matter was settled, he would affirm only that God had intervened in Mary's life, removing any tendency to sin.[7] He believed Mary to be the New Eve[8] and a perpetual virgin.[9] Her marriage to Joseph was chaste,[10] necessary to preserve Mary's reputation.[11] Indeed, God has a stronger claim to the title "spouse"—Gabriel proposes marriage, the Most High embraces, the Holy Spirit is the agent of conception and Mary conceives the Son of God. When the apostles fled Jesus, Mary remained faithful to the end—exemplifying a truly divorce-proof bond.[12] Nevertheless, Erasmus followed Augustine's contention that Mary's salvation rested on the presence of the Spirit throughout her life rather than on her maternity.[13]

Even later in life, Erasmus considered himself to be in the Marian mainstream: "No one hates more than I those yapping critics who attack the Virgin."[14] Still, he knew that he aroused suspicions because of a perceived lack of Marian devotion;[15] not even a scathing defense by Thomas More could preserve him.[16] The reason is simple: Erasmus refused to limit his frustration with Marian practice to the academy, where his ideas would have received a quieter hearing. He wrote for a broad audience, using irony and satire to skewer the sacred cows of Marian devotion that detracted from true discipleship. For instance, taking aim at those who thought devotion to Mary compensated for sin, he wrote that instead of "some particular brief prayers to the blessed Virgin. . . . How much better it would be if those who are so much frightened of sudden death were to pray to heaven for a good life!"[17] He continues: "Think of the many who set up a candle to the Virgin, Mother of God, and at midday

[6]Erasmus "1334/To Jean de Carondelet 1523" (*CWE* 9:264); see also "A Discussion of Free Will" (*CWE* 76:10). Erasmus does seem to think, however, that the Council of Basel's acceptance of the doctrine was in some way authoritative; see "Hyperaspistes Book 1" (*CWE* 76:119 n. 132).

[7]Erasmus "Hyperaspistes Book 2" (*CWE* 77:574; cf. 480, 654).

[8]Erasmus "Explanation of the Creed" (*CWE* 70:290).

[9]Erasmus "On Two Hymns of Prudentius" (*CWE* 29:176, 185-86). See also *Paraphrase on the Acts of the Apostles* (*CWE* 50:62, 88, 97 n. 41); "Explanation of the Creed" (*CWE* 70:289-93); "On Praying to God" (*CWE* 50:187-88); and "Hyperaspistes Book 1" (*CWE* 76:227-28). See especially *CWE* 76:258, where Erasmus asks Luther to explain why he believes in Mary's perpetual virginity even though it "is not expressed in Scripture and it has not been revealed by God through any miracle."

[10]Erasmus "750/To Maarten Lips 1518" (*CWE* 5:261-62).

[11]Erasmus "On the Christian Widow" (*CWE* 66:215).

[12]Erasmus "The Virgin and the Martyr" (*CWE* 69:231).

[13]Erasmus "The Handbook of the Christian Soldier" (*CWE* 66:73).

[14]Erasmus "1679/To Noël Béda 1526" (*CWE* 12:91).

[15]Erasmus "948/To Petrus Mosellanus 1519" (*CWE* 6:314-15).

[16]Thomas More "To a Monk," in *St. Thomas More: Selected Letters,* ed. Elizabeth Frances Rogers (New Haven, Conn.: Yale University Press, 1961), pp. 114-44, esp. 132-35.

[17]Erasmus "1347/To Joost Vroye 1523" (*CWE* 9:415).

too, when it isn't needed, and of the few who care about emulating her chastity of life, her modesty, and her love of heavenly things."[18] Beneath the rhetoric, the claim is simple: "No devotion is more pleasing to Mary than the imitation of Mary's humility."[19]

Nowhere was Erasmus both more popular and more confrontational than in his *Colloquies,* satirical conversations written in dramatic form. Both "Courtship" (*CWE* 39:257-68, esp. 265 lines 20-25) and "The Girl with No Interest in Marriage" (*CWE* 39:285-93) ridicule those who use Mary to claim the superiority of virginity to marriage,[20] a key plank supporting Western monasticism since Ambrose. Similarly, "A Fish Diet" complains that Mary (and the saints) has taken the place of Christ in popular devotion (*CWE* 40:677-721, esp. 719 line 12 through 720 line 31). Moreover, her followers use rites better suited to the worship of Venus[21] and practices so superstitious as to be laughable.[22] Still, Marian piety and orthodoxy persist. "The Sermon or Merdardus" defends his translation of the Magnificat against the charge that it dishonors Mary (*CWE* 40:940-53), while his "Pilgrimage for Religion's Sake" seeks a Marian middle way between the extremes of deification and elimination (*CWE* 40:621-50).

This last colloquy contains a letter from Mary to a reformer named Glaucoplutus, a fitting conclusion to this review of Erasmus's work. Glaucoplutus had a historical referent. The name compounds two Latin nouns that in English would be rendered "Owl-rich" or in German "Eul-rich." It is a play on the name Ulrich Zwingli, the reformer of Zürich. The letter falls into two parts. In the first, Mary decries the way the saints' intercessory power has been both misunderstood and abused by pious and impious alike. She thanks Glaucoplutus for his corrections. In the second, however, Mary worries that he has gone too far. Not only have the abuses stopped, so has appropriate devotion. The consequences for such a cure, she warns, may be worse than the original disease. The saints will avenge themselves, and hers will be the worst: "You

---

[18]Erasmus "Praise of Folly" (*CWE* 27:114-15, 120). Similar sentiments less scathingly expressed can be found in "On Praying to God" (*CWE* 70:224-25).

[19]Erasmus "The Handbook of the Christian Soldier" (*CWE* 66:71).

[20]Similar views are found outside the colloquies: "A virgin born from a virgin, the Lord first consecrated virginity in Mary. But, let anyone imagine that this bring contumely on marriage, he wished to be the son of a virgin but also of a married woman, so that he should be born, if not from marriage, certainly in marriage." Mary, indeed is the leader of all Christian women, whether virgins, wives or widows, for she was all three. See Erasmus "On the Christian Widow" (*CWE* 66:202, 203-4).

[21]Erasmus "The Shipwreck" (*CWE* 39:355 lines 10-18).

[22]Erasmus "Alchemy" (*CWE* 39:550 lines 10-32). See also his satire on monastic orders: "The Well-To-Do Beggars" (*CWE* 39:481 lines 19-21).

shall not eject [me] unless at the same time you eject my Son, whom I hold in my arms. From him I will not be parted. Either you expel him along with me, or you leave us both here, unless you prefer to have a church without Christ" (*CWE* 40:628 lines 10-13). Mary and Christ belong together. Appropriate devotion to the former glorifies the latter, while superstition, immorality and overreactions to abuses attack both.

Martin Luther (1483-1546). Martin Luther's writings on Mary are the most fascinating and frustrating of all the Reformers. Not only was he as prolific as he was unsystematic, but his volatile personality never truly escaped the medieval Catholicism into which it was born.[23]

Early writings show Luther to be steeped in the allegorical reading of the Old Testament and deeply devoted to the Mother of God. In his *First Lectures on the Psalms* (*LW* 11), delivered between 1513 and 1515, he understands the "land" of Psalm 85:1 to describe the earth, the human race and Mary, depending on whether one is reading literally, typologically or mystically (*LW* 11:153; see also 172). Likewise, the "mystical sense" of Psalm 87 describes both the believer's soul and the Blessed Virgin "all the way through" (*LW* 11:184-85; see similar interpretations of Ps 110 in 11:366-67). Even after the 1517 publication of the Ninety-five Theses, Luther's high view of Mary was not significantly altered. "A Sermon on Preparing to Die" (1519), for example, affirms the need to invoke Mary and the saints (*LW* 42:113), and "Against Latomus" (1521) exalts her holiness as an exceptional gift of grace (*LW* 32:157).

Still, from 1519 to 1522 Mary came to illustrate central concerns. "Freedom of a Christian" (1520) cites her willingness to undergo purification in spite of her *in partu* virginity to exemplify the obedience of faith (*LW* 31:368),[24] while "The Gospel for the Sunday After Christmas" (1521-1522) presents her as a widow whose solitary suffering (cf. Lk 2:34-35) represents Christians when confronted by those who do not believe (*LW* 52:111). She is the model of salvation by faith alone through grace alone in the "Sermon Preached at Erfurt on the Journey to Worms, John 20:19-20, April 7, 1521," where Luther maintains that even "the holy mother of God did not become good, was not saved, by her virginity or her motherhood, but rather by the will of faith and the works of God, and not by her purity, or her own works" (*LW* 51:62).

The chief work of this period is Luther's commentary on the Magnificat (1521): *The Sermon on the Mount and Magnificat* (*LW* 21:297-358). Although it begins

---

[23]William J. Cole, "Was Luther a Devotee of Mary?" *Marian Studies* 21 (1970): 100-107.

[24]Luther affirmed Mary's perpetual virginity throughout his life, commenting on it as late as 1545. See "Prefaces to the Old Testament" (*LW* 35:275).

and ends with a plea to Mary for insight,[25] Mary as example and teacher is the controlling theme. Enlightened by the Holy Spirit, Mary embodies true knowledge, love and praise of God and wholehearted devotion (*LW* 21:299-301). While he acknowledges her Davidic ancestry, perpetual virginity, poverty and humility (*LW* 21:302), Luther is captivated by her piety. She loves God for himself, not for his gifts (*LW* 21:309), and exalts God's undeserved grace (*LW* 21:314). She "does not say men will speak all manner of good of her, praise her virtues, exalt her virginity or her humility, or sing of what she has done. But for this one thing alone, that God regarded her, men will call her blessed" (*LW* 21:321). When the Magnificat is used to praise Mary's virtues, a polemic note is sounded: "They make an exception of her and set her above all examples. . . . [Now] we find those who come for her help and comfort, as though she were a divine being, so that I fear there is now more idolatry in the world than ever before" (*LW* 21:323-24). Mary is displeased when she rather than God is praised (*LW* 21:322).

As Luther's ideal Christian, Mary attributes nothing to herself and everything to God. She is preeminent among all God's creation only because God chose her to be the mother of his Son (*LW* 21:326). Mary's purity—which extends from her nativity to her glorification in heaven—does not merit the incarnation, but is a sign of the grace whose end was the conception of the Son of God. Believers may speak of Mary's merit only insofar as she was a woman, a virgin of Judah, who believed the angel. She merited her place as much as the wood merited becoming the cross by being suitable wood. The title "Queen of Heaven" used to invoke Mary (and other saints) in prayer should remind us that God is the sole source of all grace (*LW* 21:329).

In his "Personal Prayer Book" (1522), Luther speaks of the "Immaculate Virgin Mary" whose bearing of Christ did not change her spiritual or physical integrity (*LW* 43:26-27), and he approves of the Hail Mary as a spiritual discipline within limits. Believers are to repeat the first half only, using the words drawn directly from Luke's Gospel. In this way they will praise God for the grace given to Mary, meditate on the nature of that grace and call others to know and respect her. Nevertheless, this is not a prayer and ought not lead one to trust in Mary for the salvation that comes from Christ alone (*LW* 43:39-41). Luther again affirms Mary's purity (*LW* 43:40). And while he continues to hold that Mary be-

---

[25]Luther's opening prayer reads: "May the tender Mother of God herself procure for me the spirit of wisdom profitably and thoroughly to expound this song of hers, so that . . . we all may draw from it wholesome knowledge and a praiseworthy life, and thus come to chant and sing this Magnificat eternally in heaven. To this may God help us. Amen." The closing prayer asks the Lord for understanding "through the intercession and for the sake of His dear Mother Mary! Amen" (*LW* 21:298, 355).

came pregnant without sin and gave birth without pain, he is increasingly wary of excessive devotion to her, writing that "no one speaks evil of this Mother and her Fruit as much as those who bless her with many rosaries and constantly mouth the Hail Mary" (*LW* 43:40).

From 1522 on, positive remarks about Mary decline while polemics focused on devotional excesses increase. Thus, in the *Lectures on Isaiah* (1527-1532) (*LW* 16-17), Luther both insists that Isaiah 7:14 prophetically predicts Mary's *ante partum* and *in partu* virginity (*LW* 16:84) and suggests that the "sword of Simeon" may have been a moral failing (*LW* 16:322). He associates the then-common Marian interpretation of Isaiah 45:8 with abuses in the mass of the Blessed Virgin celebrated during Advent (*LW* 17:125) and stresses again that Mary did not merit the incarnation: "The sophists debated whether the blessed Virgin deserved to become a mother. I say that she was made a mother according to the promise before she was born, before she gave any thought to the matter" (*LW* 17:142).

In 1530 Luther used an open letter to defend his translation of Luke 1:28 following Erasmus rather than the Vulgate (*LW* 35:190-93). That same year, when commenting on Psalm 117, he made the "worship of Mary and all the saints" part of a long list of obstacles to and perversions of revelation (*LW* 14:23). His "Exhortation to All Clergy" complained that the "pretended church" had "Mary made a common idol with countless services, celebrations, fasts, hymns, and antiphons" (*LW* 33:54). In 1531 he accused Roman Catholics in his "Warning to His Dear German People" of substituting Mary for Christ, transforming Christ into an angry judge (*LW* 47:45-48). This was a theme that Luther was to return to regularly. For instance, a 1535 reflection on Psalm 110 contended, "They taught us to call upon the dear mother of Christ and to urge her . . . to plead against His wrath over us and to obtain his grace. And if our dear lady did not suffice, we enlisted the help of the apostles and other saints, until we finally came to the point of calling upon saints of whom no one knows whether they are holy" (*LW* 13:326).

Mary appears throughout the *Lectures on Genesis* (1535-1536) (*LW* 1-8), both positively and negatively. Positively Luther follows patristic and medieval tradition, ascribing to Mary Davidic descent (*LW* 2:72; 3:145; 5:161; 8:139). He exalts her above Abraham because, unlike him, she believed the promise before the sign was given (*LW* 3:29). He claims, in fact, that women were spared the burden of circumcision—a "seemingly foolish law"—for her sake (*LW* 3:136). He affirms Mary's personal sinlessness as necessary in order to bear Christ (*LW* 3:206) and follows the Western conclusion that Christ was preserved from original sin through his virginal conception (*LW* 4:161-62). He teaches that Mary's marriage to Joseph was chaste (*LW* 5:348-49) and refuses to comment on her assumption, noting only that Scripture is silent on Mary's death (*LW* 4:189).

Negatively Luther's most important observation is exegetical. For centuries, biblical commentators had understood Genesis 3:15 to refer to both Mary and Christ triumphing over the devil because of a mistranslation in the Vulgate (i.e., "*she* shall crush your head"). In returning to the Hebrew text, Luther insisted that the translation read not she—that is, Mary—but "it," that is, the seed or Christ. He comments, "Let us thank God that now we have also this passage unimpaired and restored. We do not want to take away from Mary any honor which is her due; but we want to remove the idolatry contained in the statement that by giving birth to Christ, Mary has destroyed all the power of Satan" (*LW* 1:192; see also 184). He also presents the loss of Christ at the temple as a test of Mary's faith (*LW* 4:94) and repudiates Marian allegories of Old Testament and pagan texts (*LW* 5:346-47). Again, however, excesses of Marian devotion specifically arouse his ire. He castigates attempts to pit the merciful Mary against her angry Son (*LW* 7:329) and repeatedly rejects the invocation of Mary and the saints as superstitious and detracting from Christ (*LW* 1:180; 4:269; 7:299).

His *Sermons on the Gospel of John* (1531-1540) (*LW* 22-24) follow a similar pattern, asserting Mary's perpetual virginity (*LW* 22:23; see also 22:214-15; 24:16, 166, 320), acknowledging her sanctity (*LW* 23:83) and proclaiming her to be the Mother of God (*LW* 24:10.7). At the same time he condemns the worship of Mary's images (*LW* 22:347), excoriates the use of her name as some kind of magical protection (*LW* 22:107), ties Marian pilgrimages to pagan religion (*LW* 22:526; see also 24:74) and ridicules the mother/judge rivalry, associating it with Bernard of Clairvaux (*LW* 22:377)—whom Luther elsewhere alludes to approvingly.[26] These reflect attempts to become children of God apart from the mediation of Christ (*LW* 22:118; see also 22:136, 142, 146, 165, 364, 368-69, 388, 490; 23:57, 59, 104, 137, 411; 24:24, 62, 69, 307).

Even in later life, however, Luther expressed an almost sentimental devotion to the Mother of God. In the 1539 treatise "On the Councils and the Church," such softheartedness comes to the fore when he writes that "Mary is the true natural mother of the child called Jesus Christ, and . . . she is the true mother of God and bearer of God. . . . Mary suckled God, rocked God to sleep, prepared broth and soup for God" (*LW* 41:93-106, esp. 100).

Reformed theologians. The three Reformed theologians have much less to say and display three main concerns: suspicion of all forms of Marian devotion,

[26]In *LW* 22:388 Bernard is mentioned with esteem. Bernard is also rebuked in Luther's "Last Sermon in Wittenburg, 1546" (*LW* 51:375).

approval of Mary's moral example and caution toward Marian doctrine. Thus, Ulrich Zwingli's (1484-1531) "Sermon on the Virgin Mary" (1522) holds that because her honor is derived from her Son's, the greatest honor that believers may bestow upon her is to honor Christ.[27] It follows that veneration of Mary apart from Christ is to be rejected. Zwingli maintains that people have turned to Mary instead of Christ and, ever concerned with the moral life of Zürich, that the repetition of Hail Marys cannot compensate for persistent sin.[28] Still, Mary is regarded as a perpetual virgin,[29] an example of faith and strength in suffering.[30]

As Zwingli's successor, Heinrich Bullinger (1504-1575) consolidated the reform of Zürich. Nevertheless, he is more positively disposed toward Marian doctrine and piety. His "Sermon on Mary," after defending Mary's perpetual virginity, offers these words of praise: "In Mary, then, everything is extraordinary and even more majestic, because it has sprung from the purest faith and burning love for God."[31] Indeed, to reject Mary is to be an enemy of Christ. This is not to say that the sermon is a wholesale endorsement of Marian developments to the sixteenth century, for it also regards the immaculate conception and the bodily assumption as open questions, saying only that it is enough "simply and straightforwardly to believe and to confess that the Virgin Mary, the holy Mother of our Lord Jesus Christ, wholly sanctified by the grace and blood of her Son and fully endowed with the gift of the Holy Spirit . . . now lives happily with Christ in heaven."[32] Bullinger also inveighs against her invocation and her mediation and rejects the understanding of Mary as mistress of the church.

John Calvin (1509-1564), the most systematic of the Reformed theologians,

---

[27]Ulrich Zwingli, "Eine Predigt von der ewig reinen Magd Maria 15. September 1522," in *Huldreich Zwinglis Sämtliche Werke,* ed. Emil Egli and Georg Finsler, Corpus reformatorum 88 (Berlin: Schwetschke, 1905), 1:391-428.

[28]See also Ulrich Zwingli, "Die erse kurse Antwort über Eks sieben Schlürich 21. Mai 1526," in *Huldreich Zwinglis Sämtliche Werke* 5:188-89.

[29]See also Ulrich Zwingli, "Jesaja-Erklärungen," in *Huldreich Zwinglis Sämtliche Werke* 14:181. He explains that perpetual virginity is a truth derived *sola scriptura* and not by church authority. Those who cannot find it lack the Spirit.

[30]Compare Zwingli's "Eine Predigt," in *Huldreich Zwinglis Sämtliche Werke* 1:410-11 with "Amica exegesis, id est: espositio eucharistiae negocii ad Martinum Lutherum. Zürich, 28. Februar 1527," in *Huldreich Zwinglis Sämtliche Werke* 5:583-85.

[31]Heinrich Bullinger, "Die Marienpredigt," in Walter Tappolet, *Das Marienlob Der Reformatoren* (Tübingen: Katzmann, 1962), pp. 274-302, quotation at 290.

[32]Ibid., p. 293. Interestingly, Bullinger himself seemed personally to believe in the bodily assumption, writing elsewhere: "Therefore we believe that the most pure chamber of the Bearer of God and Temple of the Holy Spirit, the Virgin Mary, that is her holy body, was carried to heaven by angels" ("De origine erroris libri duo," as quoted in ibid., p. 327). Tappolet also observes (p. 327) that this statement was preserved in the Dutch 1602 edition but removed from the Genevan 1549 edition.

was also the most guarded about Mary. Both his biblical and theological works show that for the Reformation's second generation she is a greater point of conflict, personifying disputes about hermeneutics, soteriology and piety. In his 1553 *Commentary on John* and 1555 *Harmony of the Gospels*, Calvin is restrained, interpreting Mary's anonymity at the Cana wedding as a warning to future Christians that honors offered to Mary ought not to obscure Jesus' glory. It is clear to him that in his context, this warning had been forgotten: "For Mary has been made Queen of Heaven, the Hope, the Life, and the Salvation of the world. . . . As if she had not all the honour that belongs to her without being made a goddess! As if it were honouring her to adorn her with sacrilegious title and put her in Christ's place!"[33] Likewise, John 19:25-27 says nothing about Mary's cosuffering or coredemption. Rather, it shows how duty to parents is to be paid: as an example to us, Jesus first attends to his divine mission and then to the welfare of his mother.[34]

Restraint also defines Calvin's understanding of the annunciation. Gabriel's announcement was entrusted to a young virgin for two reasons. First, not in order to hide the incarnation from Satan, nor because she was especially virtuous or pious, but "to test the humility of faith, and to resist the pride of the wicked."[35] Accordingly, second, the faithful must not be ashamed "to have as our teacher her who bore in her womb Christ, the eternal Wisdom of God."[36] Calvin agrees with Erasmus that Luke 1:28 describes "the free favor of God" and contends that her blessing is proof of that favor. Accordingly she is not a dispenser of grace.[37] While the "Papists" have transformed the angel's greeting into prayer, believers should not follow this practice. When they do, Calvin quips, they end up greeting someone who is not there. Further, the notion that Mary took a perpetual vow of virginity is absurd. She is blessed because of her Son.[38] Elizabeth's greeting, "the mother of my Lord," exemplifies the extent to which believers ought to honor her.

When we turn from the annunciation to the Magnificat and birth narrative, Mary ceases to be the socially inferior young girl and becomes the teacher of Christ's disciples. A close reading of her hymn reveals that Mary refuses to exalt herself "but only recognizes what she has received of God, and tells of the accep-

---

[33]John Calvin, *The Gospel According to St. John 1-10*, trans. T. H. L. Parker (Grand Rapids: Eerdmans, 1959), p. 47.

[34]Ibid., pp. 181-82.

[35]John Calvin, *A Harmony of the Gospels: Matthew, Mark, and Luke*, trans. A. W. Morrison (Grand Rapids: Eerdmans, 1972), 1:21.

[36]Ibid.

[37]Ibid., p. 22.

[38]Ibid., p. 32.

tance of His favour. . . . [It] is God's work alone that she celebrates. This shows us how far away the Papists are from her, when they deck her out with thoughtless and vain notions, and virtually disregard the benefits she received at God's hand."[39] Accordingly "praises of Mary, where the might and sheer goodness of God are not entirely set forth, are perverse and counterfeit."[40] When speaking of the birth of Christ, Calvin plays on the Marian title "Treasury of Grace" *(trésoire de la grâce),* appropriating it to highlight Mary's example. She kept the good news in her heart in order that she could pass it on to others.[41] Finally, Simeon's sword is understood to be a warning to strengthen Mary at the cross, so that her faith would not waver.[42] Throughout, Calvin's hermeneutical and theological method keeps him from speaking where Scripture is silent. To do so is to invite error.

His polemical works continue this trend. The "Articles Agreed upon by the Faculty of Sacred Theology of Paris" (1542) rejects the invocation of saints and Mary,[43] insisting that it is an "execrable blasphemy" and an insult to Mary to call her "Queen of Heaven" and "Treasury of Grace." Calvin's tone could move from the serious to the sarcastic. The "Necessity of Reforming the Church" (1543) cracks that, based on an observation of Catholic piety, some statues of the Blessed Virgin Mary and other saints are apparently more divine than others.[44] His most caustic remarks come in "An Inventory of Relics" (ca. 1544). Relics praise the doctrine of the assumption because it prevented the veneration of Mary's body. As it is, he observes, there are far too many Marian relics: "But had the breasts of the most Holy Virgin yielded a more copious supply than is given by a cow, or had she continued to nurse during her whole lifetime, she scarcely could have furnished the quantity which is exhibited."[45]

Calvin's sermons and confessional works also remain consistent. The *Institutes of the Christian Religion* (1559), while it affirms Mary's Davidic lineage,[46] rejects the veneration of the images of saints, describing the practice as idolatry.[47] It also rejects created mediation as dishonoring the singular mediation of

---

[39]Ibid., p. 35.

[40]Ibid., p. 36.

[41]Ibid., p. 80. Morrison's translation obscures this clever pun.

[42]Ibid., pp. 96, 119-20.

[43]John Calvin, "Articles Agreed upon by the Faculty of Sacred Theology of Paris," in *Calvin's Tracts and Treatises,* trans. Henry Beveridge (Grand Rapids: Eerdmans, 1958), 1:96-97.

[44]John Calvin, "The Necessity of Reforming the Church," in *Theological Treatises,* trans. J. K. S. Reid, Library of Christian Classics 22 (London: SCM Press, 1954), pp. 188-91, esp. 189.

[45]John Calvin, "An Inventory of Relics," in *Calvin's Tracts and Treatises,* trans. Henry Beveridge (Grand Rapids: Eerdmans, 1958), 1:316-19, quotation at 317.

[46]John Calvin, *Institutes of the Christian Religion,* ed. John T. McNeill and trans. Ford Lewis Battles, Library of Christian Classics 20-21 (London: SCM Press, 1960), 1:479 §2.13.3.

[47]Ibid., 1:99-116 §1.11.

Christ.[48] None of this is, by now, surprising. More interesting is the silence of the *Institutes* on the ancient ecumenical title "Mother of God." Although Calvin's Christology is not opposed to it, he justifies this silence on the grounds of misplaced devotion: "To speak of the Mother of God instead of the Virgin Mary can only serve to harden the ignorant in their superstition."[49] The "Confession of Faith in Name of the Reformed Churches of France" (1562) continues: "For many prayers have been forged full of horrible blasphemies, such as those which request the Virgin Mary to command her Son, and exert her authority over him—and which style her the haven of salvation, the life and hope of those who trust in her."[50] In this respect, Calvin and some Roman Catholic Marian apologists agree: all subsequent Marian piety evolves from the declaration of the Council of Ephesus in 431.

English Reformation. The final movement differs from those previous for two reasons. First, the English Reformation is "top-down" in structure. While there were political machinations in the Lutheran and Reformed movements, they were not initiated by politicians. Contrarily, the English Reformation hinged upon the actions of the Tudor monarchy. In Europe the Reformation was led by lawyers and monks and supported by princes; in England it was led by the crown, accomplished by an act of Parliament and supported by leading clergy.

For Luther, justification by faith alone was the article by which the church would stand or fall. For the Reformed, all other disagreements could have been settled on the basis of *sola scriptura.* In England, Henry VIII needed an heir. Catherine of Aragon's several failed pregnancies compelled him to seek a papal dispensation to annul their marriage. Henry, furthermore, believed that he had a strong case based on Catherine's previous marriage to Henry's brother, Arthur. When Arthur died, Henry VII obtained a papal dispensation to permit the remarriage of Catherine to his son, also named Henry. Henry VIII merely sought to suspend the law again. But Catherine was sister to King Phillip of Spain and aunt to Holy Roman Emperor Charles V—connections stronger than any evidence. Henry would have his heir without Rome's permission. One wonders how the English Reformation would have looked had Catherine had different relatives.

As a result we turn to confessional documents published during the reigns

---

[48]Ibid., 2:876-87 §3.20.19-27.

[49]John Calvin, *Lettres anglaises* (Paris, 1959), as quoted in O'Carroll, *Theotokos,* p. 94.

[50]John Calvin, "Confession of Faith in Name of the Reformed Churches of France," in *Calvin's Tracts and Treatises,* trans. Henry Beveridge (Grand Rapids: Eerdmans, 1958), 2:146.

of the Tudors to record Anglican attitudes toward the Blessed Virgin. Article 6 of the Ten Articles (1536), the first confession of Henry VIII's Church of England, commends the veneration of images, "especially the images of Christ and our Lady,"[51] as examples of virtue spurring the faithful to repentance. Nevertheless, to avoid idolatry, the faithful should be advised that censing, kneeling and offering before them are "done to God, and in His Honour, although it be done before the images, whether it be of Christ, of the Cross, of our Lady, or of any other saint beside."[52] Article 7 approves the honoring of saints because they are known to be elect, because they passed in godly life out of this world and because they reign in glory with Christ. Christians are to praise Christ for their example without "trusting to attain at their hands that which must be had only of God."[53] Similarly, article 8 commends saints as intercessors: "All holy angels and saints in heaven pray for us and with us, unto the Father, that for his dear Son Jesu Christ's sake, we may have grace of Him and remission of our sins, with an earnest purpose, (not wanting ghostly strength) to observe and keep His holy commandments, and never to decline from the same unto our lives' end."[54] The faithful are to pray to Mary or any other saint, provided they remember that grace and salvation are available only through Christ.

The Institution of a Christian Man: The Bishops' Book (1537) praises Mary's perpetual virginity and sanctity in terms that permit, but do not demand, the immaculate conception. It likewise approves of the Hail Mary, provided that it is said in honor of the Lord and "partly of the Blessed Virgin for her humble consent given to the angel at this salutation." The phrase "full of grace" applies to Mary's motherhood ("she conceived and bore him that is the author of all grace") and election ("this Blessed Virgin was elect to be to be the instrument of our reparation in that she was chosen to bear the Saviour and Redeemer of the world.")[55] Similar views are expressed in the *King's Book* (1543).[56]

Beginning with the reign of Edward VI and continuing under Elizabeth I,[57]

---

[51]"Articles Devised by the Kinges Highnes Majestie," in Charles Hardwick, *A History of the Articles of Religion* (London: Bell, 1904), pp. 251-52.

[52]Ibid., p. 252.

[53]Ibid.

[54]Ibid., p. 253.

[55]*Formularies of Faith Put Forth by Authority During the Reign of Henry VIII* (Oxford: Clarendon, 1825), pp. xxxvii, 203-8.

[56]*The King's Book; or, A Necessary Doctrine and Erudition for Any Christian Man, 1543* (London: SPCK, 1932), esp. pp. 20, 144.

[57]I must ignore the interregnum of the last Roman Catholic Queen of England, Mary Tudor, who undid her father's reforms.

Marian doctrine and devotion were both directly and indirectly curtailed. Directly, the books of Common Prayer published during Edward's reign (in 1549 and 1552) retained only two explicitly biblical Marian feasts: the purification of Mary on February 1 (Lk 2:22-40) and the annunciation to Mary on March 25 (Lk 1:26-38).[58] Indirectly, three of the Thirty-Nine Articles published under Elizabeth in 1571 were used to suppress Marian devotion: article 6 affirmed that Holy Scripture contained all things necessary to salvation, apparently rendering optional all forms of devotion to Mary and other saints and undermining doctrines based on tradition alone; article 15 insisted that of all the baptized only Christ is without sin, thereby seeming to question the traditional understanding of Mary's holiness; and article 22 rejected purgatory, relics, images and invocation of saints as "grounded upon no warrantie of Scripture, but rather repugnant to the worde of God."[59] But the country of Bede, Anselm of Canterbury, Eadmer, Nicholas of St. Albans, William of Ware and Duns Scotus did not lose its Marian heart entirely. Marian themes recur in the seventeenth and eighteenth centuries in the writings of Richard Hooker (died 1600), Lancelot Andrewes (died 1626), John Donne (a convert from Catholicism to Anglicanism; died 1631), James Ussher (died 1656) and Mark Frank (died 1664).[60] Only in the nineteenth century did Mary come again to the foreground in Anglican thought and piety in the works of leaders of the Oxford Movement and especially John Henry Newman.

Protestant decline to the nineteenth century. From the sixteenth to the eighteenth century, Protestant reflection on Mary weakened further. Article 21 of the (Lutheran) Augsburg Confession (1530) does not name her, but forbids the invocation of saints,[61] while the Formula of Concord (1576) amplifies only slightly, defending the title "Mother of God" and the reality of Mary's motherhood.[62] She is similarly treated in Reformed confessions.[63] Among the last Reformed theologians to treat the Blessed Virgin Mary at any length was Charles Drelincourt (1595-1680), pastor of the Reformed church of Paris. His *The Honor Due the Holy and Blessed Virgin Mary* (1633) refutes "the most widespread calumny against us, that we dishonor the Blessed Virgin and speak of her with

---

[58] *The First and Second Prayerbooks of King Edward the Sixth* (London: Dent, 1910), pp. 10-11, 336-37.

[59] "Articles, 1552-1571," in Charles Hardwick, *A History of the Articles of Religion* (London: Bell, 1904), pp. 295, 307-9, 319-21.

[60] O'Carroll, *Theotokos,* pp. 28-29.

[61] Augsburg Confession, art. 21, in Philip Schaff, ed., *The Creeds of Christendom,* vol. 3: *The Evangelical Protestant Creeds, with Translations,* 4th ed. (New York: Harper, 1919), p. 26.

[62] Formula of Concord 8.6-7 and 12.1 (*Creeds of Christendom,* 3:150, 174).

[63] Belgic Confession 28 (*Creeds of Christendom,* 3:402-3).

scorn."[64] Nevertheless, it is not a piece of Protestant polemic as much as a constructive presentation of seventeenth-century Reformed beliefs about Mary. She is rightly titled "Blessed" and "Virgin." The former because she is the Mother of God, "resplendent with virtues," and "favored beyond all the patriarchs, prophets and apostles, and exalted above all the angels and seraphim." The latter because she "remained a virgin even in and after giving birth." Reformed Christians ought to love and honor Mary, venerate her memory, celebrate her praises and praise God for the gift of Jesus through her. They are, furthermore, to treat her as both a teacher and an example. Nevertheless, when Roman Catholics use titles such as "queen," they render to her "honors that belong to the king alone." Only he is "the true gate, our advocate, the sole mediator between God and humanity." Such distortions grieve both our Lord and his mother. This is the last example of any attempt at a systematic Mariology from the Protestant side of the Reformation divide.

Throughout the eighteenth century, reflection on the Lord's mother was limited either to discussions of the incarnation (the reality of Mary's motherhood, the nature of the incarnation of God in her womb and so on) or polemics against forms of Marian doctrine and devotion (whether her perpetual virginity was a biblical doctrine).[65] As the nineteenth century dawned, however, the rationalism that had dominated European Protestant theology was declining against the advances of two rather different foes. The growth of higher methods of biblical criticism seemed to undermine the methods and conclusions of the exegesis of previous generations even as romanticism indicated a greater openness to spirituality among Europe's elite, albeit one deeply suspicious of organized expressions of (Christian) faith.[66] Where similar pressures led to a Marian revival in the Roman Catholic Church, they ended Marian reflection in Protestant churches for over a century.

The prime example of such silence is Friedrich Schleiermacher (1768-1834).

---

[64]Since Drelincourt's work was inaccessible to me, I draw on the quotations and summaries offered in Alain Blancy et al., *Mary in the Plan of God and in the Communion of Saints: Toward a Common Christian Understanding,* trans. Matthew J. O'Connell (New York: Paulist Press, 2002), pp. 40-41. The work of seventeenth-century Reformed theologian André Rivet (died 1651) titled *Apologia pro sanctissima virginie maria matre domini* is also mentioned by Blancy et al. (p. 147 n. 85), but is neither quoted nor summarized.

[65]See, e.g., the extensive summaries found in Heinrich Heppe, *Reformed Dogmatics: Set Out and Illustrated from the Sources,* rev. ed., ed. Ernst Bizer, trans. G. T. Thomson (Grand Rapids: Baker, 1978), pp. 421-28, 444; and Heinrich Schmid, *The Doctrinal Theology of the Evangelical Lutheran Church,* 3rd ed., trans. Charles A. Hay and Henry E. Jacobs (Minneapolis: Augsburg, 1899), pp. 293-309.

[66]Protestant rationalism in North America would not face similar challenges until almost a century later.

Treating criticism and romanticism as opportunities, his *Christian Faith* is an apologetic demonstration that an intellectually robust yet experientially profound Christian faith not only withstands the confrontations of both but also can incorporate their findings and attitudes.[67] Thus, where the "cultured despiser" of Christianity mocks its miracles, Schleiermacher argues that miracles are irrelevant to faith. Whereas once the miraculous may have evoked or confirmed recognition of Christ, Jesus never presented them as bases for faith.[68] Faith and reason need not conflict, for miracles are not necessary: "What takes the place of miracles for our time is our historical knowledge of the character, as well as of the scope and the duration, of Christ's spiritual achievements."[69]

The virgin birth of Christ is just such a miracle. Although its affirmation does not denigrate the faith, its denial does not challenge belief in Christ as the redeemer;[70] it has, therefore, no dogmatic value.[71] Accordingly traditional beliefs that have evolved from this doctrine (namely those regarding Mary's virginity and purity) are similarly superfluous.[72] Neither constructive nor polemical, Schleiermacher simply dismisses Mary from the conversation.

Exaltation: Roman Catholicism to the Nineteenth Century

Systematization of Mariology. The official Roman Catholic response to the Reformation, the Council of Trent (1545-1563), recognized and cemented the rupture that had taken place in Western Christianity. Nevertheless, it was surprisingly inward looking, not only explaining the Roman Catholic Church's doctrines vis-à-vis other bodies but also assessing the consequences of centuries of failed attempts at reform.[73] Given the size and scope of the issues it faced, it is not surprising that the Blessed Virgin Mary received comparatively little attention. She is mentioned only three times: the council's fifth session on original

---

[67]Friedrich Schleiermacher, *The Christian Faith,* 2nd ed., trans. H. R. Mackintosh and J. S. Stewart (Edinburgh: T & T Clark, 1928). Whether this apologetic strategy was successful, of course, is the source of ongoing debate. Nevertheless, it cannot be denied that Schleiermacher remains the most important Protestant theologian between Calvin and Barth.

[68]"That is why Christ never availed Himself of His miraculous powers in any definite connexion with the demands He made of His statements about Himself, but (in the same way as everyone avails himself of his natural powers) according as opportunity offered of doing good by them" (ibid., p. 448).

[69]Ibid. Schleiermacher therefore concludes that belief in miracles "belongs not so much to our faith in Christ directly as to our faith in Scripture" (p. 449).

[70]Ibid., pp. 403-4.

[71]Ibid., p. 404.

[72]Ibid., p. 405.

[73]Christopher M. Bellitto, *The General Councils: A History of the Twenty-One Councils from Nicea to Vatican II* (New York: Paulist Press, 2002), p. 96.

sin reaffirms that she lacked its taint;[74] the sixth session on justification proclaims her actual sinlessness;[75] while the twenty-fifth session approves of the placing of images—especially those of Christ and Mary—in churches.[76] Just as Mary was not a major feature of the first generation of Reformers, so she was not a major focus of the chief Catholic reply.

This is not to say that such replies were not forthcoming. The Reformation on the Catholic side formalized and systematized Marian doctrines, as is evidenced in the works of Peter Canisius and Francisco Suárez. Canisius (1521-1597) was an apologist, challenging Mary's critics, especially Erasmus and Luther, by arranging and commenting on extensive quotes from the church fathers and medievals. Although repetitive, Canisius's work remains significant for its (grudging) admission that certain doctrines and practices were utterly without warrant. Erasmus and Luther, in other words, did have (some) legitimate complaints. For example, Canisius refuses to defend the *Protevangelium of James* and denies that Mary had full knowledge of the mystery of the incarnation. He also seeks to articulate Marian devotional language in a way that blunts Reformers' criticisms: for Canisius, Mary is queen, mediator and even salvation, not as a rival to Christ, but beneath him, in cooperation with his will and in her role as an intercessor. Cautious approval of traditional language, however, tacitly admits that at least some Catholic preachers *did* speak in the way that the Reformers decried and needed correction.[77]

Rather than responding to critics, Francisco Suárez (1548-1617) presents Marian doctrine systematically within his Christology.[78] The treatment is painstakingly deliberate, comprising one full third of the entire work.[79] For Suárez, Mary was elected to be the Mother of God before (in logic, not in time) any consideration not only of her own merits but also of God's election to allow the Fall.[80]

---

[74]H. J. Schroeder, trans., *The Canons and Decrees of the Council of Trent* (Rockford: Tan, 1978), p. 23.

[75]Ibid., p. 45.

[76]Ibid., pp. 215-16.

[77]See Petro Vogt, *Mariae sacrosanctae et deiparae virginis vita: ex opere maiore sancti canisii de maria virgine inompaabili et dei genitrice sacrosancta* (Turin: Marietti, 1933).

[78]Thus, Suárez's Mariology arises in eighteen "disputations" in what has come to be called *The Mysteries of the Life of Christ.* It is, in fact, part of his multivolume commentary on Thomas Aquinas's *Summa theologiae.*

[79]Richard J. O'Brien, "Introduction," in Francisco Suárez, *The Dignity and Virginity of the Mother of God,* trans. Richard J. O'Brien (West Baden Springs: West Baden College, 1954), p. vii.

[80]Francisco Suárez, *Opera omnia,* vol. 19: *Commentaria ac diputationes in tertiam partem d. thomae, a quaestione xxvii usque lix, et mysteria vitae christi untrusque adventus ejus ita explicans ut et scholasticae doctrinae stuidiosis et divini verbi concionatoribus usui esse possit* (Paris: Vivès 1878), pp. 10-12 disputatio 1.3.

From this, all else follows. Sanctified from the moment of her conception,[81] she had full use of her reason[82] and had vowed to remain a virgin before her birth.[83] All her actions were deliberate and good and therefore merited even more grace, such that by the end of her life she possessed more than all angels and saints combined.[84] With respect to the sacraments, Suárez is quite confident that she received baptism, confirmation and Eucharist while she did not receive orders, penance and matrimony. He leaves the question of extreme unction open because, of course, Mary did not sin.[85] As the Virgin Mother of God, she was infused with supernatural knowledge of the nature of God, the Trinity and the plan of salvation, but not exceptional knowledge of the natural world.[86] Three days after her death, Mary was taken body and soul into heaven, where she is now a most powerful intercessor for all who call on her.[87] Her position, however, is inferior to that of Christ, and while she is the hope of sinners, the joy and salvation of the world and the mediator of grace, these expressions do not elevate Mary to divine equality. She is an exalted creature.[88]

Devotional debates. This process of formalization did little, however, to quell the devotional debates that persisted within the Roman Catholic Church until the nineteenth century. Indeed, from the seventeenth century onward, there seems to be a serious disconnect between the views of trained theologians (which tended toward moderation) and those of popular preachers and visionaries (for whom no Marian extravagance was too much).

Preachers encouraged the pious in their devotion to Mary by portraying her as a powerful help in attaining salvation. In a letter penned on July 3, 1656, noted French Roman Catholic philosopher and theologian Blaise Pascal (1623-1662) rebukes—among others—a now forgotten Jesuit priest, Father Barry, for instituting what he called "false worship of the Virgin Mary."[89] Father Barry promised access to heaven to any practitioner of even one of the devotions to Mary he proclaimed. Indeed, any finding that the repetition of words—greeting Mary, pronouncing her name often, saying the Hail Mary and so on—was too difficult can simply "wear a chaplet night and day upon the arm in the form of

---

[81]Ibid., pp. 28-30 disputatio 3.2.
[82]Ibid., pp. 70-72 disputatio 4.7.
[83]Ibid., p. 98 disputatio 6.1.
[84]Ibid., pp. 283-97 disputatio 18.2-4.
[85]Ibid., pp. 287-90 disputatio 18.3.
[86]Ibid., pp. 301-4, 306 disputatio 19.3, 5.
[87]Ibid., pp. 313-15 disputatio 21.1.
[88]Ibid., pp. 325-30 disputatio 22.2-4.
[89]Blaise Pascal, "Letter IX" in *The Provincial Letters of Blaise Pascal* (London: Griffith Farran Okeden & Welsh, n.d.), p. 136.

a bracelet, or . . . carry . . . a rosary or a picture of the Virgin."[90] Such actions will save even those who live in mortal sin. As evidence Barry relates a tale of a notoriously sinful woman who saluted Mary's image daily. Because of this devotion, Christ raised her from death in order that she might do penance.[91] Pascal retorts that Barry merely encourages "sinners in their iniquities, by imparting a false peace, but not to affect that genuine conversion which divine grace can alone produce."[92]

Second, mystics offered strange visions as disclosures of truth. Perhaps the most popular was the four-volume *Mystical City of God* by Franciscan nun Mary of Agreda (1602-1665).[93] While much of it merely embellishes the *Protevangelium of James* and the Gospels, its truly strange claims—perhaps most notoriously—held that the preexistent Mary was by divine decree exempt from the Fall;[94] that she enjoyed near omniscience from her conception;[95] that she was taken to heaven at the ascension of Christ;[96] that the city of God described by John in Revelation 21 is the Blessed Virgin returning to earth;[97] and that she enjoyed an amazing career as a teacher of the apostles, missionary and warrior against the powers of darkness until her death and (second) assumption.[98] Sister Mary's visions have had a checkered history in the Roman Catholic Church, having been banned and restored several times. The English edition of the work received the imprimatur of former Archbishop Edwin V. Byrne of Santa Fe in 1949.

Third, even mild attempts to conform piety to official church teaching were met with stiff resistance. Ludovico Muratori (1672-1750) published two works that suffered from this fate. His *Moderation in Matters of Religion* (1714) argues that the church is within its remit to define the immaculate conception, provided that "it can be deduced from Scripture or established by the constant tradition of the fathers."[99] From there, Muratori argues that while it is certainly noble to defend the doctrine in debate, blood oaths taken to preserve it to the point of

[90]Ibid., p. 138.
[91]Ibid., pp. 138-39.
[92]Ibid., p. 139.
[93]Mary of Agreda, *Mystical City of God,* 4 vols., trans. George J. Blatter (Wheeling: Corcoran, 1949).
[94]Ibid., 1:59.
[95]Ibid., 1:264.
[96]Ibid., 3:770-90.
[97]Ibid., 4:39-52.
[98]Ibid., 4:66-68.
[99]Ludovico Muratori, *Moderation in Matters of Religion,* pp. 151-52 §1.17, as summarized in Hilda Graef, *Mary: A History of Doctrine and Devotion,* vol. 2: *From the Reformation to the Present Day* (New York: Sheed & Ward, 1963), p. 72.

violence and even death were foolish. "This," he wrote, "is certainly a novel kind of martyrdom, of which our ancestors never dreamed, and which our descendants, if they are sensible, will never approve. . . . For one's blood should be shed not for our opinions, but for the divine revelations and holy laws."[100] His critics responded angrily, some even incorrectly holding that the doctrine was church teaching.[101] Muratori countered in a later work that such vows were meaningless because Dominicans were not murdering Franciscans, because Protestants had more serious problems, and because pagans had no idea what the debate was about.[102]

Immaculate conception (1854). Thus far, the Roman Catholic response to the Reformation may be stated in terms of two broad trends. On the one hand systematic theologians attenuated and formalized Marian doctrine. The Council of Trent, Canisius and Suárez show that this move was as much an apologetic response to Protestant polemics as it was a corrective to those misplaced devotions that the Reformers opposed. On the other hand preachers and mystics continued to promulgate fantastic tales while irrationally opposing the slightest criticism offered from within a shared doctrinal foundation. The picture of Marian doctrine and devotion in Catholic Europe at the beginning of the Enlightenment is one contrasting a theologically sophisticated (moderate) elite with a theologically unrefined (more extreme) populace, with laypeople and secular and religious clergy found in both groups. The singular Marian event of the nineteenth century, the papal definition of the immaculate conception in 1854, can be read as an attempt to reunite these groups by affirming a doctrine widely held among adherents of each in a way that honored Marian piety while reining in its more extreme expressions.

Reflecting the popularity of Marian mysticism and devotion of the time are the aftereffects of the visions of Catherine Labouré (1806-1876) and Bernadette Soubirous (1844-1879) among the Roman Catholic faithful. Labouré's visions occurred in 1830 during the night of July 18-19 and the evening of November 27. According to her own account, the first vision began when Sister Labouré was beckoned by a child to leave her room for the convent chapel, there to be met by the Blessed Virgin. After a time Mary appeared, seated in a chair by the chapel's altar. There ensued a conversation during which Mary told of "God's plans for her [Labouré], to warn of the trials that would come upon her, and to

---

[100]Muratori, *Moderation in Matters of Religion,* p. 268 §2.6 (Graef, *Mary,* 2:72).

[101]For a full account of the blood vow, see Julien Stricher, *Bibliotheca immaculate conceptionis,* vol. 9: *Le voeu du sang en faveur de l'immaculée conception* (Rome: Academia Mariana Internationalis, 1959).

[102]Muratori, *De superstitione vitanda* (summarized in Graef, *Mary,* 2:73).

show her how she should bear them."[103] When Mary disappeared, however, the plans had yet to be specified. The child led Labouré back to her dormitory. The second occurred at evening prayers some months later. This time Mary stood on a white ball, with a serpent under her feet. In her hands she held a golden ball surmounted with a cross and wore three rings on each finger. The golden ball, Labouré was told, represented the entire world, France and each individual; the gems in the rings represented the graces that Mary either gave or desired to give to the faithful. The vision then changed. The golden ball disappeared and Mary's hands stretched out as the entire vision was encased on an oval frame inside of which was written, "O Mary, conceived without sin, pray for us who have recourse to thee."[104] Labouré was then instructed to have a medal struck after this model. The vision then changed a second time, disclosing the reverse of the medal to be made. Dominating it was a large M surmounted by a bar and a cross, while beneath it appeared the heart of Jesus (encircled with thorns) and the heart of Mary (pierced by a sword). Twelve stars surrounded it.

Whether the vision occurred is, for our purposes, beside the point. The "Miraculous Medal," as it is now known, was struck in 1832 and became very popular with Roman Catholics around the world, not least because of the numerous miracles attributed to it. However, the vision's significance lies in the prayer it contained, specifically the phrase "conceived without sin." Even though the visionary disclosure of the medal did not become public until thirty years later, this phrase inscribed on the medal moved the immaculate conception to the forefront of imaginations worldwide and led to a growing demand to have the doctrine defined.

Bernadette Soubirous was in many ways unlike Catherine Labouré—where Catherine was twenty-four, healthy, educated and religious at the time of her visions, Bernadette was fourteen, sickly and nearly illiterate, a peasant whose faith was entirely expressed in her rosary. On March 24, 1858, Soubirous experienced what was the climax of a series of visions that had begun on February 11. In prior visionary experiences, she reported seeing a figure resembling a young girl. In previous encounters, "Aqueró," or "this thing," refused to give her name. Now, Soubirous asked the figure her name three times before she finally answered: "I am the immaculate conception." Soubirous's experiences resulted in the construction of the Church of the Immaculate Conception at Lourdes (1872) and the institution of the feast of Our Lady of Lourdes locally (1890) and

[103]Joseph I. Dirvin, *St. Catherine Labouré of the Miraculous Medal* (Garden City: Doubleday, 1965), p. 90.
[104]Ibid., p. 99.

throughout the Roman Catholic Church (1907). Today, Lourdes is the most visited Marian shrine in the world.

Again, whether Soubirous's visionary experiences were encounters with the Blessed Virgin Mary or resulted from more mundane (mental illness) or sinister (demonic) means is not germane. Rather, again, their significance lies in that, for many Roman Catholic believers both past and present, the figure whom they infer to be Mary took the title "immaculate conception" as her "name," confirming the dogmatic definition of Pius IX made four years before.[105]

Meanwhile, among Catholic Europe's elite, Enlightenment skepticism had, by the advent of the nineteenth century, begun to give way to romanticism and its greater openness toward the supernatural. When the Dominicans formally withdrew opposition to the immaculate conception in 1847, Pope Pius IX (1846-1878) took three decisive steps to clarify and define the doctrine once and for all. First, beginning in 1847 the new pope encouraged the doctrine, congratulating Father Giovanni Perrone for a book that mused whether a definition was forthcoming.[106] Second, in 1848 he initiated an official inquiry. Its preliminary report suggested that a definition was possible and recommended a consultation with all bishops. Of 603 bishops consulted, 546 favored a definition, 5 were opposed, 24 worried about the timing, 10 worried that any definition would condemn the contrary position as heresy and 18 withheld judgment.[107] In 1850 and 1851 Pius invited six theologians to give their opinions on the matter; one, Monsignor Tizzani, Bishop of Terni, was opposed. The first draft of a declaration was prepared by Father Perrone and submitted to the pope on March 26, 1851.[108]

From there, proceedings began to accelerate. Beginning in 1852 a papal commission prepared eight successive drafts for the pope's consideration. The last came on December 1, 1854. With the commission's agreement that the decree could be enacted, the debate ended and the date of December 8 was fixed for the event. The eighth draft would be revised only one more time—by the pope alone.[109] Although the bull was not finalized, the decree was issued on the ap-

---

[105]This is certainly how it is understood by Roman Catholic apologist (and Bob Jones University alumnus) Dwight Longenecker. See Dwight Longenecker and David Gustafson, *Mary: A Catholic-Evangelical Debate* (Grand Rapids: Brazos, 2003), p. 148. His evangelical dialogue partner (and fellow Bob Jones University alumnus) is—not surprisingly—not at all convinced.

[106]Rene Laurentin, "The Role of the Papal Magisterium in the Development of the Dogma of the Immaculate Conception," trans. Charles E. Sheedy and Edward S. Shea, in *The Dogma of the Immaculate Conception: History and Significance,* ed. Edward James O'Connor (Notre Dame: University of Notre Dame Press, 1958), pp. 308-9.

[107]Ibid., p. 309.

[108]Ibid.

[109]Ibid., pp. 310-11.

pointed date. The pope, invoking apostolic authority wrote the following:

> We . . . DECLARE, AND PRONOUNCE, AND DEFINE, that the doctrine which holds that the Blessed Virgin Mary, in the first instant of her Conception, has been, by a special grace and privilege of Almighty God, and in view of the merits of Jesus Christ, the Saviour of the human race, preserved and exempted from every stain of original sin, is revealed by God, and consequently is to be believed firmly and inviolably by all the faithful.[110]

In the bull itself—probably completed only in January 1855—the pope argued that this doctrine had been revealed progressively, beginning with the early church's reverence for Mary's conception by honoring it with a feast and applying to it biblical texts referring to divine wisdom.[111] He then follows with a history of the doctrine, giving what he believes to be biblical evidence, as well as support from various theologians from antiquity forward. Finally, he rehearses the steps he took and repronounces the dogma.

The theological significance of the bull lies in its twofold affirmation: from her conception Mary is exempt from original sin, while from that same instant she is saved by Christ. The former claim is explained in terms of preservation. Mary is preserved—that is, protected—from original sin by a singular grace of God. In other words, apart from grace Mary is in the same predicament as all of Adam's children. Mary herself needs to be saved. The second claim then expands on this claim. Mary's unique salvation is accomplished in view of the merits of her Son and her Savior. In this way the worries expressed variously by Anselm, Bernard, Thomas and Bonaventure have indeed been met. Mary is exempt from the stain of original sin; and Mary as much as if not more than the rest of us looks always only to Christ as the source of her salvation and ours. Even as the bull officially exalts Mary more than previously, it excludes those forms of belief and piety that placed her beyond the need of salvation.

John Henry Newman (1801-1890). The decree defining the immaculate conception marks the start of a century-long renewal in Marian theology. A movement not necessarily limited to the Roman Catholic Church, it reached its climax in 1950 with Pope Pius XII's dogmatic definition of Mary's bodily assumption. As a major theological figure in English Christianity, John Henry Newman participated in this renewal, but in almost contradictory ways. His 1845 conversion from the Church of England to Roman Catholicism marks the divi-

[110]Pius IX, *The Bull "Ineffabilis" in Four Languages,* trans. and ed. Ulick J. Bourke (Dublin: Mullany, 1868), p. 73.
[111]Ibid., p. 11.

sion.[112] As an Anglican, Newman led the recovery of Catholic doctrine and spirituality within the Church of England and was perceived—whether with appreciation or hostility—to be a Marian promoter. As a Roman Catholic, however, Newman presented to both Catholics and Anglicans a more sober, biblically grounded, patristically informed and less sentimental, speculative and tenuous understanding of the Lord's Mother than had been the case for some time.

Prior to 1845, although wary toward Roman Catholic Marian practice,[113] Newman cultivated a distinct devotion to Mary. Evidence can be found in two early sermons, both delivered on the feast of the annunciation. In the first, he chides his listeners for refusing to honor Mary simply because "some Christians exceed in their devotion, [and] become irreverent."[114] He goes on to speak glowingly of Mary's holiness and challenges his listeners to "estimate the reverence which her Son showed her" in order that they "may know how fitly to honour her memory."[115] The second sermon calls listeners to bless Mary for her role in the economy of salvation. In "bearing our Lord," this second Eve has "taken off or lightened the peculiar disgrace which the woman inherited for seducing Adam."[116] She is also blessed for her own personal sanctity. "Who can estimate," he asks, "the holiness and perfection of her, who was chosen to be the Mother of Christ?"[117] Newman then describes Mary's purity[118] in terms that led critics to assume he surreptitiously believed in the immaculate conception.[119]

One might think that, after his conversion, the suspicion with which Newman treated some aspects of Marian devotion would have withered. After all, the Catholic Newman proclaimed that Mary's privileges—including her immaculate conception, personal holiness, bodily assumption and intercessory power with God—were embryonically present in Holy Scripture, developed by the church fathers and both fitting for the Mother of God and redounding to the glory of

---

[112]Newman's own account of this conversion is now regarded as a classic religious biography; see John Henry Newman, *Apologia pro vita sua: Being a History of His Religious Opinions* (London: Longmans, Green, 1908).

[113]Ibid., p. 198.

[114]John Henry Newman, "The Annunciation: The Honour Due to the Blessed Virgin," in *Mary: The Virgin Mary in the Life and Writings of John Henry Newman,* ed. Philip Boyce (Grand Rapids: Eerdmans, 2001), p. 106. This sermon is undated, though it was certainly preached before 1832; see p. 105 n. 1.

[115]Ibid., p. 114.

[116]John Henry Newman, "The Reverence Due to the Virgin Mary," in *Mary: The Virgin Mary in the Life and Writings of John Henry Newman,* ed. Philip Boyce (Grand Rapids: Eerdmans, 2001), p. 120.

[117]Ibid.

[118]Ibid., pp. 120-21.

[119]Newman, *Apologia pro vita sua,* p. 165.

her Son.[120] But this is not the case. The fullest statement of Newman's Mariology contains both a ringing defense of the Roman Catholic Church's doctrine and a disavowal of certain popular practices.[121]

In the 1860s Newman's former Oxford Movement ally E. B. Pusey leveled charges against Newman.[122] Pusey lists many Marian beliefs that fall afoul of article 22 of the Thirty-Nine Articles: that Mary is a mediatrix without whose intercession there is no salvation, that the merciful Mary is opposed to the wrathful Christ, that she is a coredeemer, that she can bend Christ's will to her own, that she is present with Christ in the Eucharist and that Marian visions are practically accorded the status of revelation.[123] Pusey's main focus, however, was the recently defined dogma of the immaculate conception, which he critiques in detail.[124]

Newman counters Pusey's "one-sided"[125] presentation by grounding himself exclusively in the church fathers in order that he and Pusey may share the same evidence and accordingly "come to some intelligible result."[126] He then points out a distinction that Pusey failed to consider: the distinction between devotion and doctrine, contending that while the former has developed, the latter has not.[127] With respect to doctrine, Newman makes four claims. First, after an extensive exposition of the fathers' portrayal of Mary as the second Eve, Newman argues that the dogma of the immaculate conception is not an extrabiblical accretion, but "an immediate inference, from the primitive doctrine that Mary is the second Eve."[128] Second, Mary's exaltation as Queen of Heaven inevitably follows from reading Revelation 12 in its canonical context. Newman insists "that the Holy Apostle would not have spoken of the Church under this particular image, *unless* there had existed a blessed Virgin Mary, who was exalted on high, and the object of veneration to all the faithful." Furthermore, he adds, "No one doubts that the 'man-child' spoken of is an allusion to our Lord: why then is not 'the Woman' an allusion to His Mother?"[129] Third, all forms of Marian devotion are ultimately rooted in the Council of Ephesus (431) and its affirmation of *The-*

---

[120]See, e.g., John Henry Newman, "The Glories of Mary for the Sake of Her Son" and "On the Fitness of the Glories of Mary," in *Mary: The Virgin Mary in the Life and Writings of John Henry Newman,* ed. Philip Boyce (Grand Rapids: Eerdmans, 2001), pp. 149-66, 167-78.

[121]John Henry Newman, *Certain Difficulties Felt by Anglicans in Catholic Teaching Considered,* vol. 2 (London: Longmans, Green, 1900).

[122]E. B. Pusey, *An Irenicon,* 3 vols. (Oxford: Henry & Parker, 1865-1870).

[123]Ibid., 1:101-6, 150-90.

[124]Ibid., 2:301-409.

[125]Newman, *Certain Difficulties Felt by Anglicans,* 2:7.

[126]Ibid., 2:24-25.

[127]Ibid., 2:26-31.

[128]Ibid., 2:49.

[129]Ibid., 2:58.

otokos as a legitimate Marian title.[130] Fourth, the notion of Mary as a heavenly intercessor followed with beliefs about Mary's sanctity and dignity, as can be found in the earliest writings of the church fathers as well as the earliest examples of Christian art.[131]

When he moves from doctrine to devotion, however, Newman's form and tone of argument changes. First of all, he explains Marian devotion in terms of organic development. Just as all living things constantly change, growing into perfection and then declination, so Christian devotion forever evolves as it encounters differences of culture, history and so on. Helpful and harmful mutations will occur; once development stops, the organism is at its most pristine—and dead. With respect to such developments, one can choose to anticipate and prohibit excesses—"continual meddling" in Newman's view—or one may act only after an abuse comes to light.[132]

Newman then describes just what proper devotion would involve. It would understand, first, that Mary depends entirely on Jesus—even in her role as intercessor. She does not make our requests known to him; rather he, being omniscient, reveals them to her. It would maintain, second, that Mary neither indwells the devout nor may be said to be "present" to the believer in any way. Finally, it would understand that Mary neither propitiates God's wrath nor alters his judgment; being unable either to save or damn, she can be approached by believers without fear.[133]

With these guidelines in mind, Newman comes to Pusey's extensive list of Catholic quotations and repudiates "such sentences, and phrases, as these": that Mary's mercy is infinite, that God acts according to her will, that she is "safer" than her Son, that she is superior to God, that Christ is subject to her command, that she is an advocate for sinners while Christ is not, that only she can obtain a Protestant's conversion, that Christ's obedience to Mary unto death could have merited the world's salvation, that she is God's daughter by nature, that Christ is the Savior insofar as he imitates her, that he bears her image as well as that of his Father, that she gives redemption its beauty, that believers are clothed with the merits of Christ and Mary, that she is a priestess in a manner analogous to the priesthood of her Son, that she is present and received in the Lord's Supper, that priests are ministers of Christ and Mary, that the elect are born of God and Mary, that the Holy Spirit acts through her in the church and that the Holy

[130]Ibid., 2:61-67.
[131]Ibid., 2:68-76.
[132]Ibid., 2:79.
[133]Ibid., 2:82-86.

Spirit and Mary work together in the lives of individual believers.[134] Newman knows that such a lengthy rejection challenges the piety of many Roman Catholics and so qualifies it. The repudiation applies only when these phrases are understood literally—a tendency especially peculiar to Protestants.[135] Nevertheless, Newman knowingly ends up denouncing as "a bad dream,"[136] without foundation in Scripture, the church fathers, councils, theological schools, tradition, the papal teaching office or reason, the ideas of significant Roman Catholic spiritual writers, including at least one doctor of the church![137]

Newman—whether as an Anglican or a Roman Catholic—thus remains remarkably consistent in his wish to always submit himself to the teaching of Holy Scripture, definitively interpreted by the fathers and councils of the undivided church. For him this entailed rejection of much of the Marian revival that was taking place around him. In so doing, he was the vanguard of a shift in Roman Catholic Marian thought that would come to fruition only in the second half of the twentieth century.

Conclusion

The rift in sixteenth-century Western Christendom culminated in very different approaches to theology and devotion, which themselves determined the shape of doctrinal developments for subsequent centuries. This is as true for reflection on Mary as for any other theological locus or devotional practice. Among the Reformers and their descendants, the trend is one of decline into silence. In the first generation, as exemplified in Erasmus and (the early) Luther, Marian doctrines were not overtly criticized and some forms of Marian devotion were maintained. What these early critics singled out for criticism was not official church teaching per se, but those devotional Marian practices that either were regarded as base and superstitious or presented Mary as an alternative, perhaps even a rival, to her Son.

As the Reformation moved into its second generation, the criticism expanded to include officially approved Marian teachings and doctrines. By the late sixteenth and early seventeenth centuries, Mary had come to personify every theological and devotional disagreement. Where the Reformers held to justification

---

[134]Ibid., 2:113-14.

[135]Ibid., 2:113. Newman, in other words, is willing to grant these phrases a certain amount of poetic license.

[136]Ibid., 2:114.

[137]Namely, Saint Alphonsus Ligouri, whose *Glories of Mary* provided Pusey with much of his material. See Graef, *Mary,* 2:74-77, for a summary of his writings. Ligouri was named a doctor not for his devotional writings, but for his moral ones.

by grace alone through faith alone, Mary personified a soteriology of grace and merit; where they held to Scripture alone as the sole source of sacred doctrine, Mary personified unwritten apostolic tradition as a second source of revelation; where they held that salvation was through Christ alone, Mary personified an entire cult of the saints who themselves helped to mediate grace to the faithful.

Of course, there remained exceptions to this strictly polemical cast: while Zwingli, probably more for political than theological reasons, maintained the feast of the assumption, Bullinger appears actually to have believed in it, and Drelincourt attempted a constructive Mariology that remained aware of Reformation differences. Even Anglican articles 6, 15 and 22 are exceptional for their silence with respect to Mary. Article 6 extolled the truths of Scripture alone, but neither singled out Marian doctrines or devotions perceived to be contrary to its right interpretation nor said anything about devotions that were beneficial to Christian growth but not necessary for salvation. Article 15 proclaimed the universality of original sin among the baptized, but nothing about those who, like Mary, were not. Even article 22's rejection of purgatory, images and relics refuses to single Mary out.

Pressures created by the Enlightenment, however, forced the dwindling of even these exceptional circumstances. Protestant rationalism retained Mary's motherhood as a focal point when dealing with the incarnation in the face of growing philosophical arguments to abandon miracles, but in a way that did little to commend it to the romantics of the next generation. Thus, Schleiermacher undertakes to defend Christianity from its cultured despisers by repackaging it in a form they would understand: one that could plumb the depths of Christianity's spiritual experience without demanding acceptance of its miracles, including the virginal conception. With him, Mary becomes an accident of history who could be ignored without damage to the faith.[138]

When one places Roman Catholic developments alongside Protestant ones, one is immediately struck by how similar causes could lead to opposite reactions. If Protestant history is one of a gradual decline into silence, then Roman Catholic history is one of exaltation culminating in the first of two modern dogmatic definitions. Like the first generation of Reformers, the Council of Trent was content to treat Mary only in an ancillary way, rightly understanding that far more substantive issues were at stake. By the time of Canisius and Suárez, the response was well underway. For Canisius, Mary needed defending from attacks both within (Erasmus) and without (Luther), but his defense of Marian devo-

---

[138]One is forced to wonder whether, in the light of the so-called advances of liberal Protestant Christology after Schleiermacher, Mary's warning to Glaucoplutus (see pp. 213-14) was right after all.

tional language reveals a tacit agreement with these earliest Marian critics that medieval Marian devotion had become excessive, divorced from its biblical and traditional roots and now dishonoring of Christ. For Suárez, Marian thought needed to be systematized in order that devotional practice might be better related to and understood within the bounds of sound doctrine.

Given the examples offered of Marian devotion in the nineteenth century, one may wonder whether attempts like those of Canisius and Suárez to put Marian devotion on a more secure doctrinal basis had been successful. The argument between Pascal and Barry, the visions of Mary of Agreda and the treatment of Muratori by his critics seemingly coalesce to indicate that in spite of attempts at moderating devotional excess, Marian devotion among the masses continued to outstrip attempts to restrain it.

This is the context within which Pius IX's definition of the immaculate conception is best understood. Not only is it a response to romanticism's greater openness to spiritual things after the Enlightenment. It is also a deft attempt to curb Marian excess by officially defining (and therefore delimiting) what Roman Catholics ought to believe about Mary's conception. Prior to the definition, the immaculate conception had been the subject of academic debate and pious belief for centuries. Even among supporters there seem to have been several understandings, at least some of which crossed the line between excess and heresy. Pius IX not only appealed to the many Catholic faithful by defining a belief to which they already subscribed, he did so in a way that ruled out extreme interpretations, for example, the visions of Mary of Agreda, according to which Mary did not need to be saved, having been exempted from the Fall by divine decree. Pius IX definitively countered that Mary was exceptional only in the manner of her salvation. She was saved from the instant of her conception, in view of the merits of her Son. Thus the faithful were required to affirm the immaculate conception (which they already did) and to deny that Mary did not need to be saved (which at least some had affirmed until then).

The turn toward Marian sobriety, almost imperceptibly present in Pius IX's dogmatic definition, is better expressed by John Henry Newman—whether as an Anglican or as a Roman Catholic—in his insistence to say no more and no less than the church fathers. He thus gives Marian thought and devotion a patristic and biblical cast that had become obscured in the minds of many. He also serves as a bridge to the twentieth century, during which both Protestants and Catholics would turn to Mary to find not only a queen, but also a sister in the faith of all who struggle.

10

Queen of Heaven, Mother of the Church, Sister in the Struggle

Mary Through the Twentieth Century to Today

Three Marian main events quickly emerge to organize our discussion of Mariology in the twentieth century. First, the dogma of the bodily assumption of Mary into heaven, promulgated in 1950, brings a century of renewed Marian devotion to a close by officially exalting Mary to new heights. We will trace the development of this doctrine, exposit its official declaration and briefly discuss its implications. Second, the reforms initiated by the Second Vatican Council and implemented under the direction of Pope Paul VI turn away from the previous century's ever-increasing devotion. The council and the pope clearly favor an understanding of Mary more biblically and patristically grounded, more in harmony with the liturgical life of the church, more aware of the difficulties that Mary poses to other Christians and more conversant with findings in the human sciences. Third, the result of this daring initiative is a new plurality of voices speaking about Mary from the 1970s onward. Feminist theologians Elizabeth Johnson and Tina Beattie are examples of feminist thinking, and Tissa Balasuriya and Leonardo Boff are representatives of the Two-Thirds World. Protestants are slowly coming out of their long, largely self-imposed silence to reconsider Mary again. While the value of official documents and dialogues should not be discounted, perhaps more fascinating is the way in which Mary seems to grab the evangelical Protestant lay imagination.

Queen of Heaven: Bodily Assumption (1950)

When seeking to understand the bodily assumption of Mary into heaven with any degree of sympathy (this is not to say agreement), two factors need to be kept constantly in mind. The first is the doctrine's ancient roots. The Bible, of course, says nothing about Mary's death. Rather, she is last seen in the upper room, waiting for the coming of the Holy Spirit with the disciples (Acts 1:14). The continuation of that silence by the early fathers is exemplified by Epiphanius of Salamis, who insisted in the late fourth century that the church knows not how or even whether Mary died (see chap. 7). Not long after the Council of Ephesus (431), however, fanciful tales began to explain the church's silence, thereby also effectively ending it. In one of the three earliest accounts, Cyril of Jerusalem narrates how the apostles lost Mary's body as they fled a Jewish mob determined to mutilate it during her funeral procession, but says nothing of a miraculous entry into heaven. In another, a so-called eyewitness account by Bishop Evodius of Rome, Christ appears to Mary and the apostles, receives her soul at her death, only to reappear seven months later to reunite Mary's soul and body, taking both to heaven. The third—allegedly by John the evangelist—shortens the time span to three days from death to assumption. The latter proved to be the most popular and became the template for the official Western account by Melito of Sardis.[1] By the eighth century, the assumption was widely and popularly believed, even if not officially approved.

Second, the dogma of the bodily assumption may well be misunderstood if its immediate context is not also taken into account. Three items are relevant, including, first, its place in the Marian renewal that had begun a century earlier. The century between 1850 and 1950 marks "the Marian age,"[2] defined by two papal pronouncements[3] and dominated by Marian visions, some of which have been officially approved: closely associated to the immaculate conception were

---

[1]Summaries of the tales can be found in R. L. P. Milburn, "The Historical Background of the Doctrine of the Assumption," in *Women in Early Christianity,* ed. David M. Scholer, Studies in Early Christianity 14 (New York: Garland, 1993), pp. 55-66.

[2]Barbara Corrado Pope, "Immaculate and Powerful: The Marian Revival in the Nineteenth Century," in *Immaculate and Powerful: The Female in Sacred Image and Social Reality,* ed. Clarissa W. Atkinson et al. (Boston: Beacon, 1985), p. 173.

[3]Apart from the decrees concerning the immaculate conception and the bodily assumption, the popes were highly involved in the promotion of Marian piety. Donal Flanagan writes, "The popes from Pius IX to Pius XII, even when they did not directly speak on Marian doctrine, often gave an impetus to the Marian movement in other ways. Pius XI approved the legion of Mary and the feast 'Mary, Mediatrix of all graces.' Pius X indulgenced prayers to our Lady and encouraged study and practice of the 'True Devotion.' Leo XIII fostered devotion to the rosary. . . . [Such works] were preparing the ground for the astonishing upsurge in devotional practice, doctrinal effort and papal support for both which were marked features of the pontificate of Pius XII" ("The Blessed Virgin Mary, Mother of God, in the Mystery of Christ and the Church," in *Vatican II: The Constitution on the Church: A Theological and Pastoral Commentary,* ed. Kevin MacNamara [London: Chapman, 1968], p. 318).

the visions of Labouré (Paris, 1830) and Soubirous (Lourdes, 1858) (see the previous chapter); to these we now add the visions of Mélanie Calvat and Maximin Giraud (LaSallette, 1846), Eugène Barbadette (Pontmain, 1871), Lucia dos Santos (Fátima, 1917), the five children of Beauraing (1932) and Mariette Beco (Banneux, 1933).[4] As above, rendering an account of "what actually happened" in France, Portugal and Belgium is outside the scope of this study. What is germane is that many Roman Catholic Christians received them as facts—facts that, as Barbara Corrado Pope points out, are given added credence by the ancient belief that Mary was assumed body and soul into heaven: "This tenet of faith makes the possibility of her reappearance more real. An actual physical presence is something to behold, to touch and to feel."[5] They served, in other words, to strengthen belief in an ancient and already widely held doctrine.

The second item of relevance to the dogma of the bodily assumption is the Marian piety of Eugenio Pacelli—which certainly equals, if not surpasses, the Marian devotion of both Pius IX and John Paul II. Pacelli assumed the throne of Saint Peter as Pope Pius XII in 1939, at the onset of World War II. Mary played a central role in both his pastoral and teaching offices. With respect to the former, at the height of the global conflict in 1942 Pius XII consecrated the world to Mary, appealing to her as queen of the rosary and as help of Christians to intervene and "entrusting ourselves to your [i.e., her] Immaculate Heart in this fateful hour of human history."[6] With respect to the latter, the decree defining the bodily assumption is one of several important documents amplifying his Marian teaching. Among these are the 1943 encyclical titled *The Mystical Body of Christ* in which he referred to his earlier consecration and Mary's heavenly reign. A decade later, another encyclical, *Fulgens corona,* proclaimed a Marian Year to celebrate the centennial of the definition of the immaculate conception. After reiterating that earlier decree, Pius XII deliberately linked it to the assumption and strongly encouraged bishops to promote Mar-

---

[4]Accounts of the visions—with surprisingly frank assessments of their plausibility—can be found in Hilda Graef, *Mary: A History of Doctrine and Devotion,* vol. 2: *From the Reformation to the Present Day* (London: Sheed & Ward, 1963), pp. 99-106, 136-46. Interest in the visions of Lucia dos Santos was renewed by her passing on February 13, 2005. Many Roman Catholics will add this date to the evidence—which includes seemingly accurate predictions of the premature deaths of her cousins and fellow seers Francisco and Jacinta, of the Soviet Union's rise and fall and of an assassination attempt on a future pope—for the veracity of her visions, which took place on the thirteenth day of each month from May to October 1917. Certainly Pope John Paul II believed, having credited Mary with saving his life and having placed the bullet with which he was shot (again, strangely, on May 13, 1981) in the crown of the statue of Mary at Fátima.

[5]Pope, "Immaculate and Powerful," p. 190.

[6]Graef, *Mary,* 2:146.

ian devotion through sermons and pilgrimages—especially to Lourdes. The Marian Year ended with another yet encyclical, *Ad caeli reginam,* which established the feast of Mary's queenship. The apostolic constitution *Munificentissimus deus* (1950) in which the dogma was defined clearly stands as the climax of a very Marian pontificate.

The third item of relevance to the bodily assumption is the world political situation. In an essay following on the heels of the definition, Fulton J. Sheen presented the immaculate conception and assumption as directed toward political realities. The former sought to countermand the false optimism that underlay the politics of the nineteenth century. The latter was intended to appeal to people who had lived through two disastrous global conflicts, feared a (nuclear) third and accordingly adopted a false pessimism regarding human potential. If Pius IX wished to challenge the notion of the inherent goodness of the human race by reminding the world that all save two had been touched by original sin, then Pius XII wished to oppose those materialistic theories—especially communism—that began and ended in despair, by presenting the true future of the human race as foreshadowed in one singular individual.[7]

The proclamation itself, although fairly lengthy, is surprisingly straightforward and opens by narrating the steps that preceded it.[8] After acknowledging the "many cares, anxieties, and troubles" and indeed "severe calamities" that have defined the first half of the twentieth century, Pius XII observes that public devotion to Mary has been increasing.[9] This, in turn, led the Roman Catholic Church to a more serious consideration of her prerogatives and specifically the doctrine of the assumption.[10] Linking it deliberately to the immaculate conception and the definition of Pius IX in 1854, Pius XII asserts that Mary, "by an entirely unique privilege, completely overcame sin by her immaculate conception, and as a result she was not subject to the law of remaining in the corruption of the grave, and she did not have to wait until the end of time for the redemption of her body."[11] Since 1854 there has therefore been a growing demand both generally from the faithful and specifically from among "those who could speak for nations or ecclesiastical provinces" to clarify and define this doctrine.[12] This culminated in a letter issued to Pius's fellow bishops on May 1, 1946, asking them directly whether this action should be taken. The almost unanimous approval is

[7]Fulton J. Sheen, "The Assumption and the Modern World," *The Thomist* 14 (1951): 31-40.
[8]Pius XII, "Munificentissimus deus," trans. Joseph C. Fenton, *The Thomist* 14 (1951): 3-21.
[9]Ibid., p. 3.
[10]Ibid., p. 4.
[11]Ibid.
[12]Ibid., p. 5.

taken by Pius as "a certain and firm proof"[13] that this is a truth revealed by God to the church as a whole. The process of inquiry is therefore closed.

Pius XII then rehearses the "testimonies, indications, and signs of this common belief of the church" that are evident "from remote times down through the course of the centuries."[14] Throughout history the broad appeal of the assumption is shown by the number of temples dedicated to it, the many artworks depicting it, the consecration of places to her patronage and, of course, the rosary, which proposes the assumption as one of several mysteries to be contemplated.[15] It has been observed in both East and West by liturgical offices, through which the church is led into the truth. These, in turn, are based on the feast of the assumption (West) or dormition (East), which generations of popes have slowly exalted.[16] Furthermore, the earliest sermons delivered on this feast day "spoke of this doctrine as something already known and accepted by Christ's faithful"[17] while later generations of theologians employed passages from the Psalms (Ps 132:8; 45:10), the Song of Songs (Song 3:6; 4:8; 6:9), Revelation (Rev 12) and Luke (Lk 1:28)[18] and developed various arguments to support it.[19]

Pius then offers his own considerations. In Holy Scripture, Mary is intimately joined to Jesus; it therefore is inconceivable that he would not honor her by preserving her from corruption. As the New Eve, she shares in the victory of the Last Adam over the serpent; the resurrection of Christ was a sign of this victory, the glorification of Mary's body completed it. The assumption crowns Mary's preceding privileges: predestination, immaculate conception, perpetual virginity and divine motherhood. It is therefore most fitting that "she should be preserved free from the corruption of the tomb and that, like her own Son, having overcome death, she might be taken up body and soul to the glory of heaven where, as Queen, she sits in splendor at the right hand of her Son, the immortal King of the ages."[20]

The time for the declaration, Pius concludes, has arrived. In God's providence, this is the climax of his Marian actions and his entire pontificate. As a further glorification of God, he hopes that his definition will increase Marian devotion among the faithful, that she will become a sign of Christian unity, that her example will convince many of the value of devotion to God and doing

---

[13]Ibid., p. 7.
[14]Ibid.
[15]Ibid., p. 8.
[16]Ibid., pp. 9-10.
[17]Ibid., pp. 10-11.
[18]Ibid., pp. 12-13.
[19]Ibid., pp. 14-16.
[20]Ibid., p. 19.

good to others and decisively challenge materialism and the corruption of morals that it engenders and, finally, that it will increase confidence in the general resurrection at the end of time.[21] The decree (the only part of the document that may be said to be infallible) is then given: "By the authority of our Lord Jesus Christ, of the Blessed Apostles Peter and Paul, and by Our own authority, We pronounce, declare, and define it to be a divinely revealed dogma: that the Immaculate Mother of God, the ever-virgin Mary, having completed the course of her earthly life, was assumed body and soul into heavenly glory."[22]

Like *Ineffabilis deus, Munificentissimus deus* is a striking document as much as for what it does not say as for what it does. With respect to its positive content, it is surely right to tie itself to the former declaration of Pius IX as its inevitable consequence. If Mary is immune to fault—this is the core of the immaculate conception—then she is also exempt from punishment—this is the core of the assumption. It is therefore fitting that the declarations bookend the so-called Marian age. It is what the declaration does not say, however, that is far more interesting—at least to an outsider. The definition refuses to take a position with respect to Mary's death; the phrase translated "having completed the course of her earthly life" can accommodate both those who hold that Mary died and then was raised again to life and those who hold that Mary never died. More importantly, it also left a very significant debate within the first group alone, one germane to our study. By refusing to define whether she died, Pius also refused to define whether Mary died merely as a consequence of her humanity or in some redemptive way.

With respect to the former, it is possible to understand the assumption to mean that Mary died but was spared corruption. If death—the separation of body from soul—is not punishment for sin but merely the end of natural human life, then Mary died simply because she was human. Because she was also the immaculately conceived mother of the Lord, she was spared the punishment for sin—corruption—that is always associated with death and is consequent on it. On this view, Mary is a truly exceptional creature, but one beneath her Son. As for the latter, it is also possible to understand the assumption to imply that Mary's death was in some way coredemptive with that of Christ's. If death and corruption are together punishment for sin and Mary, by being assumed body and soul into heaven, was spared sin's punishment, then—goes the argument—Mary's death was neither natural nor necessary. Why then did she die? Gabriel Roschini puts it plainly: "If, *de facto,* she did die, it was, as in the case of Christ,

[21]Ibid., p. 20.
[22]Ibid., p. 21.

for the coredemption of the human race. Consequently the Blessed Virgin, like her Son, ought to have risen from death."[23] He goes on to develop an argument for understanding Mary's death, resurrection and assumption as redemptive and Mary as coredeemer in the strongest possible sense.[24]

If Roschini is right, however, it is odd that Pius XII, whether in this declaration or afterward, did not go on to spell out this implication. Thus the documents that defined the Marian age both exalt Mary and shy away from what some Roman Catholics (not to mention their Protestant critics) took to be their obvious implications. Pius IX defined the immaculate conception in such a way as to rule out those understandings that presented Jesus' mother as independent of and equal to her Son. Following Scotus he stressed that the matter had to do with not whether but how Mary was saved by Jesus. Pius XII defined the bodily assumption without taking a position on Mary as coredeemer, even though he could have and in the eyes of some should have done so. The reticence of Pius IX and John Henry Newman seen in the previous chapter was likely a portent of the Marian reforms of the second half of the twentieth century. By the Marian year of 1954, the pendulum had reached its apogee and was about to swing back.

Mother of the Church: Implementing the Second Vatican Council (1962-1965)

Pope John XXIII convened the Second Vatican Council in order to open up the Roman Catholic Church after almost two centuries during which the institution was dominated by a fortress mentality precipitated by the Reformation and the Enlightenment. While the manner of its overall success in this objective remains a matter of debate,[25] there can be no argument that its impact continues to be felt not only in Catholicism but also in global Christianity. Certainly, that is true with respect to its conclusions regarding Mary. Both its conclusions about Mary and how they were to be implemented in local Roman Catholic churches are important for our study.

---

[23]Gabriel M. Roschini, "The Assumption and the Immaculate Conception," *The Thomist* 14 (1951): 60.

[24]Ibid., pp. 61-68.

[25]The debate can be nicely framed around the editorial biases of the two major Roman Catholic theological journals founded after the council. *Concilium* was started in 1965 as a means not only to implement, but also to push the reforms begun at the council further. *Communio,* on the other hand, was founded in 1972 and seeks to appropriate the insights of the council without thereby jettisoning preconciliar beliefs and practices. According to both perspectives, Vatican II succeeded as far as it went; for the former, it failed to plot a course for further reform; while for the latter, it failed to channel theological exuberance and allowed it to become theological confusion.

In 1962 a draft text titled "The Blessed Virgin Mary, Mother of God and Mother of Men" was submitted to the bishops for consideration. It was reissued in April 1963 as "Blessed Virgin Mary: Mother of the Church." The document itself, rather than its content, soon became the focus of dispute, as the bishops quickly polarized. On one side were the Marian maximalists whose point of view is summarized by Adrian Hastings as rejoicing "in the increasing number of Marian definitions, declarations, feasts and congresses of the last hundred years" and hoping "for a further notable 'advance' in Marian teaching from the Council."[26] He maintains that this group expected the council to enshrine the Marian title "Mediatrix of all Graces." Edward Schillebeeckx similarly recalls that some even wished to see a definition of coredemptrix that understood Mary to be her Son's equal in the objective accomplishment of salvation.[27] On the other hand Marian minimalists who had already been influenced by biblical, liturgical and ecumenical movements both inside and outside Catholicism "urged the return on all sides of the Church's life to a more scriptural and liturgical way of viewing things, and it has wanted to apply this also to Marian teaching and devotion."[28] While they believed they could justify Marian theological developments, they regarded many aspects of Marian devotion as unbalanced and insisted that "the need today is not so much to advance as to deepen and purify Marian devotion."[29]

The divisive question was whether the received document should be constituted independently or treated as a chapter in the larger document on the nature of the church, with maximalists insisting on the former and minimalists on the latter option. The minimalists, indeed, were especially alarmed by a title that not only lacked in biblical and patristic warrant but seemed to place Mary over and outside the church in an inappropriate way. In a vote that was the closest of any proceeding throughout the council's duration (1114 to 1074), the bishops decided that Mary rightly belonged within the church and could not, therefore, be considered apart from it. A new theological subcommission consisting of members of both sides was struck to produce a new document reflecting this concern. The Doctrinal Commission of the council received and revised the subcommission's conclusions in March 1964. The bishops then received both the original and revised documents and used them to produce a third, which be-

[26]Adrian Hastings, *A Concise Guide to the Documents of the Second Vatican Council* (London: Darton, Longman & Todd, 1968), 1:62-63.

[27]Edward Schillebeeckx, "Mariology: Yesterday, Today, Tomorrow," in Edward Schillebeeckx and Catharina Halkes, *Mary: Yesterday, Today, Tomorrow* (New York: Crossroad, 1993), p. 13.

[28]Hastings, *Concise Guide,* 1:63.

[29]Ibid.

came *Lumen gentium* 8,[30] the council's dogmatic constitution on the nature of the church. Although born in controversy, the final document received unanimous approval.

When reading the text the reader is immediately confronted by its many scriptural and patristic citations. Although medieval and modern texts are mentioned, it is clear that the council wishes to ground Marian teaching in the earliest (common) Christian faith. According to the text, all privileges follow her motherhood and her free assent to it. Predestined to be the mother of the Son of God, Mary is also the beloved daughter of the Father, the temple of the Holy Spirit. And yet, this privilege does not make her divine. She is one of the offspring of Adam, "one with all those who are to be saved."[31] She is an exalted creature: "highest after Christ and closest to us."[32] "Therefore she is hailed as preeminent and as a wholly unique member of the church, and as its exemplar and outstanding model in faith and charity. The catholic church taught by the holy Spirit, honors her with filial affection and devotion as a most beloved mother."[33]

Although it is not a complete statement of Mariology[34] and clearly has ecumenical intentions,[35] the document does not shy away from official and unofficial Marian declarations that had proved problematic in the past. It understands the dogma of the immaculate conception as the fulfillment of the patristic parallel of Eve and Mary[36] and reiterates the dogma of the bodily assumption.[37] Still, its main objective is to understand Mary's role within the church according to which Mary is, first of all, a representative of the human race: as a daughter of Adam, she represents humanity's passive need for God; as the New Eve, she represents the potential active acceptance of God's gift. She is especially, however, the representative of all believers, for she is the church in eschatological relief.[38] She is now where all believers aim to be, and "so they turn their eyes to Mary who shines forth to the whole community of the elect as the model of virtues."[39]

---

[30]Ibid., 1:61-62.

[31]Hilda Graef et al., trans., "Dogmatic Constitution on the Church: *Lumen gentium,* 21 November, 1964," in *Vatican Council II: Constitutions, Decrees, Declarations,* ed. Austin Flannery (Northport: Costello, 1996), p. 80 §8.1.53.

[32]Ibid., p. 81 §8.1.54.

[33]Ibid., pp. 80-81 §8.1.53.

[34]Ibid., p. 81 §8.1.54.

[35]Ibid., pp. 89-90 §8.5.68-69.

[36]Ibid., pp. 82-83 §8.2.56.

[37]Ibid., p. 84 §8.2.59.

[38]Ibid., p. 87 §8.3.64.

[39]Ibid., p. 87 §8.3.65.

It is in this ecclesiological context that the council situates the notion of Mary's mediation. Mary's role as mediatrix or even coredemptrix does not elevate her to the level of Christ and remove her from the church. In these roles she remains with all the redeemed. It is part of the Christian vocation to be coredeemers with Christ; Mary is unique only in the fullness of her response to and participation in it. Her "salutary influence on men and women originates not in any inner necessity but in the disposition of God. It flows forth from the superabundance of the merits of Christ, rests on his mediation, depends entirely on it and draws all its power from it. It does not hinder in any way the immediate union of the faithful with Christ but on the contrary fosters it."[40] In her obedience to the will of God, Mary cooperated in bringing salvation to the world. And, in heavenly glory, she continues in that mediatory work. "This, however, is understood in such a way that it neither takes away anything from, nor adds anything to, the dignity and efficacy of Christ the one Mediator."[41] No creature is equal to the incarnate Word; looking to Mary as their example, all the faithful cooperate in the work of redemption that springs from one source. As a result the bishops conclude that the "church does not hesitate to profess this subordinate role of Mary, which it constantly experiences and recommends to the heartfelt attention of the faithful, so that encouraged by this maternal help they may more closely adhere to the Mediator and Redeemer."[42]

Pope Paul VI approved a new Marian title "Mother of the Church" on November 21, 1964, to summarize the conciliar teaching[43] and almost a decade later, on February 2, 1974, issued an apostolic exhortation to direct the implementation of the conciliar reforms. Titled *Marialis cultus,* the document is divided into three parts: Mary in the (Roman) liturgy, the renewal of devotion to Mary, and observations on the Angelus and the rosary.[44] While the entire exhor-

---

[40]Ibid., p. 85 §8.3.60.

[41]Ibid., p. 86 §8.3.62.

[42]Ibid., p. 86 §8.3.62.

[43]The new Marian title was, however, a point of controversy. The minimalists argued persuasively that this title—absent from both biblical and patristic sources and rarely used in the medieval era—was an unnecessary and unhelpful innovation. The bishops therefore rejected it twice—both as a title for a 1963 draft of the document that became *Lumen gentium* 8 and again as an appropriate Marian title in 1964. As a result Paul VI had to implement his own apostolic authority against that of the majority of bishops. It is ironic that a document whose intent was to present Mary as a sign of hope and comfort for all Christians (*Lumen gentium,* pp. 89-90 §8.5.68-69), in a way that did not further scandalize other Christians, should find its intent expressed in a nonbiblical, nonpatristic title imposed by papal decree. See Edward Schillebeeckx, "Mariology," pp. 15-16.

[44]Paul VI, *Marialis cultus: For the Right Ordering and Development of Devotion to the Blessed Virgin Mary,* online at <http://www.vatican.va/holy_father/paul_vi/apost_exhortations/documents/hf_p-vi_exh_19740202_marialis-cultus_en.html> (accessed March 16, 2005).

tation is fascinating, part two is most germane to our study. The pope acknowledges that "veneration of the Mother of God has taken on many forms according to circumstances of time and place, the different sensibilities of peoples and their different cultural traditions." Consequently, a renewal "that will permit them to substitute elements that are transient, to emphasize the elements that are ever new and to incorporate the doctrinal data obtained from theological reflection and the proposals of the Church's magisterium"[45] is needed. Part two offers both theological and practical guidelines according to which the Marian renewal is to be structured.

Theologically the renewal and revision of Marian devotion needs to be directed by sound trinitarian and ecclesiological principles.[46] First, Paul VI reminds the bishops overseeing the implementation of the Vatican II reforms that Christian worship is directed to the Father, through the Son, in the Spirit. Worship, he adds, may rightly be extended to Mary provided it is conducted in "a substantially different way" and in "a special manner."[47] The unique privileges that render her worthy of special veneration are not hers intrinsically but rather stem from the electing grace of the Father and the gifting of the Holy Spirit by which she was chosen and equipped to be the mother of the Son. Rightly understood, therefore, they cannot detract from the glory due to God alone, but accentuate it; they will not distract from the worship of Christ, but direct and strengthen it.

Furthermore, proper attention to Mary will keep the person and work of the Holy Spirit in the foreground, for "the sanctifying intervention of the Spirit in the Virgin of Nazareth was a culminating moment of the Spirit's action in the history of salvation."[48] Likewise, deep meditation "on the working of the Holy Spirit in the history of salvation . . . will bring out in particular the hidden relationship between the Spirit of God and the Virgin of Nazareth, and show the influence they exert on the Church."[49] Finally, the renewal and revision of Marian devotion ought to be oriented toward reminding the faithful of Mary's place in the church, namely, "the highest place and the closest to us after Christ."[50] Because of their close identification, love for one will be love for the other and vice versa.

Practically the implementation of the revitalization of Marian devotion—especially in the revision of current devotional practices or the creation of

---

[45]Ibid., §24.
[46]Ibid., §§25-28.
[47]Ibid., §25.
[48]Ibid., §26.
[49]Ibid., §27.
[50]Ibid., §28, quoting *Lumen gentium* §8.54.

new ones—is to take place following biblical, liturgical, ecumenical and anthropological guidelines.[51] First, veneration of the Mother of God should have a "biblical imprint,"[52] by which the pope means not only that biblical texts should be used more frequently, but also that "texts of prayers and chants should draw their inspiration and their wording from the Bible, and above all that devotion to the Virgin should be imbued with the great themes of the Christian message."[53] Second, devotional forms should neither replace nor be supplanted by the worship of the community. They should flow from and lead back to the church's central liturgical rite, the Eucharist.[54] Third, if they are immersed in and drawn from the Scriptures and also liturgically oriented to the Lord's Table, Marian devotions will invariably also be ecumenical.[55] Accordingly every "care should be taken to avoid any exaggeration which could mislead other Christian brethren about the true doctrine of the Catholic Church," while "any manifestation of cult which is opposed to correct Catholic practice should be eliminated."[56] Finally, renewed devotion to Mary should "pay close attention to certain findings of the human sciences."[57] The psychosocial conditions under which men and women live are changing constantly, and Marian devotion ought to be attuned to and altered in the light of such changes. This is not to espouse some sort of Marian relativism, but simply to recognize that the core of the Bible's and church's teachings will be devotionally expressed differently across history, geography and cultures.[58]

Sister in the Struggle: Mary in Recent Theology

The aftermath of the Second Vatican Council has seen a veritable deluge of writings on Mary, ranging from the devotional fringe to the highly academic. Nev-

---

[51]Paul VI, *Marialis cultus* §§29-39.

[52]Ibid., §§29-30.

[53]Ibid., §30.

[54]Ibid., §§31-32.

[55]Ibid., §§32-33.

[56]Ibid., §32.

[57]Ibid., §§34-37.

[58]Ibid., §36. Paul VI is particularly aware of how modern women may find certain forms of Marian devotion to be not only antiquated but actually immoral because of the demeaning way in which they present especially women disciples. He therefore offers a counterportrait of a strong Mary: "She is held up as an example to the faithful rather for the way in which, in her own particular life, she fully and responsibly accepted the will of God (cf. Lk 1:38), because she heard the Word of God and acted on it and because charity and a spirit of service were the driving force of her actions. She is worthy of imitation because she was the first and the most perfect of Christ's disciples. All of this has a permanent and universal exemplary value" (ibid., §37).

ertheless, among these an important trend is readily observed: the desire—in response to the invitation of Vatican II and Pope Paul VI—to understand Mary as "one of us," a pilgrim and fellow disciple. This criticism and (re)appropriation of Marian theology is expressed in feminist theology, in Third World liberation theologies and in Protestant theology.

Feminist theology. As one might expect, early feminist writings on Mary diagnose traditional thought about her as part of the problem with theology in general, namely, that it arises out of and authorizes a religious discourse in which the experiences of women and children are ignored or suppressed.[59] The course of treatment that this early stage proposed was the radical reshaping (if not rejection) of tradition in the light of women's experience. The early work of Rosemary Radford Ruether represents just such a view. For example, she challenged the "Mary of the monks," the antisexual Virgin Mother whose symbolic expression of obedience, virginity and motherhood became the ideal Christian-male definition of the Christian woman—one that no woman could match.[60] But a subversive mariological tradition may, if tapped, open up liberative possibilities for women: "the Mary of the people who is still the earth mother and who is venerated for her power over the secrets of natural fecundity"[61]—the Great Mother of pre-Christian Near Eastern religion, only baptized. Because of the power and duration of the patriarchal symbol system, however, such a liberative Mariology will in all likelihood require a different symbolic focus and expression. Another Mary—Mary Magdalene—may in Ruether's view prove to be a more worthy object of veneration.[62]

Feminist fascination with Mary, contrary to Ruether's early prediction, has neither subsided nor been supplanted by one directed to the Magdalene. Indeed, from that time until now, feminist appraisals of Mary have multiplied incredibly. A 1991 study documents no less than eleven different methodologies, with sometimes very different results, all claiming to fall within the feminist-

---

[59]My discussion of feminist theology here is limited to self-consciously Christian feminist theologians. For a post-Christian assessment of Mary, see Mary Daly, *Beyond God the Father* (Boston: Beacon, 1983), pp. 82-90.

[60]Rosemary Radford Ruether, "Mistress of Heaven: The Meaning of Mariology," in *New Woman, New Earth: Sexist Ideologies and Human Liberation* (New York: Seabury, 1975), pp. 36-62.

[61]Ibid., p. 50.

[62]Ibid., p. 59. This is not to say that Ruether was (or is) ready to relinquish the mother of Jesus. Her moving reading of the Magnificat (see *Sexism and God-Talk* [Boston: Beacon, 1983], pp. 139-58) grounds a liberation Mariology that draws criticism from some feminists for perpetuating traditional gender categories. Others, notably Elizabeth Johnson, praise it for "turning the Mary-Christ relationship into a liberating rather than repressive symbol" (*Truly Our Sister: A Theology of Mary in the Communion of Saints* [New York: Continuum, 2004], p. 37).

theological camp.[63] Two recent works—one North American, one European—have distinctive approaches.[64]

Elizabeth Johnson's *Truly Our Sister* superbly exemplifies the creative potential once North American feminist theology moves from critique to construction. It begins with an account of the experience of women with respect to the Marian symbol system that permeates the Roman Catholic Church[65] and then criticizes two mariological culs-de-sac that purport to be liberating to women (and, indeed, do offer some helpful material) but in the end are not. When Mary is presented as the "Ideal Face of Woman" or "the Maternal Face of God,"[66] what appear at first glance to be (or at least to contain) liberating proposals—Mary as the ideal feminine complementing Jesus as the ideal masculine; Mary as the symbolic expression of the divine feminine—are on further investigation theories erected on rigidly defined notions of gender constructed in, by and for a patriarchal symbol system that leaves the hierarchical structure of the church in place, the androcentric God-talk unaltered and the place of women in communities of faith unrecognized.

Johnson then departs from her earlier understanding Mary as an ecclesial symbol[67] to consider her as a "woman who actually lived a life some two thousand years ago and to honor her in a liberating way" by emphasizing "her historical reality at every point."[68] Johnson hopes thereby to present a pneumatological theology of Mary—one that treats Mary as an individual member of the community of saints living in dependence on the Holy Spirit and thereby "crafts a theology capable of promoting action on behalf of global justice and liberation, particularly empowering to the flourishing of women, coherent with elements of biblical, classical, and conciliar teaching, and productive of religious sense for our time."[69] Finding ample past precedent for this method, especially in *Marialis cultus* of Paul VI,[70] Johnson grounds it in an extensive sociohistorical analysis of the world in which Mary of Nazareth would have lived[71] and then

[63]Els Maeckelberghe, *Desperately Seeking Mary: A Feminist Appropriation of a Traditional Religious Symbol* (Kampen: Kok Pharos, 1991).

[64]There is a considerable blurring of the lines between feminist liberation theologies and Two-Thirds World liberation theologies. For the sake of clarity, I include feminist/womanist, Asian and Latino/a theologians in the latter category.

[65]Johnson, *Truly Our Sister,* pp. 3-43.

[66]Ibid., pp. 47-92.

[67]Elizabeth Johnson, "The Symbolic Character of Theological Statements About Mary," *Journal of Ecumenical Studies* 22 (1985): 312-25.

[68]Johnson, *Truly Our Sister,* p. 100.

[69]Ibid., p. 113.

[70]Ibid., pp. 114-34.

[71]Ibid., pp. 137-206.

applies it to the Marian material of the Gospels and Acts. The exegetical results are very interesting,[72] and their influence is evident in my own reading of the biblical texts above (see chaps. 1-5).

Theologically the presentation of Mary that emerges is "a woman of Spirit"[73] who "is sister to all who respond to the gift of the Spirit to their own lives, in ways seen and unseen."[74] Mary is to be read as a unique and ideal disclosure of that which the Spirit of God does in the individual lives of people and the corporate life of the church—both of which Johnson summarizes in the metaphor "communion of saints": "Interpreting Mary with her unique history within this great company locates her significance of faith amid multiple relationships of mutuality formed by the Spirit."[75] Five dimensions result from this reading:

1. In her ordinariness (as opposed to her traditionally defined sinlessness), Mary discloses the graced lives of all living members of the community. The title "saint" is not for dead examples but for all now living whom the Spirit of God makes "friends of God and prophets."[76]
2. As the mother of the pioneer of our faith—both in life and in death—Mary reminds us that while "saints" are primarily those now alive, the title does in fact extend to those who have died.
3. While Mary shows how all are saints, she—along with others—nevertheless retains a paradigmatic status. Her perseverance in faith amid the demonic structures that defined so much of her life ensures that her memory "liberates rather than diminishes the discipleship of others."[77]
4. As a woman who speaks God's prophetic message in the midst of suffering and exploitation, Mary is a companion with all who struggle—especially women and especially those who oppose patriarchal hierarchy in the church.
5. Devotion may be offered to this Mary—"truly, subversively, our sister"—especially through the frequent repetition of her own prayer (Lk 1:46-55). In this way "our relationship to God takes on an intimate liberating character which energizes action on behalf of justice."[78]

Johnson's feminism is evident in two ways. First, not surprisingly, "women's

---

[72]Ibid., pp. 209-304.
[73]Ibid., p. 305.
[74]Ibid., p. 306.
[75]Ibid., p. 308.
[76]Ibid., p. 311.
[77]Ibid., p. 314.
[78]Ibid., p. 324.

experience" is her methodological basis. Her opening account, highlighting the experiences of women outside North America and Europe, grounds her application of a hermeneutic of suspicion to the dominant Roman Catholic mariological tradition, justifies—to great effect—her exegetical focus on the "Mary of history" and maintains that justice for women ought to be the goal of any future mariological work. Second, ironically, her feminism is evident in her mariological minimalism. Following the critical path blazed by Ruether and Mary Daly, Johnson concludes that the traditional Marian motifs, including immaculate conception, perpetual virginity, bodily assumption, heavenly reign, intercession and saintly example have so historically marginalized women and promoted misogyny[79] that they cannot be redeemed—even as she once tried—by emphasizing their ecclesiological/symbolic dimension. As a result, the historically grounded, pneumatological Mary that Johnson produced is, as her title suggests, "truly our sister."

A younger generation of European feminist theologians, however, is growing impatient with the stark binary embraced both by North American feminist theologians and their conservative opponents. Finding unpersuasive the rhetorical exhortation to choose between tradition and feminism, between Mary as mother and Mary as sister, Tina Beattie's *God's Mother, Eve's Advocate* offers a deep criticism of both sides as it seeks to plumb the patristic depths of tradition from the perspective offered by French psychoanalytic feminism.[80] Beattie's aim is plain: "Rather than offering a systematic critique of Marian theology and doctrine, I insinuate myself into the cracks and gaps, developing a gynocentric narrative out of the discarded scraps of patristic theology that have been neglected or rejected in the construction of Marian theology."[81]In her view, discerning the place of the female body in salvation requires neither uncritical perpetuation nor hypercritical rejection, but the rereading of tradition.

After three extensive chapters providing a theoretical and historical context,[82] Beattie undertakes what she calls a "gynocentric refiguration of Marian symbol-

[79]Ibid., p. 314.

[80]Tina Beattie, *God's Mother, Eve's Advocate: A Marian Narrative of Women's Salvation* (New York: Continuum, 2002).

[81]Ibid., p. 6.

[82]Space does not permit a detailed exploration of Beattie's methodological and contextual work, fascinating though it may be. She weaves together Luce Irigaray and Paul Ricoeur in search of a gynocentric narrative theology (ibid., pp. 20-44), offers a genealogy of Christian thought on sexuality, indicates that early Marian theology undermines the dominant androcentric portrayal of the female body (pp. 45-70) and observes that in modern Roman Catholic theology the reification of masculinity in the male body coupled with the nonidentification of femininity with the female body leads to the presentation of the entire story of salvation in androcentric terms (pp. 71-86). This incipient androcentrism (exemplified in a male-only priesthood) is what Beattie wishes to undermine.

ism"[83] arranged around four images: mother, virgin, daughter and woman. Following Luce Irigaray's insistence on the first-order necessity of the restoration of the symbolic maternal to challenge patriarchal culture, Beattie argues that Mary's conception of the Word in her womb offers a linguistic matrix through which Christian thought did and can again out-narrate alternatives rooted in the sharp distinction between words and reality. This, in turn, is used to challenge the notion that the fatherhood of God demands a masculine priesthood.[84] Reinterpreting the patristic parallel of the Fall and annunciation narratives, Beattie then explores the ways in which patristic theology and psycholinguistic theory understand the power of language to (re)shape the world. Mary's virginity affirms women's desire in a way independent of the phallus and thus recreates a world in which sexual difference is neither primal nor obliterated, but reconciled.[85] Thus far, Mary has been defined by her maternal relationship to Christ. Left here, she cannot symbolize the redemption of women because her relationship to other women has not yet been clarified. Beattie therefore introduces a symbolic space in which Mary is defined apart from her Son—as a daughter of both Eve and Anna. Such a space, Beattie argues, permits women as daughters to recover a sense of place within Holy Mother Church.[86] Up to this point, the ancient Eve-Mary parallel has served as a subtext of Beattie's work. It now comes to the fore as she investigates how the stories of fall and annunciation, when read together, provide women with a story of salvation that they can call their own.[87] Finally, Beattie merges the images to argue that the institution of a female Marian priesthood could overcome the patriarchal association of women's bodies with impurity, violence, sex and death without violating current church teaching on sexual difference.[88]

Clearly, unlike Johnson, Beattie does not find the tradition to be a constraint to the development of a Mariology that is liberating for women (and accordingly men). It is, rather, a storehouse of symbolic images—one will find immaculate conception, perpetual virginity and bodily assumption all defended here—that contains, submerged beneath nearly two millennia of androcentrism, resources for a gynocentric reading not only of Mary, but of the entire Christian theological tradition. Nevertheless, Beattie's feminism does share important ground with Johnson's: namely, the observation that traditional understandings of Mary left

---

[83]Ibid., p. 13.
[84]Ibid., pp. 87-114.
[85]Ibid., pp. 115-40.
[86]Ibid., pp. 141-63.
[87]Ibid., pp. 164-93.
[88]Ibid., pp. 194-208.

on their own, which is to say in the hands of the Roman Catholic Church's male leadership, perpetuate false gender binaries in which the male/masculine is first essentialized and then divinized while the female/feminine remains associated at best with creatureliness and at worst with fallen humanity and its corruptive sexuality. For both, Mary must be returned to the laity.

Liberation theology. A similar concern dominates southern theologies of liberation. The rhetoric of sexuality, however, is replaced by that of class struggle. The focus is on Mary as the prophetic voice of the poor, whether the poor are found in Asia or Latin America. An example of the former is Sri Lankan theologian Tissa Balasuriya's *Mary and Human Liberation.*[89] The core of the book, a chapter titled "Mary: A Mature Adult Woman,"[90] is based on Luke's Gospel and presents Mary "as an ordinary woman of her time who went through the process of living in very difficult circumstances."[91] Balasuriya—like Johnson above—emphasizes Mary's courage and cooperation with Jesus throughout her life, even as a widow. And, like Johnson, Balasuriya pushes the traditional Marian dogmas into the background because he perceives them to have removed Mary from the life experiences of the world's poor and marginalized, a disproportionate number of whom are women and children. Balasuriya insists that what matters about Mary is "not so much that she is immaculate, a virgin, and in what form she is mother of God, but that she was intimately associated with Jesus of Nazareth, flesh of her flesh, in the beginning of the new community. This new community was to carry the message of human liberation. . . . In this, Mary is an example to all humankind."[92] She prophetically discloses the church's preferential option for the poor in her Magnificat, and for Balasuriya any dogma that blurs this disclosure is to be set aside.[93]

A very different understanding of Mary as the prophetic voice of the poor is found in Leonardo Boff's *The Maternal Face of God.*[94] On the one hand it seems as though Boff wishes to construct a Latin American liberation Mariology similar

---

[89]Tissa Balasuriya, *Mary and Human Liberation: The Story and the Text,* ed. Helen Stanton (Harrisburg, Penn.: Trinity, 1997), originally published as a double issue of *Logos* 29 (1990): 1-181.

[90]Ibid., pp. 56-78.

[91]Ibid., p. 57.

[92]Ibid., pp. 77-78.

[93]Balasuriya's construction of an either/or argument coupled with a popular and imprecise style brought him into conflict with his superiors and led eventually to his (now rescinded) excommunication from the Roman Catholic Church. See Edmund Hill, "The Balasuriya File," in *Mary and Human Liberation: The Story and the Text,* ed. Helen Stanton (Harrisburg, Penn.: Trinity, 1997), pp. 1-12.

[94]Leonardo Boff, *The Maternal Face of God: The Feminine and Its Religious Expression,* trans. Robert Barr and John Dierksmeier (Maryknoll, N.Y.: Orbis, 1987).

to Balasuriya's. In the chapter titled "Mary, Prophetic Woman of Liberation," he attends to the foundational experiences of oppression, violence and especially crippling poverty among local faith communities and how these, in turn, have shaped their understanding of the mother of Jesus. He observes that while traditional Mariology has paid little attention to the Magnificat, the poor of Latin America are transfixed by its prophetic denunciation of the powerful and declaration of God's favor toward the weak. He writes that "Christian ideology . . . has had a difficult time deciding between not ascribing any importance to Mary's prophetic words . . . and spiritualizing them."[95] In this chapter, Boff clearly reflects concerns similar to, if not the same as, those of Johnson and Balasuriya. But what is most striking about this proposal is that it does not seem to fit with the main proposal of the book.

Boff's argument is not based on the experiences of local churches as they read the Bible, but on an interweaving of the fervent devotional Marian practices of Latin American Catholicism with the theoretical emergence of the "nonrational" or "feminine" from the collective human unconsciousness to the foreground of contemporary culture.[96] By "the feminine," Boff means "the pole of darkness, mystery, depth, night, death, interiority, earth, felling, receptivity, generative force, and the vitality of the human," while the opposite pole, "the masculine," refers to "light, sun time, impulse, surging power, order exteriority, objectivity, reason." The former evinces itself in "repose, immobility, immanence, a longing for the past, and a certain darkness," while "aggressiveness, transcendence, clarity, the thrust toward transformation, the capacity to impose order and project in to the future" mark the latter.[97] When Latin American Marian enthusiasm is read through the lenses provided by Boff's "feminine," Mary—the virtual embodiment of this principle in her humility, silence and service to others—becomes the revelation of the divine feminine to the world. She functions, as it were, as an incarnation of the feminine divine.[98] Boff hypothesizes "that the Virgin Mary, Mother of God and of all men and women, realizes the feminine

---

[95]Ibid., p. 189.

[96]Ibid., p. 54.

[97]Ibid., p. 54.

[98]Boff writes (ibid., p. 91) that "Jesus the male reveals God's plan for the masculine explicitly. But he also reveals God's plan for the feminine (implicitly), since his reality, as the reality of a human being contains both the masculine and the feminine. . . . But Jesus' humanity, being male, contains the masculine and the feminine in the proportion proper to a male. Thus, while the masculine acquires an ultimate divine meaning in him directly, the feminine does so only implicitly, as the recessive component. But if there has been a full and direct divinization of the masculine—in Jesus—can we not expect the feminine to be ordered to a full and direct divinization as well?"

absolutely and eschatologically, inasmuch as the Holy Spirit has made her his temple, sanctuary, and tabernacle in so real and genuine a way that she is to be regarded as hypostatically united to the Third Person of the Blessed Trinity."[99] The result is a very high Mariology in which immaculate conception, virginal maternity and bodily assumption are supplemented with very strong notions of coredemption and comediation, for, as the incarnation of the Holy Spirit, Boff's Mary is Christ's equal. At no point does Boff attempt to harmonize this hypostatic expression of silence and repose with the active and prophetic Mary who sang the Magnificat.

Because Boff's proposal has been thoroughly criticized elsewhere,[100] we can set it aside. When considered together, our four representatives illustrate the post-Vatican II response to Mary in Roman Catholic theology. They show how experiences of the laity have come to the fore. Even though three authors (Johnson, Balasuriya and Boff) are or were active in the religious life of the Roman Catholic Church, they insist on bringing the experiences of the laity to bear on their theological constructions. Johnson and Balasuriya merit special attention from evangelical scholarship because of their close engagement with the biblical text. Beattie, as a lay theologian in her own right, freely explores lay concerns associated with the campaign to ordain women priests. In addition, all four illustrate the freedom with which post-Vatican II theologians have embraced and drawn from other disciplines to inform their work—whether it is feminist studies, a Marxist understanding of history and class struggle, theoretical anthropology or French psycholinguistics. The result is four very different portrayals of this one remarkable woman. Finally, as a result of this diversity, it is nearly impossible to identify a neat package of Roman Catholic Mariology. Johnson and Balasuriya are self-consciously minimal; Beattie and Boff are deliberately maximal—Boff idolatrously so. All four try to fall within the parameters set out by *Lumen gentium* 8 and *Marialis cultus*.

Protestant theology. Vatican II, however, has not simply kick-started a renewal of Marian thought in the Roman Catholic Church. It has also provided the

---

[99]Ibid., p. 93.

[100]Unfortunately, little of the critical interaction with Boff has been translated into English. The key articles remain Jean Galôt, "Marie et le visage de dieu," *Marianum* 44 (1982): 427-38; and J.-M. Hennaux, "L'esprit et le feminine: la mariologie de Leonardo Boff," *Nouvèlle revue théologique* 109 (1987): 884-95. Johnson presents a withering critique from a feminist perspective (*Truly Our Sister,* pp. 55-57, 81-82). She persuasively argues that whatever Boff's motivations, he has drunk too deeply from the wells of a rigidly dualistic patriarchal anthropology and that as a result he removes Mary from the realm of women's experience while his projection of patriarchal gender constructions onto the Godhead minimizes the role of Jesus Christ as the sole Savior of humankind.

impetus for Protestant biblical scholars and theologians to reconsider the Mother of God after over a century of self-imposed silence. The first facet of this recovery is the product of official or semiofficial dialogues between Protestant and Roman Catholic scholars. Primary among these remains *Mary in the New Testament.*[101] Raymond Brown and his ecumenical team were able to demonstrate just how much Protestants and Roman Catholics shared with respect to the biblical witness, even as they offered frank assessments of where and why the ecclesial traditions differed. In the latter part of the twentieth century, the U.S. Lutheran-Catholic Dialogue published a collection of fifteen essays and a common statement of convergences and divergences regarding Mary as she was understood in relation to Christ and in relation to the communion of saints.[102] In Europe, meanwhile, the Groupes des Dombes—a private association of French-speaking Lutheran, Reformed and Roman Catholic theologians—published a twofold study of Mary calling for a "conversion of the churches" in which Protestants and Catholics together would begin to consider whether their differences regarding Mary are truly church dividing.[103] The publications of the English-speaking Ecumenical Society for the Blessed Virgin Mary continue in a similar vein.

The interest, moreover, is not limited to official or semiofficial dialogues. A recent collection of essays from the Center for Catholic and Evangelical Theology offers a snapshot of the mariological concerns of a growing number of theologians from both sides of the Reformation divide whose primary concern is church unity-in-truth.[104] Perhaps most fascinating, however, is the published conversation between two alumni of Bob Jones University titled *Mary: A Catholic-Evangelical Debate.*[105] Dwight Longenecker journeyed from the Protestant fundamentalism of his youth through Anglicanism to become a Roman Catholic layman and professional apologist. David Gustafson's maturing in Christian faith led him to attend a conservative Episcopalian parish; he is a lawyer with the United States Department of Justice. Both authors are—by nature of their respective professions—good debaters and are not afraid to "score" on occasion. Nevertheless, what strikes one as remarkable about their book is its irenic tone

---

[101]Raymond Brown et al., *Mary in the New Testament: A Collaborative Assessment by Protestant and Roman Catholic Scholars* (Philadelphia: Fortress, 1978).

[102]G. Anderson et al., eds., *The One Mediator, the Saints, and Mary: Lutherans and Catholics in Dialogue VIII* (Minneapolis: Fortress, 1992).

[103]Alain Blancy et al., *Mary in the Plan of God and in the Communion of Saints: Toward a Common Christian Understanding,* trans. Matthew J. O'Connell (New York: Paulist Press, 2002).

[104]Carl Braaten and Robert Jenson, eds., *Mary: Mother of God* (Grand Rapids: Eerdmans, 2004).

[105]Dwight Longenecker and David Gustafson, *Mary: A Catholic-Evangelical Debate* (Grand Rapids: Brazos, 2004).

even as each author maintains the distinctives of his tradition. A conversation such as this would have been practically impossible prior to Vatican II. Still, a full-blown, constructive Mariology has not yet been undertaken by a Protestant theologian. What would a Protestant have to say about Mary? That is the guiding question of part three.

Conclusion

Before addressing what a Protestant Mariology would look like, conclusions to this chapter and part two need to be drawn.

Conclusion to chapter ten. Three themes emerge in chapter ten. First, within Roman Catholicism, Marian theology in the twentieth century continued to act as a restraint on acts of popular devotion. This conclusion may seem counterintuitive at first glance, but on closer investigation continues a trend established in the medieval era. The deep and abiding influence of the Augustinian doctrine of original sin on medieval Western theology implicitly restrained the acceptance and development of Eastern views of Mary's conception (see chap. 8), but it was not until 1854 that the Western church—at least officially—accepted in a way sensitive to its own Augustinian tradition what the Eastern church had taken for granted for over a millennium. This trend can also be seen in the way that the definition of the immaculate conception restricted some forms of Marian devotion. Pius IX's definition of Mary's sanctity explicitly denied Mary's exemption from the need for salvation through Christ by insisting that the immaculate conception addressed how—not whether—Mary was saved.

A similar strategy is at work in Pius XII's definition of the bodily assumption. Even as he exalts Mary by dogmatically defining a doctrine known and believed in both East and West since the fifth-sixth century, he does so in a way that curbs the devotion of some Marian enthusiasts. Even as he calls the assumption "the supreme culmination of her privileges," he refuses to define the well-known devotional titles—coredemptrix and mediatrix—despite their logical and theological association with this doctrine. These titles were considered again by the bishops at the Second Vatican Council, but in its final declaration we have a deliberate paring back of devotional excesses as Mariology comes better to be grounded in the Bible and the church fathers and begins to be articulated with the worries and sensitivities of other Christians in mind. Paul VI's personal promulgation of the medieval title "Mother of the Church" must have seemed cold comfort to at least some of those maximalists who wished to grant Mary her own conciliar document and enshrine the much older and much more controversial titles.

Second, from the Second Vatican Council onward, within Roman Catholicism

Mary is considered in dialogue in two ways. First, she is to be considered in dialogue with other Christians—not simply in dialogue with Eastern Christians, for whom the Roman doctrine of the immaculate conception is difficult not because it affirms Mary's sanctity from the first instant of her historical existence but because it presumes an Augustinian doctrine of original sin lacking in the East and for whom the doctrine of the assumption is difficult not because of its content but because of the nonconciliar manner of its promulgation. Rather, the invitation extends to those Christians with deeper Marian worries. Some are relatively minor; for example, that the modern dogmatic definitions prematurely bind the consciences of Christians and therefore make ecumenical dialogues all the more difficult. Others, however, are more serious; for example, that neither definition can claim the explicit warrant of Holy Scripture means for some not only that they may not be proclaimed as dogma but also, more strongly, that they must proclaimed as unnecessary accretions and distortions from Scripture's central message. This invitation has, over the last twenty-five years or so, begun to bear good fruit as Protestants and Catholics have come together to read the Bible, weigh the claims of tradition and engage in constructive (rather than polemical) debate even at the lay level. Mary has also been considered in dialogue with the findings of sciences outside theology. Not only has this meant greater attention to the biblical material read through the lenses provided by hermeneutical methods that Protestants, over the last 250 years, have come to take for granted. It has also meant a greater willingness to engage with the biblical and traditional material from the diverse perspectives provided by, for example, critical feminist studies, French psycholinguistic theory, theoretical anthropology and a Marxist reading of history.

Third, the eager desire with which the invitation to dialogue has been taken up by theologians within the Roman Catholic Church is increasingly matched by those outside it. And the result, for the foreseeable future, is a diversity of Marys. This is especially striking when we contrast the Marian minimalism that marks Johnson's proposal with the maximalism of Beattie's, even as both construct their Mariologies using broadly feminist categories. The same is true when Boff and Balasuriya are set against each other. Both claim to work with God's preferential option for the poor as their primary criterion, but Boff's Mary is no less than the incarnation of the Holy Spirit while Balasuriya's is our sister in the struggle for human liberation. At one level, this diversity provides exciting opportunities for theologians and Christians in general to participate in a conversation that they may otherwise have avoided. At another, however, it could become problematic. When Paul VI issued his call for Catholic thinking about Mary to take place in dialogue with other Christians and with the human sciences, he was not enshrining diversity as the goal of the strategy. While he did acknowledge that, given differences of geographical, cultural, historical location—among others—there would always be diverse devotional practices, these were to flow from and deepen the church's understanding of the Mother of God, an understanding that it held to be singularly true, even if diversely manifested across boundaries of time and place. Thus, while acknowledging Marian diversity and the challenges it affords, I do not present it as a goal to be maintained. With Paul VI, I affirm it as a stage along the way to a greater understanding of the one truth about this singular woman. I hope that my own contribution deepens rather than detracts from that understanding.

Conclusion to part two. This leads to the guidelines according to which my own proposal will be constructed. First, a recollection is in order. At the conclusion of chapter five, three proposed guidelines were drawn from and oriented toward the portrayal(s) of Mary in the New Testament. Accepting the inevitability of doctrinal development, I contended that Holy Scripture ought to be its guiding principle. I therefore suggested that developments (whether about Mary or any other doctrine) be submitted to three interrelated questions: Is this development, although overlooked by previous generations, explicitly taught in Holy Scripture? Is this development implicitly taught in Holy Scripture? Is this development logically related to other doctrines explicitly or implicitly taught in Holy Scripture? Now, at the conclusion of part two, two further guidelines may be proposed.

The first is offered in the light of the Marian developments that have taken place from 431 to 1950. From the definition of Mary as *Theotokos* to the definition of her bodily assumption into heaven, the trend has been one of exaltation. Even if plausible cases can be made that the seeds of future developments are patristic (e.g., Newman's argument that the immaculate conception is contained embryonically in the New Eve motif), each new development ends up saying something that had not been explicitly articulated before. Marian enthusiasts and critics together point out that the ancient titles "coredemptrix," "mediatrix" and "advocate" have yet to be dogmatically defined. Even as rumors abound about the possibilities of such future definitions, Gustafson is surely right to insist that saying that such terms will never come up for discussion is shortsighted.[106] It therefore seems that a Protestant Mariology has a unique opportunity to be proactive with respect to these titles. Given that we have been invited—by no less than the pope!—to the table and recognizing that he (in consultation with the theologians and bishops of the Roman Catholic Church)

---

[106]Ibid., p. 192.

will determine just what the definition will be, it is in the interest of Protestant theologians committed to the one church (and indeed, in the interest of that church) to reflect especially on these titles to see whether or in what ways they may conform to or logically derive from the explicit or implicit teaching of Holy Scripture.

The second guideline emerges as we survey how the Western church has dealt with the biblical presentation of Jesus' mother. In part one, we observed that Mary was presented in two complementary ways. In Paul, Mark and Matthew, Mary was first and foremost a person: for Paul, an anonymous guarantor of the Savior's humanity; for Mark, an (unwitting) opponent of the Gospel who misunderstood her Son's mission; for Matthew, a woman with a scandalous pregnancy. In Luke, John and possibly Revelation, this earlier "Mary the person" is overlaid by "Mary the symbol" in that Mary comes to personify the people of God. In part two, we have seen how through two millennia of development the second Mary has come almost completely to suffocate the first. The immaculately conceived *Theotokos,* the bodily assumed Queen of Heaven has very little connection to the handmaid of Nazareth who, even with the strongest purpose and best intentions, is on the edge of ostracism because of a scandalous pregnancy, indeed, who misconstrues and resists the gospel of her Son. If we are to be true to the message of Holy Scripture, greater emphasis will have to be paid to the first Mary, the Mary who hovers on the margins of her society and on the fringes of the biblical text. For the sake of that balance, this overlooked but no less biblical Mary will need to discipline the Mary bequeathed to us by the Western (Roman) tradition.

PART THREE

Toward an Evangelical Mariology

11

Virgin Mother

Mary in the Mystery of the Incarnation

The first two parts of this book concentrated on gathering the data offered in Scripture and the (Western) history of its interpretation. In order to complete the exercise, the data needs now to be assembled. The next three chapters weave together the threads of the previous parts to see whether what results is a richly compelling tapestry or a hodgepodge piece of tangled cloth. The "loom" on which this experiment will take place is provided by the guidelines suggested in the conclusions to parts one and three: the primacy of Scripture for theological development, the capacity of Scripture to correct tradition gone awry (with the corollary that tradition must be understood before it can be assessed) and the necessity of constructive as well as critical thought.

The aims of the current chapter are threefold. First, I contend against a hypothetical critic that, within the confines of the methodology stated above, Mariology is not only possible but also necessary. Having thus cleared the ground, second, I expose the soil to be cultivated later. The ground of Mariology is the first Marian title: *Theotokos,* Mother of God. If this confession is valid, then Mariology has found its theological anchor. Finally, I present Mary's virginal motherhood as the beginning of our enterprise, examining her maternity, the virginal conception of the Lord and the abiding significance of Mary's virginity. Following this, we will move backward to consider Mary's place in salvation history (chap. 12) and forward to reflect on her continuing role in the life of the church (chap. 13).

Necessity of Mariology

Were a critic to launch a theological preemptive strike against my project, now is the time to do so. Having worked through the biblical material at a very close level and having conducted a broader survey of the history of Christian thought, it may be argued that nothing of theological significance can be constructed from the data assembled. Mariology is impossible because it (a) derives not from the Bible but from tradition and (b) endorses nearly idolatrous practices that even at their best both distract and detract from Jesus as the sole source of saving grace. Both charges require a response before moving to more substantive criticism.

First, the claim that a constructive Mariology is unbiblical, in the light of the close exegetical work of part one, requires serious qualification. While Mary does not figure highly in the New Testament narratives or Epistles, to conclude that Mary is therefore insignificant is wrong. Mary is the guarantor of Christ's humanity; her virginity is the sign of his unique status in the divine economy. She is even a symbolic representation of the people of God. What matters is not the number of verses in which she is mentioned, but what those verses say and imply when considered in the light of the testimony of the whole of Scripture. This version of point *(a)* above is unsustainable.

It is not, however, the only version available. Another that accounts for the work of previous chapters would read as follows: there is insufficient biblical material to construct a Mariology of the kind of detail as has emerged in Western theological history. The validity of this objection is clear. Strands in various mariological traditions fall afoul of biblical prohibitions and cannot, therefore, pass the muster of the methodology set out above. But does it undercut the task *tout court?* I hope to show that it does not. This and subsequent chapters will maintain that the Marian material of the New Testament demands theological reflection to complete central loci in Christian theology, namely, Christology (Mary's motherhood), theology proper (the doctrine of election) and ecclesiology (Mary's role in the church). Or to put the thesis more controversially, to pass over Mariology altogether inevitably leaves other central Christian doctrines underdeveloped. Until that case is made, I invite my critic to suspend the notion that Mariology in itself is unbiblical.

The second criticism—that Mariology justifies idolatry—has more teeth. In our historical survey, we encountered several Marian practices that both lack biblical justification and contain pagan undertones. Furthermore, we have encountered questionable doctrines that, although never officially endorsed, were immensely popular. Do these warrant the wholesale rejection of Mariology? Again, the answer is no, for two reasons. First, our survey has borne out that, with respect to Mariology, doctrine did not create practice but came along after, sometimes legitimating and sometimes attenuating it. While it may well be that theologians sometimes did not speak forcefully enough to counteract abuses, the solution to aberrant practice is not silence, but right teaching. Second, our survey has shown several instances in which loyalty to the Roman Catholic Church joined a lively and profound Marian piety to find expression in the strictest possible denunciations of perceived abuses, namely, the works of Erasmus, Pascal, Muratori and Newman. Even Protestant theologians such as Luther, Zwingli, Bullinger and Drelincourt were not willing to dispense with the task altogether. And neither should we.

Ground of Mariology

If the preceding argument is valid, Mariology is not by definition unbiblical and need not justify or culminate in impiety. The question then remains where to begin. There are several possible places—all of them ancient. The confession of Mary as New Eve is first mentioned by Justin Martyr and may well have roots that predate the second century. The invocation of Mary as a special intercessor and protector of the faithful dates to the late second century. These, however, do not provide the biblical or theological *gravitas* necessary to ground our subject. Mariology naturally arises out of Christology—what the church confesses about Mary stems from and is intended to clarify what it believes about Christ. And the point at which Mariology and Christology intersect is the confession of Mary as *Theotokos,* Mother of God. Robert W. Jenson correctly writes: "If such an epithet is justified, it must also be right for there to be a subdepartment called mariology."[1]

This assertion is not uncontroversial and must therefore be unpacked further. Many evangelicals may share the worry of Nestorius, namely, that *Theotokos* smacks too much of pre-Christian goddess worship to be fully incorporated into the theological and liturgical life of the church. And while the more thoughtful of them would not go so far as he did in proposing the alternative term *Christotokos,* most would agree with Calvin that in the light of subsequent abuse, perhaps it is better to set aside the term. But this train of thought not only commits errors in logic, it also misses Cyril of Alexandria's theological point.

First, it is guilty of the genetic fallacy—of drawing a conclusion about the truth of a concept based on its origins. In this case, the argument is as follows:

a The Great Mother traditions of the ancient Near East are incompatible with Christian teaching.

---

[1]Robert W. Jenson, *Systematic Theology,* vol. 2: *The Works of God* (New York: Oxford University Press, 1999), p. 200.

b *Theotokos* originates in the Great Mother traditions of the ancient Near East.

c Therefore: *Theotokos* is incompatible with Christian teaching.

The error in this argument is exposed when we consider a parallel argument from the field of pharmacology:

a′ Poisonous materials are hazardous to my health.

b′ Antibiotic x is made of poisonous materials.

c′ Therefore: I should never take antibiotic x.

Just as the poisonous origins of the antibiotic are irrelevant to whether I should take it, so the pagan origins of *Theotokos* are irrelevant to whether it expresses a deep truth about the person of Jesus.

Second, it is guilty of the fallacy of false cause—if y follows x, then x is the cause of y. This argument is also expressed simply:

x *Theotokos* was promulgated by the Council of Ephesus in 431.

y There was a flowering of apparently idolatrous Marian devotion after 431.

z Therefore: *Theotokos* caused the flowering of apparently idolatrous Marian devotion after 431.

Again, a parallel argument from another discipline, this time biology, will help expose the error:

x′ The stork population in Europe is declining.

y′ Human birth rates in Europe are declining.

z′ Therefore: an increase in the presence of storks will increase human birth rates in Europe.

A careful reader will point out that this parallel is unfair. After all there is strong evidence of correlation in the first instance while the second is mere coincidence. Nevertheless, the exercise serves to expose that the first argument is far too simplistic. It fails to acknowledge, for example, the well-developed Marian piety that existed particularly in Syrian and Alexandrian Christianity before 431; it also fails to ask whether the flowering of Marian piety has more to do with the decline of Antiochene Christianity rather than with the dogmatic definition of one term. Once such careful historical spadework has been completed, furthermore, the question of the propriety of *Theotokos* still has not been answered. Even if the term has been abused, that does not weigh on whether it conveys something true about the person of Jesus, something without which our Christology would be impoverished.

This brings me to Cyril's main point. There can be no doubt that Cyril shared in the Marian piety that helped to distinguish Alexandrian Christianity from other forms in the patristic era. That such piety had included the frequent invocation of Mary as the Mother of God for centuries goes without saying. That it had roots extending to pre-Christian religious expression or could manifest itself in forms more reminiscent of that past than its Christian present is true. Yet, piety was not Cyril's main concern; rather, he was rightly worried that the doctrine of salvation expressed in the Nicene Creed was at stake. The councils of Nicea (325) and Constantinople (381) affirmed that the Son of God was of one substance with the Father, was incarnate by the Holy Spirit and was born of the Virgin Mary. And it was Cyril's conviction that, by assuming all that being human is in the manner described by Nicea, God the Son redeemed humanity.

From this perspective he rightly spotted that, whatever the legitimacy of Nestorius's worries, his position had the undesirable effect of sundering the union of humanity and divinity in the incarnation, effectively creating two sons in the one Jesus Christ. If Nestorius's views were to win the day, then Nicea would ultimately have to be repudiated for, even if Nestorius himself did not recognize it, his argument led to a devastating conclusion. On the one hand the human son of Mary was born, grew, suffered, died and rose, while on the other hand the divine Son of God remained eternal, impassible and (crucially) consequently uninvolved in the human condition. To maintain this position, Cyril countered, was to deny the Nicene conviction that the Son of God actually assumed a human nature. If Christians cannot confess that the incarnate God was conceived and born of Mary, then God has not embraced their lot and they are not saved. To put it in the starkest of terms, if Mary did not bear God in her womb—if she is not *Theotokos*—human beings are not saved.

If the discussion of natures and persons—let alone the Greek metaphysics underlying such terminology—cohabiting (or not) in one body sounds too bizarre, the problem can be rephrased easily to accommodate modern sensibilities. Cyril's theological worry, as expressed in the metaphysic available to him, has to do with the identity of the subject of the Gospels and just how we predicate actions or states to that subject. When we read, for instance, that Jesus became enraged and drove the merchants out of the temple, are we reading about a man or about God? When we read that he suffered death, are we reading about his humanity or divinity? Cyril's answer is that the Gospels predicate anger (or any other human emotion) and death (or any other human limitation) neither to a human nature nor to a divine one, but to a person. And that person is the incarnate God. We cannot dissect the Gospels seeking to attribute this or that emotion or act to either Jesus' humanity or divinity; we predicate them instead to the one fully divine, fully human person. The Gospels are God's own human story. The conclusion is now inescapable. If God the Son entered human time and space as a human being and if he did so by taking on the humanity given to him by his mother, then Mary is the Mother of God. No less a title will do.

This is not to sidestep the concerns of Nestorius or later Calvin and even Newman. Unlike the patriarch, the reformer and the cardinal both recognized that *Theotokos* said something profoundly right about the person of Christ; all three realized, however, that it also said something about Mary that had not been said before, namely, that Mary is not a historical accident, a mere passive object acted on in the drama of salvation. She is a subject in her own right. She was chosen; she accepted; her womb and not another contained the uncontainable God. She is not, as the ancient gnostics would have it, a mere tube who did not contaminate the divine Son with her humanity as he passed through. She is the mother of Christ. He did not assume human nature randomly, but in and through her. Calvin and Newman, further, recognized that this admission was the ground of all that came after, including the abuses—especially of devotional and sentimental language—that they decried in their unique ways.

Calvin opted for silence, Newman for correction through engagement. If the argument sketched above is correct, the former route is a mistake. To remain silent is to fail to speak where Scripture is clear—a strategy that Calvin himself usually refuses. Furthermore, according to the history of Mary after the Reformation, it has serious consequences. Is the latter route open to those who, like Cardinal Newman, are deeply suspicious about some mariological content and, unlike him, advocate a theological method that grants priority to Scripture? This question is best answered with another: How can we evangelical Protestants be true to the witness of Scripture and avoid joining our voices with those of Gabriel and Elizabeth and generations of Christians thereafter who name her blessed? Once it is granted that *Theotokos* encapsulates a profoundly biblical concept necessary for a fuller understanding of the identity of Jesus Christ, we ground Mariology. The only question is what that Mariology will look like.

Beginning of Mariology

If Christology generally and *Theotokos* specifically ground Mariology, its starting point is her virginal motherhood. For it is here that she stands both in closest relation to Jesus and in sharpest relief as a unique subject. Her place in the mystery of election (which will be discussed in chap. 12) leads to her motherhood;

her place as leader of and example to the company of disciples, both the church militant and the church triumphant (which will be discussed in chap. 13), flows from it. This final section therefore sets the stage for later chapters by reflecting first on Mary's maternity and then her virginity.

Mary's maternity. While contemporary evangelical Christians may want to begin with a staunch defense of Mary's virginity, this misplaces the theological emphasis both biblically and historically. With respect to the former, the New Testament witness concerning Mary's virginity is not universal. Paul, Mark and John, as we have seen, are silent.[2] Whether these writers did not know about it or whether it was not germane to their pastoral and theological concerns, we simply cannot say. Far more important was the need to locate Jesus not simply in salvation history but in the general world of human events. Thus, Paul stresses the humanity and Jewishness of him who was " born of a woman, born under the law." Mark presents "the Son of God" as having a mother—albeit one from whom he appears to be estranged at best. Matthew retains and considerably softens Mark's picture. Although Mary takes on symbolic overtones in Luke and John, she does so as Jesus' mother. While the testimony to her virginity is present in the New Testament, it is the reality of her motherhood (and accordingly the humanity of Jesus) that is affirmed throughout.

The writings of the church fathers from the second to the fifth centuries almost always follow the lead of the New Testament, placing the accent on Mary's maternity. And the reason is the same: they too wished to stress the humanity and history of the Savior. The battle foreshadowed in the Fourth Gospel and 1 John had erupted by the time of Ignatius of Antioch. Over against gnostic and docetic claims to a hidden knowledge secretly revealed by a purely heavenly redeemer, early Christian writers stressed the humanity of the Savior by appealing to his mother. The fathers emphasized that the Son entered our world of time and space in the most ordinary of ways—birth—and as a result his humanity was (and remains) as real as ours.

While it is most unlikely that this debate will be revived anytime soon, there is a good theological and pastoral reason for maintaining the insistence of Mary's real motherhood: it is a necessary counterweight to the tendency in traditional Christian piety to lose its grip on the humanity of Christ. This aberration is reflected in several ways. Perhaps most prevalent in evangelicalism is the

---

[2]A minority of scholars continues to hold that this is not the case, but the most that their arguments can muster are hints and allusions held to be suspect by others from across the confessional spectrum. Even if their arguments were convincing, there remains no clear statement of the miracle comparable to the narrations it receives in Matthew and Luke.

thinly veiled Apollinarianism according to which the divine Son of God assumed an otherwise dispensable human body for a period of time, intervening not to restore creation, but to rescue believers from it. Of course, doctrines never remain isolated, but always have an impact on the system as a whole. Doctrines of God that presume to speak of divine suffering apart from the human suffering of the Son, those of the atonement that understand it as a transaction taking place solely between Father and (divine) Son, reducing humanity to its object and ignoring the Holy Spirit altogether, and eschatologies that conflate the intermediate state of disembodied souls with the resurrection of the body—all have at their roots in a failure to keep the human nature and unity of Christ's person in view. Expanding on each of these, however, would take us away from our main subject. It is enough to observe the weighty christological implications attached to sound reflection on the reality of Mary's motherhood.

Mary's virginity. Christian faith affirms not only the reality of Mary's maternity, but also its singularity. She is not simply a mother, but rather *the* Virgin Mother. Packed into this title are three interrelated claims. First, the incarnate God owes his human nature to the creative agency of the Holy Spirit. Mary's motherhood is singular, in other words, because it is miraculous. Second, Mary is in some sense, *still* the Virgin Mother. Her virginity, in other words, is perpetual. Third, as Virgin Mother, Mary most closely resembles that other virgin mother, the church. She is the member of the church who best expresses the church's essential and exemplary character.

Virginal conception. At the outset a distinction between apologetics and dogmatics or systematic theology needs to be made. What follows is not an example of apologetics. I do not defend the virginal conception by contending for the propriety of belief in miracles (i.e., it is not irrational to believe it happened), divine agency in history (i.e., it is not irrational to believe that God did it) or the reliability of Holy Scripture (i.e., it is not irrational to believe it happened in the way that Matthew and Luke describe it). It is an example of systematic theology; that is, it seeks to defend and articulate the place of the virginal conception as a doctrine within a viable Christian theological system. Belief in miracles, in an understanding of divine agency that allows for them and in the reliability of Holy Scripture—while assumed in all that follows (and indeed, throughout the book)—are not my main concerns, and defending them would move well beyond the scope of this work.

In systematic theology, the legitimacy of the virginal conception has, until the last two centuries, been unquestioned. It has been a tenet of catholic faith from its earliest days that Christ was, in the language of the Apostles' Creed, "conceived by the power of the Holy Spirit and born of the Virgin Mary." This construction emphasizes both that Mary conceived in a manner outside the realm of normal human experience and that her virginity is intimately connected to the agency of the Holy Spirit. Christians across confessions have traditionally understood both halves to entail that the Holy Spirit miraculously compensated for the absence of a biological father. With the advent of the modern era, however, a growing number of theologians have questioned this previous consensus, arguing that it is not only possible but also beneficial to retain the latter claim while relinquishing the former. On the one hand the Holy Spirit is indeed the primary actor in Jesus' conception, and Mary did receive the promise as a virgin both in heart and body. On the other hand her conceiving and giving birth is gynecologically unexceptional. Jesus had a human father. This is not a simplistic rejection of the doctrine of the incarnation, but an attempt to free it from what is perceived to be an unnecessary, legendary, even harmful element.

The case relies on three streams of data. First, at the level of biblical studies, Jane Schaberg presents a solid argument for reading the birth narratives as alternatively concealing and explaining a gross sexual crime[3] that became the occasion for a most radical display of divine grace: the election of the child so conceived to divine sonship. Second, at the level of church history, Mary's gynecological virginity has been used to denigrate marriage, legitimate fears of (female) sexuality and present sexual activity as intrinsically corrupted and corrupting. The consequences of such misuse, furthermore, continue to resonate today. Third, at the level of theology, the virginal conception is regarded by some to be unnecessary to a robust traditional Christology and may actually undermine it. We have encountered the first two streams in parts one and two. The objections from the third stream are new and need further fleshing out.

According to one theological objection, one can affirm—as Wolfhart Pannenberg does—that the human Jesus had a human father and that he is God incarnate.[4] The argument is straightforward. The New Testament is not uniform in its testimony, and the birth narratives, while conveying *theological* truth, have been discredited as *history* by critical investigation. Furthermore, the orthodox understanding of incarnation as set out by Chalcedon (451)—that in the one person, Jesus Christ, divinity and humanity are united without confusion, without change, without division, without separation—is not contingent on the doctrine of the virginal conception. Biblically questionable and traditionally unnecessary,

---

[3]Jane Schaberg, *The Illegitimacy of Jesus: A Feminist Interpretation of the Infancy Narratives* (San Francisco: Harper & Row, 1987).

[4]Wolfhart Pannenberg, *Systematic Theology,* trans. Geoffrey W. Bromiley (Grand Rapids: Eerdmans, 1994), 2:318-19.

the miracle is better dismissed. The second theological charge—as developed by Arthur Peacocke—contends that if the Holy Spirit either created Jesus' human nature out of nothing or formed it by miraculously adding to Mary's genetic material, then Jesus' humanity is a sham.[5] The virginal conception endorses a form of Docetism that undermines the doctrine of the incarnation and should be left behind. Both arguments rightly highlight the hierarchy inherent in the Christian theological enterprise. They correctly affirm that the incarnation is a doctrine more vital than that concerning Jesus' human origins. If the virginal conception does not contribute to or, worse, actually harms our understanding of the incarnation, then it must be sacrificed.

The biblical case is questionable; the historical record, deeply damaging; the incarnation, unthreatened by its absence but undermined by its presence. A successful counterproposal will first need to rebut these objections. At the textual level, Schaberg alleges that the birth narratives are ideological cover-ups; Pannenberg, that they are legendary expressions of theological truth. The advantage of Schaberg's argument, like all arguments from suspicion, is that it cannot be entirely refuted. Its disadvantage, like all arguments from suspicion, is that it can never completely destroy its target. Arguments from suspicion do not construct alternatives as much as they raise questions. Schaberg must do more than that to overturn the traditional reading. Against Pannenberg is the strong historical core of the birth narratives. These are not late legends, but reflect the conviction of early Christian communities about events that, as far as they are concerned, actually happened. If the texts purport to narrate events and convey convictions about their factuality, then those following both Schaberg and Pannenberg are thrown back to a philosophical rather than biblical question: do miracles happen? But once such a question is asked, we have moved from concerns regarding the texts themselves well beyond the scope of this work.

Unlike these textual concerns, the objection from history is sound. One cannot read, for example, Ambrose's appropriation of Athanasius and not detect deep-seated, irrational fears about human (and especially female) sexuality tied however tenuously to Mary's virginity. And there is no point in denying that Ambrose's legacy has tainted a great deal of Western theological thinking.[6] Nevertheless, the abuse does not negate the use. That even someone of Ambrose's

[5]This is part of the larger case against the virginal conception argued by Arthur Peacocke in *Theology for a Scientific Age: Being and Becoming—Natural, Divine, and Human* (Minneapolis: Fortress, 1993), pp. 276-77. The scientific and other theological elements raised by Peacocke fall outside the scope of this work.

[6]Indeed, placing blame squarely at the feet of Ambrose may well lighten some of the unfairly harsh assessments of the influence of Augustine's alleged misogyny.

stature mistook, misunderstood and dreadfully misapplied the data in ways that continue to resonate does not in itself impugn the data. The abuse does, however, highlight those points at which a better theological construction will have to be advanced. Can Mary's virginity be presented in such a way that it continues to provide an example of holiness to all, whether male or female and especially to celibate Christians, without denigrating or demonizing sexual activity? That question will be taken up momentarily.

The last two objections are more difficult to handle than the first two, for they mingle sound theological observations with conclusions that are overdrawn. For instance, the distinction drawn between virginal conception and Chalcedonian Christology rightly guards against an all-too-common misunderstanding of the incarnation according to which Mary contributes the human "half" of Jesus and God contributes the divine. If this is so, then Jesus stands with Hercules and many other pagan heroes whose mothers had divine lovers. To say that the two are distinct, however, does not necessarily mean that one is disposable. The result of retaining Chalcedon while dispensing with virginal conception is the tacit endorsement of some kind of adoptionism or Nestorianism definitively ruled out by Nicea and Ephesus. If Jesus' human nature was formed by the union of sperm and ovum, then, if only for an instant, it existed as something other than the human nature of God the Son. This human nature was later either adopted into God's service at a point in time (adoptionism) or retained and shared its personhood with God the Son (Nestorianism). Either way, the Son of God did not fully embrace all that being human entails and Mary is not *Theotokos.*

Likewise, the fourth objection—that the virginal conception inevitably leads to a form of Docetism—is right to contend that if the Holy Spirit creates Christ's human nature out of nothing then the Docetism stridently opposed by Irenaeus and Tertullian results. When it adds that the Spirit's miraculous compensation for the absence of some genetic material (e.g., a Y chromosome) leads to the same unfortunate result, however, it errs. Although the fathers, lacking our understanding of human genetic makeup, do not pronounce on the problem in this fashion, they unanimously agree that Christ really is the son of Mary and that she really was a virgin at the time of his conception. We can build on this consensus and argue that, as a matter of logic, it is required for a human male only that a Y chromosome be present. Nothing need be said about how that chromosome got there.[7] There is, therefore, no Docetism necessarily implicit in

---

[7]Michael D. Bush, "Christology and the 'Y' Chromosome," in *Unapologetic Apologetics: Meeting the Challenges of Theological Studies,* ed. William A. Dembski and Jay Wesley Richards (Downers Grove, Ill.: InterVarsity Press, 2001), p. 148.

the doctrine of the virginal conception rightly understood. Although this does not constitute a full rebuttal to Peacocke's objection, the argument from this point hinges on whether it is rational to believe in a God who could intervene in the created order in such a miraculous way. And this debate, as already mentioned, is well outside the scope of this work.

The dogmatic difficulties associated with the virginal conception are not as strong as they first appeared. The biblical accounts provide reliable testimony concerning early Christian convictions about the factually of certain events. The misuse of Mary's virginity as a club to beat on a healthy view of human sexuality is granted to be just that—a misuse the recognition of which need not derail the discussion. The observation that Chalcedon is not dependent on the virginal conception, while making a valid observation, ought not to be pressed too far. And the virginal conception need not deny Christ's true humanity. Nevertheless, rebutting charges is insufficient. The miracle's abiding theological significance must also be considered if it is to maintain its place in a viable Christian theological system.

The value of the miracle lies in its status as a sign pointing both to the agency of God in the formation of Christ's human nature and, consequently, to the uniqueness of Christ's humanity. Of the three points to be unpacked further, the first is the status of the virginal conception as sign. This is to say that the miracle is neither the cause of divine sonship—as though Jesus "became" the Son of God through the sexual union of the Holy Spirit with Mary—nor its basis—as though the Son could have become a man in only this way. The first notion is one the New Testament utterly rejects. Nowhere does Matthew or Luke model Mary after the mothers of pagan demigods. The second misses the import of Matthew's use of Isaiah 7:14, according to which the pregnant virgin is a sign of God's presence, not proof of incarnation. God could have brought about the humanity of the Son in a manner other than the virginal conception. The miracle "is the sign which accompanies and indicates the mystery of the incarnation of the Son, marking it off as a mystery from all the beginnings of other human existences" (*CD* 4.1:207). As a sign, of course, its value lies not in itself, but in its ability to direct those who contemplate it to that which it signifies.

It signifies the divine agency in the formation of the humanity of the Son. It is a sign of divine omnipotence insofar as it altogether bypasses the contribution of a human father, replacing it with a divine act without human analogue. The only miracle that surpasses this one is the miracle of creation out of nothing itself. It is also a sign of divine grace. God freely and graciously gives to humanity through the Virgin Mary not simply the gift but also the very capacity to receive it. Her contribution, although real, is of itself nothing. Its merit—if that is the right word—lies only in the grace that completes and animates it. God in his grace elects, equips and makes. God gives her what she could not have procured on her own. In other words, while it is true that the incarnation as traditionally understood could have come about in another fashion, that it came about in this way signifies that he who was conceived in this way was "born, not of blood or of the will of the flesh or of the will of man, but of God" (Jn 1:13).

Following on, it also signifies the uniqueness of the Son who became man. Positively this uniqueness is expressed in the term *divine sonship.* As such, it stands as a fitting boundary at the beginning of the earthly life of the incarnate one, just as the empty tomb does its end (*CD* 1.2:182). The miracles together stand as one sign that this one life was set apart from all others. As the greatest defender of Mary's virginity in the twentieth century puts it, this life was "marked off in regard to its origin: it is free from the arbitrariness which underlies all our existences. And marked off in regard to its goal: it is victorious over the death to which we all are liable" (*CD* 1.2:182). Karl Barth therefore concludes that it "is pertinent whether his divine sonship and the mystery of His incarnation are known in any real seriousness and depth when" this sign is "unrecognized or overlooked or denied or explained away" (*CD* 4.1:207).

Negatively this uniqueness is expressed in terms of the Son's sinless humanity. At this point, Augustine's inconsistency may be addressed. Chapter seven argued that Augustine, at least at one point, believed the virginal conception to be unnecessary for incarnation. But his understanding of desire (especially as carnal desire expressed in sexual activity) led him to conclude that a sinless human nature could not be formed otherwise. The Western tradition has generally followed the latter route, as exemplified by Thomas Aquinas's (now biologically dated) argument, according to which the absence of a father entailed freedom from original sin. Matthew and Luke, however, in no way link Jesus' miraculous conception to his sinless life; Paul, Mark and John are silent even as they present Jesus as the model human. The view that virginity is somehow more virtuous and that sex is always the occasion for disordered desire has more to do with deep-seated fears of (female) sexuality among certain Western theologians wrongly imported into their readings of biblical texts. Virginity is no more the "point of connection for divine grace" than its alternative (*CD* 1.2:192).

This recognition, however, does not demand the repudiation of Augustine and the Western tradition. His and its intuition of a deep connection between the nature of Jesus' conception and the nature of the humanity conceived is sound. Only the articulation is problematic. The virginal conception is a sign of Christ's sinless life by pointing, first, to the agency of the Holy Spirit in its creation. Mary did indeed contribute everything that a mother does contribute to the formation of Christ's human nature.[8] But apart from the creative intervention of the Holy Spirit, her contribution would not have resulted in the formation of a human being, sinful or otherwise. Therefore, as Donald Macleod rightly observes, it is better to regard the Holy Spirit as the creator of Christ's human nature. Accordingly the human nature so formed would share in the essentially good character of all that God creates.[9] Sinlessness is not an addition to or reparation of Mary's humanity, but the state of a human being directly created by the Holy Spirit.

Second, the virginal conception points to the new beginning represented by Christ. Christ's human existence, unlike all others, is not "in Adam." The old Augustinian notion of original sin as a literal genetic disease passed from parent to child through the libidinous desire present in the sexual act is (thankfully) thoroughly discredited. But the Pauline notion on which it is predicated, namely, that the entire human race in some way participates in and shares in the consequences of Adam's Fall is not.[10] The virginal conception reminds us that the Last Adam stands outside the exponentially expanding cycle of sinful desire, act and consequence that has marked human beings, relationships and indeed civilizations since (almost) the beginning. Just as Christ is the Last Adam, he is also the beginning of the restoration of the original creation. As such, he stands parallel to Adam, not beneath him. All this to say that the virginal conception signifies that, from the first instant of his existence, Jesus of Nazareth stood in a unique relationship to God (understood best in terms of divine sonship) and in a unique relationship to the rest of us (understood best in terms of freedom from sin).

Perpetual virginity. There is more to the creedal affirmation that Christ was conceived by the power of the Holy Spirit and born of the Virgin Mary than the virginal conception. It entails that Mary's virginity is in some sense ongoing. Not only was she a virgin, but she remains one. This is the doctrine of Mary's perpetual virginity. Traditionally, this has been explained in terms of three chron-

---

[8]It is important to remember that the immaculate conception is formulated not to preserve Mary (and therefore Christ as the inheritor of her humanity) from original sin. Rather, it is founded on an argument from "fittingness" (i.e., it is fitting that a sinless Son should have a sinless mother). Wayne Grudem displays an all-too-common misunderstanding of the doctrine when he writes that according to the "Roman Catholic Church" Jesus did not inherit a sinful nature because "Mary herself was free from sin" (*Systematic Theology: An Introduction to Biblical Doctrine* [Grand Rapids: Zondervan, 1994], p. 531 esp. n. 3).

[9]Donald Macleod, *The Person of Christ* (Downers Grove, Ill.: InterVarsity Press, 1998), pp. 40-41.

[10]This statement says nothing about whether Adam in the Pauline sense is to be understood as an individual man, a collective symbol or both.

ological moments: Mary was a virgin at the time of Christ's conception (virginity *ante partum*), remained a virgin in the act of giving birth (virginity *in partu*) and persisted in virginity thereafter (virginity *post partum*). This belief is both ancient and catholic, not only spanning East and West but also was, until the last two hundred years or so, broadly accepted by Protestant Christians. Since that time, it has come under critical scrutiny because of the radical changes in biblical hermeneutics that marked the advent of the modern era. Biblical objections can be raised with regard to each of the three moments.

First, the notion that Mary's virginity *ante partum* was the result of a vow of chastity embedded in Luke 1:34 is, simply, a wrong reading of the text. On this point, Ambrose, for example, rightly understands that Mary's question ("how can this be, since I am a virgin?") simply alludes to her state at the time of Gabriel's announcement. It does not denote a deliberate lifelong commitment to God's service that precluded marriage (and, pace Suárez, certainly not a commitment undertaken while still *in utero*). This recognition further undermines the notion that Mary in any way merited the incarnation. Thomas Aquinas definitively repudiated the notion that by maintaining her virginity Mary earned the privilege of becoming the Mother of God. He contended, rather, that the purity or holiness by which she merited this intervention was itself a gift of grace. When God rewarded her merit, he rewarded his own gift, so to speak. In the absence of a vow of virginity, however, this argument becomes unnecessary. Luke constructs Mary's character so as to highlight just how unexceptional she is prior to God's gracious intervention. On this point, Luther's insistence that Mary "merited" her motherhood just as the wood "merited" becoming the cross seems better to conform to Luke's contention.

At first glance, more serious problems can be found with respect to Mary's virginity *in partu*. Chief of these is the weight placed by the fathers on the descriptions of Mary's delivery as found in noncanonical works, the most significant being the *Protevangelium of James*. This apocryphal work elevates Mary beyond the rest of humanity to near-goddess status by accentuating or, worse, inventing the ways in which her purity remained inviolate throughout her life—never ceremonially unclean, betrothed but never married, pregnant but a virgin, mother without normal delivery and so on. The birth narratives of Matthew and Luke, by contrast, say nothing about Mary's early life and describe her delivery of Jesus minimally, leaving no clue that it was itself an additional miracle. Furthermore, the allegorical readings of Old Testament passages (e.g., Ezek 44:2-3) are suspect because, pace Jerome, they seem to exist only to justify these noncanonical legends. Nevertheless, other evidence suggests that dismissal of the term *in partu* altogether may well be premature: the insistence of the fathers that Mary's delivery was unique insofar as it was freed from the consequences of the Fall. If Jesus stands alongside rather than beneath Adam, then it seems reasonable to assume that he stands outside the curse that has fallen on all Adam's sons and daughters, including pain in childbirth (Gen 3:16). If Jesus stands outside the mimetic cycle that theologians name original sin, then in biblical terms, we cannot shy away from naming his birth as unique even as we refuse the mythological accounts of it found in early Christian fiction. If the term *in partu* is to be retained, it ought to be for the sake of Jesus' unique humanity.

Finally, what is to be made of virginity *post partum?* Again, on the face of it, it seems that the New Testament rules it out by speaking clearly and on several occasions of Jesus' brothers and sisters. On strictly biblical terms, the most that can be said is that the semantic range of the Greek word *adelphos* can include blood siblings, stepsiblings or half siblings and close relatives. As a result the East has understood the relevant New Testament passages to refer to Mary's stepchildren while the West has taken them to denote Jesus' cousins.[11] Without arbitrating between the two traditions, are there reasons to follow them in "stretching" the elasticity of *adelphos*? Three may be given. First, we have the actions of Jesus on the cross according to John 19:26-27. If this account is both a theological account of the way in which Jesus' death creates new family bonds and an apostolic memory of Mary's presence at Calvary, then we are free to wonder with Athanasius and others just why Jesus—the firstborn—did not entrust his mother to his siblings, but to his beloved disciple. Many answers, all of them speculative, can be offered. The simplest is that there were no other family members. On its own, this is hardly compelling evidence. Two further points can and should be made.

Like her virginity *ante partum* and *in partu,* Mary's *post partum* virginity's most powerful support derives from the uniqueness of Jesus. In a recent essay, Jaroslav Pelikan observes a peculiar metonymy between John's use of *monogenēs* (cf. Jn 1:14, 18; 3:16, 18) and Mary's ongoing virginity. He presents a persuasive case, contending, first, that the best translation of the word remains "only begotten" (e.g., KJV, NKJV) and not simply "only" (e.g., NRSV, NIV). While he admits that there may be philological value to this move, it is not without its problems, chief of which is the translation of *monogenēs* as "only begotten" or "sole of its kind" in classical literature outside the New Testament.[12] This discrepancy acquires

---

[11]The difference can be attributed to the East's greater willingness to ascribe some kind of authority to the *Protevangelium of James* while the West, on this point, followed Saint Jerome.

[12]Jaroslav Pelikan, "Most Generations Shall Call Me Blessed," in *Mary: Mother of God,* ed. Carl E. Braaten and Robert W. Jenson (Grand Rapids: Eerdmans 2004), p. 8.

greater credence for Pelikan by the unanimity of the tradition that informed the earliest Christian liturgies, the councils and the creeds: "What made the Son of God . . . 'single' was this, that He was in the precise and technical sense . . . 'only begotten.'"[13] This case is buttressed if, as recent manuscript evidence suggests, John 1:18 predicates the adjective "only begotten" not to the Son but to God.[14] If the biblical reading advanced by Pelikan is sound and if theological tradition from Hilary of Poitiers to Karl Barth is correct to emphasize congruence between God in Godself and God in his act,[15] then the eternal begetting of the second person of the holy Trinity should be mirrored in his incarnate life: "He [is] the single and only begotten Son of God [and] also the single and only begotten Son of Mary."[16] In the divine economy, the corollary of the ontological description "only begotten God" is "ever-virgin" *(aeiparthenos; semper virgo).*

Virginity and example. Mary's virginity has since the patristic era provided many writers with the ultimate and exemplary expression of the church's essential character. Unfortunately, however, this has led to a repeated linkage of sanctity to chastity or virginity that has denigrated marriage in general and specifically sexual activity even within the institution of marriage. This regrettable legacy has created unnecessary confusion. On the one hand it rightly discerns a biblical linkage between Mary and the people of God, while on the other hand it articulates that linkage in unbiblical terms of sexual abstinence. The task then is to find biblical language in which to articulate the relationship between Mary and church that distances itself from previous unbiblical and even sometimes Manichean expressions.

The most immediate biblical ground for such a pairing is the Heavenly Queen of Revelation 12, which obviously symbolizes the people of God and in its canonical context has been read since the fifth century to refer in some way to Mary. Moreover, there are better if less direct biblical passages that do support this reading. The first is John 1:13. It can be no accident that a verse that in its biblical context expresses the reality of the new birth experienced by believers also "perfectly states the theology of Mary's virginity."[17] More importantly yet is the presentation of Mary in Luke 1—2 as both a prophet and a symbolic representation of the peo-

---

[13]Ibid.

[14]Compare, e.g., the NKJV: "No one has seen God at any time. The only begotten Son, who is in the bosom of the Father, He has declared Him"; with the NRSV: "No one has ever seen God. It is God the only Son, who is close to the Father's heart, who has made him known."

[15]Pelikan, "Most Generations Shall Call Me Blessed," p. 8. See also idem, *Development of Christian Doctrine: Some Historical Prolegomena* (New Haven: Yale University Press, 1969), pp. 131-36; and *CD* 1.1:479.

[16]Pelikan, "Most Generations Shall Call Me Blessed," p. 8.

[17]Jenson, *Systematic Theology,* 2:201.

ple of God, whether conceived as Israel or the church. Both are graciously chosen to bear the Word of God; both bring forth children conceived by the Holy Spirit; both are called to persevere through trial and doubt until the end. And of course, we cannot neglect the Fourth Gospel, in which Jesus' mother is almost entirely submerged in the evangelist's corporate symbolism.

As this brief rehearsal makes clear, the point of connection between Mary and church is indeed virginity—not virginity described negatively as abstinence from intrinsically sinful sexual activity, but virginity described positively as wholehearted fidelity to the prophetic calling of bearing the Word of God. Jenson nicely captures this Lukan image: "Mary is the type of the church in that the church is the prophetic community. . . . Mary is the archprophet, the paradigmatic instantiation of the church's prophetic reality."[18] Of course the relationship is not symmetrical. Mary is "beneath" the church because she is a member thereof, even if she is its most preeminent one. She bears the Word in an unprecedented manner that the church can follow only analogically at best. But insofar as she bears the Word of God to us in her words—the Magnificat—and in her body as *Theotokos,* she is a type of the community that God has by grace called into being to bear his Word to his world.

[18]Ibid., 2:202.

12

Chosen One

Toward a Doctrine of Mary's Person

The previous chapter situated Mariology within the bounds of traditional Christology, arguing for the propriety and necessity of *Theotokos* and the christological implications of Mary's maternity and virginity and suggesting that evangelical Protestants might wish to reconsider just why they are opposed to Mary's perpetual virginity and recover the ancient parallelism between Mary and the church. Now, however, we move to more difficult ground: Mary's person and, in the next chapter, her work. The structure—paralleling the traditional arrangement in Christology—is deliberate. It is intended both to recall the christological (and indeed biblical) foundations laid in the previous chapter and to highlight that all of what is said hereafter (hopefully) is properly understood as subservient to our understanding of Jesus.

In this chapter, two interrelated concerns are considered. The first is Mary's place in God's plan. Her place is intimately bound up in God's determination from all eternity to become incarnate in Jesus Christ, and this gracious election ought to determine how we think about her life. This leads to the second concern—Mary's sanctity. While immaculate conception and bodily assumption are notions closed to traditional Protestants, we can and should affirm the role of God's grace throughout Mary's life, so that, as a result of such grace, she is indeed an example to believers and that her example precisely is her grace-enabled perseverance.

Mary's Providential Place

The New Testament is silent about Mary's place in God's plan, and as a result of this silence later generations of Christians sought to fill the gaps by creating and perpetuating the most fanciful of tales, which—at least in the case of the *Protevangelium of James*—had the unfortunate effect of removing Mary from the realm of human experience, in effect, deifying her. The effects of such moves were so far reaching that J. K. Elliott rightly says that the seeds for what would become Mariology were first sown here.

To acknowledge the New Testament's silence and the legends of later centuries, however, is not to rule the question of Mary's person out of bounds. Once the christological importance of Mary is admitted—this was the task of the last chapter—it becomes perfectly natural when reflecting on the birth narratives of Matthew and Luke to pose questions such as "why Mary?" Indeed, Luke seems to have anticipated these sorts of queries. His portrayal of Mary as the foil to the extraordinarily old, barren and pious Zechariah and Elizabeth not only invites them, but directs the questioner away from a contemplation of Mary's qualities to a consideration of God's grace for an answer. As far as Luke is concerned, at least, the answer to the question "why Mary?" is "God is gracious."

Luke's emphasis on grace in Mary's life orients us to the question. Does the biblical emphasis on the priority of grace in Mary's narrative extend that narrative backward, prior to the annunciation and incarnation? The answer is yes. Mary's backstory in the Gospel narrative can and should be articulated dogmatically in terms of the preexistence of the Son and biblically in terms of the history of Israel, which is to say, the Old Testament.

The affirmation of the preexistence of the second person of the blessed Trinity presents dogmatics with a thorny problem. On the one hand an understanding of preexistence of some sort does seem to lie behind important strata of the New Testament, as we saw in chapter one. Predating the letters of Paul into which they have been incorporated, the Christ hymn of Philippians 2 and the creedal formula of Romans 1 testify that the earliest believers believed that Christ existed before his incarnation. The plainest statement of preexistence, of course, is not found in Paul, but in John: "In the beginning was the Word. . . . The Word became flesh" (Jn 1:1, 14). These passages seem to present dogmatics with a simple chronological formula according to which the Word or Son, once unincarnate, became incarnate in Mary's womb. On the other hand, however, things are rarely this uncomplicated in systematic theology.

Difficulties arise when theologians try to move beyond the bare affirmation of the Son's preexistence to articulate its nature. Robert Jenson wisely observes that there is more to the biblical description of preexistence than this simple schema would at first suggest. Although descriptions of the nature of that existence are sparse, they nevertheless disclose important insights upon sustained reflection.

First, in the Fourth Gospel the climax of the "I am" statements—"Before Abraham was, I am" (Jn 8:58)—is, on its face, a suggestion that prior to the incarnation the Son was (is?). Jenson, significantly, draws our attention not to the words so much as the speaker. Who is before Abraham? The incarnate Word, Jesus of Nazareth, himself! According to Jenson, "It is precisely the aggressively incarnate protagonist of the Gospel's narrative who says this of himself, and he puts his antecedence to Abraham in the present tense."[1] Second, Jenson also guides us to Colossians, pointing out that for its author, he who in time was "the firstborn from the dead" in whom "the fullness of God was pleased to dwell" is identical with him who from eternity is "the image of the invisible God, the firstborn of all creation" in whom "all things . . . were created" (Col 1:15-19). Neither John nor Paul conceived of preexistence apart from incarnate existence.

On the basis of New Testament passages such as these, Jenson warns against an understanding of preexistence that moves straightforwardly from unincarnate to incarnate, advising instead that the preexistence of the Son be construed in terms of the incarnation of the Son (other passages tending in the same direction include 1 Cor 8:6; 15:47; 2 Cor 8:9; Heb 5:5-6; 13:8; 1 Pet 1:20; Rev 1:8; 3:13). This is to say that from all eternity the Son of God elected the man Jesus Christ as his own identity. Of course, this is not to aver that the human nature of Christ preexisted,[2] but rather only that the identity of the one who became enfleshed in Jesus of Nazareth is an eternal one. The identity of the Son of God before the incarnation is the same as after. The eternal decision of the second person of the Trinity to assume a human nature, in other words, rendered possible this assumption in time. Karl Barth is the best-known exponent of this understanding, contending that "for God Himself, nothing can derive from any other source or look back to any other starting-point. [Jesus Christ] is the election of God before which and without which and beside which God cannot make any other choices. Before Him and without Him and beside Him God does not, then, elect or will anything" (*CD* 2.2:94).

Of course, Barth is not alone in this recognition; in evangelical theology similar statements have been made, most notably by Donald Bloesch.[3] Furthermore, contrary to some critics, it is not a theological innovation of the modern era. Perhaps its earliest exponent is, in fact, second-century theologian Irenaeus. In a

---

[1]Robert W. Jenson, *Systematic Theology,* vol. 1: *The Triune God* (New York: Oxford University Press, 1996), p. 139.

[2]Variations of this view have been expressed from time to time, notably by Origen, Caspar Schwenckfeld, Isaac Watts and Emanuel Swedenborg; see Donald Bloesch, *Jesus Christ: Savior and Lord* (Downers Grove, Ill.: InterVarsity Press, 1997), pp. 134-37.

[3]Ibid., pp. 132-43.

remarkable discussion of the anointing of Jesus by the Spirit of God, the Bishop of Lyons insists that the Word of God cannot be spoken of apart from his incarnate existence as Jesus of Nazareth.[4] It is also the inevitable conclusion of the christological insistence of Cyril of Alexandria, namely, that the incarnation is that of an eternal person—the Son of God, the second identity of God, the second person of the blessed Trinity. "The flesh," as Bloesch puts it, "was latent or implicit in the Word."[5]

With respect to Mary, a conclusion that may be as uncomfortable as it is inevitable is now clear. If the preincarnate existence of the Son of God is better construed as going-to-be incarnate rather than unincarnate or preincarnate, if his eternal identity is that of Jesus Christ, then Mary herself has from eternity been elected uniquely as the vehicle through which his assumption of a human nature would take place. Jenson expresses it well: "In the triune life, what ontologically precedes the birth to Mary of Jesus who is God the son . . . is the narrative pattern of *being going to be* born to Mary."[6] The manner of the incarnation, while distinct, cannot be separated from the eternal decision to become incarnate. If the man Jesus Christ is elect from all eternity to be the humanity of God, then the woman Mary is elect from all eternity to be the mother of that man who is God.

Mary, in other words, is no historical accident in the history of salvation. Indeed, God's gracious choice of her to be the contingent instrument of the incarnation precedes that history, for Mary's election to the role of *Theotokos* is bound up in God's determination to be who he is in his turn toward humanity in Jesus Christ—as Barth argues and as seems implied in the Christologies of both Irenaeus and Cyril. We must therefore judge the assessment of Francisco Suárez to be at least partly correct: if this understanding of election is an adequate summary of God's identity-in-act as disclosed on the pages of Holy Scripture, then Mary was chosen without consideration of any merit on her part and indeed prior (in logic, not time) to the decree to the allow the Fall. While it would be far too much to say—as Roman Catholic mystics such as Mary of Agreda did—that Mary enjoyed some sort of preexistence similar to that of the Logos, we cannot shy away from affirming with Augustine that God formed Mary in order to choose her and that he chose her in order to be formed in her. Grace marked Mary's life even when that life existed only in the mind of God.

If this understanding of Mary's place in God's plan is sound, then with New-

---

[4]Irenaeus *Against Heresies* 3.9.2-3 (*ANF* 1:422-23).

[5]Bloesch, *Jesus Christ,* p. 138.

[6]Jenson, *Systematic Theology,* 1:141.

man and indeed with the theologians of the ancient church, I affirm that Mary is to be regarded as the New Eve. Although the ascription first recorded by Justin Martyr and explored more fully by Tertullian and especially Irenaeus seems at first glance to be biblically thin, whether in terms of a literary comparison between Eve and Mary or as an extension of the Pauline Last Adam motif, in the light of our remarks it acquires a good deal of theological weight. While it is not a deduction from a particular passage (or set of passages) of Holy Scripture, it does summarize and accurately express Mary's place in salvation history. She and not another was chosen to be the Savior's mother. She and not another was the vehicle through whom God's act of restoration came to fruition, the beginning of the undoing of Adam's Fall.

Thus, if—to use Jenson's apt phrase—"the biblical Son . . . is his own presupposition in God's eternity,"[7] then God's incorporation of Mary into the plan of salvation precedes the annunciation and is indeed coterminous with and contingent on (in logic, not in time) God's eternal decision that the Son would become incarnate as Jesus of Nazareth (cf. 1 Pet 1:20). We must now push this further. The recognition that the Son's preexistence is characterized by the movement to become incarnate requires that we think of preexistence not in terms of atemporal disembodied existence, but rather as the narrative pattern of God's dealings with Israel. Jenson adds—and N. T. Wright spells out in detail—that the antecedent of the incarnate Son to which we have access is not an preincarnate or unincarnate Logos, but the narrative of Israel of which he is the climax and recapitulation.[8] Jesus' backstory, in other words, *is* the Old Testament.

Much the same needs to be said of Mary, for the narrative logic is similar. If she is, from all eternity, part and parcel of the going-to-become-incarnate pattern that defines the preincarnate existence of the second identity of God, then her own backstory ought not to be fanciful tales of a miraculously pure childhood and adolescence, but the narrative of God's dealings with that particular people—Israel. This assertion requires fleshing out.

First, relatively straightforwardly, it means that Mary's story is understood only in the light of the Old Testament—the larger narrative of which it is a part. The Gospel writers suggest this to us simply enough in several ways. Perhaps the plainest assertion of this truth is that of Saint Paul: Jesus was "born of a woman, born under the law" (Gal 4:4). If we are to understand the story of Jesus and of his mother, we need first to understand the larger story of which they are a part—the story of God's redemptive covenant with Israel through which the

---

[7]Ibid.

[8]Ibid.; N. T. Wright, *Jesus and the Victory of God* (Philadelphia: Fortress, 1996).

entire world is to be blessed. But it is found also in the genealogies of Matthew and Luke, which tie both Jesus and Mary to the key events of Israel's history—creation, Abraham and the patriarchs, conquest of the land, monarchy, exile and return. Matthew provocatively adds that Mary's pregnancy can be understood only if we at first understand the divine acceptance and redemption of sexual scandal found in the foremothers of the Messiah. It is Luke, however, who takes this logic to its extreme through his frequent allusions to the Old Testament. We have seen how, for Luke, Mary both continues and departs from the tradition of miraculous motherhood that flows through the Old Testament as a sign of God's intervention. We have seen how her acceptance of the lowly station of God's slave places her in the tradition of great female liberators of God's people. We have seen how her words in the Magnificat draw on various Old Testament prophetic utterances and mark her as the prophet par excellence. The election of Mary to her singular place from all eternity entails that her story flow from and be understood within the larger story that is the Old Testament.

The conclusion that Mary is to be understood as the culminating figure of several Old Testament motifs is now clear. It is also underdeveloped. As Timothy George rightly points out, this line of thought does not end with the recognition that Mary stands within and can be understood only in terms of the story of Israel. Rather, it drives us on to the further observation that Mary "is the kairiotic representative of the eschatological and redeemed people of God: Israel itself."[9] The typological—not allegorical—reading of the Old Testament that the fathers took for granted, according to which the "daughter of Zion" passages (e.g., Mic 4:10; Jer 4:31) referred to Mary, is thus on surer ground than may be at first apparent.[10]

The typological link between Mary and Israel in the pages of the New Testament is not, ironically, the Gospel of John, where Mary as symbol of corporate faith is most obvious, but in Simeon's blessing and warning in the Gospel of Luke. The sword that would pierce Mary's breast is in fact the sword of God's judgment spoken of by the prophet Ezekiel. There is a sense in which her response to Jesus throughout the remainder of the Gospel—with all its ambiguity, starts and stops, moments of insight and moments of confusion—mirrors the re-

---

[9]Timothy George, "The Blessed Virgin Mary in Evangelical Perspective," in *Mary: Mother of God,* ed. Carl E. Braaten and Robert W. Jenson (Grand Rapids: Eerdmans, 2004), p. 105.

[10]It is especially important not to confuse allegory and typology here. In an allegory, the meaning of the symbol is found exclusively in the thing signified, while in a typology the symbol retains its own frame of reference even as it foreshadows the thing signified. Thus, to use a common example, David is a type of but not an allegorical symbol of Christ. Much the same dynamic is going on here, where the daughter of Zion is Israel and foreshadows Mary as Israel.

sponse of Israel to the coming of Jesus Christ. In him the judgment of God visits the house of Israel, and many rise and fall with his advent. That we find Luke's Mary ultimately in the upper room is a narrative reiteration of Paul's insistence on the fundamental continuity between the two communities of faith, between the faithful remnant of Israel and the church, reminding Gentile believers that the church has a Jewish root (cf. Rom 9-11).

More germane to mariological study, the insistence on Mary's backstory being fundamentally biblical (that of Israel) rather than speculative (that of her childhood) gives us tools with which to assess and offer an alternative to traditional Roman Catholic and Orthodox understandings of Mary's holiness.

All-Holy Mary?

What is the relationship between God's gracious predestination of Mary to be *Theotokos* and her actual life? This question comes to the fore as we move away from her predestination to her sanctity. Developing an answer is fraught with ancient theological thorns. The idea that Mary, by virtue of her singular motherhood, was somehow exceptional in terms of her personal holiness emerges in the second century and finds its most developed articulation in the *Protevangelium of James*. The East widely and easily accepted Mary's fundamental holiness and the doctrines that gave it credence—doctrines that would, in the West, eventually become known as the immaculate conception and the bodily assumption. Reflection on Mary's sanctity in the West was retarded by several factors, including Jerome's staunch rejection of the *Protevangelium of James* as a baseless legend and the widespread influence of Augustine's doctrine of original sin. Ironically it was also the Augustinian insistence on God's predestination of Mary to her vocation as *Theotokos* that laid the foundation for the medieval debates through which the doctrines of immaculate conception and bodily assumption were sharpened and, in the modern era, finally defined.

In 1854 Pius IX dogmatically defined the doctrine of the immaculate conception of Mary. Mary, it asserts, was in view of the salvation accomplished by her Son freed from original sin and its consequences in a unique way, namely, from the instant of her conception. In 1950 Pius XII in a sense completed this doctrinal definition by adding that, at the conclusion of the course of her life, Mary was assumed body and soul into heaven. We may summarize these dogmatic declarations in terms of Mary's sanctity in the following way: by virtue of the salvation accomplished by her Son, Mary was preserved from the stain of original sin, never sinned during her earthly life and as a result was spared the consequences of sin at her life's end; she therefore now reigns body and soul with her Son in heaven.

Of all mariological claims, these are perhaps the most difficult, both in terms of their content and in terms of the manner of their promulgation. With respect to the former, many Christians exclude these as dogma because of the lack of explicit biblical justification. At best, they are regarded as pious options, at worst as dangerous errors. As for the latter, Christian bodies both East and Protestant—even when sometimes holding to the doctrines so defined—balk at the unilateral manner in which the definition was articulated. Expanding on the latter objection falls well outside the scope of this book; the former, however, needs further spelling out in the light of the argument developed in the previous section.

First and importantly, a note of appreciation: the dogmatic declarations concerning the beginning and end of Mary's earthly life have at their combined core an important truth: that Mary's life from beginning to end was marked by grace, which elected her to a specific—indeed utterly singular—vocation, an electing grace preceding any consideration of her merit or belief. This is the dominant theme of the annunciation (see chap. 4). Its careful situation of both Elizabeth and Mary within the overarching story of God's dealings with Israel and through it all humanity, coupled with its contrast between the exceptional Elizabeth and the ordinary Mary, are means to emphasize God's grace from first to last. Even though Mary is the central human character, Luke's story is first of all about the free, radical grace of God that preceded the annunciation, enabled her strong and free affirmation and brought the promise to its fulfillment.

Second, the recognition that Mary's canonical backstory is in fact the story of Israel renders speculation about her childhood and death simply unnecessary. The narrative context in which to take up her relationship to the rest of sinful humanity is provided not by the legends contained in the *Protevangelium of James* but in the story of God's dealing with Israel *vis-à-vis* the nations. And of course, in that narrative context, Mary's sinlessness concerns neither whether she was infected with original sin nor whether she committed actual sins, nor even the point in her life at which the Holy Spirit accomplished her purification. On these matters, Augustine's respectful silence—which is simply an echo of Holy Scripture's silence—seems far more appropriate than the speculations that find their ultimate expression in the sermons of John of Damascus in the East and in the Mariologies of the medieval theologians in the West.

Most evangelicals traditionally stop here, assuming that silence regarding the particulars of Mary's life entails a similar stance regarding the traditional subject of her sanctity. To do so, however, is to conflate two matters. Even if one correctly rejects the modern dogmas because they lack sufficient scriptural warrant, one is still required to think through Mary's relationship to the rest of us. And this is precisely what Mary's sanctity is about.

If we attend to the Synoptic presentations of Mary, two important themes emerge that must guide our thoughts concerning her holiness. First, she is perfectly and utterly ordinary. The most unflattering portrait is found in Mark. Even if, as some commentators point out, it is possible to see in Mary's attempt to restrain Jesus a depiction of strength of character and a passionate desire to protect her family, her actions clearly place her among Jesus' opponents. Surely Mark wishes to create some distance between Mary and the religious leaders, who because of their greater knowledge are that much more culpable for their rejection of Jesus and his message. Nevertheless, at least at that point in Jesus' ministry, she was styled by Mark as an outsider, unaware of Jesus' identity and seemingly blind to his message.

Preachers following John Chrysostom presented Mary's actions at the Cana wedding as selfish, manipulative and vain. Matthew engages in an elaborate apologetic that acknowledges the reality of and defends Mary from charges of sexual impropriety. Even Luke—who by far is the most positive of the Gospel writers—seems to go out of his way to reveal a Mary who is not terribly pious or well connected, who while displaying flashes of prophetic insight is not at all clear about the divine plan to which she has agreed, who will herself be visited with the sword of judgment that Jesus' presence brings on Israel.

In this history of starts and stops, insight and ignorance, Mary is clearly one of us. The Bible does not apotheosize her in the manner that later, noncanonical writings do. What sets Mary apart from us is not the specifics of her conduct; what little of it finds its way into the pages of Holy Scripture is all too familiar. Rather, it is her perseverance. When the disciples fled, it is Mary with the beloved disciple who perseveres under the cross, with Jesus until the end. After a lifetime of wrestling with ambiguity, beginning at the manger, continuing through the temple encounter and coming to a climax during Jesus' ministry, Mary is numbered among the first disciples in the upper room, awaiting the promise of the Father.

Mary's sanctity ought not to be articulated in quasibiological terms that exempt her from original sin. Neither should it be grounded in legends that magnify her purity far beyond that of any human being. Rather, biblically it is to be found in the faithfulness with which she embraced and pursued the divine commission to be the slave of the Lord through moments of ambiguity, doubt and judgment, from the annunciation through the cross and into the resurrection and the beginning of the church. This needs to be unpacked both narratively and dogmatically.

Narratively the reconception of Mary's sanctity as faithfulness to the divine vocation contained in Gabriel's announcement is to be read as the fulfillment of faithful Israel to its call to be a light to the nations. As *a* daughter of Zion, Mary is called in a general way to this specific vocation. Simply as a Jew, she is one of that people through whom all the world will be blessed. As *the* daughter of Zion, she is that vehicle through which that general vocation is specifically accomplished.

Thus, for example, the words of the prophet—"the LORD has proclaimed / to the end of the earth: / Say to daughter Zion, / 'See, your salvation comes; / his reward is with him, / and his recompense before him'" (Is 62:11)—take on new significance for believers in Jesus, for his advent forces a rereading of that text. Jesus is indeed the salvation of the daughter of Zion, and she is at once faithful Israel and Mary. Indeed, the salvation of this virgin daughter (Lam 2:13) is at several points prophetically presented as a birth. Thus, Micah writes, "Writhe and groan, O daughter Zion, / like a woman in labor; / for now you shall go forth from the city / and camp in the open country; / you shall go to Babylon. / There you shall be rescued, / there the LORD will redeem you / from the hands of your enemies" (4:10).

What ought to strike readers regarding the various daughter of Zion passages in the prophets is their moral realism. The Isaiah passage, for instance, finds its place in the midst of a larger segment dealing directly with God's judgment on and redemption of Israel. The daughter of Zion who will be rescued is she who was once termed "Forsaken" and "Desolate" (Is 62:4). Her sanctity rests not in her conduct—which has in fact brought the severest of judgments on her—but because God is faithful to his promise to the people of Israel. If the daughter of Zion is one day to be called "The Holy People" and "A City Not Forsaken" (Is 62:12), it is only because God has in his faithfulness chosen her, remained faithful to that choice and brought that choice to its fruition in her. This is especially obvious in the Micah passage, where the birthpangs that precede the rescue of Israel are in fact an image of the exile: the removal of the people from the land of promise because of their persistent sinning.

This assessment of Old Testament mariological foreshadowing ought to color the manner in which we speak of Mary's sanctity. There is no need to invent life details by which her sanctity is described and exalted beyond the range of authentic human experience, for her sanctity does not hinge on her conduct. If Mary is indeed to be read within the context of the prophets' daughter of Zion, there is, in fact, no need to ignore or tortuously reinterpret those passages of the New Testament that present her conduct in a less than flattering light. Her sanctity, like that of faithful Israel, does not depend on conduct as much as it does on perseverance to the call of God—perseverance, moreover, enabled and accomplished by grace alone.

The centrality of divine initiative in the daughter of Zion motif is the point at which we move from narrative to dogmatics, where Mary's sanctity is best understood as the paradigmatic human response to the grace of God disclosed in Christ. It is a response rooted in and enabled by grace. Mary's "here am I," with which her lifelong commitment begins, is not self-initiated but a response to the announcement of Gabriel that these things would come to pass. Mary's response is indeed free—there is nothing in the text to indicate coercion of any sort—but it arises from a freedom not inherent, but already restored through an act of God.

It highlights, furthermore, the kind of person fit to become God's servant. In his discussion of the miracle of Christmas, Barth describes the matter well: "Man is involved in the form of Mary, but involved only in the form of the *virgo Maria,* that is, only in the form of nonwilling, nonachieving, noncreative, nonsovereign man, only in the form of man who can merely receive, merely be ready, merely let something be done to and with himself" (*CD* 1.2:191). What Barth sees in the miracle of the virginal conception applies to Mary's life as a whole. Her life, in the snippets in which it is given to us, is a life lived in openness to the free and radical grace of God. Whether we find Mary assenting to the words of Gabriel, prophesying at Elizabeth's house, mulling at the manger, pondering at the temple, directing at the Cana wedding, being excluded at Peter's house, grieving at the foot of the cross or, finally, waiting in the upper room—this life is a life of trust in God in spite of events, in spite of what is not understood, full of starts and stops, whose holiness is finally found in its completion.

Conclusion

Mary's life is a faith-filled life in a very real world. Hers is a world as full of threats and challenges and joys and sorrows and moments of doubt and fear as ours. Her persistence in that world, her reliance on grace throughout it, a reliance that persisted until its course ended, marks that life as an example not only for virgins or only for women but for all who would claim the title "disciple." Speculation about how that grace was manifest at the beginning of Mary's life or its end is to tread where Scripture is utterly silent and therefore unnecessary. On this matter, Augustine's approach is the surest.

13

Advocate

Toward a Doctrine of Mary's Work

Recognition of Mary's perseverance as the ground and substance of her sanctity provides a bridge by which we can move from discussion of her person to discussion of her work, for the most obvious example of Mary's ongoing role both in the corporate life of the church and in the individual lives of believers is that of example. It is not the only one. Reflection on Mary's work also takes into consideration the more controversial issues of intercession, mediation and coredemption. Study of these issues should offer a biblically grounded and constructive understanding of Mary's work that will justify the propriety of "advocate" as a Marian title.

Mary's Example

Turning first to Mary's example, the objections and proposals of feminist and liberation theologians come to the fore. The classic objection arising from the former is that by exalting Mary to the degree and in the manner that it has, the church (especially the Roman Catholic Church) has made Mary out to be an example with hopelessly high standards. While men may be able to treat the Virgin Mother as an object of (sometimes intense) religious devotion, for women the ideal that she represents is, quite simply, impossible. When the Virgin Mother is presented as the ideal woman, Mary becomes a symbol of oppression for many women. Even when presented more sensitively as the ideal complement to the masculine Jesus or the symbolic expression of the divine feminine, Mary is often thereby removed from the actual life of faith of many Christian women and men while leaving a potentially oppressive symbol system intact.

As we have seen, strategies for addressing this imbalance differ within the feminist theological camp. Elizabeth Johnson presents a persuasive picture of Mary as a "woman of the Spirit" whose faithful response to the call of God throughout her life stands as an abiding example of discipleship not only to Christian women but also to men—an example, furthermore, that may well call into question the ways in which discipleship has become regulated and structured in Johnson's own Roman Catholic tradition. Tina Beattie, on the other hand, wants not only to leave the church's high view of Mary fundamentally intact, but indeed to expand it in order to correct (in her estimation) the very symbol system that gave Mariology life. Mariology needs not to be dismantled but pushed in new directions in order to call accepted practice into question.

Tissa Balasuriya and Leonardo Boff present parallel structures from the liberation theologies of the Two-Thirds World. The former's proposal is fundamentally similar to Johnson's: reliance on the text of the New Testament (especially Luke) over later theological developments leads to a mariological presentation in which Mary represents both the ideal disciple and God's preferential option for the poor. Boff, on the other hand, exalts Mary as an incarnation of the Holy Spirit, the divine feminine. We have seen just what kinds of difficulties this proposal leads to, not the least of which is the perpetuation of a stereotypical femininity constructed within and helping to maintain a patriarchal semiotic system.

Evangelical Protestants, because of their insistence on the primacy of the biblical text in theological construction, will likely find more common ground between feminist and liberationist scholars such as Johnson and Balasuriya and less with Beattie and Boff. This is especially the case when discussing Mary as first and model disciple, for the model to which they and we first appeal is not that of Athanasius (Mary as a symbolic expression of all the ideals of emerging Egyptian asceticism) or the later East (the queen of the heavenly court) or the West (the immaculately conceived, bodily assumed, heavenly intercessor). As a model she is first and foremost the first-century Palestinian woman delivered to us by Mark (the well-intended opponent of the gospel), Matthew (the scandalously pregnant woman) and Luke (the persistent prophet and disciple). What makes her all-holy—for this title does convey deep theological truth—is not the way in which God graciously removes her from the rest of the race, but the way in which his electing and equipping grace grants her the ability to persevere to the end, to fulfill her vocation completely.

She is a this-worldly Mary well familiar with the challenges that continue to threaten the faith of even the most postmodern of disciples: doubt, misunderstanding, almost unimaginable grief. She is a model because she rises to meet these. In a sea of doubt surfaces the faith that utters, "Here am I, God's slave, let it be to me." In the midst of events that are difficult to synthesize into a coherent narrative is the commitment to keep pondering them until their significance is disclosed, all the while treasuring them. In the midst of unimaginable grief under the cross is faith that refuses to leave until all is accomplished. And in the end is the deepest proof of trust in God's promise evident in her presence in the upper room.

This emphasis on the "historical" Mary is, left on its own, one-sided. There must also be factored into the equation the more symbolic portrayals of Luke, John and the Revelation. Here, she retains her role as model, but instead of a model of individual discipleship, it is a model of the church both militant and triumphant. With respect to the former, the following biblical images are especially evocative. As God's poor prophet, she personifies the church's proclamation of God's intervention on behalf of the poor. As the woman at the wedding, she reminds the church of its present evangelistic vocation—to point always and only to Christ with the words "whatever he says to you, do it." Under the cross, the woman of the hour is the archetype of the faithful remnant, a church true to the gospel message and Lord when all others have fled.[1] As all things are accomplished, her departure from the cross with the Beloved Disciple reminds the church that, like Mary, it has been entrusted to the care of the apostles even as it continues to guard and nurture their witness to the Word. The church lives, in other words, always under the judgment of Holy Scripture even as it honors and protects it with the lives of its members. In all these things, the Marian church is the woman pursued by the dragon—seemingly overpowered by the forces of evil and relying only on the protective power of God.

If the Marian vision of the church militant is one of faithfulness in the midst of constant satanic harassment, however, the Marian vision of the church triumphant is one of exaltation over God's enemies, which in the present entails divine protection and in the future entails victory. She expresses the ancient hope—both Jewish and pagan—that the dragon will one day be forever vanquished even as she comforts Christians with the present knowledge that the blood of the martyrs was not shed in vain. Those who are faithful unto death are not in fact noble victims of a more powerful and ruthless enemy; they are those who have "conquered him by the blood of the Lamb / and by the word of their testimony, / for they did not cling to life even in the face of death" (Rev 12:11).

Mary's Intercession

Three matters remain to be discussed—the notions that Mary intercedes for us,

---

[1]Timothy George, "The Blessed Evangelical Mary," *Christianity Today,* December 2003, p. 119.

the church militant, that she mediates grace to us and that she coredeems with Christ. These matters delve deeply into the roots of the ongoing separation between the Roman Catholic Church and the churches of the Reformation. I therefore acknowledge both the controversy and the deep sense of unease it creates for faithful people on both sides of this debate at the outset. Although the Reformation was not critically concerned with Mary in its first generation, Luther—especially as he aged—came to regard much of Marian piety with deep contempt. It is a tragedy of the Reformation that constructive attempts to move beyond such contempt, always a minority, were eventually stifled until the second half of the twentieth century. As a result, many contemporary Protestants have to overcome a history of both lobbing charges of idolatry without really understanding why and uncomfortable silence with respect to anything other than criticism.

At the same time the Reformation legacy has revealed a Marian piety on the Roman Catholic side of the divide that is sometimes regarded as immune from criticism, as though no exaltation of Mary could be considered to be too much. Even Roman Catholic thinkers such as Erasmus, Pascal, Muratori and Newman were suspected of Marian impiety when their only crime was to state clearly what was accepted, even official, church teaching against popular piety that did, in fact, justify Protestant complaints. It is only with the Second Vatican Council that we see an attempt not simply to impede the growth of Marian piety—the dogmatic decrees were just this—but actually to tie it firmly to biblical, patristic and liturgical foundations and in so doing repudiate some forms of private devotion.

As a result of this history, talking about Mary's intercession, mediation and coredemption is fraught with difficulty. But it is not impossible. There is sufficient groundwork in place to offer a biblically sound, theologically constructive and ecumenically sensitive understanding of each of these issues, which, while certainly not undoing Protestant reservations, can at least move us beyond the recitation of polemics.

Mary's intercession, on closer inspection, falls into two sets of questions. The first set has to do with the ongoing role of the church triumphant in general. Do the saints in heaven pray for us? If so, is it possible to ask for their intercessions? If it is possible, should we? Robert Jenson points out that for Magisterial churches at least there is no good reason to answer "no" to any of these questions: "Simply saying . . . that there is no scriptural mandate to address individual saints will not do."[2] Rather, he says that the case is analogous to that of infant

[2]Robert W. Jenson, "A Space for God," in *Mary: Mother of God,* ed. Carl E. Braaten and Robert W. Jenson (Grand Rapids: Eerdmans, 2004), p. 50.

baptism. Citing Luther, he observes that invoking the intercessions of the saints is an ancient practice that Scripture does not forbid.

While such an argument may accord well with Jenson's Lutheran sensibilities, it likely will not accord well with many of my readers, who will require further justification. Taking Jenson's allusion to infant baptism as a clue, I wish to develop a parallel argument with respect to the intercessions of the church triumphant for the church militant. That is, while no passage of the Bible directly justifies either the belief itself or acting thereon, a cumulative biblical case can be built to justify the doctrine even if acting thereon continues to remain problematic.

The first piece of evidence has to do with the continuity of the church across not only space, but also time—which is to say that it is not bounded by death. Indeed, to treat death as that which sunders the bonds created by our identification with Christ in baptism can (and should) be presented as an implicit denial of the resurrection of Christ, which, by our baptism, we now partly enjoy and hope one day fully to share. How can the risen Lord, the head of the body, who reigns now in his divine humanity, have that reign attenuated by the enemy he conquered when he stepped out of the tomb? Those who have died in Christ are still, after death, infused by the Holy Spirit with the resurrection life of Christ and are therefore, even as they now await the resurrection, alive to and in him. So it is that Jonathan Edwards could rightly insist that the "church in heaven and the church on earth are more *one* people, *one* city, and *one* family, than is generally imagined."[3]

The second piece of evidence has to do with the ontological status enjoyed now by those who, although dead, remain alive in Christ. If what I argued above is correct, the departed are alive in Christ not because of some doctrine of the inherent immortality of the soul, but because in baptism Christ's identity has become their own even as his resurrection life has been infused into them. It is on the basis of this shared life in Christ that Christians can and do intercede for one another across wide geographic differences. It is his life that is the basis of our communion as church, as his people, his very body. And part of that life is the mutual bearing of burdens and the pleading of God's mercy and favor on our brothers and sisters. If Christ is not only the bond of our communion, but the source of its life—a life that transcends bodily death—and if it is on the basis of our union with Christ that we intercede for each other, it is quite possible to conceive not only that the saints now in heaven pray for us, but that they can be implored to do so, much in the same way as we ask brothers and sisters here on earth.

---

[3]Jonathan Edwards, "Miscellaneous Observations" 421, in *The Complete Works of Jonathan Edwards* (Carlisle, Penn.: Banner of Truth, 1834), 2:621.

The key, of course, is to recognize the thoroughly christological dimension of our shared life. If seeking the intercessions of the saints is possible, it is not because there is some kind of traffic between souls still trapped in bodies and souls already "gone to heaven." It is possible rather because people awaiting the resurrection—whether in the body or with the Lord—remain united to each other in Christ. Jenson puts it well: "The communion of the Church is established only by communion with Christ, whatever communion the church on earth has with the church in heaven is also founded. The saints are not our way to Christ; he is our way to them."[4] The saints do not mediate Christ to us; he remains the one and only mediator through which the true unity of the time-and-space transcending community of the church is established.

Thus it is possible, based on our shared identity in Christ, both to conceive of the saints in heaven praying for the saints on earth and to invite them to do so. The last question, "should we?" is more difficult. On this matter, the Bible is silent: Scripture neither requires nor prohibits it. While the practice of the church from ancient times suggests that the answer to this question is yes, the doctrine of the church is far more circumspect. The Roman Catholic Church's latest catechism, for example, urges its adherents to do so, but does not require it.[5] At the same time most Protestant theologians, following the logic of the argument laid out above, would acknowledge that the church triumphant does in fact intercede for the church on earth. They would hasten to add, however, that because of a clear lack of a biblical commandment to seek its aid, coupled with the many historical examples of such devotion tending toward idolatry, believers ought not engage in the practice.

With respect to the actual practice of the invocation of saints, therefore, we are left with a quandary. While not directly addressed by the Bible, certain clearly biblical beliefs do appear to justify it—in a manner similar to the biblical arguments for infant baptism. In practice, however, it often appears to endorse what the Bible prohibits. In this light the best route to proceed is to allow both the practice and its denial as authentic forms of Christian witness, each supplementing the other. Thus, the practice affirms against its denial the time-and-space-transcending reality of the body of Christ, while the denial affirms against the practice the deleterious effect it has had when divorced from sound teaching.

---

[4]Robert W. Jenson, *Systematic Theology,* vol. 2: *The Works of God* (New York: Oxford University Press, 1999), p. 269.

[5]*Catechism of the Catholic Church,* 2683 (Ottawa: Canadian Conference of Catholic Bishops, 1994), p. 544.

The second set of questions can now focus more directly on Mary. Is Mary a unique case with respect to intercession and invocation? On the one hand the answer clearly is no. Mary is no more accessible to us or available to intercede for us than any other saint apart from the singular mediation of Christ. Our communion with her is exactly the same as that with other departed believers and as that with living believers. That is to say, it is a communion made possible by the source of the body's life, the body's head, Jesus Christ. "We may not ask Mary to bring us to Christ," says Jenson; but "because we are one with Christ we can address Mary."[6] This affirmation allows us to pronounce harshly on the medieval (and sometimes modern) popular notion that Mary by virtue of her motherhood could sway her Son in a way no other saint could, even to the point of suspending his justice for the sake of her mercy. If Mary takes her place with the saints beneath Christ, if he is her source of life as of ours, then the picture of a "Mother of Mercy" imploring her Son "the judge" to overturn a righteous but harsh verdict is not simply misleading but also blasphemous.

On the other hand, however, Mary is unique. Mary is invoked on the same basis as any other intercessor—that of our common life-in-Christ. Nevertheless, when we invoke Mary we do not invoke one among many saints, but that singular saint who represents the faithful people of God and is *Theotokos.* When the church on earth invokes the intercessions of Mary on its behalf, it invokes the one in whom the history of God's striving with Israel comes to its climax. To do so, therefore, is to remind both the church and God of God's promises to his people, God's reliability in bringing those promises to fruition and the faithfulness of God in striving with and in his people to bring about his desired result in and with and for them. "After all the Lord's struggle with his beloved Israel, he finally found a place in Israel that unbelief would not destroy like the temple, or silence like the prophets, or simply lose, like the Book of the Law before Josiah. This place is a person. To ask Mary to pray for us is to meet him there."[7] In her representative and maternal roles, Mary is that unique space for God, in and through whom the church continues to plead God's Word not only to God but also to itself.

Mary's Mediation and Coredemption

The remaining issues, which are perhaps the most difficult to assess dispassionately, coalesce in a single question: May the exemplary and intercessory work

---

[6]Robert W. Jenson, *Systematic Theology,* vol. 1: *The Triune God* (New York: Oxford University Press, 1996), p. 269.

[7]Jenson, "Space for God," p. 56.

be legitimately understood in some sense to be mediatory or even coredemptive? In order to treat this question properly, the discomfort it causes must be faced at the outset. It arises from two sources, the first of which is history. While Mary simply was not a major concern of the first generation of Reformers and while Luther, Zwingli and Bullinger could at times regard her quite highly, even these would have regarded the language of mediation and coredemption as attempts to undermine the singular mediatory and redemptive work of Jesus. Their worries, furthermore, are only exacerbated by future generations of Protestant theologians whose theological antennae had through years of polemics become finely attuned to any alleged talk of another redeemer. On the Roman Catholic side of the divide, it must also be admitted that given at least some expressions of popular (though unofficial) devotion, these fears were legitimate. Although this history is several centuries old, on both sides it is never far from the surface of any Marian conversation. Old emotions resonate across centuries.

The second source is methodological. Throughout this book, I attempted to base a case for an attenuated version of Mariology on the witness of Holy Scripture as it was interpreted through history. A biblical understanding of Mary's intercession—as the singular example of the intercessions of the church triumphant for the church militant—is analogous to a biblical understanding of the practice of infant baptism. While there is no explicit endorsement for either practice, what Scripture does say—in the case of infant baptism, about grace; in the case of church intercessions, about the nature of the body—does seem to justify them. On the matter of coredemption, at least, things may well be different. In chapter ten, we observed just how closely some Roman Catholic scholars tied coredemption to the dogma of bodily assumption. And, of course, the problem with this articulation is that, given the method adopted, there is nothing much for me to say about it.

Because Scripture neither says nor implies anything about the modern dogmas, apart from an appreciation of their emphasis on grace in Mary's life, silence with respect to them is the best option. Now—at least in the understanding of coredemption offered by Gabriel Roschini—we have a version erected directly on the modern dogmas: Mary was without sin from the instant of her conception; the wages of sin is death; therefore, Mary died when she did not have to. Her death, resurrection and assumption must serve another purpose: coredemption. I am driven by the biblical witness to understand Roschini's argument as a (potential) dogmatic development at least two steps removed from the Bible itself. And the logic of such steps is far from obvious to me. These are moves I cannot justify within the method I have adopted. As a result, I am left advocating silence as the best theological option.

To conclude that it is perhaps best for reasons of Reformation legacy and theology to leave these most controversial of issues alone, however, would be premature. There are very good reasons to engage in debates about mediation and coredemption. The first is straightforward: the issues have not yet been defined. While Pius XII may have regarded the definition of the bodily assumption to be the apex of Marian development, many familiar with the debate—from all sides—are not so sure. From scholars such as Roschini, immediately after the definition, to the Marian maximalists of Vatican II in the following decade, many have sensed a deep continuity between Mary's heavenly reign and her ongoing role. And I have encountered in my research no theoretical or theological reason to conclude that the train of Marian doctrinal development has come into the station. I am therefore convinced that with respect to these issues it is best to proceed on the assumption that further developments—whatever the timetable—will happen.

Second, not only have these matters not been finally defined, but a succession of popes have in various ways invited Christian theologians from outside the Roman Catholic Church to make their contributions known. Not only did Pius XII not define these terms, but his successors John XXIII, Paul VI and John Paul II have, in different ways, invited Eastern and Protestant theologians to contribute to theological conversations, including those conversations revolving around Mary.[8] It is therefore in the best interests of Protestant theologians committed to the continued vitality of the one church to pursue what may well be an unprecedented opportunity for ecumenical advance (see chap. 10). The reasons to proceed (openness and opportunity) trump those not to (history and theology).

Two concepts of Marian mediation can and should be supported, while a third must be entirely denied. First, to name Mary as mediator is appropriate in the field of Christology. Insofar as she is *Theotokos,* she does in some sense mediate God's presence on earth because she gave God the Son his human nature. From this recognition, in turn, have derived many Marian devotional titles that typically give Protestants pause: Mary is the "ladder" uniting heaven and earth; she is the "burning bush" who mediates but is not consumed by the presence of God; she is the "neck" joining head to body and so on. However foreign or even discomfiting they may sound, we must now recognize that they are in

[8]John XXIII and Paul VI issued a general invitation through the documents of Vatican II. The latter was even more specific when, in *Marialis cultus,* he observed that Marian belief and practice should not cut itself off from wider cultural and theological conversations. John Paul II issued invitations to other Christian groups throughout his remarkable pontificate, the most important for this chapter (and book) being *Ut unum sint* and *Redemptoris mater.*

some sense valid. As Christ's mother, Mary is indeed all of these things. As *Theotokos,* she physically mediated God's incarnate presence.

But, it will be asked, does Mary continue to mediate between God and people in a manner reflective of her singular mediation as *Theotokos?* The answer is a qualified yes. The distinction between "created mediation" and "uncreated mediation"—or at least one like it—made by scholars such as Jaroslav Pelikan is key. Pelikan uses the distinction carefully to circumscribe that mediation offered by Mary and the saints from the singular mediation in salvation provided by the incarnate God. Although obviously related, both in terms of kind and degree they are fundamentally different.

What then does created mediation describe? It describes a fact of Christian life with which evangelicals are deeply familiar and comfortable. It denotes the notion of a gifted intercessor. While all would recognize the need for intercessory prayer by all Christians, those from across confessional divides also acknowledge that there are specific individuals in communities of faith that are singularly able. They know "how to touch the throne of God," to use the language of evangelical pietism. Such people are "created mediators." They are vehicles through whom God has chosen to mediate his grace and favor. When speaking of Mary's mediation, it is this understanding that one ought to have in mind. On this understanding, it is simply another way of referring to Mary's intercessory role described above. Mediation, in this limited way, is synonymous with intercession.

On the other hand any presentation of mediation that whether deliberately or accidentally confuses the created mediation of the saints (whether alive or dead) with the uncreated mediation of God in Christ must be stoutly resisted. With respect to the mediation of saving grace, Jesus alone is the mediator. If the term *mediator* means one who stands alongside Jesus, one who is his equal and even alternative, then the term for both biblical and historical reasons must be rejected completely. Luther's vehement rejection of the devotional image of the Mother of Mercy who alone could alter the will of her Son the judge was and remains sound. Mary is not a mediator in this way. She is, even for the most ardent Marian devotee, beneath her Son.

The issue of coredemption is more difficult because it is a source of disagreement not only between traditional Protestants and Roman Catholics, but also among Protestants themselves. Coredemption is a slippery word, more elusive even than mediation. It refers to the possibility of cooperation between Mary and God in the salvation of the world. Roschini's argument articulates coredemption in such a way as to be closed to the Protestant theological imagination. His is not, however, the only understanding available. Two others—more securely rooted in the pages of Holy Scripture—need to be considered.

The first comes from John 19—Mary beneath the cross. To state the position simply, if Mary brought forth Jesus in joy (this is the core of her virginity *in partu*) and if she knew that her Son was the Savior of the world even as he died, then the pain she experienced at the cross was not that of grief over her Son's death, but labor (or colabor) at the birth of the church. In this sense, her suffering was coredemptive with the suffering of Christ. Both Scripture and tradition rule out this understanding of Mary under the cross. First, at no point in the text is Mary's interior disposition described. While we may rightly intuit that she experienced pain, the notion that such pain was more like labor than grief is simply forcing the text to say what it plainly does not. This understanding seems to be rooted more in the medieval tradition of the *Stabat mater dolorosa* than in the Gospel narrative itself. Furthermore, Ambrose, in his insistence that Christ needed no help in saving the world, adds his weighty voice against this understanding of Mary's place at the cross. Coredemption—however understood—cannot be rooted here, either.

Coredemption may also be raised in the annunciation in Luke and specifically in Mary's response to the angel, beginning as it does with the words "here am I." And here, the evangelical Protestant theological community is divided. All will agree that these words reflect her cooperation with God's grace in the incarnation. The question—which the text itself does not answer—is whether this cooperation is itself grace enabled. Does God's grace intervene in Mary's life in such a way that she could have said no? Synergists would answer this question affirmatively. Mary could have declined the announcement. That she accepted it is prima facie cooperation with grace in securing not simply her own salvation, but indeed, the salvation of the world. There is therefore no compelling reason for a synergist to deny Mary her title "coredeemer" insofar as it does express a truth that appears (to them at least) to be rooted in the biblical text.

On the other hand monergists affirm the sovereignty of God in his grace throughout the drama. On their reading of the biblical text, Mary did indeed freely cooperate with God's gracious intervention, but only because that same grace had chosen her from before the foundation of the world to be the instrument of the incarnation. Her freedom—and it is a real freedom—was not such that she could have declined. She was not coerced into becoming the Mother of God. She freely accepted the role to which she had been graciously predestined from eternity (see chap. 12). For monergists such as myself, coredemption—if it is to be found here at all—can be affirmed only in the weakest possible sense: Mary is coredeemer in a manner analogous to the church. Insofar as the church is the means by which God has chosen to offer his grace to the world and a sign that points to the gracious work of the Holy Spirit throughout the world, the church is itself a coredeemer. Insofar as Mary is the means by which God gave the world himself as the incarnate one, she is a sign that points to the gracious work of God in Christ.

Neither understanding elevates Mary to a position of equality with Christ. He is the redeemer without which no redemption is possible. He needed no help on the cross. Coredemption is unproblematic only if it is intended to signify the means through which that redemption is applied.

Conclusion

At the conclusion of the study, it is perhaps wise simply to list what has been accomplished alongside what has not. I have attempted to construct a Mariology within a theological method that most evangelical Protestant theologians would recognize as theirs. Some may well argue that I have placed an inordinate amount of faith in the ability of tradition to teach us how best to read Scripture, but this is not a question of the method's propriety as much as it is of its implementation. The result is an understanding of Mary squarely within and indeed beneath the rubric of Christology. Beliefs about Mary arise from and are intended to clarify our beliefs about Christ. Indeed, they are intended not to glorify Mary as much as they are intended to glorify her Son.

Those beliefs include the ongoing significance of the virginal conception for Christology, a willingness to reconsider claims to perpetual virginity and recognition of the deep symbolic connection between the Mother of God and the people of God. Added to these are convictions concerning the place of Mary in God's plan to save the world and an acceptance of Mary's sanctity defined biblically as perseverance rather than traditionally as immaculate conception. Finally, the picture is completed when we acknowledge Mary's intercessory, mediatory and coredemptive role in the plan of salvation.

Many of my readers will conclude that by presenting this picture I have signaled a belief that the Reformation was in many ways an error that now needs to be undone, that I have overlooked or conveniently forgotten the history of the controversy surrounding Mary in Western Christianity, both Protestant and Roman Catholic. To these readers I offer a reminder of those places where I believe I am constrained by Scripture not to go. I believe Scripture rightly read rejects any understanding of the election of Mary as necessary, rather than contingent on the election of God to become incarnate. I continue to hold that the two modern dogmas—which can be appreciated for their emphasis on grace—enshrine postbiblical legends about Mary's beginning and end, thereby distracting believers from the literary basis for beliefs in Mary's sanctity, namely, the

Old Testament. I remain convinced that a great deal of pious or affective language about the Blessed Virgin perpetuates a grave misunderstanding of her *subordinate* role, effectively creating an equal, alternative Savior. This is especially the case when the language of intercession, mediation and coredemption is used too loosely and in a manner abstracted from biblical roots.

So the Reformation is neither in actuality nor in my opinion about to end anytime soon. I hope, however, that I have helped to clear away some of its unhelpful polemical baggage (and each side has a truckload) in order that productive conversations may take place—conversations that articulate clearly just where we can and cannot agree, not in order to perpetuate that disagreement, but in order to prayerfully set those disagreements before the one who prayed that we might be one:

> O God Most High, who didst endue with wonderful virtue and grace the Blessed Virgin Mary, the Mother of our Lord:
>
> Grant that we, who now call her blessed, may be made very members of the heavenly family of him who was pleased to be called the first-born among many brethren; who liveth and reigneth with thee and the Holy Spirit, one God, world without end. *Amen.*[9]

[9]Collect for the Feast of the Blessed Virgin Mary, *Book of Common Prayer* (Anglican Church of Canada, 1962).

Acknowledgments

It is often said that books are not the products of authors as much as of communities. Among those that can claim some copyright here are two from academia. The board and president's cabinet of Providence College and Seminary granted me a full sabbatical for the 2004-2005 academic year. I hope they judge the freedom from classroom and committee responsibilities to have been used wisely. My colleagues there, especially Cameron McKenzie, Terry Tiessen, Michael Gilmour, Randy Holm, David Johnson and August Konkel, have stimulated my thinking not only for this project but also in all my academic work. During my sabbatical, Saint Paul University in Ottawa, Ontario, provided a studio, tremendous library resources and a collegial atmosphere, making this project pleasant. I am grateful to Prof. L. G. Bloomquist for his assistance and friendship; to the vice rector, Denis Hurtubise, for tending to the details; to Prof. J. K. Coyle for inestimable bibliographic help; and to all in the Jean-Léon Allie Library. I could neither have asked for nor found better support. Thank you.

Second, I am conscious of my debt to churches across three Canadian provinces. Early on in Manitoba, the congregations of Saint Margaret's Anglican Church, Grace Bible Church and Mitchell Community Fellowship Church allowed me to lay the groundwork for part one by inviting me regularly into their pulpits. The Rev. Dr. David Widdicombe and Val Hiebert-Friesen were especially encouraging as the vision for this project began to take shape. Throughout 2004-2005, my family and I benefited greatly from the hospitality offered by churches in Ontario and Québec, namely Grace Community Bible Church in Shawville; the Wesleyan churches in Arnprior and Shawville; the United churches in Bristol, Stark's Corners and Shawville; and the Presbyterian churches in Bristol and Fort Coulonge. Through you, I have experienced just how the body can—and ought to—care for its members. Thank you.

Third, many in the community of friends and family contributed. Among them, my editor at InterVarsity Press, Daniel G. Reid, saw promise in a proposal submitted in November 2002, helped me secure a contract and has offered sound advice ever since. Many others, including my parents, Ellard and Kathryn Perry, and other extended family and friends, including Cornie Wiens, Paul and Anita Wiens, Hugh and Norma Horner, Marjorie Horner, Revell and Helen Robinson, and Gary and Norma Graham, offered very tangible support during a year that saw two major moves and had its share of financial stresses. Glenn Horner enlivened Friday lunches with generosity, good humor and good conversation that I will miss very much. When the book was in its final stages, former students Tim Konkel and Stephen Zylstra—who remain my friends and in many ways inspirations—corrected errors and offered helpful insights and difficult questions. Thanks to you all.

Finally, my wife, Rachel, sacrificed more than I did to see this book published. It is to her that I dedicate it, knowing that it does not fully express my gratitude and hoping that it is a good beginning.

Name Index

Abraham, William J., 12
Albert the Great, 193-95
Alexander of Alexandria, 142
Ambrose of Milan, 155-61, 162, 176, 200, 276, 281
Andrewes, Lancelot, 223
Anselm of Canterbury, 177, 183-87, 193, 208, 211, 223, 232
Athanasius, 142-46, 148, 151, 152, 160, 276, 282, 297
Augustine of Hippo, 133, 153, 165-68, 174, 176, 187, 192, 198, 200, 204, 205, 208, 212, 260, 261, 279, 280, 288, 291, 292, 295
Balasuriya, Tissa, 239, 256, 257, 258, 261, 297
Barth, Karl, 278, 279, 283, 287, 288, 295
Basil the Great, 149, 150, 151
Bauckham, Richard, 49
Beattie, Tina, 239, 254-56, 258, 261, 297
Bede, 177-80, 223
Bernard, J. H., 126
Bernard of Clairvaux, 177, 189-90, 191, 193, 203, 204, 208, 217, 232
Bloesch, Donald, 287, 288
Boff, Leonardo, 239, 256-58, 261, 297
Bonaventure, 177, 193, 203-4, 232
Brown, Raymond, 43, 46, 50, 53, 259
Bullinger, Heinrich, 218, 237, 268
Bultmann, Rudolf, 25
Cappadocian Fathers, 146, 149, 151, 153, 169
Calvin, John, 23, 218-21, 269, 272
Canisius, Peter, 209, 226, 232, 237, 238
Carter, Warren, 42
Catherine of Aragon, 221
Charles V, 221
Clement of Alexandria, 138-39
Cyril of Alexandria, 169-71, 269-72, 288
Cyril of Jerusalem, 240
Daly, Mary, 254
Damasus, 128
Dibelius, Martin, 29
Donne, John, 223
Drelincourt, Charles, 223-24, 237, 268
Dunn, James D. G., 23, 27
Eadmer, 177, 187-89, 193, 204, 208, 223
Edward VI, 222-23
Edwards, Jonathan, 300
Elizabeth I, 222-23
Elliott, J. K., 286
Emerton, J. A., 126
Erasmus, Desiderius, 209-14, 219, 236, 237, 268, 299
Evodius of Rome, 240
Fitzmyer, Joseph, 25
France, R. T., 37
Frank, Mark, 223
Gaventa, Beverly Roberts, 47, 52, 53, 71
Gelasius, 128
George, Timothy, 14, 15
Graef, Hilda, 119, 126
Gregory XVI, 207
Gregory the Great, 198
Gregory of Nazianzus, 149, 150, 151, 152, 159, 169
Gregory of Nyssa, 149, 151
Grudem, Wayne, 280n. 8
Gundry, Robert, 35, 53
Gustafson, David, 259, 262
Hastings, Adrian, 246
Henry VII, 221
Henry VIII, 221, 222
Henry of Ghent, 204
Helvidius, 148, 158, 160, 163-64, 165, 176
Hilary of Poitiers, 283
Hooker, Richard, 223
Hurst, L. D., 24
Ignatius of Antioch, 120-23
Ilan, Tal, 38
Innocent I, 128
Irenaeus of Lyons, 129-33, 134, 137, 141, 287, 288, 289
Jenson, Robert W., 269, 286, 289, 299-300
Jerome, 49, 128, 161-65, 176, 192, 196, 281
John XXIII, 245, 304, 304n. 8
John Chrysostom, 148, 153-55, 196
John Duns Scotus, 177, 193, 204-7, 223, 245
John of Damascus, 18, 148, 168n. 97, 171-74, 183, 197, 292
John Paul II, 9, 241, 241n. 4, 304, 304n. 8
Johnson, Elizabeth, 239, 252-54, 256, 258, 261, 297
Johnson, Marshall, 52
Josephus, 84
Jovinian, 148, 158, 160, 176
Justin Martyr, 128-29, 134, 137, 269, 289
Labouré, Catherine, 229-30, 241
Leo the Great, 148, 168, 174-75
Lewis, C. S., 17
Longenecker, Dwight, 259

Longenecker, Richard, 27
Luther, Martin, 209, 214-17, 221, 236, 237, 268, 281, 299, 300, 305
Macleod, Donald, 280
Mary of Agreda, 228, 238, 288
Melito of Sardis, 240
Migliore, Daniel, 95
More, Thomas, 212
Muratori, Ludovico, 228, 268, 299
Nestorius, 169, 269, 271, 272
Neumann, Charles, 159
Newman, John Henry, 223, 232-36, 238, 245, 268, 272, 299
Nicholas of St. Albans, 177, 190-93, 223
Nolland, John, 86
Oden, Thomas, 10
Origen, 139-142, 151, 152
Pacelli, Eugenio. *See* Pius XII
Pannenberg, Wolfhart, 275, 276
Pascal, Blaise, 227-28, 238, 268, 299
Paul VI, 239, 248, 251, 252, 260, 261, 262, 304, 304n. 8
Peacocke, Arthur, 276, 278
Pelagius, 148
Pelikan, Jaroslav, 14, 282-83
Peter Damian, 177, 180-83
Peter of Celle, 177, 190-93
Pius IX, 209, 231-32, 238, 241, 242, 244, 245, 260, 291
Pius XII, 232, 241, 242, 243, 245, 260, 291, 304
Polycarp of Smyrna, 121, 130
Pope, Barbara Corrado, 241
Pusey, E. B., 234
Roschini, Gabriel, 244-45, 303, 304, 305
Ruether, Rosemary Radford, 251, 254
Schaberg, Jane, 275, 276
Schillebeeckx, Edward, 246
Schleiermacher, F. D. E., 209, 224-25, 237
Sheen, Fulton J., 242
Sixtus IV, 207
Socrates Scholasticus, 142
Soubirous, Bernadette, 229, 230-31, 241
Stendahl, Krister, 46
Suárez, Francisco, 209, 226-27, 232, 237, 238, 281, 288
Tertullian, 133-137, 141, 153, 160, 289
Thomas Aquinas, 177, 193, 195-203, 204, 207, 232, 279, 281
Ussher, James, 223
Wainright, Elaine, 50, 51-52
William of Ware, 177, 193, 204-7, 208, 223
Wright, N. T., 289
Zwingli, Ulrich, 213, 218, 237, 268

Subject Index

Ad caeli reginam, 242
adoptionism, 277
Against Helvidius, 163-64
Alexandria, 137-38, 270
androcentrism, 41-42
annunciation, 44, 67-73
Antioch, 153, 270
apocalyptic, 107
Apocypha, 72
Apollinarianism, 274
Apostles' Creed, 274
apostolic fathers, 120-21
Arianism, 142, 143, 148, 149, 172-73
art, early Christian, 17
Ascension of Isaiah, 123-25
atonement, 274
Augsburg Confession, 223
Augustan census, 81-82
Banneux, 241
Beauraing, 241
betrothal, 55
birth narratives, 46-58, 65-84
  apologetic nature of, 48-54
  authority of, 45
  composition of, 43
  historical value of, 42-46, 60, 65-66
  independence of Matthew and Luke, 43-45, 90-91
  Jewish roots of, 46
  Marian roots of, 65-66
  pagan roots of, 45
  sources of, 45, 65-66, 83
Bob Jones University, 259
Book of Common Prayer (1549, 1552), 223
Book of Common Prayer (Canada, 1962), 3-8
Carmelites, 206
Catechism of the Catholic Church, 17n. 5, 301
celibacy, 277, 283-84
Center for Catholic and Evangelical Theology, 14, 259
Chalcedon, 275, 277, 278
Christian Century, 15
Christian Faith, 225
Christianity Today, 15
Colloquies, 213-14
Commemoration of Mary, 144
Commentary on John, 196
concupiscence, 166
Council of Basel, 206
Council of Constantinople, 149, 271
Council of Ephesus, 13, 148, 168-71, 172, 221, 234, 240, 270, 277
Council of Nicea, 23,137, 143, 144, 148, 153, 271, 277
Council of Trent, 209, 225-26, 232, 237
created mediation, 172-73, 174, 220, 298-302, 305
De conceptu virginali, 186
Docetism, 276, 277-78
Dominican school, 193-203
Eastern Orthodoxy, 10
ecclesiology, 11
  church/synagogue dispute, 42
Ecumenical Movement, 9, 10
Ecumenical Society for the Blessed Virgin Mary, 259
ecumenism, 15, 18, 247, 250, 258-60, 260-61, 299
Enlightenment, 237, 238
evangelism, 11
evangelicalism, 15, 258, 259-60
  theological diversity of, 16
  theological method in, 17
Evangelical-Roman Catholic dialogue, 11, 16, 259-60
Evangelicals and Catholics Together, 17n. 6
"Exposition of the Angelic Salutation," 201-3
Exposition of the Gospel of Matthew, 196
Faith Today, 13
fathers of the church, 119-20
Fàtima, 241, 241n. 4
feast of the annunciation to the Blessed Virgin Mary, 223
feast of the conception of the Blessed Virgin Mary, 187-93, 204, 205, 207, 232
feast of the nativity of the Blessed Virgin Mary, 199
feast of the purification of the Blessed Virgin Mary, 223
feminism, 11, 253-54, 258, 260, 261
feminist theology, 251-56, 296
First Lectures on the Psalms, 214
Formula of Concord, 223
Franciscan school, 203-7
freedom, 11
"Freedom of a Christian," 214
Fulgens corona, 241
Glaucoplutus, 213

God's Mother, Eve's Advocate, 254-56
grace, 11
Great Mother. *See Magna mater*
Groupe des Dombes, 259
Herod, 54, 57-58, 61
Horus, 126
Ineffabilis deus, 229-32, 244
Institutes of the Christian Religion, 220-21
Institution of a Christian Man, The Bishops' Book, 222
Isis, 126
Jesus Christ, Christology, 11, 14, 22-31, 75-76, 81, 121, 129, 130, 144, 149, 170, 172-73, 197, 226, 268, 269, 271, 273-74, 275, 277, 289
  brothers (and sisters), 21, 27-28, 31, 32-36, 38, 40, 58-59, 92, 99n. 6, 99n. 7, 105-6, 136-37, 164, 281
  Davidic descent, 25, 41, 42, 47, 53, 54, 56, 57, 58, 60-61, 91, 178, 200
  deity of , 23, 74-75, 122, 142, 149-50, 169, 268, 300
  divine sonship, 26-27, 275, 279
  hour of, 98-107
  humanity of, 23, 27-28, 30, 99, 101, 105, 122-23, 135-36, 138, 142, 149-50, 160, 167, 169, 175, 268, 273-74, 277-80, 300
  humiliation, 23-24, 165
  illegitimacy of, 37, 46, 60n. 70, 61, 200
  incarnation, 23-24, 28, 30, 142, 149-50, 166-67, 178, 195, 271-72, 276, 279, 280
  Jewishness of Jesus, 29
  last Adam, 23-24, 130, 280, 289
  maleness of Jesus, 13
  Messiah, 53, 56, 57
  preincarnate existence, 23-24, 28, 30, 286-88
  recapitulation, 130-33, 166, 289-90
  resurrection, 25-26, 300
  sanctity of, 160, 166-67, 175, 196, 197, 279, 280
  sinlessness of. *See* sanctity of
  union with, 300-301
  unity of, 142
  virginal conception, 24, 25, 28, 29, 30, 31, 35, 44, 45, 53, 55, 60, 67-91, 167, 196, 197, 225, 274-80, 295
Joseph, 37, 41, 47, 54, 91, 164, 178, 200
  death of, 37, 39, 43
  genealogy of, 48-54
  righteousness of, 41, 54-57, 61
Judith, 72
LaSallette, 241
Lectures on Isaiah, 216
Lex orandi lex credendi, 143
liberation theology, 256-58, 296
Life of Antony, 145
"Liturgy of the Virgin Mother Venerated at Loreto," 211
Loreto, 211
Lourdes, 230-31, 242
Lumen gentium, 246-48, 258
Lutheran-Catholic dialogue (U.S.), 259
Magna Mater, 155, 251, 269-70
Magnificat, 76-81, 181, 213, 214-15, 219-20, 251n. 62, 253, 256, 257, 258, 290
  biblical and extrabiblical parallels in, 77-78
  Christology of, 81
  composition of, 76, 80-81
  Elizabeth as singer of 78-79
  exaltation of Mary in, 80
  Mary's self-understanding in, 81
  inspiration of, 77
  structure of 79-81
Manicheism, 158, 176, 283-84
Mariale, 193-94
Marialis cultus, 248-50, 252, 258, 304n. 8
Marian age, 232, 239, 240, 244
Marian century. *See* Marian age
Marian year, 241, 245
Mariology, 18, 39, 247, 251, 254, 257, 258, 260, 261, 262, 267-308
  beginning of, 272-84
  christological ground of, 15
  development in New Testament, 114-15
  development outside New Testament, 115, 119-20
  ground of, 269-72
  diversity in New Testament, 114
  necessity of, 267-69
  subordinate to Christology, 31, 75-76, 226
Marxism, 258, 261
Mary in the New Testament, 259
Mary
  adoration of, 75, 172
  advocate, 132, 146, 203, 262
  animation of, 195, 199, 206
  annunciation, 156, 195, 200-201, 219, 255, 289, 292, 306-7
  assumption. *See* bodily assumption
  beneath the cross, 86, 87, 100, 104-7, 156, 194, 219, 298, 306
  betrothal (marriage) to Joseph, 55, 124, 127, 141, 150, 156, 160, 163, 174, 178, 181, 196, 200, 212, 217

bodily assumption of, 14, 18, 165, 173, 189, 194, 195, 217, 218, 218n. 32, 219, 228, 232, 233, 239-45, 247, 254, 255, 256, 258, 260, 261, 262, 263, 285, 291, 295, 297, 303
childhood of, 124, 127, 292
children of, 21, 32-36, 40, 58-59, 92, 136-37, 164, 282
Christotokos, 13, 169-71, 269
coredemption of, 18, 156, 188, 193, 196, 201, 204, 211, 219, 234, 244-45, 246, 248, 258, 260, 262, 299, 302-7
Daughter of Zion, 294-95
Davidic descent of, 124, 153, 178, 181, 215, 216, 220
death of, 244-45, 292
devotion to, 10, 17, 203, 210, 213-14, 215, 217-18, 219, 222, 223, 226, 227-28, 235-36, 236, 237-38, 246, 248-50, 253, 257, 260, 262, 268, 270, 271, 299, 308
discipleship of, 63-64, 92-94, 293-94
dogma(s). *See* bodily assumption of; immaculate conception of.
doulē, 71-72, 73
election of, 95, 167, 174, 181, 193, 216, 222, 226, 243, 247, 272, 285-91, 292, 295, 306
exaltation of, 80, 126-28, 133, 153, 155, 178, 185, 186, 194, 202, 203, 214, 216, 219, 227, 235, 262, 281
example, 96, 138, 141, 144-45, 147, 151, 156, 157, 161-62, 165-66, 176, 179-80, 181-82, 194, 196, 200, 201, 204, 211, 212-13, 214, 215, 218, 219, 222, 224, 247, 248, 251, 253, 254, 256, 257, 273, 277, 283-84, 285, 293-94, 296-98, 307
faithfulness of. *See* example
faults attributed to, 133, 134, 136, 141-42, 145-46, 152-53, 154-55, 171, 216, 293
full of grace, 193-94, 196-97, 198, 199, 219, 222
guarantor of Christ's humanity, 122-23, 135-36, 143, 146, 175, 268
holiness of. *See* sanctity
immaculate conception of, 14, 18, 165, 167, 173, 177, 186-87, 188-208, 209, 211-12, 215, 218, 222, 227, 228-29, 229-32, 233, 234, 238, 240, 241, 242, 243, 244, 247, 254, 255, 256, 258, 260, 261, 263, 285, 291, 295, 297, 303, 307
incarnation of the Holy Spirit, 258, 261, 297
intercession of, 18, 100-101, 142, 177, 180, 182-83, 184, 185, 189, 192, 194, 196, 203, 204, 207, 210, 213-14, 222, 226, 227, 233, 234, 235, 254, 269, 298-302, 307
invocation of, 142, 152, 172, 184-86, 219, 222, 223, 249, 302
liberator of God's people, 72-73, 252-55, 256-58, 261
Mater dolorosa, 86
maternity of. *See* motherhood of.
mediation of, 18, 172-73, 175, 185, 189, 204, 207, 226, 234, 248, 258, 260, 262, 299, 302-7
mediatrix of all graces, 246
mother of believers, 167, 168, 175, 185
Mother of God. *See Theotokos*
Mother of Mercy, 183, 185, 189, 194, 195, 208, 210, 217, 234, 302, 305
Mother of the Church, 245-50, 260
motherhood of, 18, 75, 135, 140, 146, 147, 149-50, 167, 172, 192, 195, 196, 197, 200, 201, 212, 214, 222, 223, 224, 237, 243, 251, 258, 268, 272, 285, 290, 291
New Eve, 129, 131-33, 134-35, 138, 140, 142-43, 146, 147, 151, 152, 153, 175, 178, 179, 194, 196, 197, 199, 202-3, 204, 210, 212, 233, 234, 243, 247, 255, 262, 269, 273-74, 289
opponent of Jesus, 34-36, 38, 39-40, 293
Our Lady, 173-74, 186
perpetual virginity of, 14, 18, 27-28, 31, 38, 124-25, 127-28, 136-37, 138, 140-41, 143, 144-45, 146, 150-51, 153-54, 156, 157-61, 163-65, 165-67, 168, 174, 178, 180-81, 196, 199-200, 201, 202, 204, 211, 212, 214, 215, 216, 217, 222, 224, 227, 243, 254, 255, 280-83, 285, 306, 307
perseverance of. *See* example; sanctity of
piety. *See* Mary, devotion to
predestination of. *See* election of
preexistence of, 228, 288
pregnancy of, 48-54
prophet, 64, 76-81, 253, 256, 257, 283-84, 290, 293
purity, 126-27, 179, 190, 215
queen, 18, 109-13, 173, 175, 182-83, 186, 188, 192, 194, 195, 207, 210, 215, 219, 224, 225, 226, 234, 239-45, 241-42, 243, 254, 263, 283-84, 297
reign of, 18, 241-42, 254
relationship to church, 18, 139, 146, 161, 167, 168, 175, 246, 247-48, 249, 252, 255,

283-84, 285, 290-91, 295, 296, 298, 307
sanctity of, 155-56, 161, 167, 168, 175, 179, 186-87, 190, 192, 194, 195, 196, 197, 198-99, 202, 203, 205, 206, 207, 211, 212, 214, 216, 218, 222, 226, 227, 233, 235, 249, 253, 260, 261, 268, 276, 280, 291-95, 296, 307-8
Second Eve. *See* New Eve
sign of salvation, 150
silence of, 83, 88-89
spouse of God, Christ, 195, 212
Star of the Sea, 178, 181, 210, 211
symbol of corporate faith, 87, 94-96, 103-4, 106, 113-14, 263, 268, 283-84, 298, 302, 307
teacher, 215, 219, 224
Theotokos, 10, 138, 141-42, 150, 155, 169-71, 172, 180, 196, 201, 207, 214, 217, 221, 223, 226, 233, 234-35, 246, 250, 256, 257, 259, 262, 263, 269-72, 277, 283-84, 285, 291, 302, 304, 305, 306, 307
veneration of. *See* devotion to; invocation of; worship of.
virginity of, 24, 28, 41, 44, 45, 53, 55, 60, 123, 127, 140, 141, 142-43, 144-45, 146, 147, 149-51, 162, 163-64, 166-67, 175, 178, 181, 196, 197, 199, 200, 214, 225, 251, 255, 256, 258, 268, 273, 274-84, 285, 295
virginity *ante partum. See* perpetual virginity
virginity *in partu. See* perpetual virginity
Virginity *post partum. See* perpetual virginity
woman of faith, 75
worship of, 9, 156, 170-71, 216, 217, 218, 220, 222, 223, 249
Mary and Human Liberation, 256
Mary Magdalene, 38, 251-52
Maternal Face of God, 256-58
miracles, 98, 225, 276, 278
miraculous medal, 229-30
monergism, 306
Monologium, 184
Mother of God. *See* Mary, *Theotokos*
Munificentissimus deus, 242, 244
Mystical Body of Christ, 241
Mystical City of God, 228
Neoplatonism, 140
Nestorianism, 13, 170, 271, 277
Odes of Solomon, 125-26
ordination, 11
Oxford movement, 234
"Paean in Honour of the Virgin Mother," 210
papal infallibility, 12
Pelagianism, 161, 166
Platonism, 152
Pontmain, 241
"Prayer to the Virgin Mary in Time of Trouble," 210-11
Proslogium, 184
Protestantism, 12, 16
Protevangelium of James, 43, 126-28, 138, 146, 162, 164, 226, 228, 281, 291, 292
Pseudo-Ezekiel, 138
Redemptoris mater, 304
Reformation, 15, 18, 214-23, 299, 304, 307-8
Reformed theology, 11, 217-21
resurrection (general), 26, 274, 301
romanticism, 224-25
Saint Paul University, 14
saints, 10
Salome, 8
Satan, the devil, 122, 141, 150, 155, 174, 200, 219
Scripture, 11, 12, 18, 221
Second Vatican Council. *See* Vatican II
Sermon on the Mount and Magnificat, 214-15
Servites of Mary, 206
sexuality, 11, 13, 159-60, 161-62, 166, 175, 175, 251, 255, 275, 276, 277, 278, 279, 283-84
sin, 10, 179
original, 153, 166, 171, 172, 175, 178, 179, 186-87, 191, 195, 197, 199, 204, 205, 208, 216, 225-26, 242, 260, 261, 279, 282, 293
unpardonable, 32-33
spirituality, 11
Stabat Mater, 85-86, 306
Sub tuum praesidium, 142
Summa theologiae, 197-201
synergism, 306
sword of Simeon, 64, 85-87, 88, 89-90, 141, 178, 199, 216, 219, 290-91, 293
Ten Articles, 222
Thirty-Nine Articles, 223, 234, 237
Time, 15
tradition, 12, 17
Trinity, 26
Truly Our Sister, 252-54
Ut unum sint, 304n. 8
Vatican II, 9, 165, 239, 245-50, 251, 258, 259, 260, 299, 304

Scripture Index

Genesis
1:2, 26, 36
1:26-27, 23
3, 112
3:15, 86, 112, 217
3:16, 151, 282
12:3, 95
15:5, 68
16:15, 29
18:11, 68
19:37-38, 48
21:1, 68
21:1-14, 29
24:40, 28
25:21, 68
29:31, 68
29:32, 77
30:13, 78
30:23, 68
37:9, 110
37:10-11, 84
38, 48
38:11, 52
38:14, 51
38:26, 49
38:27-30, 51
40:16, 84
41:55, 100

Exodus
1:15-21, 72
1:22—2:4, 57
3:1-6, 151
16:4-17, 111
16:10, 127
19, 100
19:4, 111
19:9, 127
20:12, 199
24, 100

Leviticus
8, 141
15:19-20, 36
15:19-24, 127
15:19-33, 36

Numbers
3:12-13, 82
5:11-31, 127
18:15-16, 82

Deuteronomy
10:21, 78
21:15-17, 82
22:23-27, 55, 56
22:24, 56
22:27, 55
32:11-12, 111

Joshua
2, 48
2:1, 49
2:2, 51
2:17-21, 52
6:22-25, 48, 52
24:29, 72

Judges
2:8, 72
4—5, 72
6, 168
6:8, 28
11:12, 100
13, 68

Ruth
3:7, 51

1 Samuel
1, 68
1:11, 77
2:1-3, 77
2:7-8, 78
18:21, 105

2 Samuel
11:1—12:24, 48
11:4, 51, 52
11:26, 49
11:27, 49
12:10, 49
12:15, 49
22:51, 78

1 Kings
1:11-40, 52
4:32, 125
8:10-11, 127
17:1-16, 102
17:18, 100

2 Kings
3:13, 100
4:1-7, 102
4:42-44, 102

1 Chronicles
1—3, 49

2 Chronicles
35:21, 100

Nehemiah
9:14, 72

Job
7:12, 111
12:19, 78
14:1, 38
26, 111
38:8-11, 111

Psalms
1:1, 75
2:7, 105
2:12, 75
4:6, 127
8:5, 24
18:11, 127
35:9, 77
45:10, 243
51:11, 26
72:1, 57
72:10-11, 57
74:12, 111
74:13-14, 111
84:4, 75
89:3, 72
89:9-10, 111
89:9-14, 111
94:12, 75
98:3, 78
103:17, 78
104:6-9, 111
105:42, 72
107:9, 78
110, 214
110:1, 75
111:9, 78
119:11, 84
132:8, 202, 243

Proverbs
3:1, 84
8:22-31, 145
8:29, 111
31:29, 4

Song of Solomon
3:6, 243
4:8, 243
4:12, 163
6:8-9, 210
6:9, 243

Isaiah
1—5, 124
2:5, 127
6—12, 124
6:1-6, 68
7:14, 46, 55, 129, 135, 140, 150, 159, 162, 199, 216, 278
8:5-8, 111
8:14-15, 86
11, 123, 124
11:1, 162
11:1-5, 159
14:10-15, 111
17:12-14, 111
24—27, 107
26:17, 111
27:1, 111
34—35, 107
41:8-9, 78
45:8, 216
51:9-11, 111
54:1, 111
60:6, 57
61:1-2, 91
62:4, 294
62:11, 294
62:12, 294
63:10-11, 26
66:7-9, 111

Jeremiah
1:2-3, 68
4:31, 290
7:25, 28
31:12, 103

31:15, *57*
51:34, *111*

Lamentations
2:13, *294*

Ezekiel
14:17, *87, 95*
21:26, *78*
28:1-9, *111*
34:23, *72*
44:2-3, *163, 281*
44:20, *159, 180*

Daniel
4:19, *75*
6:20, *72*
7:2-28, *84*
7:8, *111*
7:20, *111*
7:24, *111*
9:20-21, *68*
10:13, *111*
10:20, *111*
12:1-2, *111*

Hosea
11:1, *57*
14:7, *103*
14:8, *100*

Joel
3:18, *163*

Amos
1:1, *68*
9:13-14, *103*

Micah
4:9-10, *111*
4:10, *290*
5:2, *57*
7:20, *78*

Habakkuk
3:8-10, *111*
3:15, *111*
3:18, *77*

Zephaniah
3:17, *78*

Zechariah
7:12, *28*
9:9, *102*
12:10, *86, 87*
13:7, *87*

Malachi
4:2, *163*
4:4, *72*

4 Ezra
9, *77*

Judith
13, *80*

1 Maccabees
2:11, *77*

Sirach
10:14, *78*
39:2, *84*

Tobit
7:12, *105*

Matthew
1, *47, 57, 140*
1—2, *47*
1:1, *47, 48, 50, 65*
1:1-2, *47*
1:1-17, *44, 47, 48, 57*
1:2, *51*
1:3, *48, 51*
1:5-7, *48*
1:6, *47*
1:11, *51*
1:11-12, *47*
1:16, *41, 43, 48, 51*
1:17, *47, 181*
1:18, *43, 44, 55, 57*
1:18-19, *127*
1:18-23, *41*
1:18-25, *54, 57*
1:18—2:23, *44*
1:19, *41*
1:20, *43, 44, 57, 135*
1:20-23, *44*
1:21, *44*
1:22-23, *135*
1:23, *44, 46, 57, 159, 199*
1:24-25, *44*
1:25, *41, 44, 47, 57, 150, 163, 164*
2, *47, 57*
2:1, *44, 47*
2:1-12, *47, 50, 57*
2:1-23, *57*
2:2, *58*
2:4, *58*
2:7, *56*
2:8, *58*
2:10, *58*
2:11, *44, 58*
2:13, *57, 58*
2:13-14, *58*
2:13-23, *47, 57*
2:14, *57*
2:16, *44*
2:20, *57*
2:21, *57*
2:22-23, *44*
2:23, *44, 47*
8:5-13, *50*
12:1-8, *59*
12:9-14, *59*
12:22-32, *59*
12:22-37, *59*
12:28, *34*
12:38-42, *59*
12:43-45, *34, 59*
12:46, *40*
12:46-50, *57, 58, 59, 106, 136, 154, 196*
12:50, *35*
13:1-53, *60*
13:53-58, *43*
13:54-58, *57, 59*
13:55, *37*
13:55-56, *40*
13:57, *91*
15:21-28, *50*
17, *141*
23:3, *42*
27:56, *105*
28:16, *66*
28:18, *47*
28:18-20, *50*

Mark
1:1, *39, 65*
1:7, *34*
1:19, *35*
1:29-30, *32*
2:1, *32*
2:6, *33*
2:16, *33*
3, *34*
3:7-19, *32*
3:13-15, *33*
3:17-18, *27*
3:18, *39*
3:19, *32*
3:19-30, *32*
3:20-21, *34, 40*
3:20-35, *39*
3:21, *33*
3:22, *33, 34*
3:23, *33*
3:23-30, *34, 36*
3:25, *33*
3:26, *34*
3:27, *34*
3:28-30, *34*
3:31, *32, 33, 35, 38*
3:31-35, *34, 37, 39, 59, 106, 136*
3:35, *35*
4:1-9, *36*
4:1-34, *37*
4:10-20, *36*
4:21-25, *36*
4:26-29, *36*
4:30-32, *36*
4:33-34, *36*
4:35-41, *36*
4:35—5:43, *37, 60*
5, *36*
5:1-20, *36*
5:21-43, *36*
5:25-34, *36*
6:1-6, *37, 43*
6:2, *37*
6:3, *27, 32, 37, 38, 40, 43, 60*
6:4, *60, 91*
6:5, *37, 98*
6:17, *33, 35*
6:45—8:27, *66*
12:12, *33*
14:1, *33*

14:50, *38*
15:40, *32, 38, 105*
15:43, *38*
15:47, *32, 38*
16:1, *32, 38*
16:7, *66*

Luke
1, *69*
1—2, *63, 283*
1:1, *45*
1:1-4, *65, 67*
1:1—9:50, *65*
1:2, *31, 65*
1:2-3, *45*
1:4, *67*
1:5, *44*
1:5-6, *70*
1:5-25, *68*
1:5-80, *127*
1:6, *74*
1:7, *69, 70*
1:9, *74*
1:11, *69, 74*
1:12, *69*
1:13, *69, 70*
1:14-17, *69*
1:15, *69, 70, 74*
1:16, *74*
1:17, *70, 74*
1:18, *69, 70*
1:19, *69*
1:19-20, *69*
1:25, *70, 74*
1:26, *44, 69*
1:26-38, *64, 67, 68, 94, 95, 223*
1:27, *43, 69, 70, 71*
1:27-34, *43*
1:28, *69, 70, 74, 95, 198, 216, 219, 243*
1:29, *69*
1:30, *69, 70*
1:30-35, *44*
1:31, *44, 69, 159*
1:32, *43, 70, 74*
1:32-33, *69, 70*
1:33, *80*
1:34, *44, 69, 70, 71, 150, 160, 281*
1:35, *44, 69, 70, 197*
1:36-37, *69*
1:38, *70, 71, 74, 79, 250*
1:39-45, *74*
1:39-56, *64, 73*
1:42, *13, 75, 79*
1:45, *70, 75, 79, 92, 94*
1:46, *78*
1:46-47, *79*
1:46-55, *74, 94, 253*
1:46-56, *76*
1:47, *77*
1:48, *77, 78, 92*
1:48-50, *79*
1:49, *78*
1:50, *78*
1:51, *83*
1:51-53, *75, 78, 79, 86*
1:51-55, *76*
1:54-55, *78, 79, 95*
1:67-80, *74*
1:68-79, *77, 79*
1:69, *79*
2, *67, 86*
2:1-5, *44*
2:1-20, *64, 81, 88*
2:1-52, *44*
2:2, *81, 128*
2:4, *43*
2:4-6, *44*
2:5, *63, 136*
2:5-6, *44*
2:8, *82*
2:11, *44, 79*
2:14, *77*
2:16, *63*
2:16-20, *83*
2:19, *83, 84, 88, 89*
2:21, *44, 84*
2:21-35, *85*
2:21-40, *84*
2:22, *44, 88, 140, 201*
2:22-40, *223*
2:29-32, *77*
2:30, *79*
2:33-34, *63*
2:34-35, *64, 95, 214*
2:35, *86, 90, 92*
2:36, *46*
2:39, *44*
2:39-40, *88*
2:41-42, *88*
2:41-52, *64, 88*
2:44-52, *88*
2:48, *63*
2:51, *84, 88, 89*
2:51-52, *88*
3:21-22, *91*
3:22, *111*
3:23-28, *44*
3:23-38, *90*
3:34, *86*
4:1, *91*
4:14-30, *136*
4:22, *37, 91*
4:24, *91*
4:31-32, *43*
6, *123, 141*
7, *67*
7:18-22, *75*
8:19-20, *40*
8:19-21, *64, 90, 92, 106*
8:21, *64, 92*
11:27-28, *64, 76, 90, 92*
11:28, *64*
12:51-53, *87*
14, *140, 141*
20:17-18, *86*
23:26-49, *86*
23:49, *105*
23:53, *82*
24:18, *105*

John
1, *98, 165*
1—10, *219*
1:1, *286*
1:1-18, *98*
1:3, *101*
1:11, *107*
1:13, *199, 279, 283*
1:14, *97, 98, 198, 282, 286*
1:18, *282, 283*
1:29-34, *99*
1:30, *97*
1:31, *75*
1:43-51, *99*
1:45, *99, 103*
2, *154*
2:1, *99*
2:1-11, *101*
2:1-12, *97, 98*
2:4, *97, 99, 102*
2:9, *101*
2:11, *98, 101*
2:12, *40, 99, 106*
3, *101*
3:16, *282*
3:18, *282*
4, *101*
4:46-54, *98, 100*
4:53, *98*
5:1-18, *98*
5:15-18, *98*
6:1-15, *98, 102*
6:14, *98*
6:16-21, *98*
6:19, *98*
6:42, *37, 99*
6:55, *202*
7:1-9, *99, 106*
7:1-10, *40*
7:4, *154*
7:5, *106*
7:8, *99*
8:20, *100*
8:58, *287*
9:1-12, *98*
9:8-12, *98*
11:38-44, *98*
11:45, *98*
11:45-53, *98*
12:20-22, *102*
12:20-36, *102*
12:23, *97, 100, 102*
12:27-32, *102*
12:33, *102*
14:26, *132*
19, *306*
19:24-25, *105*
19:25, *39, 86*
19:25-27, *38, 97, 104, 160, 219*
19:26-27, *282*
19:26-28, *105*
20, *105, 140*
20:19, *165*
20:19-20, *214*
20:25, *127*

20:26, *165*
20:30-31, *65*

Acts
1:1, *67*
1:8, *66*
1:13, *27*
1:14, *38, 40, 43, 64, 93, 94, 240*
2:18, *71, 81*
2:22-36, *79*
3:11-26, *79*
4:2, *26*
4:8-12, *79*
4:29, *71*
6:8, *198*
12:17, *27*
13:33, *25*
15:13, *27*
16:17, *71*
19:21-41, *110*
21:18-19, *27*
28:15-16, *66*

Romans
1, *286*
1—3, *130*
1—8, *21*
1:1, *71*
1:1-7, *25*
1:2, *26*
1:3, *25, 26, 27*
1:3-4, *21, 22, 24, 25, 122*
1:4, *25, 26, 27*
3, *140*
3:27, *122*
4, *120, 130*
4:7-8, *120*
4:19, *29*
5, *121, 130*
5:1-11, *130*
5:12, *197*
5:14, *130*
6:18, *71*
7, *121*
8:4-9, *25*
9—11, *291*
9:4-5, *95*
13:1-7, *82*
16:20, *112*

1 Corinthians
1:19, *122*
1:20, *122*
1:23, *122*
2:2, *25*
7:21-24, *72*
7:32, *202*
8:6, *287*
9:5, *38, 40*
14:34-35, *200*
15, *130*
15:20, *27*
15:21-58, *23*
15:47, *287*

2 Corinthians
8:9, *287*
11:3, *112*

Galatians
1:11-24, *27*
1:13-17, *27*
1:18, *27*
1:19, *21, 27, 38, 40*
2:9, *27*
2:15—4:7, *28*
3:2-3, *25*
3:28, *96*
4:4, *21, 28, 149, 289*
4:4-6, *28*
4:5, *29*
4:26, *112*
4:28-29, *21, 29, 46*
5:16-19, *25*

Ephesians
1:22, *130*
3:19, *198*
4, *121*
6, *121*

Philippians
1, *121*
2, *22, 23, 286*
2:5-11, *21, 22, 23*
2:6, *23*
2:6-7, *23, 24*
2:7, *23*

Colossians
1:15-19, *287*
1:20, *130*
2:9, *194*

2 Timothy
2:8, *25*

Titus
3:5, *198*

Hebrews
5:5-6, *287*
5:10, *163*
11:31, *49*
13:8, *287*

1 Peter
1:20, *287, 289*
2:21, *182*

Jude
1, *38*

Revelation
1—3, *108*
1—11, *108*
1:8, *287*
3:13, *287*
4—11, *108*
12, *108, 109, 110, 113, 122, 234, 243, 283*
12—20, *108*
12—22, *108*
12:1, *97*
12:1-6, *97, 107, 109*
12:7-12, *109*
12:9, *112*
12:11, *298*
12:13-17, *97, 107, 109*
13, *111*
19:15, *111*
21, *228*
21—22, *108*